# POINT-COUNTERPOINT

## Readings in American Government

*Fourth Edition*

# Herbert M. Levine

St. Martin's Press   New York

*For Albert,*
*Louise, and*
*Philippe Boudreau*

*Senior editor:* Don Reisman
*Managing editor:* Patricia Mansfield
*Project editor:* Cheryl Friedman
*Production supervisor:* Katherine Battiste
*Text design:* Mary Beth Kilkelly/Levavi & Levavi
*Cover design:* Judy Forster

Library of Congress Catalog Card Number: 90–63546

For information, write:
St. Martin's Press, Inc.
175 Fifth Avenue
New York, NY 10010

ISBN: 0–312–04905–6

## Acknowledgments

"The Constitution: Past and Present," by Thurgood Marshall. Speech at the Annual
Seminar of the San Francisco Patent and Trademark Law Association, Maui, Hawaii, May
6, 1987. Notes have been deleted.
"The Wisdom of the Framers," by William Bradford Reynolds. Speech at the Vanderbilt
University Reunion 1987 Celebration Luncheon, University Club, Nashville, Tennessee,
May 23, 1987.
"A Bicentennial Analysis of the American Political Structure," by the Committee on
the Constitutional System. *A Bicentennial Analysis of the American Political Structure:
Reports and Recommendations of the Committee on the Constitutional System.* (Washington, D.C.: Committee on the Constitutional System, 1987). Reprinted with the permission of the Committee. Requests for further reading should be addressed to the Committee at 1755 Massachusetts Avenue, NW, Washington, D.C. 20036 (Phone: 202/387-8787).

Acknowledgments and copyrights are continued at the back of the book on pages 354–
356, which constitute an extension of the copyright page.

# Preface

The debate tradition in the United States is as old as the Republic itself. Soon after the colonists achieved independence from British rule, they debated issues as fundamental as slavery, tariffs, and the policy of the United States toward the French Revolution. Some debates in U.S. history—Lincoln-Douglas and Kennedy-Nixon—have become part of the national memory, even if misremembered or embellished.

It is with this tradition in mind that *Point-Counterpoint* has been developed. The text is a collection of readings that present contending sides of important issues in U.S. government. It is designed to contribute to a democratic tradition where vigorous controversy is regarded as both proper and desirable.

The selections deal with the basic structure of the U.S. political system, political participation, civil liberties and civil rights, the power of government policy makers, and the direction of public policy. The format of the book encourages critical thinking. Part and chapter introductions provide important background information and a synopsis of the major points in each selection. For each debate question, one "Yes" response and one "No" response are given. "Questions for Discussion" follow each debate to help students formulate their own answers to the debate question. If both conflicting views on an issue seem convincing, students can then turn to the "Suggested Readings," which provide general background information as well as pro and con arguments.

Three cautionary points are in order. First, issues can rarely be broken down into a neat classification such as liberal or conservative. In this regard, it is often the case that some of the most meaningful controversy goes on among advocates of the same political philosophy.

Second, space limitations and the format of the book dictate that only two views—"Yes" and "No"—are given for each question. More often than not, other answers could be presented, such as "Yes, but . . . ," "No, but . . . ," or even "Maybe." In the process of debate, refinements can be developed. The yes-no approach, however, should provide a start toward understanding problems of U.S. government.

Third, the book does not present a single ideological perspective. As a whole, it does not take a side on the issues but presents, instead, many views. If there is an ideological commitment, it is implicit in the nature of the format: a commitment to vigorous debate as befits the democratic tradition.

## NEW TO THE FOURTH EDITION

The fourth edition of *Point-Counterpoint* includes a number of revisions to the third edition. There is a new section on civil liberties and civil rights, and there are new debate topics focusing on currently contested issues, such as fetal rights, racist speech, congressional term limitations, legalization of drugs, homelessness, direct government support to artists and writers, statehood for Puerto Rico, and U.S. foreign policy in the post–cold war era.

The fourth edition also retains some of the debates of the previous edition. These topics include the Constitution, separation of powers, campaign finance reform, and the president and foreign policy.

## ACKNOWLEDGMENTS

I am indebted to numerous people in the academic and publishing communities who helped me at various stages in the writing and production of this edition of *Point-Counterpoint*. The editorial consultants for the book offered superb suggestions and insights, including proposals for different debate topics and stylistic changes. Specifically, I want to acknowledge the following consultants for St. Martin's Press: Donald Buzinkai, King's College; Alan Clem, University of South Dakota; Jeffrey Colbert, University of North Carolina—Greensboro; Larry Elowitz, Georgia College; David H. Fozz, University of Tennessee—Knoxville; Chris J. Froke, Arkansas State University; John Geer, Arizona State University; Gerard Gryski, Auburn University; William B. Gwyn, Tulane University; Willie Hamilton, California State University—Long Beach; Valerie S. Hartman, William Paterson College; Robert Langran, Villanova University; William R. Lowry, Washington University in St. Louis; Charles Noble, California State University—Long Beach; William J. Parente, University of Scranton; Stephen L. Percy, University of Wisconsin—Milwaukee; James Perkins, San Antonio College; Wesley Phelan, Glenville State College; David Robinson, University of Houston—Downtown; Lois T. Vietri, University of Maryland at College Park; Herbert Waltzer, Miami University; Judi Ward, Coastal Carolina Community College; Laura R. Woliver, University of South Carolina; Mary D. Young, Southwestern Michigan College.

Ryan J. Barilleaux and Daniel P. Franklin, who wrote articles for the third edition, have updated their contributions. I am appreciative of their professionalism, flexibility, attention to detail, adherence to deadlines, and good will. As in the past, I thoroughly enjoyed working with both of them.

I am also indebted to Ann Hofstra Grogg, who copyedited the manuscript with her usual extraordinary skill. The St. Martin's Press staff offered expert professional guidance, and I want to thank specifically Don Reisman, senior editor; his assistant Frances Jones; and Cheryl Friedman, the project editor.

*Herbert M. Levine*

# Contents

# Part I

# Foundations of the

# United States Political System

I n 1987 the United States celebrated the two hundredth anniversary of the Constitution by drawing attention to the basic institutions and practices of the nation's political system. Political officials, leaders of private associations, and writers assessed anew the fundamental assumptions under which the U.S. political system was established; they examined how a system designed for a largely agrarian society consisting of thirteen eastern seaboard states had evolved over two centuries to meet the needs of a postindustrial society that spans a continent.

These observers often evaluated how well or how poorly the United States was living up to the ideas professed by the Framers of the Constitution. Whether positive or negative in their assessments, they focused on social, economic, and political institutions.

Those who looked favorably at the development of the past two centuries often drew attention to a number of features: the rise in the nation's standard of living; the integration of groups from diverse ethnic, religious, and racial backgrounds into a "melting pot" in which these groups could live in peace; the resilience of the Constitution in adapting to change; the expansion of democratic practices to include ever larger numbers of people; the competition of political parties for electoral success; the freedoms accorded to U.S. citizens in expressing ideas, protesting peacefully, and responding to accusations in the criminal justice system; and the promotion of the common defense.

Those who were critical of the developments of the past two centuries pointed to different facts to justify their negative conclusions: the great disparity in assets, in which less than 10 percent of the U.S. population controls 90 percent of the nation's wealth; the long history of discrimination against blacks, Hispanics, and native Americans; the use of the Constitution by the dominant economic groups to prevent or delay social or economic change; the practical means used by government to prevent or slow down the participation of lower-income groups in the political process; the limitation of choice resulting from a two-party rather than a multiparty political system; the use by government of infiltration and disruption tactics to undermine groups holding unpopular ideas; the failure of the criminal justice system to give all defendants an equal chance regardless of wealth and background; and the use of military force and secret operations in influencing nations abroad, such as in Indochina in the 1960s and 1970s and in Nicaragua in the 1980s.

The views of contending sides assessing the U.S. political system raise the most fundamental issues underlying that system. This part considers three of these issues: the role of the Framers in creating a "more perfect Union"—and how perfect was and is that Union; the efficacy of the separation of powers; and the value of federalism.

# Chapter 1

## Has the Wisdom of the Framers of the Constitution in Promoting a "More Perfect Union" Been Overrated?

The Constitution establishes the ground rules governing the political system of the United States. What the Framers believed and how they acted at the Constitutional Convention at Philadelphia in 1787 raise questions about the effect these rules may have had on political behavior thereafter.

Historians disagree sharply about the Framers of the Constitution. Characterizations of delegates to the Constitutional Convention range from self-serving men of prominence seeking to promote the interests of their own economic class to pragmatic leaders encompassing profound differences of economic interest and political philosophy.

The basic facts about the Constitution, however, are generally accepted. The Articles of Confederation, presented in Congress in 1776 but not finally ratified by all the states until 1781, established a league of friendship among the states rather than a national government. The period under the Articles was marked by widespread debt, Shays's Rebellion (a revolt of poor Massachusetts farmers), economic decay, and an inability to negotiate commercial treaties. In 1786 a Constitutional Convention was called to revise the Articles; it met in Philadelphia from May through September 1787. Most of the delegates were young, politically experienced, financially comfortable, and afraid of the common people, whom they called the "mob." Although they shared some assumptions about government and society, they disagreed profoundly about what should and should not be included in the document they were drafting.

Despite the celebration of the Framers at many civic occasions during the Constitution's bicentennial year, some observers, like Supreme Court Justice Thurgood Marshall, think the wisdom of the Framers of the Constitution has been overrated. Marshall was the first black person appointed to the Supreme Court. Earlier in his career, he was an attorney with the National Association for the Advancement of Colored People (NAACP), and he argued major civil rights cases in the courts.

In a speech sparked by commemorations of the bicentennial, Marshall faults the Framers for producing a defective document that allowed for the perpetuation of slavery and denied black people and women the right to vote. He contends that developments *after* the writing of the Constitution created a more promising basis for justice and equality than did the accomplishments of the Framers. He emphasizes the adoption of the Fourteenth Amendment ensuring protection of life, liberty, and property of all persons against deprivations without due process and guaranteeing the equal protection of the laws. Credit for change, Marshall says, should go to the people who passed amendments and laws that sought to promote liberty for *all* the people of the United States. Marshall celebrates the Constitution as a living document, evolving through amendments and judicial interpretation.

Marshall's speech prompted a direct response by William Bradford Reynolds, at that time the assistant attorney general in the Civil Rights Division of the Justice Department. Reynolds was a controversial figure in the Reagan administration because of his actions on civil rights matters. A number of civil rights leaders criticized him for his opposition to affirmative action and voting rights legislation. Reynolds's supporters defended him as a proponent of real racial equality.

In a speech delivered at Vanderbilt University, Reynolds argues that the Framers deserve the respect accorded to them in the bicentennial celebrations. Accepting Marshall's evaluation that the original Constitution was flawed, Reynolds still asserts that the Constitution marked "the greatest advance for human liberty in the entire history of mankind, then or since." Indeed, Reynolds continues, the constitutional system of divided governmental authority and separated government power eventually allowed for blacks to secure liberty. He notes that much blame for the low status of blacks in the United States should go not to the Framers but rather to those justices who failed to follow the terms of the Constitution and the laws of the land.

## ☑ YES

---

## Has the Wisdom of the Framers of the Constitution in Promoting a "More Perfect Union" Been Overrated?

---

### THURGOOD MARSHALL

### The Constitution: Past and Present

Nineteen eighty-seven marks the 200th anniversary of the United States Constitution. A Commission has been established to coordinate the celebration. The official meetings, essay contests, and festivities have begun.

The planned commemoration will span three years, and I am told 1987 is "dedicated to the memory of the Founders and the document they drafted in Philadelphia." We are to "recall the achievements of our Founders and the knowledge and experience that inspired them, the nature of the government they established, its origins, its character, and its ends, and the rights and privileges of citizenship, as well as its attendant responsibilities."

Like many anniversary celebrations, the plan for 1987 takes particular events and holds them up as the source of all the very best that has followed. Patriotic feelings will surely swell, prompting proud proclamations of the wisdom, foresight, and sense of justice shared by the Framers and reflected in a written document now yellowed with age. This is unfortunate—not the patriotism itself, but the tendency for the celebration to oversimplify, and overlook the many other events that have been instrumental to our achievements as a nation. The focus of this celebration invites a complacent belief that the vision of those who debated and compromised in Philadelphia yielded the "more perfect Union" it is said we now enjoy.

I cannot accept this invitation, for I do not believe that the meaning of the Constitution was forever "fixed" at the Philadelphia Convention. Nor do I find the wisdom, foresight, and sense of justice exhibited by the Framers particularly profound. To the contrary, the government they devised was defective from the start, requiring several amendments, a civil war, and momentous social transformation to attain the system of constitutional government, and its respect for the individual freedoms and human rights, we hold as fundamental today. When contemporary Americans cite "The Constitution," they invoke a concept that is vastly different from what the Framers barely began to construct two centuries ago.

For a sense of the evolving nature of the Constitution we need look no further than the first three words of the document's preamble: "We the People." When the Founding Fathers used this phrase in 1787, they did not have in mind the majority of America's citizens. "We the People" included, in the words of the Framers, "the whole Number of free Persons." On a matter so basic as the right to vote, for example, Negro slaves were excluded, although they were counted for representational purposes—at three-fifths each. Women did not gain the right to vote for over a hundred and thirty years.

These omissions were intentional. The record of the Framers' debates on the slave question is especially clear: The Southern States acceded to the demands of the New England States for giving Congress broad power to regulate commerce, in exchange for the right to continue the slave trade. The economic interests of the regions coalesced: New Englanders engaged in the "carrying trade" would profit from transporting slaves from Africa as well as goods produced in America by slave labor. The perpetuation of slavery ensured the primary source of wealth in the Southern States.

Despite this clear understanding of the role slavery would play in the new republic, use of the words "slaves" and "slavery" was carefully avoided in the original document. Political representation in the lower House of Congress was to be based on the population of "free Persons" in each State, plus three-fifths of all "other Persons." Moral principles against slavery, for those who had them, were compromised, with no explanation of the conflicting principles for which the American Revolutionary War had ostensibly been fought: the self-evident truths "that all men are created equal, that they are endowed by their Creator with certain unalienable Rights, that among these are Life, Liberty and the pursuit of Happiness."

It was not the first such compromise. Even these ringing phrases from the Declaration of Independence are filled with irony, for an early draft of what became that Declaration assailed the King of England for suppressing legislative attempts to end the slave trade and for encouraging slave rebellions. The final draft adopted in 1776 did not contain this criticism. And so again at the Constitutional Convention eloquent objections to the institution of slavery went unheeded, and its opponents eventually consented to a document which laid a foundation for the tragic events that were to follow.

Pennsylvania's Gouverneur Morris provides an example. He opposed slavery and the counting of slaves in determining the basis for representation in Congress. At the Convention he objected that

> the inhabitant of Georgia [or] South Carolina who goes to the coast of Africa, and in defiance of the most sacred laws of humanity tears away his fellow creatures from their dearest connections and damns them to the most cruel bondages, shall have more votes in a Government instituted for protection of the rights of mankind, than the Citizen of Pennsylvania or New Jersey who views with a laudable horror, so nefarious a practice.

And yet Gouverneur Morris eventually accepted the three-fifths accommodation. In fact, he wrote the final draft of the Constitution, the very document the bicentennial will commemorate.

As a result of compromise, the right of the Southern States to continue importing slaves was extended, officially, at least until 1808. We know that it actually lasted a good deal longer, as the Framers possessed no monopoly on the ability to trade moral principles for self-interest. But they nevertheless set an unfortunate example. Slaves could be imported, if the commercial interests of the North were protected. To make the compromise even more palatable, customs duties would be imposed at up to ten dollars per slave as a means of raising public revenues.

No doubt it will be said, when the unpleasant truth of the history of slavery in America is mentioned during this bicentennial year, that the Constitution was a product of its times, and embodied a compromise which, under other circumstances, would not have been made. But the effects of the Framers' compromise have remained for generations. They arose from the contradiction between guaranteeing liberty and justice to all, and denying both to Negroes.

The original intent of the phrase, "We the People," was far too clear for any ameliorating construction. Writing for the Supreme Court in 1857, Chief Justice Taney penned the following passage in the *Dred Scott* case, on the issue whether, in the eyes of the Framers, slaves were "constituent members of the sovereignty," and were to be included among "We the People":

> We think they are not, and that they are not included, and were not intended to be included. . . . They had for more than a century before been regarded as beings of an inferior order, and altogether unfit to associate with the white race . . . ; and so far inferior, that they had no

rights which the white man was bound to respect; and that the negro might justly and lawfully be reduced to slavery for his benefit. . . . [A]ccordingly, a negro of the African race was regarded . . . as an article of property, and held, and bought and sold as such. . . . [N]o one seems to have doubted the correctness of the prevailing opinion of the time.

And so, nearly seven decades after the Constitutional Convention, the Supreme Court reaffirmed the prevailing opinion of the Framers regarding the rights of Negroes in America. It took a bloody civil war before the 13th Amendment could be adopted to abolish slavery, though not the consequences slavery would have for future Americans.

While the Union survived the civil war, the Constitution did not. In its place arose a new, more promising basis for justice and equality, the 14th Amendment, ensuring protection of the life, liberty, and property of *all* persons against deprivations without due process, and guaranteeing legal protection of the laws. And yet almost another century would pass before any significant recognition was obtained of the rights of black Americans to share equally even in such basic opportunities as education, housing, and employment, and to have their votes counted, and counted equally. In the meantime, blacks joined America's military to fight its wars and invested untold hours working in its factories and on its farms, contributing to the development of this country's magnificent wealth and waiting to share in its prosperity.

What is striking is the role legal principles have played throughout America's history in determining the condition of Negroes. They were enslaved by law, emancipated by law, disenfranchised and segregated by law; and, finally, they have begun to win equality by law. Along the way, new constitutional principles have emerged to meet the challenges of a changing society. The progress has been dramatic, and it will continue.

The men who gathered in Philadelphia in 1787 could not have envisioned these changes. They could not have imagined, nor would they have accepted, that the document they were drafting would one day be construed by a Supreme Court to which had been appointed a woman and the descendent of an African slave. "We the People" no longer enslave, but the credit does not belong to the Framers. It belongs to those who refused to acquiesce in outdated notions of "liberty," "justice," and "equality," and who strived to better them.

And so we must be careful, when focusing on the events which took place in Philadelphia two centuries ago, that we not overlook the momentous events which followed, and thereby lose our proper sense of perspective. Otherwise, the odds are that for many Americans the bicentennial celebration will be little more than a blind pilgrimage to the shrine of the original document now stored in a vault in the National Archives. If we seek, instead, a sensitive understanding of the Constitution's inherent defects, and its promising evolution through 200 years of history, the celebration of the "Miracle at Philadelphia" will, in my view, be a far more meaningful and humbling experience. We will see that the true miracle was not the birth of the Constitution, but its life, a life nurtured through two turbulent centuries of our own making, and a life embodying much good fortune that was not.

Thus, in this bicentennial year, we may not all participate in the festivities with flag-waving fervor. Some may more quietly commemorate the suffering, struggle, and sacrifice that have triumphed over much of what was wrong with the original document, and observe the anniversary with hopes not realized and promises not fulfilled. I plan to celebrate the bicentennial of the Constitution as a living document, including the Bill of Rights and the other amendments protecting individual freedoms and human rights.

 **NO**

*Has the Wisdom of the Framers of the Constitution in Promoting a "More Perfect Union" Been Overrated?*

## WILLIAM BRADFORD REYNOLDS
### The Wisdom of the Framers

Let me start with the observation that I regard myself to be most privileged to be a public servant at a time when we celebrate the 200th Anniversary of the Constitution—a magnificent document that has, in my view, no equal in history and every reason to be feted. It is by now no revelation that the Framers would be aghast at the size and reach of government today; but they would also be enormously proud of how much of their legacy has endured. The vitality of the original Constitution, and its various amendments, is reflected by its ability to withstand spirited debate over its content and meaning, a process that thankfully has been taking place with more and more enthusiasm in town meetings and forums all around the country, involving students, public officials, and citizens of every variety in evaluating how well our Constitution has served us over the past two centuries. I find it remarkable—and an enormous tribute to the Constitution—that in every instance about which I have read, these gatherings have been hard-pressed to think of ways in which to improve it in any meaningful manner.

That is not to say that the original Constitution of 1787 was flawless. And in our celebration of the document, we must not overlook its flaws and our long and painful struggles to correct them.

If there was any tendency to do so, it was no doubt corrected a few weeks ago when Justice Thurgood Marshall spoke in Hawaii on the Constitution's Bicentennial celebration. Whatever degree of disagreement one might have with Justice Marshall's comments, he has invigorated the debate on the meaning and vitality of constitutional principles in a focused way that can only serve to underscore the importance of the document itself and why it is so deserving of this Bicentennial celebration.

In recounting his remarks, I will rely on Justice Marshall's own words. He began by warning against what he called the "tendency for the celebration to oversimplify" the adoption and meaning of the Constitution of 1787 and to "overlook the many other events that have been instrumental to our achievements as a nation"—events that, as he explains, included the Civil War and the amendments added to the Constitution in its wake. Thus, he rejected what he described as a complacent belief that the "vision of those who debated and compromised in Philadelphia yielded the 'more perfect Union' it is said we now enjoy." Justice Marshall remarked further that he does not believe—and I quote—that "the meaning of the Constitution was forever 'fixed' at the Philadelphia Convention"; nor does he find "the wisdom, foresight, and sense of justice exhibited by the Framers particularly profound." The government the Framers of 1787 devised, he declared, "was defective from the start, requiring several amendments, a civil war, and momentous social transformation to attain the system of constitutional government, and its respect for the individual freedoms and human rights, we hold as fundamental today."

More specifically, Justice Marshall faulted the original Constitution because, as he put it, the Framers "did not have in mind the majority of America's citizens." The Preamble's "We the People," the Justice said, included only whites. Justice Marshall observes that the Constitution tacitly addressed the slavery issue in two ways: in Article I, section 2, by counting "other Persons" as three-fifths of "free Persons" for purposes of Congressional representation; and in Article I, section 9, by protecting the authority of states to continue importing slaves until 1808. Because the original Constitution was defective in this manner, Justice Marshall holds that "while the Union survived the civil war, the Constitution did not." Taking its place, he said, was "a new, more promising basis for justice and equality, the 14th Amendment, ensuring protection of the life, liberty, and property of *all* persons against deprivations without due process, and guaranteeing equal protection of the laws." For Justice Marshall, it is this new Constitution that we should celebrate; not the old one, which contains "outdated notions of 'liberty,' 'justice,' and 'equality.' " Thus, Justice Marshall declines to participate in the festivities with "flag-waving fervor," but rather plans to celebrate the Bicentennial of the Constitution as a "living document, including the Bill of Rights and the other amendments protecting individual freedoms and human rights."

Justice Marshall chose to focus almost exclusively on the most tragic aspects of the American experience, but he is absolutely right to remind us of them. For the Constitution was intended to be the culmination of a great struggle for the natural rights of men—a philosophy whose cornerstone is the absolute guarantee of equality under the law. When the Framers sought to protect in the Constitution the fundamental rights of man but failed to guarantee explicitly those rights to every individual, they introduced a self-contradiction that preordained struggles and conflicts we continue to confront today.

I am concerned, however, that what Justice Marshall has encouraged is far more than a simple mid-course correction in our celebration of the Constitution. It is one thing to be reminded of the compromise on slavery during the making of the Constitution. It is quite another, however, to encourage the view that there are two constitutions, the one of 1787, the other consisting of the Bill of Rights and the 14th Amendment; that the old one is so thoroughly defective that it did not survive the Civil War, and that the new one alone is worthy of celebration. Certainly, we ought to understand and appreciate the original Constitution in light of its weaknesses as well as its considerable strengths. But in the process, we ought to respectfully decline the invitation to consign it to the dustbin of history. That is a judgment as wrong as any on the other side of the ledger that uncritically praises the document of 1787. We indeed need what Justice Marshall called for—a "proper sense of perspective."

Notwithstanding its very serious flaws, the Constitution in its original form constituted the greatest advance for human liberty in the entire history of mankind, then or since. Indeed, it was only by preserving our underlying *constitutional system*—one of divided governmental authority and separated government powers—that blacks could enjoy the fruits of liberty once that self-contradiction I alluded to was corrected.

Fresh from the experience of subjugation under the British crown on one hand, and the failure of the Articles of Confederation on the other, the Framers understood that there is an interdependent relationship between fundamental rights and the structure and powers of government. Thus, they crafted a government of limited powers, grounded in natural law principles and deriving its authority from the consent of the governed. They designed a system to protect individual rights through a balance and separation of governmental powers, which would forever ensure that the new national government would not exceed its enumerated powers. Not the least of these checks against governmental invasions of individual rights was the creation in Article III of an independent judiciary as a guardian of constitutional values.

Many of the Framers were not satisfied to protect individual rights merely by limiting the power of national government; they insisted upon a Bill of Rights to safeguard explicitly those rights they deemed most fundamental. Although the Bill of Rights was separately adopted, it would be [an] error to view the original Constitution apart from the first ten amendments, for the Framers agreed from the outset that the rights enumerated in the Bill of Rights were the object of government to protect. Beyond setting forth specific rights essential to a free people, the Framers established in the Ninth and Tenth Amendments a decentralized federal structure to more fully secure the free exercise of individual rights and self-government.

This was the basic structure of government the Framers deemed necessary to vindicate the principles of the American Revolution as set forth in the Declaration of Independence; and that, in my view, is the unique and remarkable achievement we celebrate today. But in celebrating the triumph of the Constitution, I am in full agreement that we must not overlook those parts of the constitutional experiment that were not noble and which, fortunately, have long since been corrected. Indeed, the experience of the Framers' compromise on the issue of "equality under law" provides us with important lessons even today.

From our historical vantage point, there is certainly no excuse for the original Constitution's failure to repudiate slavery. In making this deal with the devil—and departing from the absolute principle of "equality under law"—the Framers undermined the moral legitimacy of the Constitution.

But we ought to recognize that on this issue the Framers were faced with a Hobson's choice. The Constitution required unanimous ratification by the states, and at least two of the states refused to consent unless the slave trade was protected. James Wilson explained the dilemma: "Under the present Confederation, the states may admit the importation of slaves as long as they please; but by this article, after the year 1808, the Congress will have power to prohibit such importation. . . . I consider this as laying the foundation for banishing slavery out of this country." We know now that this hope was far too optimistic; and indeed, it would take the Civil War to rid the nation of that evil institution.

But even as the Framers were acceding to this compromise, they were sowing the seeds for the expansion of freedom to all individuals when circumstances would permit. James Wilson, for example, emphasized that "the term *slave* was not *admitted* in this *Constitution*." Instead, the term "Person" was used, suggesting that when the slaves became "free Persons," they would be entitled to all the rights appertaining to free individuals.

Indeed, many abolitionist leaders argued that the Constitution, by its omission of any mention of slavery, did not tolerate slavery. Noting that the Constitution nowhere mentions the word "slave," Frederick Douglass declared that "[i]n that instrument, I hold there is neither warrant, license, nor sanction of the hateful thing." Yet such arguments were tragically unheeded by the United States Supreme Court in the *Dred Scott* decision, which provided succor to the notion that there are justifications for exceptions to the principle of "equality under law"—a notion that despite its sordid origins has not been totally erased to this day.

Indeed, the *Dred Scott* decision illustrates that a significant part of the responsibility for our failure to make good on the principle of "equality under law" can and should be assigned less to shortcomings in the original Constitution—as Justice Marshall would have us believe—but to those who sat where Justice Marshall now sits, charged with interpreting that document.

Justice Marshall apparently believes that the original flaws in the Constitution dictated the result in *Dred Scott*. I am more inclined toward the view of my colleagues at the Department of Justice, Charles J. Cooper and Nelson Lund, who argue that Chief Justice Taney's constitutional interpretation was "loose, disingenuous, and result-oriented." Justice Curtis' dissent sounded a warning over this type of judicial interpretation unattached to constitutional moorings that is as compelling now as it was 125 years ago:

Political reasons have not the requisite certainty to afford rules of interpretation. They are different in different men. They are different in the same men at different times. And when a strict interpretation of the Constitution, according to the fixed rules which govern the interpretation of laws, is abandoned, and the theoretical opinions of individuals are allowed to control its meaning, we no longer have a Constitution; we are under the government of individual men, who for the time being have power to declare what the Constitution is, according to their own views of what it ought to mean.

The judiciary's tragic failure to follow the terms of the Constitution did not occur in this one instance only. Indeed, the Civil War amendments and civil rights legislation passed in that era were in the next several decades emptied of meaning by the Supreme Court in decision after decision. In *Plessy* v. *Ferguson*, to cite but one example, the Court once again stepped in and, over the lone, brilliant dissent of the elder Justice Harlan, shamefully sacrificed the principle of "equality under law."

I daresay that had the Court fully honored its mandate under the original Constitution in *Dred Scott*, or under the Fourteenth Amendment in *Plessy* v. *Ferguson*, we could well have escaped much of the racial strife and social divisiveness that Justice Marshall lays at the doorstep of the Constitution itself. Indeed, the tragic legacy of those decisions—the deadening consequences that so regularly flow from a compromise (no matter how well intended) of the principle of "equality under law"—provides a sobering lesson for the present Court as it struggles with similar issues involving race and gender discrimination. These are issues that no less so than in an earlier era leave hanging in the balance the overarching question of whether the liberating promise of the Constitution, as originally understood and subsequently articulated in explicit terms by ratification of the Civil War amendments, will or will not be fulfilled for all Americans.

Justice Marshall, I would respectfully submit, too casually brushes so weighty a concern to one side in contending that the Constitution did not survive the Civil War. One would think that this assertion would at least invite from some quarter the obvious questions: Did separation of powers survive the Civil War? Did the executive branch and the Congress? Did, indeed, the institution of judicial review?

I must admit to quite a different reading of history, one that has an abiding appreciation of the fact that our Constitution did survive so cataclysmic an upheaval as the Civil War. In all too many instances of internal strife among a People, one form of subjugation is ultimately replaced by another. But the Civil War produced a far different (indeed unique) result: its consequence was to more perfectly secure and extend to all Americans—through the Thirteenth, Fourteenth, and Fifteenth Amendments—the blessings of liberty as set forth in the Declaration of Independence, blessings of liberty that had already been secured for other Americans in the original Constitution and Bill of Rights. It is revisionist history of the worst sort to suggest that the Fourteenth Amendment created a blank constitutional slate on which judges could write their own personalized definition of equality or fundamental rights. The Civil War Amendments were a logical extension of what had come before: they represented *evolutionary,* not *revolutionary* change.

To be sure, the Fourteenth Amendment does offer support for Justice Marshall's claim that the Constitution is "a living document," but only in the sense that the Constitution itself provides a mechanism—namely, the amendment process—to reflect changing social realities. Indeed, this orderly process for constitutional "evolution" is a part of the original Constitution's genius, for it provides a mechanism to correct flaws while safeguarding the essential integrity of our constitutional structure. But the existence of this mechanism—coupled with the system of checks and balances among the three branches of the federal government and the strong endorsement of federalism principles embodied in the Tenth Amendment—makes it abundantly clear that the Framers gave no license to judges (members of the Branch regarded, to borrow from Alexander Hamilton, as the "least dangerous" of the three) to construe constitutional provisions as they see fit.

There is good reason for this confluence of restraints on judicial activism. The Constitution is not a mass of fungible, abstract principles whose meaning varies with time; rather, it comprises a broad societal consensus on certain fundamental, absolute principles necessary for the protection of individual liberty. The Framers believed that these constitutional values should not be lightly disturbed or set aside. Accordingly, the Constitution was structured so as to require that any change reflect the broadest expression of societal consensus.

This does not leave the Supreme Court or lower federal courts unable to apply the Constitution to circumstances never contemplated by the Framers. But the Judges are not free to disengage from our constitutional moorings in furtherance of their own social agendas; they are not free to determine that the constitutional principles themselves are unwise or obsolete.

Indeed, the very premise on which rests the notion that the Constitution as originally framed has no relevance today is fatally flawed. For the fact remains that the core structure upon which the Constitution was based—a government of limited powers, federalism, separation of powers, protection of fundamental individual rights—has proven in the past two centuries far superior to any other governmental system in protecting human freedoms. And where proponents of change have successfully secured the broad consensus necessary to amend the Constitution, they have expanded and perfected those protections. But judicial activism as an illegitimate substitute for the amendment process can only jeopardize our fundamental freedoms by denigrating the structural underpinnings vital to their survival.

Justice Marshall's contrary thesis is gerry-built on a regrettable overstatement of perceived flaws in the Constitution without so much as a passing reference to the qualities that have endured for the past two hundred years: a governmental structure that has withstood the test of time, weathered turbulent conflicts, and proven itself to be the greatest engine for individual freedom in the history of mankind. That remarkable accomplishment is certainly worth the celebration it is receiving, and much, much more.

Let us not be content with less than a complete appreciation for this document on which our Republic stands. Let us accept Justice Marshall's invitation to explore fully the lessons of the past two centuries. But let us decline his invitation to break the Constitution into two, and to reject the document of 1787 and accept only that which followed the Civil War. We are under a Constitution; it is the original Constitution together with its twenty-six amendments that we must seek to understand and uphold. Let us never forget that the Constitution is in its entirety the Supreme Law of the Land, and all of the branches—the executive, legislative, and judicial—are subordinate to it. We must embrace the Constitution as a whole: not uncritically, but not unlovingly either. Our task, in this Bicentennial year, should be that of loving critics. For our Constitution has provided this great nation of ours with a charter for liberty and government that has enabled us to move ever closer to that "more perfect Union" the Framers envisioned.

In conclusion, it is fitting that I call on the words of former Chief Justice Warren Burger, the Chairman of the Bicentennial Commission. He said it best when he remarked that the Constitution "isn't perfect, but it's the best thing in the world." Our Constitution embodies the American spirit, the American Dream, and America's doctrinal commitment to civil rights—those fundamental rights we all hold equally as American citizens. For this reason, I respectfully part company with Justice Marshall in my view that it is indeed our Constitution as framed two centuries ago, and amended thereafter from time to time, that stands tall today as "the source of all the very best that has followed." Let us not hesitate to celebrate.

## Questions for Discussion

1. How did the political system adopted by the United States in the late eighteenth century compare to the political systems in other countries during the same period in terms of ensuring individual freedom?
2. What would have been the consequences to the political development of the United States had the Framers included provisions outlawing slavery and granting political equality for blacks?
3. What were the assumptions of the Framers about the relationship between individuals and the government?
4. What effect did the constitutional prescription to divide power between a central government and the states and between the different branches of the central government have on the condition of black people?

5. What evidence can you supply to accept or reject the proposition that the Constitution did not survive the Civil War?
6. What impact should the intent of the Framers have on Supreme Court justices in deciding cases today? What are the reasons for your answer?

## Suggested Readings

Beard, Charles A. *An Economic Interpretation of the Constitution of the United States.* New York: Free Press, 1986. [Reprinted, originally published New York: Macmillan, 1913.]

Berns, Walter. *Taking the Constitution Seriously.* New York: Simon & Schuster, 1987.

Currie, David P. *The Constitution in the Supreme Court: The First Hundred Years, 1789–1888.* Chicago: Univ. of Chicago Press, 1985.

Farrand, Max, ed. *The Records of the Federal Convention of 1787.* New Haven: Yale Univ. Press, 1937.

Goldwin, Robert A. *Why Blacks, Women, and Jews Are Not Mentioned in the Constitution and Other Unorthodox Views.* Washington, D.C.: American Enterprise Institute for Public Policy Research, 1989.

Hamilton, Alexander, James Madison, and John Jay. *The Federalist Papers,* edited by Clinton Rossiter. New York: New American Library, 1961.

Ketcham, Ralph, ed. *The Anti-Federalist Papers; and the Constitutional Convention Debates.* New York: New American Library, 1986.

Loury, Glenn C. " 'Matters of Color'—Blacks and the Constitutional Order." *Public Interest,* no. 86 (Winter 1987), 109–123.

McDonald, Forrest. *We the People: Economic Origins of the Constitution.* Chicago: Univ. of Chicago Press, 1958.

Mee, Charles L., Jr. *The Genius of the People.* New York: Harper & Row, 1987.

Morris, Richard B. *Witnesses at the Creation: Hamilton, Madison, Jay and the Constitution.* New York: New American Library, 1986.

Storing, Herbert J., with the assistance of Murray Dry, eds. *The Complete Anti-Federalist.* 7 vols. Chicago: Univ. of Chicago Press, 1981.

# Chapter 2

# Does the Separation of Powers Need to Be Changed?

It is generally accepted that without compromise the Constitutional Convention would have failed. One important conflict was between the large states, which favored representation based on population, and the small states, which wanted each state to have equal representation. This conflict was resolved by establishing a House of Representatives constituted on the basis of population and a Senate represented on the principle of state equality. Another conflict involved popular participation in the political process. This division was resolved by permitting the House of Representatives to be elected by popular vote and the Senate to be elected by the state legislatures (the Seventeenth Amendment ratified in 1913 required the direct election of senators).

The Constitution provided for a stronger central government than had existed under the Articles of Confederation. That new government was to be a republic in which the president and Congress would be elected directly or indirectly by the people. The Constitution also provided for the establishment of the basic institutions of the national government: the presidency, the Congress, and the Supreme Court. Specific provisions were made for how leaders would be chosen for these offices and how their authority would be limited.

The Framers feared the concentration of power in the hands of a few, but they also wanted to avoid "mob rule" by the majority. A fundamental feature of the new Constitution was, therefore, a system of shared power. Each branch of the federal government has primary power in one area, but that power is not total. Congress, consequently, has primary legislative power; the president, primary executive power; and the Supreme Court, primary judiciary power.

Each of these powers, however, is shared. The president exercises some judicial power (the nomination of judges to the Supreme Court) and some legislative power (the vetoing of legislation). Congress has some executive power (Senate confirmation of executive appointments) and some judicial power (impeachment by the House of Representatives). The Supreme Court, too, has some legislative power (the interpretation of laws) and some executive power (the administration of laws to ensure compliance with judicial decisions).

But this central feature of the Constitution is itself under debate. The Committee on the Constitutional System (CCS), a nonpartisan organization composed of present and past government officials and private citizens, argues that the system is outmoded. The CCS is chaired by Senator

Nancy Landon Kassebaum, Republican from Kansas; C. Douglas Dillon, former secretary of the treasury and undersecretary of state; and Lloyd N. Cutler, former counsel to the president. Its purpose is to study and analyze the U.S. constitutional system.

In its *Report and Recommendations,* the CCS points to strains in the constitutional system, such as the mounting national debt, conflicts between Congress and the president over foreign policy, and malfunctions of the modern electoral system. The report places principal blame for these developments on the diffuse structure of the separation of powers and the decline in party loyalty and party cohesion at all levels of the political system. It notes the adverse effects of the system: a brief "honeymoon" between president and Congress, divided government, lack of party cohesion in Congress, loss of accountability, and lack of a mechanism for replacing failed or deadlocked government. It presents proposals adopted by the CCS and additional proposals worth considering. According to the CCS, such proposals would strengthen party cohesion, improve collaboration between the executive and legislative branches, and reduce the costs of campaigning for election.

In essence, the CCS would like the U.S. constitutional system to pattern itself after the British parliamentary system. In the British system the prime minister is a member of Parliament; the majority party or a majority coalition of parties controls the House of Commons—the chief legislative institution; and party members in the House of Commons generally vote the way the party decides. A losing vote in the House of Commons results in new elections for all members of that chamber.

James Q. Wilson, Collins Professor of Management at the University of California at Los Angeles, argues that the criticisms against the existing constitutional system are not valid. He contends that the national deficit, failures of economic policy, and conflicts between the executive and legislative branches on foreign policy matters are not caused by the separation of powers and that proposed reforms will not solve the inherent problems. He notes that there are two fundamental arguments for a constitutional system of separate institutions sharing powers: "It helps preserve liberty and it slows the pace of political change." In his view these arguments are as valid today as they were when the Constitution was written.

Both selections mention political parties, a political institution not mentioned in the Constitution because formal parties did not exist when the Constitution was drafted. Like some other institutions not mentioned or emphasized in the Constitution—the committee system in Congress and the bureaucracy, for example—political parties have evolved to meet the needs of a changing society and have come to play an important role in the U.S. political process, as we shall see in Part II.

## Does the Separation of Powers Need to Be Changed?

### COMMITTEE ON THE CONSTITUTIONAL SYSTEM

## A Bicentennial Analysis of the American Political Structure

Two hundred years ago, the founders of the American republic decided that the governmental system that had guided them safely through the War for Independence was in need of change. They became convinced that nothing short of a new constitution would meet the demands that lay ahead.

Having reached this conclusion, they did not hesitate to take the necessary action. The result was the framing and ratification of the United States Constitution.

As we approach the bicentennial of the Constitution, Americans are eager to honor the framers' work, which is truly one of the great achievements of human history.

The system designed in 1787 has proven remarkably adaptable to the changing demands of a growing nation. Political leaders have been imaginative and bold in finding ways to adapt the system to meet evolving national responsibilities and needs. Hamilton, Jefferson and Madison themselves took the lead in creating the party system, building greater cohesion and efficiency into the lawmaking process.

As the United States shifted from an agricultural to an industrial society and the regulation of commercial and financial markets became too complex for a government of separated powers, a later generation of politicians invented the independent regulatory commission, combining rule-making, administrative and adjudicatory powers in a single governmental body.

During the 1930s, new signs of strain began to appear. In response to the Great Depression, the government embarked on a vast set of programs to manage the growth of our modern industrial economy and provide a measure of social justice for those who suffered from its malfunctions. Then dangerous challenges to American security arose in Europe and the Far East and in our own national defense, and we had to assume global military and foreign policy responsibilities. These developments, domestic and foreign, required the federal government to undertake new tasks that were unprecedented in kind or scope and could hardly have been foreseen by the framers.

Thoughtful observers soon realized that the governmental structure was straining under this enormous additional load. A series of commissions chaired by Louis Brownlow, Herbert Hoover and Roy Ash made sweeping recommendations that became the basis for extensive modernization of the executive branch. Distinguished panels in the Senate and House chaired by Mike Monroney and Robert LaFollette, Jr., Richard Bolling, Adlai Stevenson III and William Brock

19

brought about important changes in the procedures and committee structure of Congress. Groups outside the government (such as the National Academy of Public Administration, the Committee on Political Parties of the American Political Science Association and the Committee for Economic Development), as well as individual analysts and authors, offered other suggestions for reform.

Though most of these studies confined themselves to recommending adjustments within the existing framework, many recognized that the twentieth-century problems confronting our eighteenth-century American political system might require changes in the constitutional structure. Changes in statutes and party rules are of course less difficult to make and ought to be tried before changes in the Constitution itself. Changes in the Constitution should not be shunned, however, if critical modern problems cannot be solved by other means.

In the last Federalist Paper, Alexander Hamilton urged that the Constitution be ratified despite the objections that were being raised, because there would be opportunity later to make amendments as experience revealed the need. James Madison and Gouverneur Morris likewise acknowledged imperfections in the framers' brilliant work.

For example, the same document that established the Bill of Rights also countenanced the continued practice of slavery. When that contradiction became apparent over the next century, the resulting constitutional crisis produced a terrible civil war. Abraham Lincoln called a distracted nation to attention with the words, "We must disenthrall ourselves." "The dogmas of the quiet past," he added, "are inadequate to the stormy present. . . . As our case is new, so we must think anew, and act anew." And the Constitution was amended to outlaw slavery, root and branch.

Thomas Jefferson considered the amendment process one of the Constitution's most important features. "I am certainly not an advocate for frequent and untried changes in laws and constitutions," he wrote. "But I know also that laws and institutions must go hand in hand with the progress of the human mind. As that becomes more developed, more enlightened, as new discoveries are made, new truths disclosed, and manners and opinions change with the change of circumstances, institutions must advance also and keep pace with the times."

As Jefferson foresaw, we too face unprecedented challenges. If aspects of the system framed in 1787 prevent the national government from meeting its present responsibilities, we must identify the outmoded features, separate them from the good and durable parts of the system and make the necessary modifications.

To do so is not to reject the great work of our forebears. It honors their spirit in the most sincere way: by seeking to emulate it.


## SIGNS OF STRAIN

As the bicentennial draws near, the signs of strain in our governing processes are unmistakable.

Perhaps the most alarming evidence is the mounting national debt, fueled anew each year by outsized and unsustainable deficits that defy the good intentions of legislators and Presidents.

Consistency in our foreign and national security policies is also frustrated by an institutional contest of wills between Presidents and shifting, cross-party coalitions within the Congress. Over forty treaties submitted to the Senate for ratification since World War II have either been rejected or have never come to a vote. Among those that have never come to a vote are SALT [Strategic Arms Limitation Treaty] II, the 1974 and 1976 treaties on underground nuclear tests and explosions, maritime boundary treaties with Mexico and Canada, several UN [United Nations] and OAS [Organization of American States] human rights conventions, and a wide variety of bilateral trade, tax and environmental treaties. Meanwhile presidential concern over "leaks" and frustration with congressionally imposed restrictions have led Presidents and their staffs to launch important diplomatic, military and covert activities in secret and without consulting Congress.

Further problems—particularly damaging in a nation dedicated to the principle of self-government—stem from malfunctions of the modern electoral system: the high cost of running for office, the corroding influence of campaign contributions from single-interest groups, the stupefying length of campaigns (for the presidency, usually several years from initiation to inauguration), and persistently low turnout rates (among the lowest in the world for nations with competitive elections).

## CAUSES

Sensing the failures and weaknesses in governmental performance, people tend to blame particular politicians or the complexity of the modern world. But our public officials are no less competent, either individually or as a group, than they used to be. Nor do our problems, as complex as they are, defy rational solutions consistent with our basic constitutional liberties. The difficulty lies mainly in the diffuse structure of the executive-legislative process and in the decline of party loyalty and cohesion at all levels of the political system.

The separation of powers, as a principle of constitutional structure, has served us well in preventing tyranny and the abuse of high office, but it has done so by encouraging confrontation, indecision and deadlock, and by diffusing accountability for the results.

Ideally our two-party system should counteract the centrifugal tendencies of the separation of powers, with each party's politicians committed to a common philosophy of government and to specific program goals for which they stand accountable at the next election. In fact, throughout most of the nineteenth century and until after the end of World War II, the loyalty of most politicians to their party was deeply felt. They ran for office on a ticket selected by the party's leaders. Once in office, they recognized a common stake in the success of their party's governance and their joint accountability as candidates of the party at the next election.

In recent decades, however, political reforms and technological changes have worked together to weaken the parties and undermine their ability to draw the separated parts of the government into coherent action. Beginning in the late nineteenth century, Congress enacted a series of measures that redistributed functions previously performed by the parties. Civil service systems stripped the parties of much of their patronage.

The rise of the welfare state took away many opportunities for service by which the parties had won and held the loyalty of their followers. The secret ballot replaced the "tickets" which had previously been prepared by the parties and handed to the voters to cast into the ballot box. The 17th Amendment (ratified in 1913), which required the direct election of Senators, dealt another blow to party cohesiveness. So did the direct primary, which came to dominate the nomination of presidential candidates, particularly after 1968.

Modern technology has enabled candidates to appeal to voters directly, through television, computer-assisted mailings and telephone campaigns, and by quick visits in jet airplanes, all of which have lessened their dependence on party organizations and leaders. The key to these technologies is money, but candidates found they could raise it directly for themselves better than through the party organization. At the same time, interest groups found they could exercise more power over legislative votes by contributing directly to selected candidates rather than to a party.

The habits of voters also changed in this new environment. Party loyalty had been the rule for most of the nineteenth century, but by the last quarter of the twentieth century, one-third of all voters were registered as independents, and even among voters registering with parties, ticket-splitting became the norm.

Many of these changes resulted from laudable reforms and were, in any case, inevitable. No one wants to roll the clock back to the time when party bosses and local "machines" dominated the political process.

Nevertheless, we need to recognize that the weakening of parties in the electoral arena has contributed to the disintegration of party cohesion among the officials we elect to public office. Members of Congress who owe their election less to their party than to their own endeavors and their own sources of funds have little incentive to cooperate with party leaders in the Congress, much less their party's incumbent in the White House. And the proliferation of congressional committees and subcommittees has increased the disarray. There are now so many that almost every member is the chairman or ranking minority member of at least one committee or subcommittee, with all the political influence, proliferating staffs, publicity and fund-raising potential needed to remain in office.

## EFFECTS

Because the separation of powers encourages conflict between the branches and because the parties are weak, the capacity of the federal government to fashion, enact and administer coherent public policy has diminished and the ability of elected officials to avoid accountability for governmental failures has grown. More specifically, the problems include:

### Brief Honeymoons

Only the first few months of each four-year presidential term provide an opportunity for decisive action on domestic problems. By the second year, congressional incumbents are engrossed in the mid-term election and defer difficult decisions that will offend any important interest group.

The mid-term election usually results in a setback for the President's party that weakens his leadership and increases the stalemate and deadlock in the Congress. After the mid-term election, the government comes close to immobility as the President and Congress focus their energies on the imminent presidential election.

### Divided Government

We have had divided government (one party winning the White House and the other a majority in one or both houses of Congress) 60 percent of the time since 1956 and 80 percent of the time since 1968, compared to less than 25 percent of the time from the adoption of the Constitution until World War II.

This has led to inconsistency, incoherence and even stagnation in national policy. Affirmative policy decisions, as well as the nondecisions resulting from frequent deadlocks that block any action at all, are reached by shifting majorities built out of cross-party coalitions that change from one issue to the next.

Divided government in turn reflects the decline in party loyalty and the growing practice of ticket-splitting among the electorate. In 1900 only four percent of all congressional districts were carried by one party's presidential candidate and the other party's candidate for Member of the House. By 1984, because of the growth of ticket-splitting, this happened in 44 percent of all congressional districts.

One of Woodrow Wilson's themes during the campaign of 1912—a time of divided government—was that only party government (with one party successfully bridging the separated powers by winning control of the presidency and both houses of Congress) could carry a coherent program into effect. The voters in 1912 responded by choosing party government, and Wilson's New Freedom program was successfully legislated.

## Lack of Party Cohesion in Congress

Even in times of united government, disunity persists between the branches—and between and within the two houses of Congress—because many members of both the President's party and the opposition party reject the positions taken by their leaders. Legislators today have less reason to stick with their party's position and more reason to follow the urgings of non-party political action committees, which provide more of their campaign funds than the party does. The summary rejection of President Reagan's budget in 1986, even by members of his own party in the Republican-controlled Senate, dramatically illustrates the lack of party cohesion in the current political environment. This lack of cohesion induces Presidents and their staffs, as noted above, to conceal important foreign policy initiatives even from the leaders of their own party in Congress.

## Loss of Accountability

Divided government and party disunity also lead to diffused accountability. No elected official defends the sum of all the inconsistent policy decisions made by so many shifting cross-party coalitions, and each successfully shifts the blame to others. Polls show the public is dissatisfied with the governmental institutions—especially Congress and the bureaucracy—that legislate and administer this hodge-podge of policies. But the public seldom holds a party accountable for these failures, and it hardly ever holds individual legislators responsible.

Since World War II, 90 percent of each party's incumbent legislators who sought another term have been reelected, even in years when their party lost the White House. In 1986 the figure was 97 percent. Benjamin Franklin's famous maxim, "We must all hang together, or assuredly we shall all hang separately," no longer applies to the Members of Congress of either party.

## Lack of a Mechanism for Replacing Failed or Deadlocked Government

Presently there is no way between our fixed election dates to resolve basic disagreements between the President and Congress by referring them to the electorate. The only way to remove a failed President is by a House impeachment and Senate trial for "treason, bribery, or other high crimes and misdemeanors." And between the fixed election dates there is no way to reorient a Congress in which one or both houses obstruct an important and popular presidential program.

## REMEDIES

In seeking to adjust the constitutional system to modern conditions, we must be careful to preserve its enduring virtues. We must continue to respect the Bill of Rights, protected by an independent judiciary, and we must continue to insist that elected officials be able to monitor one another's performance and call one another to account.

Consistent with these principles, it should be possible to design improvements that would encourage party cohesion and lessen the deadlock between the executive and legislative branches without sacrificing essential checks and balances. The Committee on the Constitutional System offers the following proposals as sufficiently meritorious to warrant national consideration and debate. Some of these proposals call only for adopting new party rules or statutes, while others would require amendments to the Constitution.

## PROPOSALS WHICH COMMAND MAJORITY SUPPORT AMONG OUR MEMBERSHIP

### Strengthening Parties as Agents of Cohesion and Accountability

*1. THE PARTY PRESIDENTIAL NOMINATING CONVENTION* The parties should amend their rules for the presidential nominating conventions so as to entitle all winners of the party nominations for the House and Senate, plus the holdover Senators, to seats as uncommitted voting delegates in the presidential nominating convention. This would give the congressional candidates of the party a significant voice in selecting the presidential candidate, increase the loyalties between them in the election campaign, improve cohesion between the President and the legislative incumbents of his party and tend to make them jointly accountable to the voters in the next election.

*2. OPTIONAL STRAIGHT-TICKET BALLOTING* Congress should enact a statute requiring all states to include a line or lever on federal election ballots enabling voters, if they so desire, to cast a straight-line party ballot for a party's candidates for all open federal offices.

A recent survey shows that nineteen states, including Illinois, New York and Pennsylvania, already have such statutes and that ticket-splitting is less common in those states. This would encourage party loyalty at the voter level and among a party's federal candidates. To the extent that it reduced ticket-splitting, it would lessen the likelihood of divided federal government, while still leaving voters free to split their tickets if they chose.

**3. PUBLIC FINANCING OF CONGRESSIONAL CAMPAIGNS** Congress should amend the campaign financing laws to create a Congressional Broadcast Fund similar to the existing Presidential Campaign Fund. This fund would be available to each party under a formula similar to that used for the Presidential Campaign Fund, on condition that the party and its candidates expend no other funds on campaign broadcasts. Half of each party's share would go to the nominees themselves. The other half would go to the party's Senate and House campaign committees, which could apportion the funds among candidates so as to maximize the party's chances of winning a legislative majority.

By requiring candidates to look to the party for a substantial part of their broadcast funds, this proposal would help to build party loyalty and cohesion. It would also provide a constitutional way of limiting expenditures on the largest single component of campaign financing costs.

## Improving Collaboration between the Executive and Legislative Branches

**1. FOUR-YEAR TERMS FOR HOUSE MEMBERS AND EIGHT-YEAR TERMS FOR SENATORS, WITH FEDERAL ELECTIONS EVERY FOURTH YEAR** The present system of staggered elections has the effect of pulling the branches apart. Members of the House, who run every two years, feel a political need to demonstrate their independence from the White House, particularly in off-year elections. So do the one-third of the Senators who face an election within two years. Every other time an incumbent in either house runs for reelection, there is no presidential campaign.

The effect is to encourage legislators to distance themselves from the President and from presidential programs that may involve a difficult, short-term adjustment on the way to a worthwhile, longer-term result.

The Constitution could be amended so that the President and Members of the House would serve concurrent, four-year terms, and one Senator from each state would be elected for an eight-year term at each presidential election. This would eliminate the present House and Senate elections in the middle of the presidential term. It would lengthen and coordinate the political horizons of all incumbents. Presidents and legislators could join to enact necessary measures with the promise of longer-run benefits, without having to worry about an imminent election before the benefits were realized.

With fewer elections, the aggregate cost of campaign financing should go down, and legislators would be less frequently or immediately in thrall to the interest groups on whom they depend for funds. The honeymoon for enacting a President's program would be longer. With a four-year life for each Congress, the legislative process for the budget and other measures could be made more orderly and deliberate.

*Alternatives.* If the eight-year term for Senators were deemed too long, the Senate term could be shortened to four years, concurrent with the terms of the President and the House, which would also eliminate the mid-term election. Or, if the Senate would not accept a shortened term, we could keep the present six-year term. This would retain a limited mid-term election (for one-third of the Senate), permitting a partial referendum on government policy, at the cost of shortening the political horizon of one-third of the Senate.

**2. PERMITTING MEMBERS OF CONGRESS TO SERVE IN THE CABINET** The Constitution now bars members of Congress from serving as heads of administrative departments or agencies or holding any other executive-branch position. This provision was intended to prevent the President from dominating Congress by offering executive positions to key legislators. But its principal effect has been to deprive the nation of administrators who would have the confidence of both the executive and legislative branches.

If the barrier were removed from the Constitution, Presidents would have the option of appointing leading legislators to cabinet positions, and legislators would have the option of accepting such offers, without being required to give up their seats in Congress. Such ties between the branches might encourage closer collaboration and help to prevent stalemates. They would broaden both the range of talent available to a President in forming his administration and the base of political leadership in the executive branch.

Under such an amendment, of course, a President would not be obliged to appoint any members of Congress to his cabinet, nor would they be obliged to accept.

Woodrow Wilson strongly favored this amendment, as a means to encourage closer collaboration between the branches. While modern legislators may have less time and incentive to join the cabinet than earlier generations, there is no longer any reason for a constitutional barrier to an experiment that has considerable promise and little risk.

**3. RELAXING THE REQUIREMENTS FOR TREATY RATIFICATION** The ability to enter into formal agreements with other nations is vital to effective national government in an increasingly interdependent world. The present constitutional requirement that treaties require the approval of two-thirds of the Senate has been a major barrier to the use of treaties and has led to evasion of the treaty process by way of executive agreements.

To restore an appropriate congressional role in the making of agreements with foreign powers, this provision should be amended to require that treaties can take effect with the approving vote of a constitutional majority of both houses. If the Senate does not join in proposing such an amendment, it should at least approve an amendment reducing the present requirement of approval by two-thirds of the Senate to 60 percent.

## Reducing the Costs of Campaigning for Election

The lack of any legal limit on total campaign expenditures has led to a spiraling, competitive escalation in campaign costs. In the 1986 mid-term election, the legislative candidates raised and spent $342 million, up 30 percent over 1984. The cost of campaigning has put a contested seat in Congress beyond the means of everyone who is not either personally wealthy or willing to become dependent on well-heeled special interest groups. The Supreme Court's interpretation of the First Amendment seems to prohibit Congress from limiting private campaign expenditures by legislation, although the Court has authorized public financing on the condition that candidates who accept it limit their expenditures to these federal funds.

A constitutional amendment allowing Congress to set reasonable limits on campaign expenditures would not endanger the freedom of expression guaranteed by the First Amendment. If such an amendment were adopted, many able citizens who now reject the idea of standing for election might be attracted to political office, and the divisive influence of interest group contributions might be reduced to the point where more cohesive government would again become feasible.

## ADDITIONAL PROPOSALS WORTH CONSIDERING

The changes recommended in the previous section command majority support among members of the Committee on the Constitutional System. A number of other ideas have found less than majority support to date, but some members believe they are important enough to deserve further discussion. They fall into four categories.

## Strengthening Party Cohesion and Party Accountability

### 1. ENCOURAGING PRESIDENTIAL APPEARANCES BEFORE CONGRESS

Congress and the President should work out mutually agreeable voluntary arrangements for periodic presidential appearances before major congressional committees. These appearances would be used to present presidential positions and to answer congressional questions about presidential actions and proposals. Such arrangements would be consistent with the provision in Article II that the President "shall from time to time give to the Congress information on the State of the Union." They would also encourage greater cohesion between the President and the members of his party in Congress.

### 2. CREATING A SHADOW CABINET FOR THE LEGISLATIVE OPPOSITION

Legislators of the party losing the presidential election should organize a "shadow cabinet." The party's leaders in each house might alternate annually as leader and spokesman of the shadow cabinet, and the party's chairman or ranking member of the major committees in each house might alternate annually as shadow spokesmen in their particular fields, with their counterparts in the other house serving as deputy spokesmen. The shadow cabinet could coordinate party positions on legislative issues and act as party spokesmen before the public.

## Reducing the Likelihood of Divided Government

For 20 of the last 32 years—and for 14 out of the last 18—the White House and at least one house of Congress have been controlled by opposing parties. Some of the measures suggested above should reduce the likelihood of divided government, but they may be insufficient to eliminate it. If divided government is recognized as the preeminent cause of interbranch conflict and policy stalemate and deadlock, two stronger approaches are worth considering.

### 1. MANDATORY STRAIGHT TICKETS

The first approach is to make straight-ticket voting not merely easier, as suggested above, but compulsory. By constitutional amendment, each party's nominees for President, Vice President, Senate and House could be placed on the ballot as a single slate, with the voter required to cast his or her vote for one of the party slates in its entirety.

The drawback to this idea is that Americans are strongly committed to voting for the person rather than the party. They would not be easily convinced to sacrifice this freedom in the interest of party loyalty and cohesion.

**2. SEQUENTIAL ELECTIONS**  The second approach is for Congress to enact a statute providing for sequential elections in presidential years, with the voting for President and Vice President to be conducted two to four weeks before the voting for members of Congress. Under such a proposal voters would already know, at the time they balloted for members of Congress, which party they have entrusted with the presidency. This would give the newly elected President an opportunity to persuade voters to elect a majority of the same party to Congress and thus give the party a better opportunity to carry out its program.

The drawbacks here are that in the congressional election Americans might still vote for the person rather than the party. Also, there would probably be a considerable fall-off in the number of voters in the congressional election.

## Calling New Elections in the Event of Deadlock or Governmental Failure

If it were possible for a President to call new elections, or for Congress to do so, we would have a mechanism for resolving deadlocks over fundamental policy issues. Indeed, the very existence of such a mechanism would be an inducement to avoid a deadlock that could trigger new elections. It would also make it possible to reconstitute a government that had palpably failed for any other reason.

There are formidable obstacles to incorporating such a device in our present system. Should the President alone, or Congress alone, or both the President and Congress be empowered to call for new elections? How soon should they follow after the passage of the resolution calling for them? Are we prepared to vote in a month other than November? Should there be full new terms for the winners (perhaps adjusted to the regular January expiration dates), or should they fill just the unexpired terms?

These questions can probably be answered. The real questions are whether we need such a strong device for breaking deadlocks or for removing Presidents who have failed for reasons other than impeachable conduct, and whether it is likely that in a special election the electorate would break the deadlock or would simply reelect all the incumbents.

Most constitutional democracies employ such a device, and it deserves serious consideration. It is not inconsistent with separated powers, and it might well operate to encourage cooperation between the branches in order to forestall the ordeal of special elections.

## Reexamining the Federal-State Relationship

The weaknesses of the federal government are in large part the result of over-load. This overload could be lessened by a better division of responsibility among federal, state and local governments.

A special convocation could be held every ten years with delegates to be selected in equal numbers by federal, state and local governments in a manner to be determined by Congress, to make recommendations to achieve a more cooperative, equitable, efficient, accountable and responsive federal system, under procedures requiring Congress and the state legislatures to vote on each recommendation.

## MINORITY PROPOSAL FOR A POSSIBLE PACKAGE

Further discussion of these measures, and others that may be advanced, may well produce a package offering total benefits greater than the sum of the individual parts.

Some of our members believe, for example, that the following measures could be combined into a desirable package.

1. Adopting four-year terms for House members and eight-year terms for Senators, with elections in presidential years.
2. Empowering the President (perhaps with the consent of a specified number of members of one or both houses) or the Congress (by a special or regular majority of both houses, or perhaps even by an absolute majority of the members of one house) to call for a prompt election to all federal offices for new, full terms.
3. Permitting the President to appoint members of Congress to the executive branch without requiring them to give up their seats.
4. Allowing Congress, by constitutional amendment, if necessary, to place reasonable limitations on the total that may be spent in a political campaign.
5. Holding a federal-state-local convocation every ten years to make recommendations for improving the federal system.

## A WORD ABOUT PROCEDURES

Article V of the Constitution sets forth two procedures for amending the Constitution. The first is for Congress, by two-thirds majorities of both houses, to submit proposed amendments for ratification by the states. The second is for the legislatures of two-thirds of the states to petition Congress to call a convention for the purpose of proposing amendments. In either case, the proposed amendments do not become part of the Constitution until ratified by three-quarters of the states.

The former method has been used for each of the twenty-six amendments currently in the Constitution. It is a proven way to insure thoughtful consideration for proposed reforms.

The only time in American history when the alternative method may have served a useful purpose was in the drive for the 17th Amendment, which provided for the direct election of United States Senators. Resistance to passage in the Senate led backers to attempt the alternate route. Eventually, the Senate capitulated and helped to frame a congressional resolution that was subsequently ratified.

The Committee on the Constitutional System strongly favors the traditional congressional method for proposing constitutional amendments. We hope that Congress will soon initiate a study to determine whether the Constitution in its present form can provide effective, accountable government for a third century, whether perceived weaknesses in our political structure can be remedied by changes in party rule and statutes, or whether changes in the Constitution itself may be desirable. . . .


## CONCLUSION

In presenting this analysis and list of proposals, the Committee wishes to stress its central conviction. The best way to honor the framers of the Constitution during this bicentennial era is to follow their example.

When the parlous state of affairs under the Continental Congress raised doubts about the fitness of the new nation's frame of government, George Washington and his associates took steps to meet the challenge. They adopted the changes necessary (in the words of the resolution that called the Convention of 1787 into being) to "render the federal constitution adequate to the exigencies of government and the preservation of the union."

Two hundred years later, we stand in awe of their achievement. We disserve their memory, however, if we ignore signs that our political system today faces challenges that it is not equipped to meet.

We need to face up to these shortcomings in the capacity of our two-hundred-year-old political structure to cope with a global economy and prevent a nuclear war. We may ultimately conclude that these shortcomings can be remedied without major structural changes, or that any major changes needed to correct them would create even greater problems. But we cannot be confident of having reached the right conclusions until we confront the problems, trace them to their roots and examine the alternatives.

It is in this spirit that we offer these proposals.

---

*Does the Separation of Powers Need to Be Changed?*

---

## JAMES Q. WILSON

### *Does the Separation of Powers Still Work?*

If one is asked to explain why the American government acts as it does with respect to almost any policy issue, the chances are probably eight in ten that the right answer is the separation of powers. The existence of three separate institutions with independent constitutional standing and, in two cases, distinct electoral constituencies is what distinguishes American government from parliamentary democracies. The separation of powers is the source of the enormous influence that Congress exercises over both the broad outlines and minute details of public policy, an influence that has led Daniel Patrick Moynihan to remark that the United States is the only major government with a legislative branch and that leads many European observers to doubt that this country is really governed at all. The separation of powers is also at the root of the courts' authority to declare presidential and congressional acts unconstitutional and thus is a major cause of one kind of judicial activism.

If one is asked what is wrong with American government, the odds are great—maybe not eight in ten, but better than one in two—that the reply will refer to some aspect of our politics that can be explained by the separation of powers: "The president cannot negotiate for the United States on delicate foreign policy matters." "Congress meddles in the work of bureaucratic agencies." "There are too many governmental leaks to the press." "The Pentagon is not under strong, unified management." "There are too many patronage (i.e., political) appointees in government agencies." "There are too few policy-oriented (i.e., political) appointees in government agencies."

If one makes a list of the most frequently proposed alterations in our constitutional arrangements, the odds are high that these proposals will call for a reduction in the separation of powers: "Let the president put some members of Congress in his cabinet." "Have the president and members of Congress who are from the president's party run as a team." "Allow the president to dissolve Congress." "Allow Congress to call for a special presidential election." "Curb the power of judicial review."

If one listens to the reflections of presidents and their aides, no matter whether they are liberals or conservatives, the most common complaint is that the president does not have enough power. Roosevelt, Truman, Eisenhower, Kennedy, Nixon, Carter, Reagan: All have remarked on how little the president can do compared to what the public expects him to do. Roosevelt, Truman, and Nixon appointed commissions (the President's Commission on Administrative Management [PCAM], the Hoover Commission, and the Ash Commission)

33

to advise them on how best to extend their control over the bureaucracy; Nixon (like many presidents before him) tried to impound funds that Congress had ordered him to spend; Carter made a largely futile effort to weaken congressional control over the bureaucracy; Ford and Reagan have argued that the War Powers Act, which requires congressional participation in presidential decisions to commit armed forces, is unconstitutional. And on and on.

It is as if almost everybody were expressing devotion to the Constitution in general but not to the central principle on which it rests. Does anybody like the separation of powers? Can anything good be said for it?

## THE SEPARATION OF POWERS IN THE COURTS

There is one group devoted to the principle: the Supreme Court. It may be activist in interpreting the Bill of Rights, but on the separation of powers it has adopted the most literal readings of the Constitution. In 1926, it held that Congress cannot deny to the president the right to remove an executive official he has appointed[1] (nine years later the Court modified that ruling to allow congressional restrictions on presidential appointments to independent regulatory commissions).[2] In 1975, it held that President Nixon could not impound (i.e., fail to spend) funds appropriated by Congress.[3] The following year it decided that Congress could not appoint members of the Federal Election Commission.[4] In 1983, it overturned the legislative veto, a procedure whereby Congress had granted discretionary authority to the president or subordinate officials subject to the right of Congress to block a proposed exercise of that authority by adopting a resolution.[5] Three years later it struck down a part of the Gramm-Rudman deficit reduction act because the across-the-board spending reductions mandated by the act were, under certain circumstances, to be executed by the Comptroller General. It seems that, because the Comptroller General can be removed by Congress, he is subservient to Congress and so cannot exercise "executive powers."[6]

From time to time, the Court recognizes that the Founders never intended to create a government based on a strict separation of powers but rather one based, in the words of Richard E. Neustadt, on separate institutions sharing powers. But whenever the Court finds a statement specifying how those powers are to be shared, it tends to give to those words the most narrow construction. For example, its objection to the legislative veto was that such congressional resolutions have the force of law even though they are not signed by the president (never mind that the president may have signed a law creating the system of legislative vetoes); a law, to be a law, "shall be presented to the President of the United States" for his signature or veto as required by the language of Article I. And in the Gramm-Rudman case, the Court was unimpressed by the fact that the Comptroller General, since the creation of the post in 1921, has been a largely nonpartisan and neutral officer who serves a fifteen-year term and who can only be removed for cause and with the assent of both the president and Congress.

It is hard to find an area of constitutional law in which the Court has been as nonactivist as with respect to the separation of powers. The uncharitable may argue that the Court's faithfulness to text on this issue is necessary to empower it to be activist on other issues, for without strict adherence to the doctrine of separated powers the Court itself might not be able to assert the authority, nowhere mentioned in the Constitution, to declare acts of Congress unconstitutional. Perhaps; certainly *Marbury* v. *Madison* (1803), the first case to announce the Court's power to invalidate acts of Congress, was also the first case to argue that Congress had violated the separation of powers (by attempting to enlarge the original jurisdiction of the Court).

Whatever the Court's motives, its words echo hollowly in the halls of contemporary political debate. Scarcely any other voice is raised in praise of the separation of powers, except in the most abstract sense. Separated powers are a fine idea, it would seem, except when they prevent me from having my way.

Of course, it was precisely to prevent officials from having their way that powers were separated in the first place. As Chief Justice Burger said in the Court's opinion in the Gramm-Rudman case, the institutions of government were deliberately arranged to create a system that "produces conflicts, confusion, and discordance." Few presidents probably cared for that arrangement very much, but their complaints were of little moment during the century and a half or so when the national government played a minor role in public affairs (except in wartime, and then the Court, with only a few exceptions, allowed the president quite sweeping powers free of any but the most essential congressional checks). Once the national government began—or tried to begin—to play a large role, presidents, and people who looked to the president for action, visibly and audibly chafed under their constitutional restraints.

## THE CASE AGAINST THE SEPARATION OF POWERS

There have always been two distinct, though often intertwined, strands in the case against the separation of powers. One is the liberal case: The federal government should play a large and active role in human affairs by supplying services, reducing economic inequality, and catering to the demands of those who find themselves at a disadvantage in the marketplace. During most of this century, presidents have been more sensitive to the urban and industrial constituencies who make these demands than has Congress. Therefore, the powers of the president should be enlarged and those of Congress (or those parts of Congress that are "obstructionist") should be reduced. From this perspective, it made sense to weaken the authority of congressional committees, or at least the committees headed by powerful conservatives (such as the House Rules Committee under the leadership of the legendary Judge Howard Smith of Virginia).

It also made sense to call, as did James MacGregor Burns and E. E. Schattschneider, for strong political parties headed by the president, or presidential candidates, that would be able to command the loyalty of party members in Congress to the president's program and supplant the loyalty those members gave to committee chairmen. When Burns wrote of the "deadlock of democracy," he was writing of the political barriers to the enactment of a liberal agenda.

The other case is the rationalist one. Whether policies are liberal or conservative, they should be made decisively, efficiently, and on the basis of comprehensive principles. The public interest was not well served by simply adding up individual preferences into a "patchwork" or "crazy quilt" of inconsistent programs administered in "wasteful" ways by "duplicative" agencies. The public interest was better served by having a unitary view of what was good for the nation "as a whole." Only a single official could design and propose an internally consistent set of policies based on some overriding principle. In our system that person is the president. Therefore, the president should have more power. In this view, it made sense to give the president firmer control over the bureaucracy, equip him with sufficient staff to develop programs and oversee their administration, empower him to recognize government agencies, and strengthen his hand in dealing with Congress. In theory, a rationalized national government could serve either liberal ends (by enacting broad welfare and regulatory programs) or conservative ones (by cutting waste, reducing spending, and simplifying or minimizing regulation). The rationalist view especially emphasized the foreign policy role of the president. With Tocqueville, it noted that diplomacy is especially difficult in a democracy owing to the need for secrecy, speed, and unity of action, all hampered by the fact that the president must share power with Congress.

The existence of two arguments against checks and balances helps explain why a liberal, Harry Truman, could appoint a conservative, Herbert Hoover, to recommend ways of improving government; why presidents of all stripes have been able to make plausible cases in favor of enhancing their powers; and why movements for constitutional "reform" are able to recruit conservative businessmen as well as liberal academics into their ranks.

These reform movements, though they have helped change aspects of the presidency, have not had a fundamental impact on the separation of powers. To the extent the separation of powers has been altered, it has been the result of events more than plans, events that helped liberals more than rationalists.

Liberals achieved the enactment of a large part of their agenda as a consequence of two windows of opportunity that opened thirty years apart. The Great Depression enabled an overwhelming Democratic majority in Congress, aided (after 1935) by a slim but solid majority on the Supreme Court, to lay the foundations for the modern welfare state. In 1965, a landslide electoral victory by Lyndon Johnson and the arrival of a liberal majority in both houses of Congress set the stage for a vast expansion of the welfare state and the enactment of dozens of consumer- and environmental-protection laws.

Rationalists made some gains in wartime, when the president gained enhanced authority over the government and the economy, but most of these gains faded with the return of peace. Otherwise, rationalists have had to plug away at small, painfully won changes—the passage of the Budget and Accounting Act in 1921 (that created the Bureau of the Budget and the General Accounting Office), the acquisition by the president in 1935 of the power to reorganize by executive order (subject to a legislative veto), the expansion of the White House office pursuant to the recommendations of the PCAM, the passage of the Legislative Reorganization Act of 1946 that reduced the number of standing committees of Congress and laid the groundwork for the growth in congressional staff, and the creation in 1978 of the Senior Executive Service (SES) to permit more flexible use of high-level bureaucrats. Some of these changes, especially the creation of the Bureau of the Budget and the attendant growth of presidential control over the budget and the legislative agenda, were of great moment, but many proved to be short-lived or chimerical gains. The power to reorganize expired, and now that the legislative veto has been deemed unconstitutional, it probably cannot be revived. The White House staff has grown so much that it has become a bureaucratic problem in its own right. The reduction in the number of congressional committees was quickly followed by the growth in the number of subcommittees, leaving authority in Congress at least as decentralized as it had once been. The Senior Executive Service has been a disappointment: Not many top-level bureaucrats moved from one agency to another, rarely was a SES member fired, and the availability of cash bonuses did not seem to enhance performance.

Moreover, the very success of the liberals in supplying the agenda for and expanding the role of the federal government was achieved at the cost of major setbacks for the rationalist cause. The government became big before the president became institutionally (as opposed to personally) powerful. What Roosevelt and Johnson created, their successors could not easily manage. Moreover, the liberal gains in the late 1960s and early 1970s were accompanied by a radical decentralization of Congress. Liberal majorities in the House and Senate confronted the conservatives holding power as chairmen of certain key committees, such as the House Rules Committee and the House Ways and Means Committee. To move their agenda onto the floor where its passage was assured, liberals had to unseat committee chairmen they regarded as obstructionist, enhance the power of individual members at the expense of committee chairmen, modify the rules to make it harder to bottle up legislation in committee, and (in the Senate) alter, slightly, the cloture rule to reduce the threat of a filibuster. The effect of these changes, chiefly wrought by the House Democratic caucus, was to increase the power of individual congressmen and reduce the power of congressional leaders.

Politically, if not constitutionally, powers became more rather than less separated. The president now was held responsible for every imaginable domestic and foreign problem, but his capacity to make a systematic response to these problems was reduced by two changes: The growth in the size of the government had contributed to the growth in the number and variety of interest groups that sought to block presidential initiatives, and the decentralization of Congress reduced the president's ability to negotiate with a handful of congressional leaders who could help build legislative majorities.

Critics of the separation of powers could have made one of two responses to this state of affairs. The rationalist might have argued for a reduction in the size and scope of the federal government on the grounds that our policy commitments now exceeded our capacity to manage them. Or the rationalist could have reaffirmed his alliance with the liberals by arguing for more profound and sweeping changes—necessarily involving constitutional revision—in order to reduce the separation of powers sufficiently to permit the president to direct affairs in the new order. By and large, rationalists have chosen the second course, and so we have such groups as the Committee on the Constitutional System (CCS), led by Lloyd Cutler, C. Douglas Dillon, and Senator Nancy Landon Kassebaum. Thirty or forty years ago, I surmise, such a group would have been arguing for a stronger Bureau of the Budget, a bigger White House staff, a more effective civil service system, fewer congressional committees, and (perhaps) stronger political parties. Most of those things happened, but now they seem inadequate to the task of directing a vast federal government. And so the call has gone out for constitutional reform.

To the CCS and its supporters, the need for fundamental change is almost self-evident. Perhaps that is why so little of their writing is devoted to making the case for change. The most important essay, Lloyd Cutler's "To Form a Government,"[7] is almost the only systematic effort to explain why we need to modify the separation of powers. Given their premises, of course, the need for change *is* virtually self-evident. To them, the public interest is a discoverable set of principles and goals from which right actions can be inferred. The means to achieve these ends must be comprehensively and efficiently related to those ends. This is more easily done by one mind than by 535, by an official responsible to a national electorate than by one beholden to many small electorates, and by a person able to carry out his policies subject to the check of electoral defeat than by one who cannot carry out any policies at all without first overcoming countless checks by subcommittees, committees, interest groups, and houses of Congress. The rationalist position, like rationality itself, seems to require little defense.

## THE INTENT OF THE FRAMERS

But of course the Framers of the Constitution were not trying to create a government that would discern national goals and serve them efficiently and with dispatch; they were trying to create a limited government that would serve only those goals that could survive a process of consultation and bargaining designed to prevent the mischief of factions and the tyranny of passionate majorities or ambitious politicians. The CCS and its allies understand this but argue that conditions have changed since 1787: Public affairs today are more complex, interdependent, and fraught with peril than they were in the nineteenth century, and so we must modify our governing arrangements in order to meet these new challenges.

It is not difficult, of course, to produce a litany of difficulties facing the nation: a large budget and trade deficit, the threat of nuclear war, a complex array of international commitments, an economy painfully adjusting to new kinds of international competition, the cancer of crime and drug abuse, and so on. But it is not clear that these "new realities" are fundamentally different from the kinds of problems faced by Washington's first administration and it is certainly far from clear that they constitute a case for constitutional change.

The first administrations had to salvage a disrupted economy, pay off or otherwise settle a crushing war debt funded by worthless paper, worry about the presence of hostile British forces in Canada and a British navy at sea, cope with French control of the Mississippi River valley and Spanish control of Florida, put down a rebellion of Pennsylvania farmers protesting the tax on whiskey, reconcile the deep ideological divisions stirred up by the French Revolution, make legitimate the government in the eyes of skeptical Anti-Federalists and Jeffersonian Democrats, do battle with Indians waging war on the periphery of the new republic, and settle the hotly contested Jefferson-Adams presidential race by going to thirty-six ballots in the House of Representatives. Hardly simple times; hardly an easy test for the new constitutional order. It survived.

Today, the case for constitutional change is being made to a nation prosperous and at peace whose political institutions enjoy unquestioned legitimacy. Decision making is as contentious and protracted now as it was two hundred years ago, but under circumstances that are far more conducive to success and popular support than once was the case. In 1986, one can only be amused to reread the 1974 essay by Charles Hardin on why our government was then in crisis and why only major "constitutional surgery" could correct it. Watergate, the supposedly "imperial presidency," and popular distrust of government were the crisis; the cure required these changes: electing the president and Congress for coterminous four-year terms, abolishing the office of vice president, allowing Congress to remove a president by a vote of no confidence, giving the president an automatic majority in the House of Representatives, and so on. Of course, the "crisis" ended without any of these "cures." Watergate was handled by the normal constitutional procedures—congressional investigations, criminal trials, and the prospect of impeachment—and the presidency and the president are once again in high repute.

## REAL AND IMAGINED PROBLEMS

But generalities cannot settle the matter. Let us look at the specific ways in which the constitutional system is allegedly defective: the deficit, economic policy, and foreign affairs.

## 1. The Deficit

C. Douglas Dillon has argued for a parliamentary democracy because, unlike our system, it would more effectively address the problem of the deficit. There are two things wrong with his argument. The first is that there is no evidence at all that the deficit is a consequence of the separation of powers. At the President's request, taxes were cut. At the President's request, defense spending was increased. At the President's request, the Social Security system was preserved intact, with minor adjustments in tax and benefit levels. At the President's request, budgets were submitted that were not in balance. There are important differences between what the President has requested and Congress has approved with respect to many spending bills, but all of these differences, if resolved in the President's favor, would not produce a balanced budget. The deficit would be somewhat less, but not substantially so, if all presidential requests were automatically enacted by a subservient Congress. If Mr. Dillon is worried about the deficit, he need not vote for constitutional reform; he need only have voted against Mr. Reagan.

The second difficulty with the Dillon argument is immediately apparent when we examine the budgets of parliamentary democracies. There are important conceptual problems in comparing deficits across nations—consider, for example, the problem of comparing governments that do and do not own major industries, or that of comparing deficits between high- and low-inflation countries. Taking into account all these problems, Vito Tanzi of the International Monetary Fund, using data from the Organization for Economic Cooperation and Development (OECD), produces estimates for the 1984 deficit, measured in percentage of gross national product, that are arranged from high to low in Table 1.

Every nation on this list with a fiscal deficit except ours has a parliamentary democracy; that is to say, it is not governed in accordance with the separation of powers. Japan, Germany, and Norway have deficits smaller than ours; Italy, Ireland, Belgium, Greece, Denmark, the Netherlands, Spain, and Canada have much larger ones; France, Sweden, and the United Kingdom are about on a par with us. The safest conclusion that can be drawn from this list is that form of government has no effect on the size of the deficit.

A bolder inference, for which a case might be made, is that parliamentary regimes, by concentrating power in the hands of the executive, facilitate the adoption of new spending measures designed to satisfy the constituencies that brought the prime minister and his party into power. David Cameron has shown, for example, that government spending as a percentage of the gross domestic product and the rate of increase in that spending over the last twenty years or so has been higher in Belgium, France, Italy, the Netherlands, Norway, Sweden, and West Germany than in the United States. Only in Spain and Japan did the government spend less, and the rate of increase in spending in these countries was faster than it was in this country.[8] Moreover, much (but not

Table 1.  Deficit Comparison across
Nations for 1984[a]

| Country | Percentage of GNP |
| --- | --- |
| Italy | 12.4 |
| Ireland | 12.3 |
| Belgium | 10.3 |
| Greece | 9.8 |
| Denmark | 6.0 |
| Netherlands | 5.9 |
| Spain | 5.7 |
| Canada | 5.3 |
| France | 3.5 |
| Sweden | 3.5 |
| UNITED STATES | 3.1 |
| United Kingdom | 2.8 |
| Japan | 2.3 |
| Germany | 1.4 |
| Norway | −2.4 |

[a]*Source:* Vito Tanzi, "The Deficit Experience in Industrial Countries," in Phillip Cagan, ed., *The Economy in Deficit* (Washington, D.C.: American Enterprise Institute, 1985), pp. 94–95.

all) of the difference between high- and low-spending nations is associated with leftist party control of the government. In any nation, liberals can win elections; in the United States, it is harder for them (or for conservatives) thereby to win control of the government. Parliamentary democracies may have the ability to make the "hard choices" the rationalists want, but it is far from clear they have any desire to do so. What is clear is that it is easier for them to make the easy choices.

## 2. Economic Policy

We are constantly reminded that we live in an interdependent world undergoing rapid technological and economic change. Those who remind us of this situation claim that the United States does not respond to that change very well. We save and invest too little. We import too much. We allow jobs to be destroyed by Asian competitors. We fail to rebuild our smokestack industries. We regulate in cumbersome ways. We have too many small farmers. Our legal system imposes costly delays.

The implication of these criticisms is that there is a correct economic policy that a bold president would implement. (Among my students at UCLA there is a widespread belief that a sufficiently bold president would turn out to be either Lee Iacocca or Peter Ueberroth.) If the right president can be found, then he should be given the freedom to design and carry out his economic policy. If he fails, the voters will punish him at the next election; if he succeeds, the voters will reward him (unless, of course, constitutional reformers have succeeded in limiting him to a single six-year term).

In support of the virtues of greater decisiveness and comprehensiveness in economic policymaking, one can point to the fact that many other industrial nations have been more successful than the United States in taxing consumption (for example, the value added tax) and rewarding investment (for example, by not taxing capital gains). There is also evidence from several studies of other countries that their system of environmental regulation is less adversarial and less legalistic but just as effective as that in the United States.[9]

These are weighty arguments, but it is not clear they weigh in favor of movement toward a parliamentary regime. First, it is not obvious what economic policy is correct. Of course, advocates of a rationalist governing system will respond that, though no one knows for certain what policies will work, at least a strong, executive-centered system will permit us to try a given policy. Their view is that a yes-or-no referendum by the public is a better check on economic policymaking than a detailed scrutiny and amendment by Congress. I am not convinced. We may make new economic policy in half-hearted steps or tolerate inconsistent economic programs, but we thereby hedge our bets and avoid the extreme swings in policy that are characteristic of some other regimes. Britain nationalized, denationalized, renationalized, and then denationalized again several of its basic industries. France appears on the verge of doing the same.

Second, it is increasingly implausible to use "deadlock" as a word to describe American policymaking in America. After many decades of increased regulation of prices and conditions of entry in such industries as domestic banking, aviation, securities trading, and telecommunications, a more or less measured and careful process of deregulation has begun that, though far from constituting a revolution, has revealed this nation's capacity for learning and self-correction. After decades during which Democrats demanded steeply progressive tax rates and Republicans went along in return for extensive deductions, the president and Congress renegotiated the terms of that old compact in favor of a system with less steep rates and fewer loopholes.

Third, the adversarial and legalistic nature of economic regulation here, while indisputable, reflects many factors in addition to the separation of powers. No doubt the separation of powers intensifies the adversarial nature of our regulatory system by empowering congressional critics of current regulatory law and enabling the courts to play a large role in reviewing and reversing regulatory decisions. But we live in an adversarial culture, the product of centuries devoted to defining politics as a struggle over rights. We are deeply imbued with a populist suspicion of the sort of behind-the-scenes negotiations that characterize regulatory policymaking in England and Sweden. The central-ized nature of political and economic life abroad facilitates the settlement of issues by negotiations among peak associations, whereas here the decentral-ized political order and the more competitive economic one make it impossible to commit either the government or economic actors to the syndicalist pattern of decision making so often seen in Europe.

## 3. Foreign Policy

Lloyd Cutler makes much of President Carter's inability to get the Senate to ratify the SALT [Strategic Arms Limitation Treaty] II treaty in 1979. A president able to "form a government" would have been able to commit this country to such a treaty. Cutler points out that no prime minister is faced with the need to obtain senatorial ratification of treaties.

True enough. But one moment: The Senate rarely fails to ratify a treaty. It has approved something approaching a thousand treaties and turned down about twenty and just five in this century, of which only the Treaty of Versailles, establishing the League of Nations, was an important defeat. Of course, it can talk a treaty to death, as it almost did with SALT II (the *coup de grace* was not Senate but Soviet behavior—the USSR invaded Afghanistan before the treaty could come to a vote). But in general the Senate tends to go along.

The crucial question should not be whether the president should have more power over the Senate but whether the treaties that failed ratification were in the public interest. Just before describing Carter's problems with SALT II, Cutler speaks of the need for "making those decisions we all know must be made." Was SALT II such a decision? If so, Cutler leaves the argument unstated. Strong arguments can be and were made against it. Many thoughtful people believed that it was a bad treaty. The notion that ratification should be made easier so that the real check on the success of the president's policy is public reaction at the next election is chimerical: People rarely, if ever, vote for or against presi-dents because of the treaties they have signed, for the obvious reason that, barring some dramatic incident, the people have no way of knowing whether the treaty was a good or bad idea.

Foreign policy is more than treaties, of course. It is not hard to think of circumstances in which one would want the president to have a freer hand. It is not hard to think of ways of giving him a freer hand. If constitutional reformers are so keen on supplying a freer hand, it is curious that they spend so much time discussing quasi-parliamentary procedures and so little time discussing the virtues of repealing the War Powers Act, modifying congressional supervision of the Central Intelligence Agency, and eliminating the legislative veto over arms sales, none of which requires a constitutional amendment. One wonders whether the rationalists are really rationalists and not actually liberals in ratio-nalist clothing, eager to have a president powerful enough to sign arms-control and nuclear-test-ban agreements but not strong enough to commit troops to Grenada or Lebanon or provide aid to anti-Marxist rebels in Central America or Angola.

Still, a strong case can be made that in negotiating with foreign powers, the president of the United States is in an awkward position, not simply or even mainly because he must get the Senate to ratify his treaties, but because he must publicly negotiate simultaneously with both Congress (and congressionally amplified domestic pressures) and the foreign power. When President Nixon was negotiating with the North Vietnamese to end the war in Southeast Asia, he had to make concessions to both Congress and the enemy, reducing any incentive the enemy had to make concessions in return. As President Reagan negotiates with the Soviet Union over arms control, it would be difficult for him to make credible and useful offers to constrain deployment of anti-satellite weapons or the "Star Wars" defense system if Congress, in advance of the negotiations, places, on its own initiative, constraints on these weapons. It is hard to play poker if someone on your side frequently proclaims that you will give away certain chips regardless of what your opponent may do.

But it is unlikely that any of the most frequently discussed constitutional changes would materially improve the president's bargaining position. Putting members of Congress in the cabinet, letting the president serve a six-year term, or having the president and House members run as a team would leave the president and Congress in essentially the same relationship as they are now: rivals for control over the direction of foreign policy.


## THE UNWRITTEN CONSTITUTION

There are two fundamental arguments for a constitutional system of separate institutions sharing powers: It helps preserve liberty and it slows the pace of political change. Those arguments are as valid today as they were in 1787. Individual liberties are more secure when the actions of one part of the national government can be checked by, or appealed to, another. Political change is slower, and so the growth of new programs and public spending is slower, when any new proposal must survive the political obstacle course of bureaus, subcommittees, committees, and houses of Congress.

Rationalists may view the delays, confusion, and inconsistencies produced by this system as costly, as of course they are. But they should not assume that if the costs were reduced or eliminated by reducing or eliminating the separation of powers, the advantages of this system would remain. Even Lloyd Cutler recognizes that a congressional system has some advantages over a parliamentary one; for one thing, the former permits investigations of executive misconduct that the latter does not. Watergate comes quickly to mind, but there are many other examples—Teapot Dome, defense procurement scandals, civil rights abuses, and organized crime. On a smaller scale, one cannot complain to one's congressman about an injustice and have much hope of redress if the power of Congress has been reduced.

Liberal proponents of reducing the separation of powers know full well that it impedes political change and that, I believe, is the major reason they favor such a reduction. At one time they might have worried that an executive-dominated system would threaten liberty, but they have become accustomed (and with good reason) to looking to the courts for the protection of personal liberty, and so this worry no longer seems as serious. That it is a larger state they wish and not simply a more efficient one is evident from the fact that, whereas they have often been eager to curb the independence of Congress, they have never (since 1935) been eager to curb the independence of the courts. Yet judicial independence is probably as much a source of delays, confusion, and uncertainty as is congressional independence (consider how court review af-fects the operation of public schools, the management of prisons, or the settle-ment of personal injury claims). If over the last half century the courts had been under the control of conservative rather than liberal activists (or even under the control of conservatives, period), I imagine that liberal enthusiasm for constitu-tional reforms would not stop at the courthouse door.

Defending the principle of separation of powers is not the same as defending the practices that have developed around these constitutional principles. Don K. Price, like me, argues against constitutional change but argues in favor of changes in the "unwritten constitution," those customs and arrangements that allow a government of separate institutions to work at all.[10]

The most important provision of the unwritten constitution is the internal organization and procedures of Congress. The Constitution requires that the House and the Senate as a whole enact legislation, but it is silent on how many additional "enactments" must occur within the House and the Senate. At one time, there were virtually no congressional committees and no chairmen, at another time there were many powerful chairmen; at one time members of the House had great autonomy, at another time they yielded immense authority to the Speaker; at one time the House Rules Committee dominated the legislative process, at another time it played a smaller role; at one time seniority alone determined who should be chairman, at another time the party caucus influ-enced the choice of chairmen.

## LEADERSHIP IN THE STATES

The variety of unwritten constitutions that can exist within a system of separate institutions is revealed by the experience of American state legislatures. No one can understand the politics of California by reading its constitution, because nowhere does it mention the extraordinary power exercised by the speaker of the assembly. Willie Brown is not elected speaker by the voters of the state, yet next to Governor George Deukmejian he is the most powerful official in that state.

People accustomed to think of a lieutenant governor as a political nobody would not be prepared for the extraordinary power enjoyed by the lieutenant governor of Texas, who not only presides over the state senate but chooses the members and chairmen of its committees. If you went to Mississippi to do business with the state, you might think it important to meet the governor, but most people there will tell you that it is more important to meet with the speaker of the House. Like his counterparts in California and several other states, Speaker C. B. "Buddie" Newman of Mississippi can control the composition and leadership of key committees and determine the fate of much legislation.

The Congress of the United States, by contrast, is extremely decentralized and individualized. Speaker Sam Rayburn during the 1950s was not nearly as powerful as Speaker Thomas Reed in the 1890s, but he was far more powerful than Speaker Tip O'Neill in the 1980s. Congress, especially the House, has chosen to have weak leadership; in principle it could choose to have strong leadership. The methods are neither obscure nor unconstitutional: vest in the speaker or the majority leader the power to select and remove committee chairmen; change campaign finance laws so that the House and Senate campaign committees could raise and spend large sums of money on behalf of individual candidates and place control of these entities firmly in the hands of the speaker or majority leader; reduce the ability of individual members to create their own political action committees or to receive funds directly from the political action committees of others; and strengthen the power of the speaker or the majority leader to choose which committees shall consider bills and which bills will come to the floor for a vote. All of these things are done in state governments operating under essentially the same separation-of-powers principles as shape the national government.

It is not entirely clear why state legislatures (including such progressive ones as those in California, Massachusetts, and New York) should have resisted the tides of individualization and decentralization that have engulfed Congress. But two things are clear: First, the weakening of congressional leadership has been accomplished chiefly at the initiative of liberals who regarded strong leaders and chairmen as a barrier to liberal policies. Second, that weakening has reduced, or at least vastly complicated, the ability of the president to negotiate effectively with Congress. If one wishes to preserve the system of checks and balances but facilitate the process of bargaining and reciprocity essential to its operation, it makes more sense to enable the president to negotiate with four or five congressional leaders who can make commitments than to require him (or his legislative affairs staff) to negotiate with scores or even hundreds of individual members, none of whom can commit anyone but himself.

I am not optimistic that Congress will restore strong leadership. As I have written elsewhere,[11] there are very few examples in American history of people who possess certain powers voting to give them up or of people deciding they favored less democracy rather than more. And even if congressional leadership is strengthened, the president will certainly not be able to dominate the leaders who emerge. But it is in this area of the unwritten constitution that remedies for the defects of the separation of powers must be found. There are no constitutional remedies short of the abolition of the principle itself, and that is a price that two hundred years of successful constitutional government should have taught us is too high to pay.

---

NOTES

1. *Myers* v. *United States,* 272 U.S. 52 (1926).

2. *Humphrey's Executor* v. *United States,* 295 U.S. 602 (1935).

3. *Train* v. *City of New York,* 420 U.S. 35 (1975).

4. *Buckley* v. *Valeo,* 424 U.S. 1 (1976).

5. *Immigration and Naturalization Service* v. *Chadha,* 103 S. Ct. 2764 (1983).

6. *Bowsher* v. *Synar,* 106 S. Ct. 3181 (1986).

7. Lloyd N. Cutler, "To Form a Government," *Foreign Affairs,* Fall 1980, pp. 126–143.

8. David R. Cameron, "Does Government Cause Inflation? Taxes, Spending, and Deficits," in Leon N. Lindberg and Charles S. Maier, eds., *The Politics of Inflation and Economic Stagflation* (Washington, D.C.: Brookings Institution, 1985), pp. 230–232.

9. David Vogel, *National Styles of Regulation* (Ithaca, N.Y.: Cornell University Press, 1986); Steven J. Kelman, *Regulating America, Regulating Sweden* (Cambridge, Mass.: MIT Press, 1981).

10. Don K. Price, *America's Unwritten Constitution* (Baton Rouge, La.: Louisiana State University Press, 1983).

11. James Q. Wilson, "Political Parties and the Separation of Powers," in Robert A. Goldwin and Art Kaufman, eds., *Separation of Powers—Does It Still Work?* (Washington, D.C.: American Enterprise Institute, 1986), pp. 18–37.

## Questions for Discussion

---

1. What changes would have to be made in the Constitution for the United States to adopt a British-type parliamentary system?
2. Who would be the winners and losers of such changes?
3. To what extent has the changing character of the United States from a small agrarian society to a large postindustrial society made the system of separation of powers outmoded?
4. Would the adoption of a parliamentary political system in 1787 have changed the course of U.S. history? If so, how?
5. Is a parliamentary system more accountable to the people than a system of separated powers? What are the reasons for your answer?
6. What would be the effect of the calling of a new constitutional convention in the 1990s to remedy the alleged defects of the U.S. political system?
7. What light do recent events, such as the savings and loan bailout and the U.S. response to the Iraqi invasion of Kuwait in the years of the Bush administration, shed on this debate? Do you think that they support the arguments of the CCS or Wilson? Explain.

## Suggested Readings

Bonafede, Dom. "Reform of U.S. System of Government Is on the Minds and Agendas of Many." *National Journal,* 17, no. 26 (June 29, 1985), 1521–1524.

Cutler, Lloyd N. "To Form a Government." *Foreign Affairs,* 59, no. 1 (Fall 1980), 126–143.

Fisher, Louis. *The Politics of Shared Power: Congress and the Executive.* 2nd ed. Washington, D.C.: CQ Press, 1987.

Goldwin, Robert A., and Art Kaufman, eds. *Separation of Powers—Does It Still Work?* Washington, D.C.: American Enterprise Institute for Public Policy Research, 1986.

Hardin, Charles M. *Constitutional Reform in America: Essays on the Separation of Powers.* Ames, Iowa: Iowa State Univ. Press, 1989.

Koh, Harold H. *The National Security Constitution: Sharing Power after the Iran-Contra Affair.* New Haven, Conn.: Yale Univ. Press, 1990.

Price, Don K. "The Parliamentary and Presidential Systems." *Public Administration Review,* 3, no. 4 (Autumn 1943), 317–334.

Robinson, Donald L., ed. *Reforming American Government: The Bicentennial Papers of the Committee on the Constitutional System.* Boulder, Colo.: Westview Press, 1985.

Scarrow, Howard A. "Parliamentary and Presidential Government Compared." *Current History,* 66, no. 394 (June 1974), 264–267, 272.

Sundquist, James L. *Constitutional Reform and Effective Government.* Washington, D.C.: Brookings Institution, 1986.

U.S. Cong. *Political Economy and Constitutional Reform.* Hearings before the Joint Economic Committee, 97th Cong., 2nd Sess., 1982. 2 vols.

Weaver, R. Kent. "Are Parliamentary Systems Better?" *Brookings Review,* 3, no. 4 (Summer 1985), 16–25.

*See also* Suggested Readings for Chapter 1.

# Chapter 3

## *Does Federalism Encourage Good Government?*

An understanding of the federal system today requires an examination of what federalism is, why it was established, and how it has evolved. Federalism is a system of government under which power is distributed between central and regional authorities in a way that provides each with important power and functions. The United States is but one of many federal systems around the world. Canada, India, and the Federal Republic of Germany are examples of nations that have federal systems. In the United States the central authority is known as the federal government, and the regional authorities are the state governments.

Federalism is a structural feature not necessarily coterminous with democracy. A federal system divides power. A unitary system, in contrast, concentrates power. In a unitary system power is controlled by the central authorities, as it is, for example, in Great Britain and France. In Great Britain, regional governing authorities are created, abolished, or rearranged by the central government at Westminster. In the federal system of the United States, however, state governments cannot be so restructured. No state boundary can be changed by the government in Washington, D.C., acting on its own authority. (An exception occurred during the Civil War when the state of West Virginia was created out of Virginia.)

A federal system was adopted in 1787 because a unitary structure would have been unacceptable to the people of the United States, who had strong loyalties to their states. In addition, the Framers of the Constitution wanted a government that would be stronger than the one existing under the Articles of Confederation, but they feared a central government that was too powerful. The federal system allowed for a compromise between those who favored a strong central government and those who supported a weak central government.

The central government was given some exclusive powers (e.g., to coin money and to establish tariffs). The states and federal government shared some powers (e.g., to tax and to spend money). The Tenth Amendment to the Constitution provides that "the powers not delegated to the United States by the Constitution, nor prohibited by it to the States, are reserved to the States respectively, or to the people."

The Constitution is not so clear, however, about where the powers of the central government end. Two centuries of conflict over this issue of states' rights have marked U.S. history. In general, the trend has been away from states' rights and toward national supremacy.

Those who argue for states' rights contend that the Constitution must be interpreted strictly. Congress should legislate only in those areas that are specifically delegated to it in the Constitution and should leave all those powers not mentioned to the states. Those who argue for national supremacy maintain, however, that the Constitution establishes a strong central government with vast authority. They support a broad interpretation of the federal government's powers.

National supremacy proponents have won victories, although they have always been under attack by states' rights advocates. In 1819, for example, in *McCulloch* v. *Maryland*, the Supreme Court upheld the power of the federal government to create a bank despite the fact that the Constitution does not grant an expressed power to the national government for this purpose. The Court held that Congress was granted broad scope through Article I, Section 8, Clause 18 of the Constitution, which gives Congress the power "to make all Laws which shall be necessary and proper" to carry out its enumerated powers.

As the character of U.S. society has changed, so, too, have the institutions of government. The relationship between the states and the national government has been influenced by these changes. With the emergence of large corporations whose activities transcend state boundaries, the role of the federal government in regulating interstate commerce has increased. Other economic problems, such as unemployment and inflation, can no longer be satisfactorily handled at the state level and require the federal government's attention.

States' rights became the slogan of groups who benefited from decentralized control—such as big business and segregationists—while national supremacy was heralded by groups that received strong support from Washington—such as labor unions and civil rights advocates. In those instances in which the states were unable or unwilling to meet the needs of a changing industrial economy and to respond to the pressures of social problems, the national government asserted its authority—often at the expense of the states. The courts have upheld the right of the federal government to move into areas previously dominated by the states—such as education, housing, commerce, and employment.

Because the issue of states' rights has become so prominent in the course of U.S. history, it would be wrong to conclude that the relationship between the federal government and the states is best categorized as a zero-sum game; that is, whatever one side gains, the other side loses. Today *cooperation* rather than *conflict* characterizes the relations between the two levels of government.

Liberals tended to support—and conservatives to oppose—the authority of the federal government over states' rights so long as racial segregation and economic regulatory matters were of central concern. But with integration and Supreme Court decisions favoring a federal government role in the economy in place, liberals have become more supportive of states' rights. Liberals appreciate that some states guarantee broader rights to citizens than are found in the Bill of Rights. Liberals also approve of the vigorous environmental and consumer protection laws that some states have enacted. Conservatives have traditionally supported states' rights. At times, however, some conservatives have preferred a federal government rather than a state government role in economic and environmental matters.

Although beneficiaries of a federal system may change, a continuing question is whether federalism encourages good government. In the debate presented below James Bryce, a British statesman and scholar who wrote in the late nineteenth and early twentieth centuries, makes a classical defense of federalism in general and of the U.S. federal system in particular. In his book *American Commonwealth* (1888), he argues:

1. Federalism furnishes the means of uniting commonwealths into one nation under one national government without extinguishing their separate administrations.
2. Federalism supplies the best means of developing a new and vast country.
3. Federalism prevents the rise of a despotic central government.

Bryce then lists the benefits that he ascribes to decentralized government:

1. Self-government stimulates the interest of people in the affairs of their neighborhood and promotes civic responsibility.
2. Self-government secures the good administration of local affairs.
3. Federalism enables a people to try experiments in legislation and administration that could not be safely tried in a large centralized country.
4. Federalism diminishes collective risk.
5. Federalism relieves the central government of burdensome problems.

Writer Michael Kinsley argues that the federal system should wither away. His article appeared in 1981, the first year of the presidency of Ronald Reagan. It is a critique of Reagan's preference for strengthening state governments at the expense of the federal government.

Kinsley contends:

1. Federalism unnecessarily increases litigation and judicial involvement in the political system.
2. It denies equal justice under the law.
3. It produces inefficient government.
4. It strengthens the special interests over the public interest.
5. It results in unequal public services.
6. There is no evidence that state governments are more efficient than the federal government.

## Does Federalism Encourage Good Government?

### JAMES BRYCE

### *The Merits of the Federal System*

I do not propose to discuss in this chapter the advantages of Federalism in general, for to do this we should have to wander off to other times and countries, to talk of Achaia and the Hanseatic League and the Swiss Confederation. I shall comment on those merits only which the experience of the American Union illustrates.

There are two distinct lines of argument by which their Federal system was recommended to the framers of the Constitution, and upon which it is still held forth for imitation to other countries. These lines have been so generally confounded that it is well to present them in a precise form.

The first set of arguments point to Federalism proper, and are the following:—

1. That Federalism furnishes the means of uniting commonwealths into one nation under one national government without extinguishing their separate administrations, legislatures, and local patriotisms. As the Americans of 1787 would probably have preferred complete State independence to the fusion of their States into a unified government, Federalism was the only resource. So when the new Germanic Empire, which is really a Federation, was established in 1871, Bavaria and Wurtemberg could not have been brought under a national government save by a Federal scheme. Similar suggestions, as every one knows, have been made for re-settling the relations of Ireland to Great Britain, and of the self-governing British colonies to the United Kingdom. There are causes and conditions which dispose independent or semi-independent communities, or peoples living under loosely compacted governments, to form a closer union in a Federal form. There are other causes and conditions which dispose the subjects of one government, or sections of these subjects, to desire to make their governmental union less close by substituting a Federal for a unitary system. In both sets of cases, the centripetal or centrifugal forces spring from the local position, the history, the sentiments, the economic needs of those among whom the problem arises; and that which is good for one people or political body is not necessarily good for another. Federalism is an equally legitimate resource whether it is adopted for the sake of tightening or for the sake of loosening a preexisting bond.

2. That Federalism supplies the best means of developing a new and vast country. It permits an expansion whose extent, and whose rate and manner of progress, cannot be foreseen to proceed with more variety of methods, more adaptation of laws and administration to the circumstances of each part of the territory, and altogether in a more truly natural and spontaneous way, than can

be expected under a centralized government, which is disposed to apply its settled system through all its dominions. Thus the special needs of a new region are met by the inhabitants in the way they find best: its special evils are cured by special remedies, perhaps more drastic than an old country demands, perhaps more lax than an old country would tolerate; while at the same time the spirit of self-reliance among those who build up these new communities is stimulated and respected.

3. That Federalism prevents the rise of a despotic central government, absorbing other powers, and menacing the private liberties of the citizen. This may now seem to have been an idle fear, so far as America was concerned. It was, however, a very real fear among the great-grandfathers of the present Americans, and nearly led to the rejection even of so undespotic an instrument as the Federal Constitution of 1789. Congress (or the President, as the case may be) is still sometimes described as a tyrant by the party which does not control it, simply because it is a central government: and the States are represented as bulwarks against its encroachments.

The second set of arguments relate to and recommend not so much Federalism as local self-government. I state them briefly because they are familiar.

4. Self-government stimulates the interest of people in the affairs of their neighborhood, sustains local political life, educates the citizen in his daily round of civic duty, teaches him that perpetual vigilance and the sacrifice of his own time and labour are the price that must be paid for individual liberty and collective prosperity.

5. Self-government secures the good administration of local affairs by giving the inhabitants of each locality due means of overseeing the conduct of their business.

That these two sets of grounds are distinct appears from the fact that the sort of local interest which local self-government evokes is quite a different thing from the interest men feel in the affairs of a large body like an American State. So, too, the control over its own affairs of a township, or even a small county, where everybody can know what is going on, is quite different from the control exercisable over the affairs of a commonwealth with a million of people. Local self-government may exist in a unified country like England, and may be wanting in a Federal country like Germany. And in America itself, while some States, like those of New England, possessed an admirably complete system of local government, others such as Virginia, the old champion of State sovereignty, were imperfectly provided with it. Nevertheless, through both sets of arguments there runs the general principle, applicable in every part and branch of government, that, where other things are equal, the more power is given to the units which compose the nation, be they large or small, and the less to the nation as a whole and to its central authority, so much the fuller will be the liberties and so much greater the energy of the individuals who compose the people. This principle, though it had not been then formulated in the way men formulate it now, was heartily embraced by the Americans. Perhaps it was because they agreed in taking it as an axiom that they seldom referred to it in the subsequent controversies regarding State rights. These controversies proceeded on the basis of the Constitution as a law rather than on considerations of general political theory. A European reader of the history of the first seventy years of the United States is surprised how little is said, through the interminable discussions regarding the relation of the Federal government to the States, on the respective advantages of centralization or localization of powers as a matter of historical experience and general expediency.

Three further benefits to be expected from a Federal system may be mentioned, benefits which seem to have been unnoticed or little regarded by those who established it in America.

6.  Federalism enables a people to try experiments in legislation and administration which could not be safely tried in a large centralized country. A comparatively small commonwealth like an American State easily makes and unmakes its laws; mistakes are not serious, for they are soon corrected; other States profit by the experience of a law or a method which has worked well or ill in the State that has tried it.

7.  Federalism, if it diminishes the collective force of a nation, diminishes also the risks to which its size and the diversities of its parts expose it. A nation so divided is like a ship built with water-tight compartments. When a leak is sprung in one compartment, the cargo stowed there may be damaged, but the other compartments remain dry and keep the ship afloat. So if social discord or an economic crisis has produced disorders or foolish legislation in one member of the Federal body, the mischief may stop at the State frontier instead of spreading through and tainting the nation at large.

8.  Federalism, by creating many local legislatures with wide powers, relieves the national legislature of a part of that large mass of functions which might otherwise prove too heavy for it. Thus business is more promptly despatched, and the great central council of the nation has time to deliberate on those questions which most nearly touch the whole country.

All of these arguments recommending Federalism have proved valid in American experience.

To create a nation while preserving the States was the main reason for the grant of powers which the National government received; an all-sufficient reason, and one which holds good to-day. The several States have changed greatly since 1789, but they are still commonwealths whose wide authority and jurisdiction practical men are agreed in desiring to maintain.

Not much was said in the Convention of 1787 regarding the best methods of extending government over the unsettled territories lying beyond the Alleghany mountains.[1] It was, however, assumed that they would develop as the older colonies had developed, and in point of fact each district, when it became sufficiently populous, was formed into a self-governing State, the less populous divisions still remaining in the status of semi—self-governing Territories. Although many blunders have been committed in the process of development, especially in the reckless contraction of debt and the wasteful disposal of the public lands, greater evils might have resulted had the creation of local institutions and the control of new communities been left to the Central government.[2] Congress would have been not less improvident than the State governments, for it would have been even less closely watched. The opportunities for jobbery would have been irresistible, the growth of order and civilization probably slower. It deserves to be noticed that, in granting self-government to all those of her colonies whose population is of English race, England has practically adopted the same plan as the United States have done with their western territory. The results have been generally satisfactory, although England, like America, has found that her colonists have been disposed to treat the aboriginal inhabitants, whose lands they covet and whose persons they hate, with a harshness and injustice which the mother country would gladly check.

The arguments which set forth the advantages of local self-government were far more applicable to the States of 1787 than to those of 1887. Virginia, then the largest State, had only half a million free inhabitants, about the present population of St. Louis. Massachusetts had 450,000, Pennsylvania 400,000, New York 300,000; while Georgia, Rhode Island, and Delaware had (even counting slaves) less than 200,000 between them.[3] These were communities to which the expression "local self-government" might be applied, for, although the population was scattered, the numbers were small enough for the citizens to have a personal knowledge of their leading men, and a personal interest (especially as a large proportion were landowners) in the economy and prudence with which common affairs were managed. Now, however, when of the forty-four States twenty-seven have more than a million inhabitants, and four have more than three millions, the newer States, being, moreover, larger in area than most of the older ones, the stake of each citizen is relatively smaller, and generally too small to sustain his activity in politics, and the party chiefs of the State are known to him only by the newspapers or by their occasional visits on a stumping tour.[4]

All that can be claimed for the Federal system under this head of the argument is that it provides the machinery for a better control of the taxes raised and expended in a given region of the country, and a better oversight of the public works undertaken there than would be possible were everything left to the Central government.[5] As regards the educative effect of numerous and frequent elections, . . . elections in America are too many and come too frequently. Overtaxing the attention of the citizen and frittering away his interest, they leave him at the mercy of knots of selfish adventurers.

The utility of the State system in localizing disorders or discontents, and the opportunities it affords for trying easily and safely experiments which ought to be tried in legislation and administration, constitute benefits to be set off against the risk . . . that evils may continue in a district, may work injustice to a minority and invite imitation by other States, which the wholesome stringency of the Central government might have suppressed.

A more unqualified approval may be given to the division of legislative powers. The existence of the State legislatures relieves Congress of a burden too heavy for its shoulders; for although it has far less foreign policy to discuss than the Parliaments of England, France, or Italy, and although the separation of the executive from the legislative department gives it less responsibility for the ordinary conduct of the administration than devolves on those Chambers, it could not possibly, were its competence as large as theirs, deal with the multiform and increasing demands of the different parts of the Union. There is great diversity in the material conditions of different parts of the country, and at present the people, particularly in the West, are eager to have their difficulties handled, their economic and social needs satisfied, by the State and the law. How little Congress could satisfy them appears by the very imperfect success with which it cultivates the field of legislation to which it is now limited.

These merits of the Federal system of government which I have enumerated are the counterpart and consequences of [the] limitation of . . . central authority. . . . They are, if one may reverse the French phrase, the qualities of Federalism's defects. The problem which all federalized nations have to solve is how to secure an efficient central government and preserve national unity, while allowing free scope for the diversities, and free play to the authorities, of the members of the federation. It is, to adopt that favourite astronomical metaphor which no American panegyrist of the Constitution omits, to keep the centrifugal and centripetal forces in equilibrium, so that neither the planet States shall fly off into space, nor the sun of the Central government draw them into its consuming fires. The characteristic merit of the American Constitution lies in the method by which it has solved this problem. It has given the National government a direct authority over all citizens, irrespective of the State governments, and has therefore been able safely to leave wide powers in the hands of those governments. And by placing the Constitution above both the National and the State governments, it has referred the arbitrament of disputes between them to an independent body, charged with the interpretation of the Constitution, a body which is to be deemed not so much a third authority in the government as the living voice of the Constitution, the unfolder of the mind of the people whose will stands expressed in that supreme instrument.

The application of these two principles, unknown to, or at any rate little used by, any previous federation,[6] has contributed more than anything else to the stability of the American system, and to the reverence which its citizens feel for it, a reverence which is the best security for its permanence. Yet even these devices would not have succeeded but for the presence of a mass of moral and material influences stronger than any political devices, which have maintained the equilibrium of centrifugal and centripetal forces. On the one hand there has been the love of local independence and self-government; on the other, the sense of community in blood, in language, in habits and ideas, a common pride in the national history and the national flag.

*Quid leges sine moribus?* The student of institutions, as well as the lawyer, is apt to overrate the effect of mechanical contrivances in politics. I admit that in America they have had one excellent result; they have formed a legal habit in the mind of the nation. But the true value of a political contrivance resides not in its ingenuity but in its adaptation to the temper and circumstances of the people for whom it is designed, in its power of using, fostering, and giving a legal form to those forces of sentiment and interest which it finds in being. So it has been with the American system. Just as the passions which the question of slavery evoked strained the Federal fabric, disclosing unforeseen weaknesses, so the love of the Union, the sense of the material and social benefits involved in its preservation, appeared in unexpected strength, and manned with zealous defenders the ramparts of the sovereign Constitution. It is this need of determining the suitability of the machinery for the workmen and its probable influence upon them, as well as the capacity of the workmen for using and their willingness to use the machinery, which makes it so difficult to predict the operation of a political contrivance, or, when it has succeeded in one country, to advise its imitation in another. The growing strength of the national government in the United States is largely due to sentimental forces that were weak a century ago, and to a development of internal communications which was then undreamt of. And the devices which we admire in the Constitution might prove unworkable among a people less patriotic and self-reliant, less law-loving and law-abiding, than are the English of America.

---

NOTES

1. In 1787, however, the great Ordinance regulating the North-West Territory was enacted by the Congress of the Confederation.

2. The United States is proprietor of the public domain in the Territories, and when a new State is organized the ownership is not changed. The United States, however, makes grants of wild lands to the new State as follows:—(1) Of every section numbered 16 (being one thirty-sixth of all) for the support of common schools. (2) Of lands to endow a university. (3) Of the lands noted in the surveys as swamp lands, and which often are valuable. (4) It has usually made further grants to aid in the construction of railroads, and for an agricultural college. The grants commonly leave the United States a much larger landowner within the State than is the State itself, and when all the dealings of the National government with its lands are considered, it is more justly chargeable with squandering the public domain than the States are.

3. I give round numbers, reduced a little from the census of 1790.

4. To have secured the real benefits of local self-government the States ought to have been kept at a figure not much above that of their original population, their territory being cut up into new States as the population increased. Had this been done—no doubt at the cost of some obvious disadvantages, such as the diminution of State historical feeling, the undue enlargement of the Senate, and the predominance of a single large city in a State—there would now be more than two hundred States. Of course in one sense the States are no larger than they were in the early days, because communication from one part to another is in all of them far easier, quicker, and cheaper than it then was.

5. It must be remembered that in most parts of the Union the local self-government of cities, counties, townships, and school districts exists in a more complete form than in any of the great countries of Europe. . . .

6. The central government in the Achaian League had apparently a direct authority over the citizens of the several cities, but it was so ill defined and so little employed that we can hardly cite that instance as a precedent.

## Does Federalism Encourage Good Government?

### MICHAEL KINSLEY

### The Withering Away of the States

Speaking of the glories of federalism, as President Reagan has been doing lately, have you heard the one about Howard Hughes? Hughes was born and raised in Texas. He spent most of his adult life and made most of his fortune in California. Then he bought up a large chunk of Las Vegas (that's in Nevada) and moved into a hotel there. He spent his last few years flitting mysteriously around the world, and was on a plane heading back to Texas when he died in 1976.

In our glorious federal system, inheritance is one of many matters left entirely to state law and state courts. Now then. Who was to run Hughes's vast business empire while his affairs were being settled? Each of these "united" states has its own complex rules and precedents on this question. Each state also has its own rules and precedents about which state's rules and precedents to follow. Hughes's relatives persuaded a court in Delaware to appoint one of them administrator. Delaware? Almost all of Hughes's assets were in a company called Summa Corporation. Each state makes its own laws governing corporations, and Delaware turns a pretty penny making its own laws the most accommodating. So Summa, like most major U.S. corporations (General Motors, the *New Republic,* and so on), is incorporated in Delaware. But the stock certificate reflecting Hughes's ownership of Summa was in the Bank of America headquarters in Los Angeles. Los Angeles is in California. So a California official challenged Delaware's right to appoint an administrator. Litigation ensued.

Meanwhile, the famous "Mormon will" popped up. In Utah. Wills must be approved by the state where the decedent was "domiciled" and by every state where his assets are located. Where was Hughes "domiciled"? Unclear. A court in Nevada held a trial and ruled that the will was a fake. Then the issue had to be retried in California. And again in Texas. Since all three states came to the same conclusion, that the Mormon will was a fake, that particular issue was finally settled last month after only five brisk years of litigation.

So Howard Hughes died without a will. Each state, naturally, has its own set of rules about what happens in such a case. California and Nevada have the same rules, but Texas's rules are different. The states are in miraculous agreement on the general rules about whose rules should apply, but each state has its own doctrines and precedents on specific cases, and each applies them in its own courts. Believe it or not, Hughes's relatives settled this one among themselves without litigation! There was plenty to go around.

But wait. There is the matter of inheritance taxes. The federal government has one. So do most of the states. For this reason, Texas and California both claim the late Mr. Hughes as one of their own. Delaware (remember Delaware?) also has designs. All of these taxes would add up to more than 100 percent of the estate. Nevada has no death tax; the heirs are convinced that cousin Howard always thought of Las Vegas as "home." This issue has been bouncing around the country like a billiard ball. In 1978 a Texas jury determined in a Texas court that Hughes was a Texan. California was unpersuaded. It asked the U.S. Supreme Court to decide.

In nations not blessed with a federal system there is a sad scarcity of courts and a straightforward hierarchy among them. In this country there are 51 independent court systems, and the relationship among them is one of infinite complexity and beautiful subtlety of doctrine, weaved by legal artisans over 200 years. The U.S. Supreme Court decided that it did not have the power to decide the Hughes case, but several justices suggested that a federal district court could decide it. A federal district court in Texas decided that it could not decide. Then a federal appeals court decided that the district court could, too, decide. California has asked the Supreme Court to decide that the Texas district court cannot decide after all. If the district court does ultimately decide, the matter will then head up to the Supreme Court for the third time.

How many lawyers have been involved in all this? "Literally hundreds," says one of them. At what cost? Reticent pause. Millions and millions? "Oh, certainly." The conclusion is several years away.

We don't all face the problem of being heirs to Howard Hughes's fortune, but we all suffer the nuisance of living in a federal system. Now President Reagan wants to reverse the trend of 200 years and give the states a larger role in governing our lives. He hasn't yet explained why. It's clear he wants less government *in toto*, but how will shifting functions between levels of government achieve this? Some see racist intent in Reagan's revival of the term "states' rights." Others argue that transferring social services "back" to the states, which never provided them in the first place, is just a sneaky way of canceling them. Reagan's people insist otherwise. But if Reagan really thinks that transferring functions and authority from Washington to the states is a sensible way to make government more efficient, more responsive, less obtrusive, and so on, he should consider how federalism really works in 1981. Anyone truly concerned about making America more productive, more democratic, less wasteful, less bureaucratic, would want to hasten the withering away of the states as quickly as possible.

Everyone knows, for example, that America fritters away far too much brainpower on legal matters while the Japanese are inventing computers that design robots that build automobiles and so on. One main reason is federalism. Half of the standard three-year legal education could be wiped out if we had a single government with a single set of laws. Almost that many lawyers could be wiped out, too. There are elaborate constitutional doctrines about what the states can and cannot do because they are joined in a nation, and what the central government can and cannot do because we are 50 sovereign states. The gears of litigation grind endlessly over what court a particular quarrel belongs in and what law that court should apply. (Should a federal court sitting in Minnesota use Indiana conflict-of-law rules to decide whether an Ohio automobile guest statute should apply to a crash in Texas between a car from Alabama driven by a Louisiana woman and a truck owned by a Delaware corporation? That sort of thing.) This country also makes many important governmental decisions through the awkward and costly procedure of letting the states and the federal government sue one another. Unfortunately, in this litigation-crazed nation, agencies of the federal government regularly sue one another, so eliminating the states wouldn't eliminate this problem. But it would help.

On most important matters, each state makes its own laws and settles its own arguments. When a large airplane crashes, for example, lawyers may have the pleasure of debating the safety of some wing bolt or cargo hatch in dozens of courts and of researching obscure doctrines of negligence under dozens of independent legal systems. Every law student learns to quote Mr. Justice Brandeis about why this is a good thing: "It is one of the happy incidents of the federal system that a single courageous state may, if its citizens choose, serve as a laboratory; and try novel social and economic experiments without risk to the rest of the country." Its citizens seldom so choose. Instead, there is something called the National Conference of Commissioners on Uniform State Laws, which has been beavering since 1892 to bring about some kind of consistency in matters on which there is no earthly reason why the states need to disagree. Some of the commission's monuments include the Uniform Simultaneous Death Act, the Uniform Facsimile Signatures of Public Officials Act, the Uniform Division of Income for Tax Purposes Act [UDITPA] and so on. This last one, for example, tackles the fascinating question of how to apportion the income of a multistate corporation for the purpose of collecting state income taxes. The Uniform Commissioners struggled bravely and here, in part, is the formula they came up with:

> Section 9. All business income shall be apportioned to this state by multiplying the income by a fraction, the numerator of which is the property factor plus the payroll factor plus the sales factor, and the denominator of which is three.

> Section 10. The property factor is a fraction, the numerator of which is the average value of the taxpayer's real and tangible personal property owned or rented and used in this state during the tax period and the denominator of which is the average value of all the taxpayer's real and tangible personal property owned or rented and used during the tax period.

Unfortunately, no state is required to accept UDITPA or the other uniform acts, and those that do generally fiddle with them first.

Mr. Reagan, with his fondness for bromides, probably believes in equal justice under the law. Federalism makes this impossible in the United States. A recent survey by the National Law Journal found that an American will spend more time in prison for robbery in South Carolina than for willful homicide in half a dozen other states; that the average felony conviction leads to 13 months in jail in South Dakota and 58 months in Massachusetts; and so on. The biggest disparity is that some states have capital punishment and others don't.

Anyone who believes that enhancing federalism is a sensible way to reduce the cost of government should look up "national" and "state" in that great political science treatise, the Washington, D.C. telephone book. The founding fathers thought that the Senate could adequately represent the interests of the states to one another and the central government. Reagan may think that's still how it works. In fact, untold millions are spent every year in the attempt to coordinate 50 sovereignties within a single nation.

Thirty-two state governments, at last count, have offices in Washington. Many of these are located in the "Hall of the States," an office building on Capitol Hill that also houses the National Governors Association and the National Conference of State Legislatures. But that's just the beginning. The state of California has 21 separate governmental offices in Washington. They include the state office itself, with a dozen staff members ("middle-sized," says one of them), and offices for Alameda County, Los Angeles County, San Bernardino County, San Diego County, Santa Clara County, Inglewood County, the California County Supervisors Association, Los Angeles City, six other cities and city groupings, the League of California Cities, the California university, state college, and community college systems, the California Department of Education, and the California legislature.

Besides the governors and state legislatures, there are separate National Associations (or "Assemblies" or "Conferences" or "Centers" or "Leagues") of (or "for" or "on"): Community Arts Agencies, State Art Agencies, State Units on Aging, Conservation Districts, Consumer Agency Administrators, Counties (downtown and Capitol Hill branches), Criminal Justice Planning Directors, Government Communicators, Regional Councils, State Alcohol and Drug Abuse Directors, State Aviation Officials, State Boards of Education, State Boating Law Administrators, State Budget Offices, State Credit Union Supervisors, State Departments of Agriculture, State Development Agencies, State Directors of Special Education, State Lotteries, State Mental Health Program Directors, State Mental Retardation Program Directors, State Savings and Loan Supervisors, State Universities and Land Grant Colleges, Tax Administrators, Towns and Township Officials, Urban Flood Management Agencies, City Councilmen, State Courts, and so on. And then there is the Advisory Commission on Intergovernmental Relations, a creature of the federal government itself, with a staff of 37 dedicated to grinding out fat reports on federalish topics. It may be expected to survive the Stockman [Budget Director David Stockman] ax.

Well, this is a big and complicated country, federalism or no. But these offices don't replace the coordinating function of a single central government. Most of them duplicate a whole hierarchy of federal offices on matters like historic preservation, mental health, criminal justice, and so on. These state offices generally perform two functions. One is to deal with the special problems created by federalism: 50 separate buildings codes, professional licensing procedures, criminal records systems. A more important function is to lobby the federal government.

Reagan and his people seem vividly aware of how "special interest groups" thwart the functioning of democracy, clog the wheels of government, and subvert the assertion of the general will. But they seem unaware of how much federalism aggravates this problem. It turns lower levels of government from units on an established hierarchy into independent duchies, free to join with or join battle with all the other special interests. If, say, federal mental health bureaucrats want to protect or expand their turf, they must more or less go through channels, and in theory someone may even give them a fairly expeditious "no." State mental health bureaucrats may open a Washington office, hire professional lobbyists, and, if all else fails, start filing lawsuits. The people who pay state taxes are the same ones who pay federal taxes, yet the question of how much our society as a whole should spend on mental health or criminal justice or historical preservation gets [settled] by various governmental units slugging it out as if they had nothing to do with one another. Millions of your state tax dollars are being spent every day in efforts to affect how your federal tax dollars are spent, while millions of your federal tax dollars are spent fending them off. This is efficient government?

Speaking of your taxes, federalism makes a mess of them. Having different levels of government raising revenues independently not only makes life needlessly complicated. Taxation depends on the government having a monopoly. A rational and fair tax system is impossible when governments must compete with one another. The growth of multinational corporations has made this an insoluble problem among nations. The Balkanization of our tax system creates a perfectly needless problem in this country.

Every state has an office called something like the Industrial Development Division. The job of these offices is to entice business into the state—sometimes from abroad, but usually from other states. The main weapon is tax favors. A thick packet from the state of Michigan, for example, promises "significant tax incentives" to industries setting up in Michigan. These include exemptions from property tax for up to 12 years, a modified corporate income tax, special exemptions for things like pollution control equipment, and so on. Michigan, like most states, also offers to raise money through federal tax-exempt bonds and relend it to corporations that settle there. Thus ordinary, stationary taxpayers finance this competition through both their state and their federal taxes.

The March 10 [1981] *New York Times* contained a full-page ad from the New York State Department of Commerce asserting in 144-point type, "NEW YORK VOTES 'YES' FOR BUSINESS," and bragging about all the taxes that have been lowered to make New York "the best place in the world to do business." The same paper had a page-one article about how just one of these tax breaks is costing the state $100 million a year with no perceptible benefit. Certainly very little new business is generated by the nation as a whole by letting corporations play the state legislatures off against one another. In fact, the process undoubtedly makes our economy less efficient and less productive by adding artificial considerations to business investment decisions. A company that ought to be locating a new plant near its suppliers or near its markets will instead plunk it down in whatever state is temporarily ahead in the game of tax-incentive leap-frog.

State-level regulation of business creates similar absurdities. On the one hand, an entrepreneur (and we're all terribly solicitous of entrepreneurs these days) who wishes to raise money for a new product must hire a lawyer to shepherd his scheme through 51 different securities regulatory systems. Hardly good for productivity. And when you're following a truck on the interstate highway, you may observe the consequence of federalism plastered all over its rear end.

On the other hand, federalism makes sensible regulations impossible to apply and enforce. There are two reasons for this. First, we do have open state borders, for the moment, and air and water currents remain unimpressed by the doctrine of states' rights. This means that matters like gun control and pollution standards simply cannot be addressed on the state level. Assertions by Reagan people that they should be are simply fatuous. Second, regulation, like taxation, must be a monopoly to work right. This may sound undemocratic, but it's actually the essence of democracy. Almost everybody in the country might agree that a certain regulation is desirable, but no state will be able to pass it for fear of losing business.

The catalog of bribes sent out to business prospects by the Texas Industrial Commission contains the usual promises about "one of the most favorable tax systems in the entire U.S.," industrial development loans, lack of troublesome regulations, and so on. It adds an interesting twist with a discussion of the severance tax (the tax on minerals extracted from the ground) on gas and oil wells:

> Although the number of Texas firms subject to severance tax is relatively small, the revenues provided are significant and are at least partially responsible for the favorable tax structure industry enjoys. In 1979 Texas collected $1,025,550,000 in severance taxes. While this tax accounted for more than 17 percent of the state's total tax revenue, it also represented 35 percent of all severance taxes collected in the United States.

In other words, Texas is able to entice business from other states by keeping taxes low and offering other inducements like free job-training programs because it happens to have lots of oil. Is it rational and productive, is it the best way to stimulate growth and jobs, is it one of the glories of federalism, that businesses having nothing to do with oil should be bribed away from the job-hungry northeast by the use of oil revenues?

Federalism makes the government a much better deal for some people than for others. This is not a question of letting local areas decide how much government they want. Government Balkanization lets some people get more services for less money. This can be seen most clearly in metropolitan areas, where rich suburbs are able to have lower tax rates but higher per-capita expenditures than central cities, which often must support area-wide services like museums and zoos. But there are equally dramatic disparities across the nation. For example, while the New York state and city university systems are raising tuition and cutting back on services, the University of Texas is keeping tuition low and has embarked on a lavish building program. This is not because the people of Texas have democratically decided to tax themselves more heavily to support higher education, but because late in the last century the Texas legislature assigned the universities some useless grazing land, which turned out to contain oil. As a result, the "Permanent Fund" shared by UT and Texas A&M is $1.3 billion (larger than Harvard's endowment) and growing fast.

The energy crisis has dramatized what was previously a rather academic question: who should benefit from the great mineral wealth of this country? Obviously the main beneficiaries are those lucky enough to own some of it. But often it is owned by the government, and even when it isn't, the government can and does appropriate some of it through taxes for the benefit of . . . whom? Everybody in society? or just those who happen to live nearby? Right now, the system goes out of its way to keep the benefits nearby. For example, as coal production gears up in the west, various states are applying stiff severance taxes to coal mined on *federal* land. Meanwhile, the federal windfall profits tax *exempts* all oil produced on *state*-owned land. Why?

President Reagan not only is untroubled by anomalies like this, he wants to increase them. He has claimed "a very warm feeling in my heart for the 'sage-brush rebellion,' " and has endorsed that movement's principal aim, which is to transfer vast areas of federal land—much of it with valuable resources—to state ownership. This is bad policy and, worse, it is bad leadership. It feeds a dangerous growth in geographical chauvinism. Regional pride is a fine thing, but that is not what is behind the recent developments like the sagebrush rebellion, Alaska's scheme to rebate oil money based on how many years people have lived there, Texas bumper stickers that say "Let 'Em Freeze in the Dark," or proposed state laws in the industrial midwest that would forbid plants to move elsewhere. Economic stress is eroding our feeling of national community. The president should be trying to reinforce it, working to apportion the suffering and benefit equitably. Instead, Reagan is encouraging insularity and grabbiness.

Why is he doing this? Reagan claims to believe that, to the extent we must have government, state government is inherently more efficient than the federal government, and less prone to the dreaded waste, fraud, and abuse. There is no evidence to support this belief. All the growth in government employment in recent years has come on the state and local level. In 1960 there were 2.3 million people working for the federal government. In 1979 there were 2.8 million. By contrast in 1960 there were over six million state and local government employees, and today there are almost 13 million. State and local governments, in other words, have more than doubled over the past two decades, while the federal bureaucracy has increased by less than 20 percent.

Anyone who reads almost any local paper will find the notion laughable that the state government is better run than the national government. One of my local papers is the *Washington Post*. It covers two state governments and one jurisdiction that would like to be a state, and certainly has taken to behaving like one. In the first four days of March, the *Post* Metro section contained the following stories:

- "Study Says Most City Assessments Wrong," reporting that more than two-thirds of residential properties in the District of Columbia are assessed inaccurately.
- "Ethical Considerations in Annapolis," about a Maryland state legislator, also a tavern owner, who is sponsoring a bill to forbid teenagers from buying alcohol anywhere except in a tavern. "His case is far from isolated," says the article. "This year, as always in this part-time legislature, there are tavern owners sponsoring drinking bills, insurance agents promoting eased guidelines for their work, and lawyers and doctors whose bills would increase the business and benefits of their professions." Mention is made of a "thick new ethics law" passed last year.
- "2 Figures in Probe Get New Posts," about how the chairman and staff director of the D.C. Alcoholic Beverage Control Board, both being investigated by a federal grand jury for bribery and extortion, were given new city jobs with full pay.
- "City Housing Rehabilitation Unit Stripped of Funding," about a D.C. agency accused of "an alleged history of program foul-ups, shoddy construction, staff conflicts of interest with private contractors and improper use of city money."
- "Bill to Lower Probate Fees Opposed," about how lawyers in the Maryland legislature are preventing cheaper administration of wills.

In four whole days, there was not a single story of corruption, stupidity, waste, or other outrage by the state of Virginia! And, mind you, the Richmond legislature *was* in session. Perhaps we should turn the federal government over to Virginia.

Or perhaps we should drop it. Federalism, I mean. It was great fun, but it was just one of those things. We don't need to do anything so drastic as abolishing the states. They could remain as reservoirs of sentiment and employers of last resort for people's brothers-in-law. But billions could be saved by both the government and the private sector if we were to nationalize huge chunks of the law such as negligence, incorporation and business regulation, and professional licensing. Justice and economy would be served by unifying the court system and the punishment of crime. A single national taxing authority would put thousands of lawyers and accountants out of work. (States could still set their own tax rates, but Uncle Sam would make the rules and do the collecting for everybody.) National authority over social concerns like welfare and environmental rules would assure that society as a whole makes rational, democratic decisions about issues that affect society as a whole.

At the very least, someone should sit down with President Reagan and explain to him that he is confounding his great and universal theme of the individual versus government with the issues emerging from a particular historical oddity. It will be no triumph for freedom to get the federal government off our backs, only to have 50 state governments climb back on.

## Questions for Discussion

1. Which is closer to the people: the state or the federal government? Why?
2. What criteria can be used in evaluating whether a policy area properly belongs to the states or to the federal government?
3. What constitutional provisions would have to be changed for the United States to become a unitary system?
4. What are the advantages and disadvantages of the United States becoming a unitary system?
5. Which would "special interest" groups prefer: a federal or a unitary system? Why?

## Suggested Readings

Caraley, Demetrios. "Changing Conceptions of Federalism." *Political Science Quarterly,* 101, no. 2 (1986), 289–306.

Conlon, Timothy. *New Federalism: Intergovernmental Reform from Nixon to Reagan.* Washington, D.C.: Brookings Institution, 1988.

Cooper, Charles J. "The Demise of Federalism." *Urban Lawyer,* 20, no. 2 (Spring 1988), 239–283.

Derthick, Martha. "The Enduring Features of American Federalism." *Brookings Review,* 7, no. 3 (Summer 1989), 34–38.

Dye, Thomas R. *American Federalism: Competition among Governments.* Lexington, Mass.: Lexington Books, 1990.

Howard, A. E. Dick. "A Historical View: Federalism at the Bicentennial." *Journal of State Government,* 62, no. 1 (January/February 1989), 12–19.

Keller, Morton. "State Power Needn't Be Resurrected Because It Never Died." *Governing,* 2, no. 1 (October 1988), 52–57.

Lieberman, Joseph. "Modern Federalism: Altered States." *Urban Lawyer,* 20, no. 2 (Spring 1988), 285–299.

Neumann, Franz. "On the Theory of the Federal State." In *The Democratic and* the *Authoritarian State,* edited by Herbert Marcuse, pp. 216–232. Glencoe, Ill.: Free Press, 1957.

Vedlitz, Arnold. *Conservative Mythology and Public Policy in America.* New York: Praeger, 1988.

Walker, David B. "American Federalism: Past, Present and Future." *Journal of State Government,* 62, no. 1 (January/February 1989), 3–11.

Wilmarth, Arthur E., Jr. "The Original Purpose of the Bill of Rights: James Madison and the Founders' Search for a Workable Balance between Federal and State Power." *American Criminal Law Review,* 26, no. 4 (Spring 1989), 1261–1321.

# Popular Participation

D emocracies pride themselves on the freedom of people to participate in the political process. Such participation takes many forms, including forming private associations known as interest groups, getting involved in political campaigns, voting, working for political parties, and expressing ideas through speech or the mass media.

The traditional definition of an interest group is a collection of people with common interests who work together to achieve those interests. When a group becomes involved in the activities of government, it is known as a political interest group.

More than a century ago, Alexis de Tocqueville observed that the people of the United States have a propensity to form associations. This observation has become as valid a description of the 1990s as it was of the 1830s. The United States has a large number of political interest groups—business, labor, professional, religious, and social reform. At the same time, many citizens do not belong to organizations other than religious and social groups, which in some cases have no significant political role.

Interest groups engage in a variety of activities, including making financial contributions to candidates for public office and to political parties, getting their viewpoints known to the general public and to other groups, organizing demonstrations, and influencing government officials. Legitimate political behavior in a democracy allows for great freedom to participate in these ways. The First Amendment to the Constitution is often cited as the basis for such political behavior. That amendment states:

> Congress shall make no law respecting an establishment of religion, or prohibiting the free exercise thereof; or abridging the freedom of speech, or of the press; or the right of the people peaceably to assemble, and to petition the government for a redress of grievances.

One form of political activity is involvement in political campaigns and elections. In a democracy people are free to support candidates of their choice. Such support may consist of merely voting in an election, but it may also include organizing meetings, soliciting support for candidates, raising and spending money for candidates, and publicizing issues.

An effective democracy requires that information be widely disseminated. The same First Amendment that protects the rights of individuals and groups to engage in political activities also safeguards the press and other media such as television, radio, and magazines. Television, particularly, has become the chief source of news for many people.

What people do and what they think are of vital importance to government officials. In democracies (and even in many dictatorships) government makes every effort to know what public opinion is on many issues. Sometimes government leads and sometimes it follows public opinion.

Although modern dictatorships rely on political participation, that participation is generally controlled by the ruling elite. Interest groups are not spontaneous organizations designed to be independent from government but are linked to government primarily through government-controlled leadership. And so, for example, trade unions are not free to strike or engage in protest activities—at least not legitimately. People are not free to form competitive political parties, and often there is only one political party that dominates elections. That party is regarded as having a special role in mobilizing the masses.

In many modern dictatorships elections do take place, but they are generally rigged. Where opposing candidates are permitted to compete, there is generally no significant difference between the candidates on issues. Protest movements and mass demonstrations are broken up, sometimes ruthlessly, unless those movements are controlled by the government. To be sure, protest movements and demonstrations do exist in some modern dictatorships, but government tries to control or suppress them.

In modern dictatorships, moreover, the media are not free to report the news in an objective manner. Instead, the media reflect the wishes of the ruling dictators. News is suppressed; opposition newspapers are closed down. There is only one truth—that of the government—disseminated through television, radio, magazines, and newspapers.

Many people in the world live in dictatorships. Since 1989 and 1990, however, democracy has made great gains and has replaced or diminished dictatorial rule in the Soviet Union and in most Eastern European countries. Democracy has also made significant advances in Latin American countries. And South Africa, long under white minority rule, is experiencing change through greater political participation by its black community.

Although democracies are fundamentally different from dictatorships, even democracies do not always live up to the standards of freedom they cherish. In this regard, the political behavior of nongovernmental organizations in the United States poses problems for those interested in protecting democratic processes. Although it is relatively easy to discuss democracy in the abstract, actual practices in the U.S. political system raise thorny questions about the application of democracy to concrete situations. This part considers four issues pertaining to popular participation in the democratic process: the importance and impact of registration requirements on voting turnout, the ways in which contributions by special interest groups may or may not influence the democratic process, the abolition of the Electoral College, and the role of the mass media in shaping public opinion.

# Chapter 4

# Will Voter Registration Reforms Increase Voter Turnout?

A central feature of political democracy is universal suffrage. The United States today has a voting system based on universal suffrage. With the exception of people under the age of eighteen, felons, or the insane, every U.S. citizen has the right to vote. Restrictions based on registration and residence impose the only limits on this right.

Restrictions on the right to vote have existed throughout most of U.S. history. Under Article I, Section 4, of the Constitution, the states can determine the "Times, Places, and Manner" for holding elections, but Congress is permitted to alter such regulations "except as to the Places of chusing Senators." (Until 1913, senators were chosen by state legislatures.) In the early years of the Republic only white male property owners were allowed to vote in most states. The trend has been to expand the franchise to include groups previously excluded. At first property ownership as a voting requirement was eliminated. The Fifteenth Amendment to the Constitution, adopted in 1870, forbade any state to deny or abridge the right to vote "on account of race, color, or previous condition of servitude."

States, however, found ways to prevent blacks from voting. In effect, blacks were excluded from exercising their votes in the South through such devices as literacy tests, the white primary, and the poll tax, which required the payment of a fee to vote. Intimidation by some whites made it unlikely that blacks would organize for the purpose of exercising the right to vote. According to the Supreme Court, political parties were considered to be "private organizations" and, consequently, not subject to the Fifteenth Amendment. Some of these restrictions also effectively disfranchised some whites. The poll tax kept poor whites from voting, and literacy tests were used to keep immigrants from voting.

The twentieth century brought major changes. The Nineteenth Amendment allowed women to vote. The Twenty-fourth Amendment, adopted in 1964, made the payment of a poll tax or any tax illegal in federal elections, both primaries and elections. The Voting Rights Act of 1965 assured that black people could vote in every state. The Twenty-sixth Amendment, adopted in 1971, established eighteen as the minimum age for voting. Supreme Court decisions and state legislation eliminated literacy tests. As a result of all these measures, the right to vote is virtually universal in the United States.

Yet many U.S. citizens do not exercise that right. In the 1988 general election, for example, the turnout rate of voters was 50.16 percent, compared to 54.4 percent in 1976 and the post–World War II high of 62.8 percent in 1960. In state and local elections the turnout is generally lower than in national elections.

Nonvoting has been explained as resulting from the decline of political parties, the media's focus on personalities rather than political issues, and the absence of perceived meaningful choices between candidates of the two major parties. Some observers say that nonvoting is no threat to the democratic process since nonvoters must be essentially satisfied with the way the U.S. political system is functioning. Other observers say that nonvoting is a sickness of democracy, a sign that citizens feel powerless to change the course of U.S. politics.

In 1989 and 1990, Congress considered reforming registration procedures to increase voter turnout but failed to enact a law on the subject. In order to vote in U.S. elections, citizens must first register. But registration procedures vary from state to state. In some states citizens must go in person to a state election agency and register to vote. In other states the procedure is handled by mail. States vary, too, in considering whether people who have registered but who have not voted for a period of years must reregister.

Should voter registration be reformed? Washington attorney Robert Deyling argues that it should. He contends:

1. About 75 percent of the people who are registered to vote cast their ballots, but only about 60 percent of all eligible voters are registered.
2. The pool of registered voters would be enlarged.
3. Current registration procedures disproportionately impede voting by low-income and minority citizens.

Political consultant Edward S. Hochman argues against the value of voter registration reform, stating:

1. The current practice in registering to vote is no difficult task.
2. Purging state voter lists helps prevent fraud.
3. In earlier decades, the same voting registration procedures did not lead to low voting turnout.
4. Voting turnout can be increased by other means.

*Will Voter Registration Reforms Increase Voter Turnout?*

## ROBERT DEYLING

### Knocking Over Voter Barriers

Congress will soon take a vote that could open the doors of democracy to millions of Americans.

In the 1988 presidential election, only about 50 percent of eligible voters cast a ballot, the lowest turnout in any national election since 1924. Voter participation in national elections has been in slow but steady decline since 1964, a fact not explained by apathy alone.

Despite the elimination of obviously discriminatory barriers to voting, such as poll taxes and literacy tests, more subtle and often unintended impediments persist. By establishing uniform national standards for voter registration, Congress may soon remove many of these remaining bureaucratic roadblocks.

Voter turnout is directly related to the number of people registered to vote. About 75 percent of those who are registered can be expected to vote in a presidential election. However, only about 60 percent of all eligible voters are registered. While we can't be positive that more people would vote if more were registered, expanding the registration rolls would enlarge the pool of potential voters.

In part, that is the motivation behind the National Voter Registration Act of 1989, a proposal to reform state voter registration practices. The bill, S 874, now pending in the Senate, would make available to all citizens a number of innovative registration options that are already in place in many states. These include registration by mail, registration through the driver's license application process, and expanded registration at offices of state and federal government agencies.

The bill would also strictly limit the "purging" of voter rolls, which is used in some states to disqualify people who do not vote in every election. Eleven states, encompassing nearly 20 percent of the nation's population, currently delete names from their voter lists after only two years of non-voting; almost all states purge their lists of people who have not voted for four years. Although list-purging is defended as an anti-fraud measure, critics contend that it disproportionately affects low-income and minority voters. Those groups tend to vote less frequently and change addresses often, making it more difficult for registrars to confirm their eligibility to vote.

Nearly 90 percent of Americans have a driver's license or state identification card. The Senate bill would make voter registration automatic for people who apply for or renew their license or ID card, unless the individual specifically declines the option.

Thirteen states now provide some form of "motor voter" registration. The licensing procedure can be easily adapted to allow convenient but verifiable registration. Most states already use the driver's license as the source document for their central record-keeping, and the license application collects most of the information needed to determine eligibility to vote.

There are other models for reform as well: Twenty-four states allow registration by mail. Some type of agency-based registration is permitted in 21 states, about 10 of which allow registration at the motor vehicle department.

In hearings before the Senate Rules and Administration Committee this past spring [1989], witnesses stressed the urgent need for reform. Rep. Al Swift (D-Wash.), chairman of the House Administration Subcommittee on Elections—which is considering legislation similar to the Senate bill—cited a *New York Times* poll conducted in November 1988, in which 40 percent of the respondents said they had not voted in the last election because they were not registered. The League of Women Voters noted that "while there have been improvements in voter registration administration in many states, the state-by-state approach to reform has left a confusing array of practices."

Others complained that states retain outdated rules that hinder registration. According to the American Civil Liberties Union, for example, in Virginia most people must register at the offices of city or county registrars, some of which are open fewer than five days a week.

The Senate also heard about the disproportionate burden onerous voter registration places on racial minorities and low-income people. The National Association for the Advancement of Colored People reported, based on its registration drives across the country, that inconvenient sites and restricted hours deter low-income people from registering. Looking beyond those who apply for driver's licenses, the NAACP contended that a truly inclusive system would also focus on "those places that reach or service persons who do not drive or own cars—the public assistance offices, the unemployment offices."

Of course, S 874 has critics. Some state officials fear the bill would require expensive changes in election administration. Florida officials have estimated that election costs there would rise 50 percent under the new registration rules. One idea that has surfaced is for the federal government to pick up the tab—which, the Congressional Budget Office estimates, could be $25 million per year.

And some officials attack the bill's requirement that states amend driver's license applications to permit voter registration. They claim that many people, including those under 18, would mistakenly apply to register by checking the wrong box on the application and that some applicants would be ineligible to vote because they were not citizens or had criminal convictions.

Despite the criticisms, most states appear ready to take on the challenge of increasing access to the ballot box. In 1987, the National Association of Secretaries of State issued a report calling for a wide range of reforms. And Kentucky officials have asked the Senate to amend S 874 to exert even greater federal control over the registration process, proposing a system of nationwide registration by postcard. That approach, now used to register members of the military and other Americans living overseas, would require the U.S. Postal Service to deliver registration forms to every residence in the country at least once a year.

Some of the witnesses before the Senate committee hearing suggested that, in light of the costs and procedural changes the bill would impose, Congress may not have the constitutional power to pass the legislation. The Justice Department has expressed opposition, questioning whether difficult registration requirements really cause low voter turnout and attacking the bill as congressional meddling in an area of "legitimate state discretion."

But the legislation is clearly a legitimate exercise of Congress' power under Article I, Section 4, of the Constitution to "make or alter" state laws that affect elections of senators and representatives. Indeed, in 1979, the Carter Justice Department, testifying about a proposal that would have forced the states to allow same-day registration for all federal elections, concluded that registration reform was a proper exercise of Congress' power to override state laws concerning the "times, places, and manner" of holding federal elections.

According to the League of Women Voters, the United States remains the only major Western democratic nation that does not automatically register its citizens to vote. The Voting Rights Act of 1965 and its amendments have been essential in fighting blatant forms of discrimination in the voting process. By enacting a bill like S 874, Congress can finish the business of registration reform and eliminate many of the remaining obstacles to voting.

 $\checkmark$ N O

*Will Voter Registration Reforms Increase Voter Turnout?*

## EDWARD S. HOCHMAN

### Tuned-out Voters Won't Turn Out at Polls

As a political consultant who has been involved in more than his share of voter-registration drives, I am amazed that the same drivel continues to be spouted regarding low voter turnout. (See "Knocking over Voter Barriers" by Robert Deyling, *Legal Times*, Sept. 18, 1989, Page 35.) Just once, let's try to displace fallacy with fact.

## 1. REMOVING OBSTACLES TO REGISTRATION

While requirements vary from state to state, registering to vote is neither an intimidating nor a cumbersome rite. In fact, as most voters may recall, the process is easier than obtaining a driver's license, an undertaking that most non-registered people manage to accomplish.

As a teenager, I registered to vote in about 10 minutes. Admittedly, I had to take a bus to city hall, but that one-time inconvenience hardly seemed onerous. Subsequently, I've also registered people during voter drives at their homes, shopping centers, bus stops, etc.

Frankly, it's time we stop making excuses for those who won't get off their buttocks to register. If an 18-year-old can pass both a written and a driving test to obtain a license, he or she can drive to city hall to sign onto the voter rolls.

## 2. PURGING VOTER LISTS

I've seen the "dead" attempt to vote, including one shill who tried to convince me (when I was a poll watcher) that he was my late neighbor. Unquestionably, purging stale voter lists helps prevent fraud.

Most states don't purge until *after* the fourth full year of non-voting in *any* election. In my home state of New Jersey, there are often four elections (April school-boards, May municipals, June primaries, and November generals) and, occasionally, other special elections.

If a person can't get to the polls for at least one of the 12 to 20 elections held during the four-year period, keeping his or her name on the list (a) won't turn that person into a religious voter, but (b) will invite the very mischief that purging aims to prevent.

As for the disingenuous claim that minorities are prejudiced because "they tend to vote less frequently," this certainly is less a criticism of efforts to ensure the integrity of the voter rolls than an indictment of those groups that a quarter-century ago held massive marches to secure the very rights they now neglect to exercise.

## 3. ASSESSING VOTING TRENDS

Allegedly archaic registration practices have been blamed for leading to lower voter turnouts, but that very premise refutes the argument. These practices have been in existence for *decades,* and it's only since the mid-1960s that voting rates began to decline. Before the mid-1960s—before the age of television, electronic mail, and many other means of mass communication—these very same practices never served as impediments to impressive voter turnouts.

If those concerned with low turnouts wish to find a scapegoat, they'd be better advised to look elsewhere.

Now the League of Women Voters complains that "the state-by-state approach to reform has left a confusing array of practices." So what—in how many states does the league expect a person to register?

Moreover, my two best friends, both white, middle-class, Jewish professionals—the very stereotype of a likely voter—inexcusably refuse to register. One doesn't want to be bothered with "political junk mail," while the other fears jury duty. As this suggests, the reasons why many don't vote may be a bit more complicated than well-meaning but misguided reformers would have us believe.

## 4. INCREASING VOTER TURNOUT

If the reformers are sincere in wishing to encourage greater turnout, they should consider the following:

### A. Limit the Number of Electoral Cycles

The seemingly endless number of elections has numbed far too many voters. To take my own region as an example, no sooner had the 1988 presidential election been concluded than the candidates for the New York mayoralty, New York citywide positions, New Jersey governorship, and New Jersey legislature all began bombarding the public with their 30-second banalities. Next year, no doubt, we'll be subject to more of the same.

In the name of common decency, we should be given a break.

I submit that any state limiting its elections to even-numbered years (which would mean modifying the terms of its odd-year posts) would see a dramatic increase in voter turnout.

### B. Consolidate Elections

To take New Jersey—which is not unique—there is no justification for the boredom, expense, and inconvenience spawned by a minimum of four separate elections each year.

School-board, municipal, and primary elections should all be held on the same day. The financial savings alone would warrant the change.

### C. Increase Patronage and Party Discipline

Provided that their appointments meet a minimum level of competence, we should welcome back the patronage system—at least to a small degree. Although this is a complicated issue, there probably is a strong causative relationship between the breakdown of political machines (a term not intended to be pejorative) and the decline in voter turnout. No doubt there are other factors—decreasing union membership, dispersion to the suburbs of traditional ethnic voting blocs, and so on—but the concerted effort by so-called reformers to destroy the infrastructure of our two major political parties has also been a villain. Indisputably, the patronage system was the most continuously successful system for ensuring a large voter turnout.

## D. Reform the Primary and Convention Delegate-Selection Process

Given the widely voiced gross dissatisfaction with the choice of candidates, is there any wonder that the voting rate is dropping? At least the much-maligned backroom bosses had the foresight to give us Roosevelt-Willkie, Truman-Dewey, Eisenhower-Stevenson, Kennedy-Nixon, Johnson-Goldwater, and Nixon-Humphrey—all undeniably able men who could excite their partisans with cogent philosophies and crisply defined agendas. In the 20 years of "reform" since, we've been treated to the mediocrities of George McGovern, Jimmy Carter, Gerald Ford, a pathetically time-warped Walter Mondale, and, most recently, George Bush vs. Michael Dukakis.

How many people who voted from 1948 through 1968 can honestly say that the candidates from 1972 to 1988 moved them with equal passion?

Blasphemous as this may sound, the enactment of open primaries, the ratification of self-destructive delegate-selection processes, the deliberate diminution of the power of party leaders and regulars, all have led to the repeated inability of the major parties to nominate candidates who could be affirmatively embraced by the majority of the electorate. Instead, the primary process is now dominated by the crazies on both ends of the political spectrum, much to the disservice of the American people.

If we once again give the voters decent choices, they'll vote in decent numbers.

## E. Limit the Campaign Season

Anyone who by now doesn't understand the need for this can hardly be trusted to vote anyway.

Perhaps when public funding for major offices finally is enacted, a provision can require that any candidate accepting such funding, *inter alia,* must agree not to start his or her campaign more than six months prior to the election.

Sadly, virtually all recent suggestions to increase voter turnout have been gimmick-ridden fluffs that fail to address the core problem. Their advocates just won't admit that the main reason so many potential voters aren't buying is because the product is too often poorly packaged and probably not worth examining anyway.

Apart from the constitutional minefield in which they would have to tread, the reformers would better their cause by giving the political parties the tools to produce good candidates and the means to energize voters, while consolidating elections so that the voters can better focus on a few campaigns. Then the reformers should keep their mitts off the system and watch as the voting percentages rise.

## Questions for Discussion

1. Why do people vote?
2. What are the socioeconomic characteristics of the people who do not vote?
3. How do registration procedures affect voting turnout?
4. How would registration reforms affect voting fraud?
5. What role should the national government play in registration, and what responsibilities should be left to the states? What are the reasons for your answer?
6. How can voting turnout be increased?
7. Does it matter whether half the eligible voters do not vote? Why?
8. Should eligible voters be penalized by fines if they do not vote? Why?

## Suggested Readings

Alston, Chuck. "The Maze of Spending Limits: An Election Field Guide." *Congressional Quarterly Weekly Report*, 48, no. 21 (May 26, 1990), 1621–1626.

Avey, Michael J. *The Demobilization of Voters: A Comprehensive Theory of Voter Turnout*. New York: Greenwood Press, 1989.

Bennett, Stephen Earl. "The Uses and Abuses of Registration and Turnout Data: An Analysis of Piven and Cloward's Studies of Nonvoting in America." *PS: Political Science & Politics*, 23, no. 2 (June 1990), 166–171.

Ginsberg, Benjamin, and Martin Shefter. *Politics by Other Means: The Declining Importance of Elections in America*. New York: Basic Books, 1990.

Piven, Frances Fox, and Richard A. Cloward. "National Voter Registration Reform: How It Might Be Won." *PS: Political Science & Politics*, 21, no. 4 (Fall 1988), 868–875.

———. *Why Americans Don't Vote*. New York: Pantheon, 1988.

Powell, G. Bingham, Jr. "American Voter Turnout in Comparative Perspective." *American Political Science Review*, 80, no. 1 (March 1986), 17–43.

Reichley, A. James, ed. *Elections American Style*. Washington, D.C.: Brookings Institution, 1987.

Teixeira, Ruy A. *Why Americans Don't Vote*. New York: Greenwood Press, 1987.

U.S. Cong., House of Representatives. *Voter Registration*. Hearings before the Subcommittee on Elections of the Committee on House Administration, 100th Cong., 2nd Sess., 1988.

"Voter Registration: Pros & Cons." *Congressional Digest*, 69, no. 4 (April 1990), 97–128.

# Chapter 5

## *Does Private Funding for Congressional Elections Give Undue Influence to Political Action Committees?*

For most of U.S. history the funding of political campaigns was left entirely to private sources. Unlike the practice in countries where the government underwrites the expense of campaigning, in the United States political parties and candidates have had to attract donations from individuals and groups.

In the twentieth century, campaign contributions have come under greater government regulation. In 1907 Congress passed a law prohibiting corporations from using their own funds in federal election campaigns. A similar prohibition was enacted for labor unions in 1943. Between 1947 and 1962 the law governing campaign expenditures forbade both corporate and union contributions and expenditures in federal primaries, general elections, and nominating conventions.

A number of laws were passed in the 1970s to deal with campaign finance. Many resulted from the revelations of illegal corporate contributions to the Committee to Reelect the President, the campaign organization for the reelection of President Nixon. Successful challenges to some provisions in these laws resulted in Supreme Court decisions invalidating some restrictions on campaign finance in federal elections.

Today, campaign finance laws require that all federal candidates must disclose their campaign contributions. For presidential contests, a system of matching grants and public financing was established, and expenditure limits were set. No limits were placed on how much a congressional candidate's campaign committee could spend on the candidate's campaign.

One of the consequences of the campaign reform legislation was the growth of political action committees (PACs). A PAC is a private organization concerned with promoting economic, social, or ideological goals in public policy through electoral and other forms of political activity. PACs contribute money to candidates for public office. In addition, some of them help with getting out the vote and with voter registration.

PACs originated with trade unions in the 1930s. Their real development occurred in the 1970s and thereafter as a result of campaign finance reform. The Federal Election Commission (FEC), the government unit charged with enforcing federal election laws, classifies PACs under six categories: corporate PACs, labor PACs, trade/membership/health PACs, nonconnected PACs, cooperative PACs, and corporation without stock PACs.

According to the FEC, there were 608 PACs at the end of 1974. By July 1990 the number of PACs had increased to 4,192.[1] Not only has the number of PACs increased, but so, too, have PAC expenditures. FEC figures show the increase. For the election cycle of 1977–1978, PACs contributed $77.4 million to candidates. In the 1989–1990 election cycle, PACs contributed $372.4 million.[2]

Bills have been introduced into each chamber of Congress to replace private funding of congressional campaigns with a system of public funding. Although both chambers of Congress passed bills on campaign finance reform in 1990, a conference committee never met to resolve the differences and, consequently, no campaign finance reform legislation was passed that year. The Senate bill would have eliminated PACs, set up voluntary campaign spending limits, and provided low-cost campaign mail and free television time to the candidates. The House bill would have limited spending in House contests to $550,000 per candidate for the general election and would also have offered low-cost campaign mail and free broadcast time.

In the debate that follows, Mark Green and Joseph J. Fanelli express differing views on congressional campaign finance reform. Both selections are statements submitted to the Senate Committee on Rules and Administration, which was considering reform legislation on campaign finance in 1986.

Green, formerly president of the Democracy Project on Campaign Reform and currently consumer affairs commissioner of New York City, argues against the current system of campaign finance. Specifically, he contends:

1. Money buys influence, access, and even votes themselves.
2. Special interest money can paralyze Congress.
3. Special interest PACs discriminate against the groups that do not have PACs.
4. The PAC process is an incumbent-protection process.

He then refutes the arguments that have been made to defend PACs.

Joseph J. Fanelli, president of the Business-Industry Political Action Committee, makes the case for PACs. Specifically, he denies the assertions of the PAC critics and argues:

1. The political system of the United States is based on individual involvement in political campaigns. Restrictions against PACs would harm a fundamental principle of that system.
2. It is fundamentally wrong to use tax revenues for political candidates taxpayers might oppose.
3. In a period of high federal government deficits, it is wrong to add a new government program requiring additional revenues.
4. The FEC would not be able to administer public finance.
5. Public finance would encourage incompetent candidates to run for office.

6. The public is opposed to public funding in congressional campaigns.
7. It would be impossible to produce a fair system of disbursing funds to campaigns in different regions of the country.

NOTES

1. Federal Election Commission News Release, "FEC Releases Mid-Year PAC Count," July 25, 1990.
2. Federal Election Commission News Release, "PAC Activity Falls in 1990 Elections," March 31, 1991. It should be noted, however, that for the first time since 1977, a decrease in PAC financial activity was recorded during an election cycle. The 1989–1990 election cycle revealed a decline of 3 percent in receipts from the comparable figure in the 1987–1988 cycle.

 ☑ YES

*Does Private Funding for Congressional Elections Give Undue Influence to Political Action Committees?*

## MARK GREEN
### *The Case against Political Action Committees*

This is the eighth time I have testified before Congress on the subject of campaign finance reform. The first time was in 1974, two years after my book *Who Runs Congress?* was first published. That year, campaign spending for congressional elections was $72 million, and political action committees spent $12 million. In the last election, congressional campaign spending rose to $377 million. And PACs [political action committees] gave a staggering $100 million—almost a thousand percent increase over 1974.

It is evident that such unrelenting growth in campaign spending in general and PAC spending in particular affects how the legislature works—and doesn't. First, money buys influence, access, or even votes themselves. When I testify at these hearings and imply that people "give to get"—that there is legislatively interested money—I sometimes encounter angry public denials. Yet privately, we all acknowledge the truth of Rep. Barney Frank's observation that "We are the only human beings in the world who are expected to take thousands of dollars from perfect strangers on important matters and not be affected by it."

Second, special interest money can paralyze Congress. In an institution that has more than 300 committees and subcommittees, it is not hard for monied interests to find a beachhead in one or more committees in order to stop legislation from going forward. Those of us who lobbied Congress or state legislatures know how hard it is to get legislation enacted—and how easy it is to get legislation stymied. A vivid example is the extraordinary volume of spending (and lobbying) prompted by the merest whiff of tax reform.

Third, special interest PACs discriminate against the PAC-less. Who has access to PACs? Is it the Hispanic child on the lower east side of Manhattan who has a PAC? Is it an unemployed teenager in Buffalo, a small farmer going under, a consumer paying more for goods because of an antitrust exemption? And who has access to PAC money? It is not the first-time women or minority candidates, who might not have gone to school with the men who dominate PAC spending decisions. This is not a partisan point. For it was Majority Leader Robert Dole who noted, "There's no Poor PAC."

And finally, the PAC process is a true incumbent-protection system, for the money goes predominantly to one party, the incumbency party, as Common Cause president Fred Wertheimer calls it. According to *What Price PACs?*, a Twentieth Century Fund study conducted by political scientist Frank Sorauf, in House elections in 1982, 67 percent of all PAC money went to incumbents; in the Senate, 64 percent went to incumbents. "Most PACs have parent organizations, and most of those organizations have legislative interests and Washington representatives," observes Sorauf. "Supporting incumbents is thus a strategy of risk avoidance, of consolidating and protecting influence already won; it is the strategy of the already influential."

## THE AVALANCHE OF EVIDENCE

Today, the Senate is seriously considering campaign finance reform for the first time since 1977. At this hearing and at prior sessions in the Fall, you have heard testimony about the rising costs of campaigns and the increasing role of political action committees. But the most persuasive testimony has come from Senators and Representatives themselves.

In response to a challenge from Bernadette Budde, the director of Business-Industry PAC (BIPAC), to "show me the bodies" of members of Congress who were influenced by campaign contributions, I interviewed twenty-nine Representatives and Senators in 1982. Not surprisingly, the laws of human nature have not been repealed. Here is the avalanche of evidence:

Republican Representative Claudine Schneider of Rhode Island in 1982 tried to persuade a Republican colleague to oppose more funding for the Clinch River Breeder Reactor. He declined, explaining, "Westinghouse is a big contributor of mine."

Another Republican Representative, Jim Leach of Iowa, tells how he once suggested to an urban Democrat with no dairy constituency that it might be politically wisest for him to oppose a dairy price support measure, and was told, "Yeah, but their PAC gave me money. I have to support them."

A New York Democrat admitted that he voted for the Alaska Gas Pipeline, even though he opposed it on the merits, because "I didn't want the construction unions contributing to my opponent."

In the mid-1970s, a labor union that gave Rep. Leon Panetta (D-CA) a

$1500 contribution asked for support of pending "cargo preference legisla-
tion." When Panetta asked about the substance of the bill, he was told, "I
don't have to tell you anything substantively—we gave you money. We support the bill, and we expect you to." Panetta kicked the lobbyist out of his
office, and voted no.

According to one PAC manager, a certain liberal Democratic Representative,
unsure how to vote on the recent Reagan tax increase, was told by a business
PAC that if he supported the bill, "the slate would be wiped clean" between
them. The Democrat voted for the bill, for reasons having nothing to do with
the business lobby. Yet when the PAC sent him a $500 check, he angrily
returned it, telling the PAC manager, "It was like leaving a 20 cent tip." The
PAC then doubled the contribution, which the Congressman accepted.

When Representative Dan Glickman of Kansas asked a colleague several
years ago to join him in opposing a measure that would stop the Federal Trade
Commission from regulating auto dealers, he was told, "I'm committed. I got a
$10,000 check from the National Automobile Dealers Association. I can't
change my vote now." (In a separate incident, the Iowa Beef PAC began a letter
asking for Glickman's support on a bill by noting, "As we trust you will recall,
the Political Action Committee of Iowa Beef Processors, Inc., has heretofore
supported your candidacy. . . ." Glickman sent back their $250, and then
voted for the measure, as he originally intended to.)

A drug industry lobbyist told an aide to Representative Barney Frank of
Massachusetts that if Frank could co-sponsor an industry-sponsored Drug Pat-
ent Act, the lobbyist would come to Frank's first fund-raiser in Washington,
D.C. Frank told the lobbyist, "Go to hell."

Former Representative Millicent Fenwick recalled, "I wasn't down here but
two months [in 1974], at a dinner for Alvin Toffler, when I sat down next to a
reformer in Congress and asked if he'd be overriding a President Ford veto. He
said, 'Are you kidding? I took $58,000 from labor, and they want it.' "

Representative Mike Synar, Democrat of Oklahoma, says, "I go out on the
floor and say to a member, 'I need your help on this bill,' and often he will say,
'I can't do that, I got $5,000 from a special interest.' So I no longer lobby
Congressmen. I lobby the lobbyists to lobby the Congressmen."

We are all familiar with the correlation studies conducted by Common Cause
and Public Citizen's Congress Watch. These studies have found that when
specific economic interests invest substantial amounts in a large number of
legislators before key votes, the dividends roll in.

And the past few years have seen numerous journalistic accounts, all persuasively documenting the impact that campaign money has on our democracy
and our legislature. You are undoubtedly familiar with them: Elizabeth Drew's
*Politics and Money: The New Road to Corruption;* sociologist Amitai Etzioni's
*Capital Corruption;* and perhaps most impressively, the previously mentioned
study conducted for the Twentieth Century Fund by political scientist Frank
Sorauf, *What Price PACs?* These exposés usually appear as the election cycle
reaches its apogee, so we can expect further documentation soon to come. And

with every article, every book, public confidence in our democratic institutions diminishes.

We err if we look for a "smoking gun"—a Watergate tape of [a] Dita Beard memo that will sensationally convince even the most self-interested skeptic that the system needs to change. *For the system itself is the smoking gun.*

## THE CASE FOR PACS

Despite this damning and irrefutable empirical case, some beneficiaries of the PAC process cast about for rationales for the current system. In recent years, their arguments have been widely heard. Despite all appearances, they argue, PACs actually *increase* participation and democracy. Their arguments deserve scrutiny lest they become accepted by default. Like popcorn, they contain a kernel of truth puffed up beyond recognition.

Let me walk through some of them with you.

*PACs are merely exercising the right of free speech.* This assertion has been made by, among others, Eugene McCarthy, the American Civil Liberties Union and that well-known champion of the Bill of Rights, Mobil Oil. "When you cut through all the anti-PAC rhetoric," stated a Mobil advertisement, "it becomes obvious that PAC opponents don't really want the voices of average citizens to be amplified."

Are PAC contributions free speech? Although money talks in American politics, that has always been the *problem,* not the goal. Money isn't speech; speech is speech.

And if money were speech, would bribery be constitutionally protected? If so, large contributors could effectively overturn the Supreme Court's reapportionment decisions; instead of one person, one vote, the standards would be many dollars, many votes. If a contribution can buy a legislative result and drown out the voices of thousands of citizens, free speech has been stifled, not encouraged.

*PACs account for only a small part of all political contributions.* As Richard Armstrong, head of the Public Affairs Council, a pro-business group, wrote in *Newsweek* a few years ago, "The truth is that all PACs combined, including those of labor, contribute less than one-fourth of the aggregate amount spent on election campaigns."

But a PAC need not bankroll an entire campaign to be remembered by a politician after the votes are counted. Furthermore, aggregate statistics are misleading because the inclusion of candidates who get almost no PAC money pulls down the average. In any event, PACs have supplied over 40 percent of the campaign treasuries of winning House candidates in recent elections.

Finally, PAC money, like snow in the mountains, gathers at the peaks. A large portion of it goes to committee chairs and party leaders who are most able to return favors. In 1984 the House minority leader, Robert Michel, received 58 percent of his campaign funds from PACs; House Ways and Means Committee chairman Dan Rostenkowski filled 63 percent of his coffers with PAC money.

*"If you take inflation into account, campaign spending has increased only 20 percent or so in the last five years."* So wrote Robert Samuelson in a review panning Elizabeth Drew's book in the *New Republic.*

Actually campaign spending has skyrocketed. Between 1972 and 1982, while the Consumer Price Index doubled, spending for House races increased 450 percent and for Senate races, 500 percent. In 1972 the average first-term representative spent less than $100,000; in 1982, about $300,000.

Consider the cases of John Culver and Peter Kostmayer. In the 1974 Iowa contest for the Senate between Culver and David Stanley, the opponents' combined expenditure was $807,037; when Culver ran for re-election against Charles Grassley in 1980, it was $3.9 million—a 487 percent increase in just one term. Kostmayer spent $58,000 to win his House seat in 1976, lost in 1980 and then spent $600,000 to win again in 1982—more than a 1,000 percent increase.

*Business isn't monolithic, so business contributions have a diffuse impact.* "Business rarely takes a uniform position on any political issue," wrote Armstrong. PAC critics, he added, "forget the conflicts within the business community itself—big business versus small business, industry versus industry, free trade versus protectionism, and so on."

It's true that divisions can occur within an industry on specific issues—such as airline deregulation, for example. More frequently, however, business does present a united front. Is any chemical company lobbying for a stronger Superfund? Did any commodities traders' group oppose the bill that gave a tax break to commodities traders? And as the securities industry and the banks fight it out to shape the future of our financial system, where is the PAC that fights for depositors and small investors?

*PAC gifts aren't inducements for future votes; they're rewards for a prior record.* According to Representative Beryl Anthony, when he gets $5,000 from a PAC it "means somebody has approved of my prior service in Congress" and nothing more. If a legislator's support for the special interest group's position preceded the contribution, how could it have *resulted from* the contribution?

Then why do so many PACs cross-examine candidates in questionnaires and in person about their positions on pending matters? As Amitai Etzioni points out, "Unlike rocks, people can anticipate; they can act now in anticipation of payoff to follow." And according to Jay Angoff, when he was an attorney at Public Citizen's Congress Watch: "Whether a member votes for legislation because he has received money from a certain group or receives money because he has voted for legislation sought by the group, it makes no difference to the consumer. Either way, people who vote to further the interests of the business lobbies that contribute to their campaign continue to get ahead."

*The average PAC gift is too small to make a difference.* Since PAC gifts to candidates average around $600, even a lawmaker eager to sell out would be unmoved by a typical gift. Political scientist Michael Malbin observes that while several banking PACs gave Senator John Tower a total of $90,000 when he ran for re-election in 1978, his campaign spent $4 million; so banking PACs accounted for 2.5 percent of the total. Malbin asks, "Can anyone seriously argue that Tower's positions were influenced by his greed for that bit of money?"

Even in Senate races, which are far more expensive than House races, $90,000 is still $90,000. And for a House candidate, $10,000 out of total costs of $300,000, say, is surely memorable, especially if it comes early in the campaign, when a candidate needs to show credibility—or late, for that crucial media buy. Six years after I ran for the House in Manhattan, I still remember everyone who gave me $1,000 contributions and at what stage in the campaign. How many members of Congress can't?

*Even a $5,000 gift isn't enough to buy a member of Congress.* According to a Mobil advertisement, "That's hardly enough to corrupt a legislator, even if he or she were disposed to be corrupted."

To that Representative Tom Downey (D-NY) quipped, "You can't buy a Congressman for $5,000, but you can buy his vote." No PAC gift would sway Senator Proxmire (D-WI) in his support of the Genocide Treaty or Representative Henry Hyde (R-IL) in his opposition to abortion, but most of the 600-odd votes a year in Congress do not involve such deep moral or philosophical commitments. As a Democratic lawmaker told *Newsday's* Judith Bender, "If you're on the fence and it doesn't matter to you or your constituents which way you vote, but it matters to some of your biggest contributors, your mind is going to be made up very easily, because the vast majority of issues are not war and peace, equity and justice. They are really very different shades of gray."

*PACs are public.* They are at least an improvement over Watergate-era practices like passing cash-filled shopping bags and making secret infusions from corporate treasuries. "The signal virtue of the 1974 election law was that it required full disclosure of who is giving how much to whom," editorialized the *New Republic* in 1984. Critics should "concentrate on looking through the campaign finance and Congressional voting records to see who is in bed with whom."

No one is advocating a return to the days of Bobby Baker and Maurice Stans, but disclosure, however necessary, is not a sufficient step toward cleaning up the campaign financing process, for several reasons.

PAC men in bed with legislators do not receive the same media attention as, say, cohabiting movie stars. And disclosure isn't good enough if *both* candidates in a race are equally in hock to interest groups—a not uncommon occurrence, since almost all candidates accept PAC gifts. Finally, a Democracy Project study found that 20 percent of contributions to Republicans in close House races in the 1980 election came from business PACs that gave after the October 15 filing deadline. While legal, such quiet gifts evade the intent of campaign finance laws, for they avoid public scrutiny until after the election.

*PACs increase political participation.* According to a survey by Herbert Alexander, the political scientist and campaign finance expert, 100,000 people gave to business PACs between 1979 and 1980. An advertisement sponsored by United Technologies calls this phenomenon "a welcome shift toward the grassroots."

Individual PAC donors, however, participate in the least participatory way. PACs take small contributions from donors, but the donors have little if any say over how the money is disbursed. Representative Leach worries that since "groups seldom reflect the same collective judgment as their members, [the views of PAC managers], not the small contributors to their associations, become the views that carry influence."

And the way PACs raise money is frequently coercive. Consider how Dart-Pac dunned Dart Company executives with "donation guidelines," follow-up letters pointing out that contributions were being compared with salary, group sessions and finally one-on-one grillings. In 1978, according to Nicholas Goldberg in the *Washington Monthly*, 83 percent of Dart executives contributed, giving an average of $1,030, as opposed to 0.06 percent of the company's stockholders, who averaged $27.45 each.

PAC defenders are trying to perform the political equivalent of making water run uphill. Despite the best efforts of cloistered academics and corporate public relations aides, it is impossible to deny that the swelling volume of PAC money is distorting if not corrupting the legislative process. It is my impression that after hearing these counter-arguments, the public and Congress itself have concluded that the case for PACs falls short.

 ☑ *N O*

Does Private Funding for Congressional Elections Give Undue Influence to Political Action Committees?

JOSEPH J. FANELLI

*The Case for Political Action Committees*

## FICTIONAL PROBLEMS IN OUR PRESENT SYSTEM

It is charged that congressional votes are bought and sold with PAC [political action committee] contributions as the medium of exchange. Where is the proof? Where have specific allegations been made, let alone verified?

There is that special brand of false syllogism which proceeds in this manner; first, several members of a House or Senate Committee voted for certain legislation; second, a PAC that was interested in that legislation made contributions to several of those members; third, therefore (as though it were proven beyond a doubt) their votes had been "bought" by campaign contributions.

It is charged that PAC contributions have caused the inflation of campaign costs. Rather, the elements that go into a campaign these days cost considerably more than ever: media, printing, postage, travel, salaries, telephones, computers, the need to engage the professional services of campaign consultants, lawyers and accountants in order not to run afoul of the Federal Election Commission. Then there are the wealthy candidates who are willing to spend millions and millions of dollars of their personal fortune in their own campaigns.

Another misconception is that PACs give very large sums of money to candidates. First, there is the legal limit of $5,000 per candidate, per race. But very few PACs have the resources to give the maximum in very many races. Based on our 1985 survey of business employee PACs contributing in the 1983–84 election cycle, of those responding, the average business employee PAC gave a total of $47,194 to congressional candidates. Eighty-seven percent of the business employee PACs contributed under $100,000.

Our survey also showed the average business employee PAC's contribution to House candidates was $295; the average to Senate candidates was $1,103. Are such modest amounts going to "buy" influence with candidates whose campaigns cost many, many times those amounts? And even if the average were considerably higher, where is the justification to presume that members of the House and Senate could be "bought"? Is it accurate or fair to imply that every member has his or her "price"?

It also has been charged that the contributions of PACs are responsible for keeping incumbents in office and insulating them from the voters. For several decades over 90 percent of House incumbents have been getting reelected. So this phenomenon began long before the proliferation of PACs came about. The record for Senate incumbents contrasts with that of the House; there is much more turnover. As recently as 1980 only 56 percent of the Senators seeking reelection were successful.

Contributors to PACs are said to be coerced into giving. Again, where is the proof? The participation rate of employees in most business-related PACs according to our survey is only about 31 percent, which would indicate a purely voluntary process.

PACs are said to dominate the elections for Congress. Is that possible when the total contributions of all PACs still amount to less than 30 percent of the money spent in congressional campaigns? This includes all PACs—business, labor, membership, ideological, non-connected, trade and professional associations, etc. They serve many different purposes, many conflicting purposes. Their force is diffused; their voice is muted.

Still the critics continue to talk as if all of the varieties of PACs had just one purpose and one clearly defined course of action.

That is patently false.

To continue to lump all PACs together can only be done for purposes of propaganda; it cannot be excused on grounds of ignorance.

Mr. Chairman, I repeat all of this with some degree of frustration. These facts have been told many times before. But the drumbeat of allegations continues, and it seems there are so many whose minds are made up and who refuse to be bothered about the facts. . . .

We at BIPAC [Business-Industry Political Action Committee] are opposed to public, or taxpayer, financing of election campaigns on both theoretical and practical grounds and we have testified several times before House and Senate Committees expressing our opposition.

We believe that our political system is predicated on the personal involvement of individuals, and anything that would weaken the prerogatives or incentives for individual voter participation would in turn weaken our democratic system.

We believe all citizens have the right to devote time, talent and/or resources to help elect candidates of their choice. Some may choose to do this by going door-to-door distributing information about favorite candidates or by the time-honored "stuffing of envelopes" at campaign headquarters. Others may devote special talents writing speeches and press releases, designing campaign literature, or speaking; still others may offer their accounting or computer skills and many others, whose time and talents are directed otherwise, may wish to provide financial resources to help support those candidates whose views they share.

This is a basic, fundamental right in our participatory democracy.

So is the right to join with other like-minded citizens to support certain candidates or groups of candidates, whether in a political party, a club or organization, a political action committee or an ad hoc group.

We are always mystified that some people purport to see this basic American exercise—which is essential to our system—as somehow undermining our electoral process.

To deny citizens this right, or to supplant it with federal funds taken from taxpayers, violates the electoral system on which this Nation was founded.

We also believe it is fundamentally wrong to take tax revenues derived in part from "Citizen Jones" to give financial support to "Candidate Smith," whom Jones would never support of his own volition.

We further believe that public (taxpayer) financing, even "partial" financing, would tend to decrease individual participation in the political process. Surveys taken among PAC contributors, for instance, have reported repeatedly that persons are drawn into political involvement, in part, by means of participation in political action committees. The PACs help to educate voters, about candidates, issues and forthcoming elections; they stimulate their interest. Similarly, the ability of individuals to make a financial contribution directly to the candidates of their choice fosters their interest in participating further in the electoral process.

There also are practical problems concerned with taxpayer financing of elections. Faced with the present federal deficit, and the cutbacks taking place in many segments in government, this is hardly the time to adopt a new area of public expenditures. The private sector can and is providing campaign financing.

The Federal Election Commission, still virtually overwhelmed with the administrative burden imposed by the presidential and congressional finance laws, would be completely overwhelmed if it were also given responsibility for funding and monitoring congressional races, in which thousands of candidates would be seeking nomination and election to office.

We also believe the availability of public funds would encourage some candidates to run for office whose qualifications are so meager that they would never run if they had to rely on voluntary contributions. Candidates who never could hope to attract sufficient support to compete because of their lack of qualifications and/or extreme views, surely would be tempted if they could get publicly-funded support in the primary or in the general election.

Moreover, public opinion surveys have shown general opposition to taxpayer financing of congressional campaigns, but proponents apparently refuse to accept these results with which they do not agree.

It also has been pointed out that the economic, demographic and geographical makeup of congressional districts and states differ greatly; the financial needs for effective campaigning vary greatly, for instance, from a rural district with few media outlets and an urban district in the midst of a high-priced media market. No one has produced a formula for allocating funds from the Federal Treasury which would remotely approach fairness on this score.

Notwithstanding all these facts, taxpayer financing is still offered by some as a panacea for problems in the current congressional campaign financing system, some of which are real and many of which are totally fictional. . . .

## PROBLEMS IN THE U.S. ELECTION SYSTEM

Mr. Chairman, there are several areas of legitimate concern with regard to our electoral system in addition to the cost of campaigns and the proper role of political action committees.

Here are some areas that I believe need to be studied:

1. Poor voter turnout.
2. The substantial advantage incumbents have over challengers; i.e., the franking privilege, newsletters, staff, etc.
3. The setting up of PACs by Senators and Members of the House for the purpose of distributing funds to colleagues.
4. The setting up of PACs by Presidential candidates for the ostensible purpose of contributing to Senatorial and Congressional campaigns but which actually are used in support of their own presidential candidacies.
5. The "privilege" of Members of the House who were elected before the 1980 election to convert left-over campaign funds to personal use.

## *ELECTION PRACTICES SHOULD BE REVIEWED IN TOTO*

From the above list of problem areas, which certainly is not exhaustive, it would seem a thorough review of the way in which our Congress is elected would be desirable. Preferably it should be done by a mix of persons who are not themselves directly part of the process and by those in the process; it should be a truly objective, impartial assessment of current practices and what might be done to remedy shortcomings.

Studies by appointed commissions, even so-called "blue ribbon" groups, tend to be downgraded by the cynical. Too often they conclude with reports of the obvious and with recommendations that are impractical or unachievable.

In this case, a commission might do much to clear the air. I believe an objective study of campaign finance would conclude, as many have, that PACs are a positive force in the electoral system—the means by which millions of Americans have been brought into the political process and whose awareness and commitment have been enhanced. I think the supposed corrupting influence of PACs would be shown to be non-existent.

The report of such a Commission would likely conclude that the present reporting and disclosure requirements of the Federal Election Commission have produced a system where campaign giving and spending are better known than ever before, and that any proposed changes should be weighed carefully to be sure they will not do more harm than good.

Of course the possibility of public or taxpayer financing of Congressional elections also should be reviewed. Public opinion surveys continue to show that the voters reject this alternative by better than 60 percent. It has had its "never-say-die" advocates for a decade, but they have failed to rally public support for the idea. And the Congress has rejected it whenever it has been presented for a vote.

Taxpayer funding has serious flaws and should bear the most careful study.

Picking on PACs is a favorite sport for some critics, but it does not address the real problems in our system. I urge the Senate Rules Committee to look at the total picture, and not tinker with just one element that is working well.

## *Questions for Discussion*

1. Why does Green worry about PACs?
2. How would you determine whether PACs unduly influence members of Congress?
3. How would you determine whether members of Congress unduly influence PACs?

4. Who are the principal beneficiaries of the current system of campaign finance for members of Congress? Why?
5. Who would be the principal beneficiaries of public financing for congressional campaigns? Why?

## Suggested Readings

Ashdown, Gerald G. "Buying Speech: Campaign Spending, the New Politics, and Election Law Reform." *New England Law Review*, 23, no. 2 (Autumn 1988), 397–420.

Center for Responsive Politics. *Money and Politics*. Washington, D.C.: Center for Responsive Politics, 1988.

England, Robert S. "Coming to Terms with Campaign Reform." *American Spectator*, 22, no. 11 (November 1989), 22–25.

Etzioni, Amitai. *Capital Corruption: The New Attack on American Democracy*. San Diego, Calif.: Harcourt Brace Jovanovich, 1984.

Garvey, Ed. "It's Money That Matters." *Progressive*, 53, no. 3 (March 1989), 17–21.

Jacobson, Gary C. "Parties and PACs." In *Congress Reconsidered*, edited by Laurence C. Dodd and Bruce I. Oppenheimer, pp. 117–152. 4th ed. Washington, D.C.: CQ Press, 1989.

"Limiting Political Action Committees: Pro & Con." *Congressional Digest*, 66, no. 2 (February 1987), 33–64.

Nelson, Candice J., and David B. Magleby. "Congress and Campaign Money: The Prospects for Reform." *Brookings Review*, 7, no. 2 (Spring 1989), 34–41.

Sabato, Larry. *PAC Power: Inside the World of Political Action Committees*. New York: Norton, 1985.

Salmore, Barbara G., and Stephen A. Salmore. *Candidates, Parties, and Campaigns: Electoral Politics in America*. Washington, D.C.: CQ Press, 1989.

Stern, Philip M. *The Best Congress Money Can Buy*. New York: Pantheon Books, 1988.

U.S. Cong., Senate. *Campaign Finance Reform*. Hearing before the Subcommittee on the Constitution of the Committee on the Judiciary, 100th Cong., 2nd Sess., 1988.

# Chapter 6

## Should the Electoral College Be Abolished?

When citizens vote in presidential elections, they do not cast their ballot for presidential candidates but for electors who are pledged to support particular candidates. These electors constitute the Electoral College, which officially elects the president.

The Framers of the Constitution created an Electoral College because they feared popular election as the means for filling the nation's highest office. Instead they hoped that wise electors would make independent judgments. Today electors are committed to supporting their party's candidate, but they are not uniformly required to do so. Still, citizens can be generally certain that electors will vote as pledged.

In the Electoral College the number of electors for each state is equal to the number of senators and representatives from that state. Heavily populated states have more electors than sparsely populated states because they have more representatives. The slate of electors that gets the largest number (even a plurality, rather than a majority) of popular votes gets *all* the Electoral College votes of that state. To become president, a candidate must win a majority of the votes in the Electoral College. If no candidate wins a majority, the House of Representatives makes the choice from the three candidates with the largest number of electoral votes. In this runoff election state delegations vote as units, each state having one vote.

Even if an election is not thrown into the House of Representatives it is possible for a person to become president with less than a majority of the popular vote. In 1876, for example, Samuel J. Tilden received more popular votes than Rutherford B. Hayes, yet Hayes became president. Grover Cleveland experienced the same kind of loss to Benjamin Harrison in 1888.

The effect of the Electoral College system on the distribution of power has been to give advantages to the heavily populated states, like New York, California, and Illinois, because these states have large electoral votes. Presidential candidates usually devote their attention to these more populous states because of the Electoral College's winner-take-all system.

From time to time, Congress has conducted hearings about changing the Electoral College system. Three new procedures for electing the president have been proposed:

1. Require electors to vote for the candidates to whom they are pledged.

2. Replace the winner-take-all system with a system in which candidates get the same proportion of a state's electoral vote as they received in its popular vote.
3. Eliminate the Electoral College altogether and establish direct popular election of the president.

The debate below considers the value of the Electoral College. Political scientist Lawrence Longley argues that it should be abolished. He points out that:

1. Faithless electors may vote for anyone they please rather than the candidates to whom they are committed.
2. The system gives too much power to voters in the large states.
3. The system prevents all popular votes from being counted equally.
4. The failure of a candidate to obtain a majority in the Electoral College may lead to a chaotic situation in which the House of Representatives elects the president.
5. The winner of the popular vote can lose the election.

Political scientist Judith Best argues against changing the system. She points out that:

1. Faithless electors have never had a practical effect on any election.
2. It is unlikely that an election will be thrown into the House of Representatives.
3. The Constitution does not require a system of strict political equality.
4. The Electoral College operates in equilibrium with the rest of the nation's institutions.

 *YES*

---

*Should the Electoral College Be Abolished?*

---

### LAWRENCE LONGLEY

## The Case against the Electoral College

The Electoral College is a fatally flawed means of selecting the president. Its operations are at best neither certain nor smooth and at worst contain the potential for constitutional crisis. It should be abolished.

The flaws of the contemporary Electoral College are many, but five major shortcomings stand out. The first is the possibility of a faithless elector. This stems from the fact that the Electoral College today is not the assembly of wise and learned elders envisioned by its creators, but is rather little more than a motley state-by-state collection of political hacks and fat cats. Neither in the quality of the electors nor in the law is there any assurance that an elector will vote as expected.

Indeed, in six of the nine most recent presidential elections, individual electors have cast votes contrary to the expectations of those who elected them. Even more disturbing is the possibility that this could occur in a narrow race, one in which one or two votes would determine the victor. A faithless elector might attempt to barter or deal for the presidency either for personal gain or to get attention for pet causes. The presidency should be determined by the American people, not soiled by the actions of faithless electors.

The second problem of the contemporary Electoral College lies in the almost universal custom of granting all of a state's electoral votes to the winner of a state's popular vote plurality—not even a majority. This winner-take-all determination of state electors magnifies tremendously the relative voting power of citizens of the largest states. Each of their voters decides not just his own vote, but how 36 or 47 electoral votes are cast (if electors are faithful). The Electoral College does not treat voters alike—a thousand voters in Scranton, Pennsylvania are far more electorally important than a similar number of voters in Wilmington, Delaware. Consequently, the Electoral College has a major impact on candidate strategy. Voters in large states are courted vigorously because of where they reside and vote.

A third feature of the Electoral College lies in the apportionment of electors among the states. The constitutional formula is simple: one vote per state per senator and representative. Inhabitants of very small states thus have some advantage because they have at least three electoral votes, while their population might otherwise entitle them to but one or two votes. This weighting by states, not by population, provides another way the Electoral College ensures that the votes of citizens for president will not be counted fairly or equally.

The fourth problem of today's Electoral College is probably the most dangerous in terms of the stability of the political system: what if the election is inconclusive or deadlocked? If no candidate wins an electoral vote majority on election day, the election might be bartered in the Electoral College five weeks later. If the Electoral College itself should fail to produce a majority, the election would then be thrown into the House of Representatives for final decision. They would begin deliberation on January 6, only 14 days before Inauguration Day. Chaos and confusion mixed with sordid deal-making could result as the nation approached Inauguration Day uncertain who the president would be—or what price he had finally paid to win that office.

The fifth and final flaw is that under the present system, there is no assurance that the winner of the popular vote will win the election. This problem is a fundamental one. Can an American president operate effectively in our democracy if he has received fewer votes than the loser? The effect upon the legitimacy of a contemporary presidency would be disastrous if a president were elected by the Electoral College after losing in the popular vote. The chances of this may be remote, but it has happened and in a bitter election would be dangerous. In 1888, Grover Cleveland's 100,000 vote plurality turned into just 42 percent of the electoral vote. One hesitates to contemplate the consequences of a contemporary president being inaugurated despite having been rejected by a majority of the American voters.

These defects of the contemporary Electoral College cannot be dealt with by patchwork reforms such as abolishing the office of elector to solve the problem of the faithless elector. This distorted and unwieldy counting device must be abolished, and the votes of the American people—wherever cast—must be counted directly and equally in determining who shall be president of the United States.

 **NO**

## Should the Electoral College Be Abolished?

### JUDITH BEST

### The Case for the Electoral College

Every four years the opponents of the Electoral College march in front of us a parade of horribles. We hear about faithless electors, the possibility of elections thrown into the House of Representatives and filled with intrigue, or of presidents who have won only a minority of the popular vote. It sounds as though something is truly wrong, and we had better fix it before it is too late.

But the appearance is far from the reality. None of these imaginary horrors has ever affected a presidential election, and the chance of them is outweighed by the Electoral College's contribution to constitutional government. Faithless electors, for example, arouse our moral indignation, but they have never come close to having a practical effect on any election. More than seventeen thousand electoral votes have been cast since 1789 and just about ten of them could be called miscast.

The threat of an election thrown into the House of Representatives is a fantasy. We have not had one since the Electoral College system assumed its modern shape over one hundred fifty years ago. Because the operation of the Electoral College makes it a reliable plurality system, we are unlikely to have one in any event. There is a multiplier effect in the electoral vote that gives the winner of a national plurality a higher percentage in the electoral vote than in the popular vote. This always produces a winner in the Electoral College.

Because this multiplier effect works to the advantage of the winner of the plurality, a president representing a minority of voters is highly unlikely unless a candidate runs a sectional or regional campaign. Under the rules of the existing system, a regional concentration of popular votes is both undesirable campaign strategy and undesirable politics. There are worse things than a runner-up as president, and one of them would be a president who received all of his support from one region of the country. As the election of 1860 suggests, that is a formula for civil war.

Although the opponents of the Electoral College attack it on many grounds, their major objection is that it is unfair because it does not give each citizen one equally weighted direct vote for president. This is the kind of argument that Alexander Hamilton called "a very crude notion as well of the purposes for which government was instituted as of the true means by which the public happiness may be promoted." This crude notion is that we are and were intended to be a simple democracy, and that limitations and qualifications of the rule of the arithmetical majority are unjust. This is false both to the Framers and to the principles of the Constitution.

Our government is complex and is filled with devices and intermediary institutions to secure liberty, to protect minorities, and to prevent majority tyranny. To mention just the most important ones in the Constitution, there are the amendment procedure, the Senate, the Supreme Court, and, of course, the Electoral College. All of these directly or indirectly impose limitations on arithmetical majorities. None of these institutions or procedures operates under the principle that gives each citizen one equally weighted direct vote. The Constitution itself was not ratified in this way. Of course, the Constitution can be altered, but under the amendment procedure each state has one vote regardless of its population. The vote of a state with half a million people counts as much as the vote of a state with twenty million.

One half of the legislative power of the national government is exercised by the Senate, where again voters in the least populous state have the same number of Senators as the voters in the most populous state. One third of the power of the national government is exercised by the Supreme Court. The nine justices are neither selected by nor subject to removal by the direct popular votes of the people. If the Electoral College is unfair, so are all these institutions and procedures. The American idea of democracy is not and never has been government by adding machine.

Speaking in opposition to a direct election system, then-Senator John Kennedy said, "It is not only the unit vote for the Presidency we are talking about, but a whole solar system of governmental power. If it is proposed to change the balance of power of one of the elements of the solar system, it is necessary to consider all the others." The Electoral College is an integral part of our governmental solar system, for it requires successful presidential candidates to create the broad cross-sectional majorities that are moderate and able to govern the continental, heterogeneous nation. Like our other national institutions and procedures it adds a federal and geographic component to the rule of arithmetical majorities. The system is complex, but we are a complex, not a simple, democracy. The system is federal, but we are a federal republic.

The Electoral College operates in equilibrium with the rest of our national institutions. To change one part of this system and not the others could upset its delicate balance. To make the president the recipient of the only direct national mandate would change the balance in the executive-legislative relationship to the great advantage of the president. A truly plebiscitary president, who could claim to speak directly for the general will, could destroy the authenticity of the voice of Congress, which speaks only for federal concurrent majorities. Direct election of the president, far from enhancing democracy, could undermine democracy itself.

## Questions for Discussion

1. How would direct election of the president affect the two-party system?
2. How would direct election affect the power of racial minorities in the United States?
3. If a president were elected with a minority of the popular vote but a majority of the Electoral College vote, how would popular support of the presidency be affected?
4. How would a system of direct election of the president affect the political campaigning strategy of presidential candidates?
5. Which groups benefit and which are hurt by the Electoral College system?

## Suggested Readings

Barnes, James A. "Republican Tilt." *National Journal*, 20 (November 12, 1988), 2845–2848.

Bickel, Alexander M. *Reform and Continuity: The Electoral College, the Convention, and the Party System.* New York: Harper & Row, 1971.

Diamond, Martin. *The Electoral College and the American Idea of Democracy.* Washington, D.C.: American Enterprise Institute for Public Policy Research, 1977.

"The Geography of U.S. Presidential Elections." *Scientific American*, 259 (July 1988), 44–51.

Peirce, Neal R. *The People's President: The Electoral College in American History.* New York: Simon & Schuster, 1968.

Polsby, Nelson, and Aaron Wildavsky. *Presidential Elections: Contemporary Strategies of American Electoral Politics.* 7th ed. New York: Free Press, 1988.

"The Proposal for Direct Election of the President: Pro & Con." *Congressional Digest*, 58, no. 3 (March 1979), 65–96.

Sayre, Wallace F., and Judith H. Parris. *Voting for President.* Washington, D.C.: Brookings Institution, 1970.

Slonim, Shlomo. "The Electoral College at Philadelphia: The Evolution of an Ad

Hoc Congress for the Selection of a President." *Journal of American History*, 73 (June 1986), 35–58.

U.S. Cong., Senate. *The Electoral College and Direct Election.* Hearings before the Committee on the Judiciary, 95th Cong., 1st Sess., 1977.

Weinhagen, Robert F., Jr. "Should the Electoral College Be Abandoned?" *American Bar Association Journal*, 67 (July 1981), 852–857.

# Chapter 7

# Do the Mass Media Have a Liberal Bias?

By most accounts the mass media—television, newspapers, magazines, and the radio—play a central role in the U.S. political system. Some observers believe the media's influence is so powerful that they function as the fourth branch of government. The media's perception of political leaders and events affects what people believe, so that political leaders neglect the media at their peril. In May 1987, for example, reporters for the *Miami Herald* staked out the Washington townhouse of then Democratic presidential frontrunner Gary Hart, after the newspaper received information that a woman was staying with Hart while his wife was in Colorado. Media attention to that event was strong enough to make Hart withdraw from the campaign. Although he subsequently returned to the campaign, his organization suffered setbacks in support and funding.

Whether allegations made against Hart on the subject of sexual morality in this and other instances were accurate or not, the reporting of such a matter had a profound impact on this candidate and the entire presidential campaign as well. In previous years newspapers had adhered to a professional code that forbade reporting on certain aspects of the private lives of public figures.

The media's influence is based not only on the stories presented but on the prominence given them. An analysis of the media's reporting on a single day will show a diversity of emphases. News, or the importance of particular items of news, is not so self-evident that everyone in the journalistic profession agrees on what is, and what is not, significant. Some critics of the media have noted the importance of emphasis in coverage of the Vietnam War, coverage they claim was detrimental to U.S. foreign policy interests. Stories—particularly those filed on television that highlighted the killing of Vietnamese civilians or the use of drugs by GIs—brought the war home to viewers in a manner unfair to U.S. policy makers. These critics argue that U.S. journalists were biased, for they were not able to expose the enemy's actions and problems for balanced coverage, and in addition they were much less sensitive to U.S. government needs than had been their counterparts covering World War II.

Supporters of the media counter that these critics simply do not like the news and so are "killing the messenger." All the reporters are doing, media supporters contend, is reflecting what is happening. They add that political leaders try to dominate the news and resent when reporters get the true stories.

Media critics often contend that the media have a bias, but they differ about what the bias is. The debate below reflects these differing views. Media analyst Brent H. Baker sees the major mass media as tilting toward the left. He contends that the media portray conservative policies and actions as failures and look favorably on the liberal alternative viewpoint. He explains the liberal bias as reflecting the personal views of journalists, editors, producers, and news division executives. Many key executives in the press, Baker notes, once worked for liberal public officials.

Noam Chomsky, a radical critic of U.S. domestic and foreign policy, argues that the media in the United States constitute an awesome propaganda machine serving the corporate and government establishment. In an interview for the magazine *Humanist,* he makes the following main points:

1. The media focus on matters that will discourage popular participation in the political process.
2. The media are careful to cover controversial issues, such as the Watergate scandal and the Iran-Contra affair, in a manner that does not threaten the established order.
3. The media feign dissent at the same time that they support the existing system.

 *Y E S*

## Do the Mass Media Have a Liberal Bias?

### BRENT H. BAKER

#### Media's Liberal Slant on the News

For years, conservatives have argued that major American news organizations present the news with a liberal bias. Members of the media have rejected the contention, countering that the press simply reflects an anti-establishment bias. Who is correct? A look at how big media outlets—specifically ABC, CBS, and NBC; the three national news magazines; the *Washington Post;* and the *New York Times*—covered controversial issues over the past few years makes it clear that political reporting often reflects a tilt to the left. That does not mean every story slights the conservative position, but that, almost every time a report is unbalanced, it favors the position promoted by liberals.

Whether the issue is aiding the Contras, the results of economic policy, how George Bush conducted his presidential campaign, who is to blame for homelessness, or virtually any other hotly debated topic, one thing remains true— someone relying solely on the information dispensed by big media could not help but see conservative policies and actions as failures and look positively toward the liberal alternative viewpoint.

There is no grand conspiracy at work here. The reason is simple enough. The views held by journalists naturally influence their reporting, and poll after poll has found that liberal positions hold the allegiance of most. The 1981 Lichter-Rothman survey of big media members determined 81 percent voted for George McGovern in 1972 and a large majority preferred Jimmy Carter over Gerald Ford four years later. A 1985 *Los Angeles Times* poll of reporters for large newspapers found three times as many consider themselves liberal as conservative. Less than 25 percent of them voted for Ronald Reagan in 1984.

On every issue, most reporters took the liberal side. Over 80 percent favored a woman's right to have an abortion, 66 percent opposed prayer in school, 78 percent wanted stricter gun control, 80 percent were against higher defense spending, and 75 percent rejected aid to the Contras. Another poll, by the Associated Press Managing Editors Association, revealed that barely 15 percent of journalists identified themselves as Republicans. The evidence has become so irrefutable that media pundits long ago gave up debating it. Instead, they fall back to another line of defense. However, as *New Republic* senior editor Fred Barnes wrote, in so doing, these "defenders of the press rely on precisely the sort of argument they would reject if made by others. Even if most journalists are liberal, then professionalism prevents this from influencing their stories. Now, what if a judicial nominee said he was a racist but that this wouldn't affect his views on civil rights cases." Who would believe that? Certainly, today's adversarial press would not.

Big media stars would not hesitate to question the objectivity of a newscast if all the producers and reporters once worked for the Heritage Foundation, a conservative Washington think-tank, and they would be right. Yet, people with equally strong convictions in the opposite direction already hold such key positions. Indeed, the Media Research Center [MRC] has compiled a list of over 110 reporters, editors, producers, and news division executives who have connections to liberal Democratic causes or politicians. In contrast, just 25—less than 25 percent—have any ties to conservatives or Republicans of any kind.

These people are not just lowly assistants—far from it. Top news executives at the three networks worked for well-known Democrats before obtaining media jobs. David Burke, who became president of CBS News in 1988 after 11 years with ABC News, served as chief of staff to Sen. Edward Kennedy (D.-Mass) from 1965 to 1971. The CBS News political editor since 1985, Dotty Lynch, was Gary Hart's pollster in 1984 and is a veteran of Sen. Kennedy's 1980 presidential attempt. Lynch's predecessor brought similar political preferences to his job. Wally Chalmers was running Kennedy's political action committee, the Fund for a Democratic Majority, when tapped by CBS just before the 1984 campaign.

The same pattern applies to the other networks. ABC's 1988 political coverage was run by vice president Jeff Gralnick, who served as press secretary to Sen. George McGovern in 1971. Barely a month after the 1984 election, NBC News hired Tim Russert, former chief of staff to Sen. Patrick Moynihan (D.-N.Y.) and counselor to New York's proudly liberal Gov. Mario Cuomo. Russert soon became the vice president overseeing the content of the "NBC Nightly News" and the "Today" show. He is now NBC's Washington bureau chief.

Most of those with Republican affiliations get behind-the-scenes public affairs jobs or become commentators, not reporters. ABC's George Will and CNN's Patrick Buchanan are good examples.

Numerous reporters dedicated themselves to promoting liberal policies before making a career change. ABC's Jeff Greenfield, frequently seen on "Nightline," wrote speeches for Sen. Robert Kennedy. Rick Inderfurth, who covers national security issues for ABC News, gained his expertise by working for Senators McGovern and Hart in the mid-1970s. ABC's chief foreign correspondent, Pierre Salinger, was Pres. Kennedy's press secretary. In key behind-the-scenes positions, the same holds true. The producer of "Face the Nation," the Sunday morning interview show on CBS, once toiled for Massachusetts Gov. Michael Dukakis. Deborah Johnson, executive producer of the CBS show "Nightwatch," helped found the far-left magazine *Mother Jones* in 1975.

This preference for Democrats goes beyond the electronic media. *Time* magazine senior writer Walter Shapiro covered the 1988 campaign. His experience included writing speeches for candidate Jimmy Carter in 1976, and he was rewarded with a job under Labor Secretary Ray Marshall. *Newsweek* reporter Timothy Noah worked for a Democratic Congressional candidate before joining the magazine's Washington staff. Foreign affairs reporter Douglas Waller served as an aide to liberal Congressman Ed Markey (D.-Mass.) until joining *Newsweek* in 1988. At *U.S. News & World Report*, where former Reagan aide David Gergen served as editor until recently, senior editor James Killpatrick left in 1987 to handle press relations for Democrat Paul Simon's presidential campaign. Judith Miller, a *New York Times* editor, began her career as a reporter for *The Progressive* magazine.

Given the preponderance of liberals in newsrooms, it's no surprise their reporting shows little understanding of conservative views. Take the problem of homelessness. A story on the "CBS Evening News" is representative of how most journalists approach the topic. Susan Spencer reported that cuts in Federal housing subsidies were a key cause. She also considered that the minimum wage has not been increased "since 1981, while inflation has pushed up prices nearly 34 percent" as another reason. When the producer of the story was asked why the conservatives' explanation for the problem—that rent control artificially has reduced the supply of low-income housing in big cities—was not even mentioned in the supposedly balanced story, he responded: "I don't understand your point." In other words, he never even heard the argument before.

Reliance on sources of information that match the reporter's preconceptions also frequently results in the same one-sided story. A Thanksgiving Day, 1988 report on CBS offers an excellent case study. Bob McNamara began his piece: "Seattle, the Pacific Northwest's most polished, prosperous city. With the rich bounty of its nearby waters, and its orchards, on the face of it these seem like the best of times. But here, as elsewhere, times could hardly be worse for thousands. Today, soup kitchens feed more people than ever, and sadly, more families, more children."

McNamara acknowledged 16,000,000 new jobs have been "created across the country in this decade, but there's a cruel hitch. A recent Senate committee report says that, of those new jobs, half of them pay wages below the poverty level for a family of four." McNamara failed to tell viewers one key fact—it was prepared by the Democratic staff of the Budget Committee. With a little research, he would have learned the same Census Bureau statistics the Democrats used show just the opposite after eliminating the Carter years from the average. Since 1982, 61 percent of these new jobs pay $20,800 a year or higher, twice the poverty level for a family of four.

McNamara's story represented much coverage on how America fared during eight years of Reagan's conservative economic policies. Far from serving as an uncritical conduit for Reagan to manipulate the public, national news outlets had a negative verdict on Reaganomics. "Are You Better Off?," *Time* asked. "For much of the middle class," it asserted, "the answer is no." Just like McNamara, *Time* accepted some very questionable statistics. The "middle class has been shrinking," the magazine argued, and "Reagan's tax cuts only worsened the skew." In fact, IRS figures that *Time* didn't mention show that the wealthy now pay a larger share of taxes collected and the working poor a smaller one. In addition, a 1988 Bureau of Labor Statistics study determined: "America's middle class has been shrinking since 1969, but mainly because more families have moved to the upper class." Reports which contradict the media's line conveniently are overlooked.

Since creating the term "Reaganomics," big media reporters have made it synonymous with negative developments. In 1987, the Media Research Center asked the Nexis news data retrieval system to locate the frequency of use of the term by the *Washington Post*, the *New York Times, Newsweek, Time,* UPI, and AP between 1981 and 1986. The findings were startling. As the 1981–82 recession deepened, reporters continually referred to "Reaganomics," using the term 1,957 times to blame the President's supply-side economic policies for stagnation and high unemployment. With the recovery in 1983–84, as Reagan's policies began taking effect, "Reaganomics" nearly dropped from the media's vocabulary. It was mentioned just 96 times by 1986. In fact, during the period examined, "Reaganomics" use directly followed the unemployment rate path.

In 1988, ABC weekend anchorman Sam Donaldson inadvertently revealed how the big media sees the world. Reviewing current events, he referred to "Soviet leader Gorbachev" and "Cuban leader Fidel Castro." He suddenly changed his tune and became far more descriptive when it came to Chile: "In Chile, a country ruled by military dictator Augusto Pinochet, demonstrators opposing his rule drew police tear gas and other riot control measures." Donaldson's double standard in labeling symbolized the troubling tendency of many reporters—looking critically at our nation's allies while overlooking the evils of our enemies.

The Media Research Center examined how ABC, CNN, CBS, and NBC covered six Sandinista statements promising compliance with peace accords vs. 10 instances when the regime violated peace agreements or publicly rejected Democratic reforms. Pledges for improvement were covered by at least three of the four networks every time, but actions which contradicted those pledges either barely were mentioned or completely ignored. Consequently, viewers saw more than five times as many stories portraying the Sandinistas as earnestly trying to develop a pluralistic society than instances when they reaffirmed their totalitarian nature.

For example, the *Miami Herald* reported Sandinista dictator Daniel Ortega publicly proclaiming that the Contras "should be thankful that we're not offering them the guillotine or the firing squad, which is what they deserve." The four TV networks did not consider the threat worth mentioning. When the Sandinistas claimed they would allow free speech and release all political prisoners, promises they subsequently failed to fulfill, all the networks covered the story.

Several years ago, Lucy Spiegel, a CBS News producer based in Managua, stated: "Personally, I think the Contras are worthless." That just might explain why Americans have seen far more TV reports detailing the human rights violations of the Contras while Sandinista violations rarely were raised.

"CBS This Morning" sent co-host Kathleen Sullivan to Cuba just before Christmas, 1988, but Castro's denial of basic human rights to his people did not interest her. Instead, viewers were treated to two days of glowing reports about life on the island. Sullivan referred to Cuba's "model health care program and lively arts scene." Her most incredible claim was that its young adults "all have benefited from Castro's Cuba." Can you imagine a network star uttering such a positive statement about a right-wing dictator while ignoring everything negative?

Some inevitably will argue these examples simply are carefully selected anecdotes that fail to prove a larger point. However, the coverage of two nearly identical events, the presidential conventions in 1988, provided findings that are more illuminating.

Media Research Center analysts watched over 100 hours of network coverage of the conventions. The study found that, far from displaying balance, TV correspondents labeled Republicans "conservative" more than four times as often as they noted the liberal views held by Democratic attendees the month before. The networks did not hesitate to raise repeatedly the Iran/Contra affair, the stalemate with Panama's Manuel Noriega, and the Republican "sleaze" factor, as well as presenting two prime-time nights focused almost exclusively on Dan Quayle's background. Lloyd Bentsen's PAC fund-raising scandal and the criminal investigations of Dukakis' state appointees were ignored.

Indeed, from day one of the GOP convention, TV reporters echoed Democratic campaign themes and demanded that Republicans respond. NBC's Tom Brokaw, for example, asked Quayle one night: "You're opposed to abortion in any form. You have opposed the ERA and you're opposed to increasing the minimum wage, which is important to a lot of women out there. Aren't you going to have a hard time selling Dan Quayle to the women of this country?" In total, network reporters challenged Republicans with Democratic-issue questions on 128 occasions, two and one-half times more often than they posed Republican ones to Democrats.

Finally, the constant refrain of "Bush's gender gap problem" could be heard from liberal politicians as they argued he had little support from women. The networks picked up on the liberal agenda item and frequently raised the issue in campaign stories. Yet, when the facts quieted Bush's opponents, the media fell right in step, never conceding it was a party to an unfounded political myth.

CBS News reporter Bob Schieffer devoted a story to how women are "a big problem for George Bush because [they] don't seem to like him much." Schieffer cited a CBS News/*New York Times* poll which found "women favor Dukakis overwhelmingly, 53 to 35 percentage points, what some call a 'gender gulch.' " NBC's Lisa Myers was quick to explain why later that month. "In 1980, when he ran for president the first time, Bush didn't have problems with women," she asserted. "But then he became Reagan's vice president and changed positions on key women's issues." Now, he supports "an amendment banning abortion" and opposes the ERA.

However, when the Bush gender gap started disappearing, so did the issue from TV screens. A September, 1988, CBS News poll determined Bush led among women 43 to 41 percent. Men preferred Bush by 53 to 37 percent, nearly the identical margin Dukakis held with women in June. How did the "CBS Evening News" handle the Dukakis gender gap among men? Lesley Stahl summarized the poll, but didn't consider the Dukakis problem worthy of mention, and NBC's Myers never retracted her earlier claim.

These are just a few examples of reporting that has made it impossible for the big media ever to squelch charges its reporting and selection of stories show a bias in favor of liberal politicians. With few in the newsroom who hold or even understand conservative views, reporters can't help but reflect the way they look at the world. As a result, the media won't be able to gain credibility as an impartial source of information until it makes a concerted effort to hire enough conservatives to bring balance to the newsroom and executive corridors.

## Do the Mass Media Have a Liberal Bias?

### NOAM CHOMSKY
#### Bewildering the Herd
**An Interview by Rick Szykowny for *The Humanist***

Reading the mainstream media, you'd never know that, for over 20 years, Noam Chomsky has been considered by many to be the most important political thinker in the United States. He is the author of *American Power and the New Mandarins, Towards a New Cold War, On Power and Ideology, The Culture of Terrorism,* and *Necessary Illusions,* to name but a few, and coauthor (with Edward S.

Herman) of *The Political Economy of Human Rights* and *Manufacturing Consent*. Taken together, these works present an extraordinary critique of state and corporate power in the United States—particularly its influence on the media and American foreign policy. For his troubles, Chomsky has been virtually exiled from the media mainstream, as well as repeatedly vilified.

In 1939, while attending an experimental Deweyite school in his hometown of Philadelphia, Noam Chomsky published his first article: an editorial in the student newspaper on the fall of Barcelona during the Spanish Civil War. It was a few weeks after his tenth birthday.

By the time he was 30, Chomsky had already revolutionized the fields of linguistics and cognitive science with his theories of "transformational" or "generative" grammar and language acquisition. By the time he was 40, he had become one of this nation's most forceful and articulate opponents of the Vietnam War, which in turn led to his decades-long commitment to political and social activism. It was around this time that Chomsky published his celebrated essay, "The Responsibility of Intellectuals," in the *New York Review of Books*, which read in part:

> It is the responsibility of intellectuals to speak the truth and expose lies. Intellectuals are in a position to expose the lies of government, to analyze actions according to their causes and motives and often hidden intentions. In the Western world at least, they have the power that comes from political liberty, from access to information, and from freedom of expression. For a privileged minority, Western democracy provides the leisure, the facilities, and the training to seek the truth lying hidden behind the veil of distortion and misrepresentation, ideology, and class interest through which the events of current history are presented to us.

In 1988, just short of his sixtieth birthday, the Inamori Foundation announced that Chomsky had won the Kyoto Prize (often called the Japanese version of the Nobel Prize) in the basic sciences. *The Humanist* talked to Noam Chomsky on September 7, 1990.

**The Humanist:** You take the average American who gets his or her information on the world at large from, say, the network news, from wire service reports in the daily newspaper, and maybe—if he or she is feeling especially dutiful—from CNN or "Nightline." How good a picture do they actually have of what's really happening in the world?

**Chomsky:** They get a good picture of how the state-corporate nexus in the United States would like to *depict* the things that are happening in the world . . . and occasionally more than that.

**The Humanist:** Occasionally more than that?

**Chomsky:** Yeah. But not most of the time. Most of the time the press is very disciplined.

**The Humanist:** Well, in short, what I'm asking is how well served are Americans by the mainstream media?

**Chomsky:** If you follow the mainstream media with great care and skepticism and approach it with the right understanding of how propaganda works, then you can learn a lot. The normal viewer or reader gets fed a propaganda line.

**The Humanist:** You've frequently stated that the Western media constitute the most awesome propaganda system that has ever existed in world history. But at the same time, the press tries to cultivate a mythology or popular image of itself as tireless, fearless seekers after the truth. You have them taking on the politicians, such as Dan Rather challenging George Bush on the air, or even toppling them from office, as Woodward and Bernstein allegedly did with Nixon. That's the public image of the media, and I think many people are going to be surprised to hear that they are being fed a line of propaganda.

**Chomsky:** Well, I doubt that many people would. Most polls indicate that the majority of the population regards the media as too subservient to power. But it's quite true that for educated people it would come as a surprise. And that's because they are the ones most subject to propaganda. They also participate in the indoctrination, so therefore they're the most committed to the system. You mentioned that the media cultivate an image of a tribune of the people fighting power. Well, that's natural. How would a reasonable propaganda institution depict itself? But in order to determine the truth of the matter, you have to look at the particular cases. I think it is one of the best established conclusions in the social sciences that the media serve what we may call a propaganda function—that is, that they shape perceptions, select the events, offer interpretations, and so on, in conformity with the needs of the power centers in society, which are basically the state and the corporate world.

**The Humanist:** So, in other words, an adversarial press doesn't really exist in this country.

**Chomsky:** It exists out on the margins, and *occasionally* you'll find something in the mainstream. I mean, for example, there are cases where the press has stood up against a segment of power. In fact, the one you mentioned— Woodward and Bernstein helped topple a president—is the example that the media and everyone else constantly use to show that the press is adversarial.

But there are very serious problems with that case that have been pointed out over and over again. In fact, what the example actually shows is the subordination of the media to power. And you can see that very clearly as soon as you take a look at the Watergate affair. What was the charge against Richard Nixon, after all? The charge against Nixon was that he attacked people with power— he sent a gang of petty criminals for some still unknown purpose to burglarize the Democratic party headquarters. Well, you know, the Democratic party represents essentially half of the corporate system. It's one of the two factions of the business party which runs the country. And that is real power. You don't attack real power, because people in power can defend themselves. We can easily demonstrate that that's exactly what was involved; in fact, history was kind enough to set up a controlled experiment for us. At the very moment of the Watergate exposures, there was also another set of exposures: namely, the FBI COINTELPRO operations which were exposed using the Freedom of Information Act right at the same time. Those were infinitely more serious than the Watergate caper. Those were actions not by a group of crooks mobilized by the president or a presidential committee but by the *national political police*. And it was not just Richard Nixon; it ran over a series of administrations. The exposures began with the Kennedy administration—in fact earlier, but primarily with the Kennedy administration—and ran right through the Nixon administration. What was exposed was extremely serious—far worse than anything in Watergate. For example, it included political assassination, instigation of ghetto riots, a long series of burglaries and harassment against a legal political party—namely, the Socialist Workers party, which, unlike the Democratic party, is not powerful and did not have the capacity to defend itself. That aspect of COINTELPRO alone, which is just a tiny footnote to its operations, is far more important than Watergate.

So what we can look at is how the media responded to these two exposures: one, the relatively minor crookedness of the Watergate caper; and, two, a major government program of harassment, violence, assassination, attacks on legal political parties, and efforts to undermine popular organizations over a long period. The Watergate affair became a major issue, shaking the foundations of the republic. The COINTELPRO exposures are known only to a handful of people; the press wasn't interested in it. And that tells you exactly what was involved in Watergate: people with power can defend themselves, and the media will support people with power. Nothing else is involved.

**The Humanist:** Well, that's interesting, because you have the media reinforcing a false picture of what was going on then. I mean, they did not——

**Chomsky:** What I just said is virtually a truism. Here is something close to a controlled experiment. Two exposures at exactly the same time: one, an exposure of a very minor attack on people with power; the other, the exposure of a very major attack over a long period of time—with all sorts of ramifications—against a large part of the population, including political parties, without power. And how did the media respond to these two cases? Well, basically, they cared nothing about the major attack on the people without power, and they made a huge fuss about the minor attack on the people with power. So, what does a rational person conclude from this? Well, a rational person concludes from this example—which illustrates it rather dramatically—that the media serve power.

**The Humanist:** Well, I think it's especially pernicious, since Watergate was then touted as an example of the system working.

**Chomsky:** That shows how beautifully the propaganda system operates. It takes an example which proves its subordination to power and turns it into a demonstration of its adversarial role. That's brilliant.

**The Humanist:** You've made the continual argument that the function of the media is actually to *obscure* what's happening in the world.

**Chomsky:** To obscure . . . it's more complex than that. I mean, the media, after all, have a complex role. In fact, you can't put the media into a single category. First of all, let's make a rough distinction. On the one hand, there are the mass popular media—that includes everything from sports and sitcoms to network news and so forth—and their task is basically to divert the population, to make sure they don't get any funny ideas in their heads about participating in the shaping of public policy. On the other hand, there are the "elite" media, which are directed to what is sometimes called the "political class": the more educated, wealthy, articulate part of the population, the "managers"—cultural managers, political managers, economic managers. I'm talking here about the *New York Times* and the *Washington Post*—at least their front sections. Now, those media have a somewhat more complicated task. They have to instill proper attitudes that serve as a mechanism of indoctrination in the interests of power. But they also have to present a *tolerably* realistic picture of the world, since, after all, their targets are the people actually making decisions, and those people better have a grasp of reality if the role they play is actually going to benefit those who wield power.

**The Humanist:** But you mean a *specific* kind of reality——

**Chomsky:** Well, you have to have some grasp of the real world, otherwise you get into trouble. So, take an investment banker or a state manager—someone involved in government—if those people don't have some grasp of reality, they're going to make moves which will be very harmful to the people who really pull the levers. So, therefore, they better have some grasp of reality. But that has to be shaped in the interests of power, and that's a delicate task. Universities have the same problem.

**The Humanist:** These are all the things you refer to as the *ideological professions.* But their version of reality is not necessarily my or your version of reality.

**Chomsky:** No, in fact, it's often quite different. And that's what you find in any system of power—the totalitarian state, the democratic state, and so on. In fact, it's just entirely natural that, where you have institutions with a degree of centralized power, they're going to use that power in their own interests. I don't think there's an exception to that in history. Now, we happen to live in a system with a very high degree of centralized power—primarily in the corporate world, which has enormous influences over all other institutions, including government and obviously the media; in fact, the media are major corporations. They have a point of view and shared interests and concerns—of course, there's some diversity within them—and naturally they are going to try to ensure that everything in their political, cultural, and ideological realm is going to be influenced to satisfy their needs. It would be astonishing if that were not true, and the evidence is overwhelming that it *is* true.

**The Humanist:** There have been a number of people, such as W. Lance Bennett in his book *News: The Politics of Illusion,* who have argued that the American people were somewhat better served by the media in the early days of the republic, when the press consisted of numerous small journals and newspapers, all with what would today be considered their own bias or partisan position or political axe to grind. What do you make of the deification or cult of objectivity that characterizes mainstream news reporting today?

**Chomsky:** Well, first of all, I think you want to be very careful about comparing different historical eras; it's a tricky question. It's certainly true that there was a lot more diversity in earlier years; you don't have to go back very far to find a lot of diversity.

On the other hand, it was also highly skewed toward power. For example, let's take the American Revolution. The position of noted American libertarians, such as Thomas Jefferson and the founding fathers, was that there should be no tolerance at all for positions antagonistic to their own. The range of debate and discussion that was permitted in Nicaragua in the last 10 years while the country was under foreign attack was incomparably greater than anything Jefferson would have allowed—or that the United States has allowed under far less threatening circumstances.

As for the cult of objectivity, here, too, we have to be careful. Surely the media describe themselves as deeply committed to objectivity, but what propaganda institution would not make that claim? A serious person would want to ask if that were true. And the answer is that it's not true—it's very far from true.

**The Humanist:** A related question then is why do the media continually concentrate on the individual personalities involved in the issues rather than the institutional actors, which is something you yourself scrupulously avoid. For example, in the Iran-contra scandal, the media pretty willingly acquiesced to Reagan's efforts to make Oliver North and John Poindexter the fall guys.

**Chomsky:** Well, they also concentrated on Reagan himself. Remember, the big question was: did Reagan know—or did he remember—what the policies of his administration were? The reason the media concentrate on these matters is that they're irrelevant. And insignificant. What they obscure is the institutional factors that, in fact, determine policy. And in the Iran-contra affair, it was rather striking to see the way major issues were almost completely obscured. So, let's just take one of the obvious questions: you asked why they do that. Well, that's just in the service of their propaganda function. One of the main purposes of any ideological system is to divert attention away from the actual workings of power and to focus on marginal phenomena. Individuals can be replaced, and then these institutions can continue to function as they do. So, if you take a look at the Iran-contra thing, once again there are perfectly obvious questions that were never asked, which takes remarkable discipline.

For example, the Iran-contra affair focused on what had happened since the mid-1980s—from 1985, 1986 on—with regard to the U.S. sale of arms to Iran. Well, an obvious question arises: namely, what was going on before 1985? And there's an answer to this. Before 1985, the United States was authorizing the sale of arms to Iran via Israel—exactly as it was doing *after* 1985. Now at that time, remember, there were no hostages. So what's going on? If the whole operation was supposed to be an arms-for-hostages deal, how come we were doing exactly the same thing before there were any hostages?

Well, that's another obvious question, and there's an answer to that one, too. It's not a secret; for example, I was writing about it in 1982 and 1983. And the answer is that the United States was authorizing arms sales to Iran via Israel in an effort to find elements within the Iranian military with whom they could establish contacts and who might be able to carry out a military coup to overthrow Khomeini. That was frankly, openly, and publicly admitted by top Israeli officials, including people high in the Mossad and others. And all the people who were later exposed in the Iran-contra affair were speaking quite publicly about this in the early 1980s. One of them, Uri Lubrani, said that, if we can find somebody in the military who is willing and able to shoot down 10,000 people in the street, we'll be able to restore the kind of regime we want, basically meaning the Shah. That's standard policy whenever there's hostility to some government: cut off aid to that government but arm the military in the hopes that elements within the military will carry out a coup. That was done in Chile, Indonesia—in fact, that's just normal. And it was being done in Iran in the early 1980s.

So, was there any discussion of this in the Iran-contra hearings? No, because, even though the question "What was happening *before* 1985?" was so obvious that it could hardly fail to come to the mind of anybody looking at the issues, the trouble is, if you ask it, you get the wrong answers. Better not to ask it. Therefore, this became one of the many aspects of the Iran-contra affair that were effaced in what was, in fact, a coverup operation by Congress and the media.

**The Humanist:** I think it's kind of interesting to note in your discussions of American government that when you do refer to the government you almost invariably mean the executive. Do you consider Congress a confederacy of political eunuchs?

**Chomsky:** Well, I do discuss Congress to some extent, but it doesn't vary very much. I mean, there's a little diversity in Congress. If you get down to the House of Representatives, you'll find a scattering of people who will raise hard questions, such as Henry Gonzalez of Texas or Ted Weiss of New York or Ron Dellums and various people in the Black Caucus. I mean, there's a scattering of people who raise questions that barely make it to the media. But, by and large, Congress is very much constrained within the same very narrow elite consensus.

**The Humanist:** Well, do you feel also . . . I mean, I know that you have advanced these arguments and a number of other people have also advanced these arguments—they are there to be found by anyone who wants to seek them out. . . . But at the same time, I think there's a great effort in the mainstream media to write these arguments off as conspiracy theory.

**Chomsky:** That's one of the devices by which power defends itself—by calling any critical analysis of institutions a conspiracy theory. If you call it by that name, then somehow you don't have to pay attention to it. Edward Herman and I, in our recent book, *Manufacturing Consent,* go into this ploy. What we discuss in that book is simply the institutional factors that essentially set parameters for reporting and interpretation in the ideological institutions. Now, to call that a conspiracy theory is a little bit like saying that, when General Motors tries to increase its market share, it's engaged in a conspiracy. It's not. I mean, part of the structure of corporate capitalism is that the players in the game try to increase profits and market shares; in fact, if they didn't, they would no longer be players in the game. Any economist knows this. And it's not conspiracy theory to point that out; it's just taken for granted. If someone were to say, "Oh, no, that's a conspiracy," people would laugh.

Well, exactly the same is true when you discuss the more complex array of institutional factors that determine such things as what happens in the media. It's precisely the opposite of conspiracy theory. In fact, as you mentioned before, I generally tend to downplay the role of individuals—they're replaceable pieces. So, it's exactly the opposite of conspiracy theory. It's normal institutional analysis—the kind of analysis you do automatically when you're trying to understand how the world works. And to call it conspiracy theory is simply part of the effort to prevent an understanding of how the world works.

**The Humanist:** Well, I think also the term has been assigned a different meaning. If you look at the root of the term itself—*conspire,* to breathe together, breathe the same air—I mean, it seems to suggest a kind of shared interest on the part of the people "breathing together." It just seems that the world has been coopted for a different use now.

**Chomsky:** Well, certainly, it's supposed to have some sort of sinister meaning; it's a bunch of people getting together in back rooms deciding what appears in all the newspapers in this country. And sometimes that *does* happen; but, by and large, that's not the way it works. The way it works is the way we described in *Manufacturing Consent.* In fact, the model that we used—what we called the *propaganda* model—is essentially an uncontroversial guided free-market model.

**The Humanist:** An uncontroversial——

**Chomsky:** Guided free-market model—the kind that's *virtually* uncontroversial.

**The Humanist:** Hmmm. Well, can you say what issues the media reliably *don't* cover? I mean, are there a series of issues that——

**Chomsky:** Well, take some of the issues that we've mentioned. Any issue—anything that's going on—the media will shape and modify so that it serves the interests of established power. Now, established power may have several components, and these components may even be in conflict in some way, so you will get a diversity of tactical judgments.

Let's take, for example, the *major* foreign policy issue of the 1980s: Nicaragua. There was an elite consensus that we had to overthrow the Sandinistas and that we had to support murder and terror in El Salvador and Guatemala—that was a given. But within that consensus, there were some tactical variations. For example, how do you overthrow the Sandinistas? Do you do it by terror and violence, the way the Reaganites wanted? Or do you do it by economic strangulation and a lower level of terror and other sorts of pressures, the way the "doves" wanted? That was the debate. That was the *only* debate. And the media kept to that line. In fact, I've done a rather detailed analysis of this. The fact is that in news reporting, in editorials, and even in opinion columns—which are supposed to reflect a diversity of opinion—the commitment to this position approached 100 percent. So, if you take a look at, say, the opinion columns in the

*New York Times* and the *Washington Post,* as I did during the peak periods of debate, you'll find close to 100 percent support for the position that the Sandinistas have to be overthrown and a debate over how it should be done. Now, that's the kind of uniformity you find in a totalitarian state, and it's the same with all the other issues that I've looked at. Ed Herman and I and others have looked at a very wide range of cases, and that's what you find throughout.

**The Humanist:** You speak of the media engaging in a practice that you call *feigning dissent.* Is this an example of it?

**Chomsky:** Yes. For example, let's take the question of how to overthrow the Sandinistas. In 1986, a poll revealed that about 80 percent of the people called "leaders"—which includes corporate executives and so on—were opposed to the contra option and thought that other means should be used to destroy the Sandinistas and restore the rulers of their choice. Other forceful and illegal measures—but not contras. The reason was simply cost effectiveness. They recognized that the contras are—as the liberals put it—an "imperfect instrument" to achieve our goals. Now, if the media were simply reflecting corporate interests, then about 80 percent of the commentary would have opposed the contras. Actually, it was about 50 percent, which means that the media were more supportive of the government's position than a propaganda model would predict. So, if you want, there *was* a defect in our model—namely, that we *underestimated* the degree of subordination of the media to the government. But that's about it.

**The Humanist:** Do you think right now that the media are helping to lead us into war in the Persian Gulf?

**Chomsky:** Definitely. It's a complicated story, but the options are basically either war or a negotiated settlement. Now, what are the opportunities for a negotiated settlement? Well, there have been opportunities which have not been explored. And it's very interesting to watch the way the media treated them. For example, on August 12 [1990], Iraq apparently offered to withdraw from Kuwait as part of a general withdrawal from occupied Arab lands. That would mean, with the withdrawal of Syrian troops from Lebanon, the withdrawal of Israeli troops from Lebanon, and the withdrawal of Israeli forces from the occupied territories, they would give up Kuwait. Well, that's not an entirely unreasonable proposal; you can imagine a basis for discussion. *It was dismissed.* It was dismissed in the *New York Times* in one sentence—in the course of a news article on another topic. TV news just laughed about it.

On August 19, Saddam Hussein suggested a general settlement treating the problem of Kuwait as an Arab problem to be settled by the Arab states in the manner of Syria in Lebanon and Morocco in the western Sahara. Well, that, too, was rejected at once—this time on the very plausible grounds that, in that arena, Iraq could have prevailed because it's the most powerful force in that part of the world. Well, that's correct, but there's a small point we're missing here: namely, that Saddam Hussein was just stealing a leaf from our book. Every time a U.S. intervention takes place in the Western hemisphere, we immediately warn the world to keep away, even vetoing U.N. Security Council resolutions condemning U.S. aggression on the grounds that it's a hemispheric issue and others should not be allowed to interfere. Well, sure, it's a hemispheric issue because, in the hemisphere, we are so powerful compared to anyone else that we expect to prevail. If it's wrong for Saddam Hussein—as it is—then it's wrong for us.

Take a more striking case: on August 23, an offer was transmitted to Washington from Iraq by a former high U.S. official with Middle East connections. That offer was an interesting one. According to memoranda and the testimony of the people involved, which was basically recognized as accurate by the administration, the offer included complete withdrawal from Kuwait, Iraqi control of the Rumailah oil field, which is almost entirely in Iraq except for a small corner in Kuwait—Iraq claims, maybe rightly, that Kuwait has been draining its resources, so they want a settlement which would guarantee them control over that oil field—general negotiations over security issues, and so on. They didn't even mention U.S. withdrawal from Saudi Arabia. Well, that's an interesting offer. What was the reaction to it? Well, first of all, it wasn't published. Six days later, Newsday—which is not the national press—published it very prominently as the cover story and gave all the details. The next day, the New York Times—the newspaper of record—mentioned it in a small paragraph on the continuation page of a story on another topic. The Times opened by quoting the government as saying that the offer is baloney. Then, after having framed the issue properly—in other words, that the offer is baloney—it went on to concede quietly that the Newsday story was accurate and that the Times had had the same information a week earlier but hadn't published it. And that was the end of that story.

This reveals some things about the media. First of all, it shows that, outside the national press, you occasionally do get deviations. So, for example, the Newsday report was an exposure of information not wanted by those people in power who are trying to avoid negotiations. So, these deviations can happen, and, when they do, you move to the phase of damage control. The way you deal with this information is by marginalizing it. First you present it as baloney; then you quietly concede it's true and that you knew it all along but were suppressing it. And that's the end of the story.

Well, what does that tell you? The choice again is a negotiated settlement or war. And we see the way the possibilities for a negotiated settlement are being dealt with. Well, that happens to be Washington's priority at the moment, so therefore it's the media's priority.

**The Humanist:** Washington's priority is war?

**Chomsky:** Washington's priority is not war but, rather, to achieve our ends by the threat or use of force.

**The Humanist:** That brings up another question: how much of a crisis is there really in the Persian Gulf?

**Chomsky:** If it did explode into war, the consequences could be catastrophic.

**The Humanist:** I don't mean after Bush inserted the troops into Saudi Arabia; I mean before.

**Chomsky:** Even then it was serious; Iraq's invasion of Kuwait was a very serious matter, and everything should be done to get them out of there. I mean, on grounds of principle and international law, it's not fundamentally different from the U.S. invasion of Panama or the Israeli invasion of Lebanon or a dozen other cases we can think of where we didn't care or we supported the aggression. But on the grounds of, say, human rights, it doesn't begin to compare with the Indonesian invasion of Timor, which led to near genocide and which we tacitly supported. So, the only "principle" involved here is that might does not make right unless we want it to, and in the other cases we wanted it to. But this is significant because it involves energy. The Arabian peninsula is the major energy reserve of the world, and it's been a major commitment of the United States since World War II that we or our clients control that source of energy and that no independent indigenous force is allowed to have a significant influence. Actually, years ago, at the time of the first oil crisis, I referred to this as "axiom one" of international affairs. These resources are controlled by the United States, U.S. corporations, and U.S. clients like Saudi Arabia, and we're not going to tolerate any indigenous threat to that control. A large part of our foreign policy turns around that issue. And there's absolutely no doubt whatsoever that Saddam Hussein is a monster and just as much a monster and a gangster six weeks ago when he was a favored client of the United States—in fact, the United States was his largest trading partner, and the Bush administration had gone out of its way to offer him loans, credits, and so on. All of this was suppressed—virtually suppressed—by the media for a long time. He was just as much of a monster then. He's still a monster. Now, however, his monstrous acts happen to be harming U.S. interests, so therefore he's *portrayed* as a monster in the media.

**The Humanist:** I have a feeling that so much of the country has been conditioned now by this demonization in the press of Saddam Hussein that they would say, "Why should we even take these proposals seriously?"

**Chomsky:** We should take them seriously because he's frightened. The demonization for once happens to be accurate; he is a demonic character, just as he was when the press was looking the other way. But the fact of the matter is that he got in over his head and he now realizes it, apparently. We don't know, incidentally, if these offers are genuine; there's only one way to find out—and that's to pursue them. And that's what Washington does not want to do. You can't miss the fact that the United States is isolated on this issue. Who else has troops in the region?

**The Humanist:** Well, it looks like the United States is bribing Egypt to put some troops in.

**Chomsky:** We're trying to turn the screws on other countries to get them to participate, which in itself is very striking. Right now, as you and I are talking, the U.S. government—Nicholas Brady and James Baker—are flying around the world trying very hard to get people to contribute. What does this mean that we're trying to *get* them to contribute? So far, they've refused, but, if we have to *make* them contribute, that shows our isolation. Yesterday [September 6],

Germany announced that they would not pay anything for the American forces in Saudi Arabia—that this was a bilateral arrangement between the United States and Saudi Arabia and had nothing to do with Germany. Japan, the other major economic force in the world, has been saying that maybe they'll give some financial support to the countries that are being harmed by the embargo, or, you know, maybe they'll send a couple of jeeps. Egypt, which is a big, populous country with a very large army—a third of a million men—has sent 2,000 men armed with light weapons and jeeps. Hell, I can round up more than that from the people I know. As for Saudi Arabia, there were big headlines in this morning's paper saying that Saudi Arabia agrees to share the costs for the American soldiers. How very exciting. I mean, here are American soldiers sent to preserve the Saudi Arabian monarchy, and the Saudis are willing to pay some of the costs. Boy, that's really impressive.

**The Humanist:** Well, the United States wants to forgive Egypt its $7 billion debt and also make the Soviet Union a most-favored trading partner if they play along.

**Chomsky:** *Play along* just means give us a diplomatic cover—that's what it amounts to. Why is the United States so desperate for a diplomatic cover? In fact, why is everyone else in the world backing off from armed confrontation? These are things that a really objective media would want to be exploring. And again you find no discussion of it. And then you find an outraged editorial in the *New York Times* saying, "How come the world is playing the part of the bad guy?" But try to find some analyses of why that's true. Well, there are reasons; the reasons are pretty obvious. You know, the United States for a long period was the dominant force in the world—both economically and militarily. It was agreed on all sides that, when the United States was intervening in the Third World, it was "politically weak" but economically and militarily strong. And you tend to lead with your strength. We had military and economic strength. Now, we are only one out of three. It's a tripolar world from an economic point of view. But the United States is still unique in military force. Nobody comes close; we are *the* military power. And with the withdrawal of the Soviet Union from world affairs, we're freer to use military force than before, because the Soviet deterrent has disappeared. And there's a natural temptation to lead with your strength, which in our case happens to be military. Germany and Japan have different interests, and the resolution of the issue by the exercise of force is not in those interests.

**The Humanist:** Do you think that there was any good reason for Bush to put all those ground troops into Saudi Arabia?

**Chomsky:** Not really, no. I mean, I think there were reasons for the world community to make it clear that it would not tolerate Iraqi aggression, it would not tolerate the takeover of Kuwait, and it would certainly not tolerate any threat to Saudi Arabia. I think to make that clear and explicit was absolutely valid and right, and I think that Bush really knows there's agreement about that in the world. The question is where do you go from there?

**The Humanist:** But my question is was there any real need for those troops to be committed? And didn't that dangerously raise the stakes?

**Chomsky:** We could argue that; I'm not completely convinced that there was. But you could argue that a military presence was necessary. It would have been far preferable to do it under the U.N.'s [United Nations] auspices. That also was not pursued. Or, rather, it was pursued, but the U.N. would not go along; in fact, the other world powers still have not really agreed to enforce the embargo. After a lot of arm-twisting, we finally got a U.N. Security Council resolution, but it was a very cautious one: it refused to authorize even the minimal use of force. Again, the United States is relatively isolated.

**The Humanist:** I think it's interesting that in the media you see a different sort of picture. For example, you were talking earlier about how weak and frightened Hussein actually is at this point—or at least frightened.

**Chomsky:** Well, he looks it. But again, you don't know whether this is bluster and posing—just an effort to get what he can—or if he really is frightened. And, as I said, there's only one way to find that out—and that's to pursue a negotiated settlement.

**The Humanist:** So, do you think Hussein is militarily as powerful as the media have presented him?

**Chomsky:** On this issue, I think the media are pretty accurate. If you look closely at the military analysis, you'll see that his military power is partly papier-mâché. The army has poor morale, a limited capacity . . . but it depends by what standards you're judging. By Middle Eastern standards, it's a very powerful army. But if there's a war with the United States, Iraq will lose. If we wanted, we could blow the country out of the universe.

**The Humanist:** And what about the media's newfound appreciation of the United Nations now that it's allegedly voting on our side?

**Chomsky:** Well, that's an interesting story. The U.N. has come in for some quite unaccustomed praise. There's been article after article about how, with the end of the Cold War, and with the Russians no longer dragging their feet, the U.N. can finally function in the way it was originally designed to function. There's one slight problem, though. Certainly for the last 20 years, the U.N. has not been able to function because the United States has blocked it. We're far in the lead—far, far in the lead—in terms of Security Council vetos. On a whole range of issues—including the Middle East, the observance of international law, disarmament, the environment, you name it—the United States has vetoed Security Council resolutions repeatedly and has voted alone, or along with one or two client states, in the General Assembly. That's happened over and over again.

So, what does that tell you? Well, if you look at the attitude toward the U.N. in the United States, you find that, in the late 1940s, the U.N. was regarded quite favorably. At that time, after World War II, the United States was overwhelmingly dominant in the world and the U.N. could be counted on to follow U.S. orders on virtually everything. So, at that time, the U.N. was a fine thing, and the Russians—who were being outvoted because we were using the U.N. as an instrument against them—were the bad guys. Then the U.N. gradually fell out of favor, as U.S. dominance in the world declined. And as Third World countries gained independence and were able to join, the U.N. fell under what we call the "tyranny of the majority"—otherwise known as democracy— because it was no longer following U.S. orders. So, slowly, over the years, we lost interest in the U.N. By about 1970, the situation had gotten to the point where the United States was becoming increasingly isolated. And, by that time, the U.N. was just bad news; it was full of irrational anti-Americanism and so forth.

It's interesting to see how the discussion changed over those years. In the 1950s, the debate was why are the Russians so awful? By 1985, the debate was why is the *world* so awful? You had stories in the *New York Times Magazine* by its U.N. correspondent asking how come the whole world seems to be out of step. I mean, they're voting against us on everything; so, what's the matter with the world? And there were a number of thoughtful ruminations on *that* topic. Now, in this one instance, the U.N. is more or less acting in accordance with U.S. wishes—more or less. So, all of a sudden, the U.N. is a wonderful institution.

Well, anybody looking at this record would regard it as a comedy. Any sane person would. The U.N. is considered favorably to the extent that it follows U.S. orders; to the extent that it doesn't, it is looked upon unfavorably. Further- more, for the past 20 years, the Soviet Union has, by and large—in fact, overwhelmingly—voted with the majority, the large majority. Those are the facts of the matter. Try to find a report in the press that even comes close to describing that. Well, that again shows you what a remarkable institution of distortion and deception the media are.

**The Humanist:** Not only that but . . . I don't know if you've been watching "Nightline" recently?

**Chomsky:** I don't watch it.

**The Humanist:** Well, Barbara Walters was on hectoring a German journalist and a Japanese trade ministry representative about whether or not they were going to contribute money. There was Barbara Walters, you know, speaking almost on behalf of the American people, asking them where's their damn money.

**Chomsky:** Well, an obvious question arises; namely, why . . . let's say she's the voice of the American government, not the American people . . . why does she have to hector representatives of Germany and Japan about giving us money? Why do we have to twist their arms to get them to pay for this? After all, they're more reliant on Middle East oil than we are. So, what's the matter? Well, maybe this says something about us. The possibility that there's some- thing wrong with our policy, our commitment . . . that's something that can't be raised. I mean, it's just a law of logic that we're right in whatever we do. And even if the whole world disagrees with us—not just on this but on many other issues—the world is wrong. The world is not on the "team," you know, if it doesn't go along with us. We just take that for granted.

**The Humanist:** I brought that up because it wasn't as if this journalist had the keys to the German treasury. It wasn't news; it wasn't analysis. It just seemed to be a lot of posturing. Actually, this leads me to my next question. You concentrate mainly on the print media; is there any reason for that?

**Chomsky:** Yeah, I don't have the resources to cover television. Don't forget that, on this side of the fence, we don't have many resources. Everything I do is on my own time, mostly with my own money. On the other side of the fence, you have ample resources. And if you really want to cover television seriously, you have to go through the transcripts, which really takes time. Furthermore, to the extent that there have been studies of television—there have been some by others—it's almost invariably the case that the framing of the news on television is largely within the bounds set by the national print media. You can pretty well predict what's going to be on network television on any given evening by looking at the front page of the *New York Times* or the *Washington Post*.

**The Humanist:** Sure, even people within television freely admit that. Do you think there's any difference in terms of the effectiveness of indoctrination between broadcast media and the print media?

**Chomsky:** Yeah, for most of the population, television news' framing of the issues is probably much more influential.

**The Humanist:** Gore Vidal, among others, has suggested that people who are inundated by television news are easier to manipulate. Do you buy that?

**Chomsky:** Well, I think we again ought to make the distinction between the political class—those who are more active in political, economic, and cultural management, a minority of some 20 percent—and the rest of the population whose function is to be passive observers. For the large mass of the population, I suspect that the main impact of television comes not through the news but through mechanisms to divert their attention. That means network programming—everything from sports to sitcoms to fanciful pictures of the way life is "supposed" to be. Anything that has the effect of isolating people—keeping them separated from one another and focused on the tube—will make people passive observers.

Remember, after all, that this is basic liberal democratic theory—I'm not making it up. If you read, say, Walter Lippmann, the dean of American journalism, who is also considered a leading progressive, democratic theorist, his argument is that, for a democracy to function properly, there are two different roles that have to be played: one is the role of what he called the *specialized class*—the responsible men, a small minority—and the other is the role of the public, whom he described as a "bewildered herd." The role of the public, then, is to be spectators, not participants; their role is just to watch and occasionally to ratify. The decision-making has to be in the hands of the elite. That's democracy.

**The Humanist:** And that was to be consciously directed?

**Chomsky:** Oh, well, I'm quoting Lippmann and he means it to be completely conscious. You can trace this to the founding fathers: the public are to be observers. The country was founded on the idea that . . . Well, John Jay [the president of the Constitutional Convention and the first chief justice of the Supreme Court] put it very concisely: "Those who own the country ought to govern it." That's the way the country was established, and that's the way it's been run.

**The Humanist:** Do you think things are getting better or worse in terms of the people's access to alternative news sources?

**Chomsky:** Oh, I think it's better.

**The Humanist:** Better?

**Chomsky:** For one thing, I think the media are better than they were 20, 25 years ago, and more open. I've been talking about how narrow they are, but it's a lot better than it was 25 to 30 years ago.

**The Humanist:** Why did this change occur?

**Chomsky:** Mainly because of the way everything changes—social change. Why do we have free speech? Not because anybody wrote it down on paper but because of centuries of struggle—popular struggle. Every social change comes about through a long-term process of struggle—whether it be the peace movement, the civil rights movement, the women's movement, or whatever.

And in the 1960s, there was a substantial popular awakening, which improved enormously the cultural and intellectual level of a large part of the population. And that's had an effect. There's been a tremendous effort to stamp it out, but I don't think it's working. It's had its effect on popular dissidence during the 1980s, which was greater than it has been in our recent history. And it's had an effect on the media and Congress. Many people have filtered into the system who came through that experience—and that's had an effect. So, now you have people in the media whose formative influences were in the 1960s' ferment—and sometimes you can see their effect. And the same thing holds true with Congress. Take the congressional human rights campaign, which is mistakenly attributed to the Carter administration; a lot of the initiative for it came from young people and grew out of the 1960s experience.

**The Humanist:** So, you think that people are getting——

**Chomsky:** I think it's marginally better in the mainstream institutions. Also, there are lots of alternatives. Take something like community-based radio, which is pretty widespread over the country—well, that really offers an alternative. Communities that have a community-based radio station are significantly different from others in terms of the liveliness and openness and vitality of the political discussion. I travel around the country a lot, and for me the difference is palpable.

**The Humanist:** So, you think that people are getting *less* manipulable then?

**Chomsky:** Yeah, I think so. You could see it in the 1980s. For example, when the Reagan administration came in, they expected to be able to carry out worldwide interventions the way the Kennedy administration did; Kennedy was their model. And the Kennedy administration was quite brazen about it; some of what they did was clandestine, but most of it was quite open. When they started bombing South Vietnam, it was on the front pages. When they sent troops to Vietnam, it was overt. The Reagan administration couldn't do that; they had to move at once to clandestine warfare—in fact, they mounted the largest campaign of clandestine terror in modern history, probably. Well, the scale of clandestine operations is a good measure of popular dissidence. Clandestine operations aren't secret from anybody except the domestic population. And they're inefficient. Any state will use overt violence if it can get away with it; it'll turn to covert violence when it can't get away with it.

**The Humanist:** Do you have any advice on how to escape this pervasive and continual indoctrination offered by the media?

**Chomsky:** People have to understand that it's necessary to undertake what you might call a course in intellectual self-defense. You have to understand the nature of the material that is being imposed upon you and its institutional sources. When you do that, you can make corrections. It's very hard to do that as an isolated individual. But in solidarity with others, in communication with others, it can be done. It was done, for example, by the Central American solidarity movement, which was a very effective movement in the 1980s, and also by the anti-apartheid network, by the "green" movement, and by the women's movement. That's the way you combat it. An isolated individual— unless he or she is really heroic—can't prevail.

## Questions for Discussion

1. What criteria should be used in determining whether a newspaper or television program is biased in presenting the news?
2. How does the approach used in presenting the news affect the receiver of the information?
3. If there is a media bias, what is it? What is your evidence?
4. How do political leaders attempt to shape the news? Are they successful?
5. How does corporate ownership affect the presentation of the news?
6. How do the attitudes of the journalists, producers, and executives affect the shape of the news?

## Suggested Readings

Cooper, Marc, and Laurence C. Soley. "All the Right Sources." *Mother Jones,* 15, no. 2 (February/March 1990), 20–27, 45–48.

Donaldson, Sam. *Hold on Mr. President.* New York: Random House, 1987.

Fischer, Raymond L. "Manipulating the Media and America: The Negative 1988 Campaign." *USA Today* (magazine), 117, no. 2526 (March 1989), 20–22.

Goldstein, Tom, ed. *Killing the Messenger: 100 Years of Media Criticism.* New York: Columbia Univ. Press, 1989.

Hess, Stephen. *The Washington Reporters: Newswork.* Washington, D.C.: Brookings Institution, 1981.

Iyengar, Shanto, and Donald R. Kinder. *News That Matters: Television and American Opinion*. Chicago, Ill.: Univ. of Chicago Press, 1987.

Lichter, S. Robert, Stanley Rothman, and Linda S. Lichter. *The Media Elite*. Bethesda, Md.: Adler & Adler, 1986.

Parenti, Michael. *Inventing Reality: The Politics of the Mass Media*. New York: St. Martin's Press, 1986.

Rusher, William A. *The Coming Battle for the Media: Curbing the Power of the Media Elite*. New York: William A. Morrow, 1988.

Starker, Steven. *Evil Influences: Crusades against the Mass Media*. New Brunswick, N.J.: Transaction Publishers, 1989.

Thimmesch, Nick, ed. *A Liberal Media Elite?* Washington, D.C.: American Enterprise Institute, 1985.

# Civil Liberties

# and Civil Rights

P olitical systems make rules that are binding upon their members. But political systems differ in the amount of freedom permitted to citizens. In twentieth-century totalitarian dictatorships, the state imposed severe restrictions on individual liberty. Not only was it concerned with what people did, but it sought to mold people's minds to a government-approved way of thinking.

Modern democracies permit a large amount of individual freedom. As a modern democracy, the U.S. government accepts the principle of civil liberties, recognizing that individuals have freedoms the government cannot take away. Among these are freedom of speech, freedom of the press, and freedom of assembly. The Constitution as originally written in 1787 contains some protections for the individual against the encroachment of government, but the most important are set forth in the first ten amendments to the Constitution, known as the Bill of Rights and adopted in 1791. They are also found in federal government laws and court decisions, as well as in state constitutions and laws.

As the arbiter in constitutional disputes between the government and the individual, the Supreme Court is often at the center of the storm when it tries to determine whether government has overstepped the bounds and illegally violated the liberties sanctioned by the Constitution. And so, the Court has decided issues such as whether the government can force a person whose religion forbids worship of graven images to salute the flag (it cannot) and whether the government can ban obscene books, magazines, motion pictures, or television programs (it can).

The Court's decisions on privacy have been particularly controversial. Privacy is the right of an individual to deal with his or her personal life without government interference. The Constitution does not specifically mention a right of privacy. The Court, however, decided that such a right can be inferred from the First, Fourth, Fifth, Ninth, and Fourteenth Amendments to the Constitution. The right of privacy has been a consideration in the Court's decisions allowing for the right of a woman to have an abortion under certain conditions. And it is now central to cases involving fetal rights.

Court decisions on freedom of speech issues have also been very controversial. The Court has often supported the rights of unpopular groups, such as Nazis and communists, to make speeches advocating their political ideas. It has at times also set limits on speech.

Like many modern democracies, the United States contains citizens of different religions, races, and ethnic backgrounds. In addition to promoting civil liberties, the U.S. government is committed to protecting civil rights—those rights that assure minority group equality before the law.

As the speech by Thurgood Marshall in Chapter 1 indicates, the record of civil rights protection for African Americans has been a sorry one. Brought to the New World as slaves, black people were not granted U.S. citizenship until after the Civil War. And even after the adoption of the Thirteenth, Fourteenth, and Fifteenth Amendments, which eliminated slavery and gave legal and political rights to black people, those rights were often denied in practice until the 1960s.

Although the formal barriers to civil rights have largely fallen, many African Americans believe that the nation still does not adequately promote genuine equality. They point to discrimination in employment, housing, and professional advancement as examples of unfinished business.

Part III deals with three issues of civil liberties and civil rights: the right of the state to intervene to protect the life of the fetus, the limits of freedom of speech in making racist statements, and the wisdom of the civil rights agenda.

# Chapter 8

## *Should Legal Sanctions Be Imposed to Protect Fetal Rights?*

Few issues in U.S. society have divided the nation's citizens as much as abortion. Since the Supreme Court decided in *Roe* v. *Wade* (1973) that during the first trimester of a woman's pregnancy the state has no right to impede her from getting an abortion, opponents and defenders of the decision have made their viewpoints known from Main Street to the halls of Congress.

The abortion controversy has focused attention on the legal status of the fetus. Does the fetus have legal rights? If the fetus has legal rights, do they take precedence over the rights of the mother? Does the state have a right to impose civil and criminal sanctions in cases of what has become known as "fetal abuse"?

Fetal-abuse issues have also been focused by increasing information about the consequences of drug and alcohol abuse. A pregnant woman taking crack, a highly addictive form of cocaine, risks not only her own life but that of the fetus as well. Some babies born to crack-addicted women will have severe physical and mental disorders for the rest of their lives. Scientists have also discovered that use of alcohol and tobacco during pregnancy can cause fetal defects. Even mild alcoholic consumption by a pregnant woman may result in serious physical problems for the child.

Does the government have the right or responsibility to intervene to protect the fetus? State legislatures and courts have wrestled to reconcile the rights of the mother with the rights of the fetus. The issue has involved not only privacy rights but the First Amendment guarantee of freedom of religion as well. For example, a hospital successfully received court permission to force a woman who was a member of the Jehovah's Witnesses to have a blood transfusion against her will in the belief that the transfusion was necessary to save the life of the eight-month-old fetus.

The issue of fetal rights is a subject of great interest to women. Feminists who favor abortion rights see the fetal-rights movement as an attack on *Roe* v. *Wade.* They object to its invasion of privacy and its criminal focus on women to the exclusion of men, although some supporters of fetal rights also support punishment of men who contribute to harming a fetus by actively aiding a pregnant woman's drug or alcohol abuse.

The debate below considers whether legal sanctions should be imposed to protect fetal rights. Attorneys Bruce Fein and William Bradford Reynolds argue that they should. They contend:

1. A legal shield is necessary to deter dangerous conduct of no social utility.
2. Preventable prenatal harms should not be permitted to set back a child's natural starting point.
3. The nation's educational, physical, and economic strength is diminished when unborns are mentally or physically impaired.

In the view of the authors, tort law should be expanded to penalize both fathers and pregnant mothers who show reckless disregard for the fetus they have created. They also assert that criminal sanctions against pregnant mothers who disregard the consequences of their actions to the fetus should be imposed and that negligent fathers be subject to similar punishment. The penalties would have to be drawn carefully, the authors say, lest they generate undesirable social consequences.

Attorneys Kary L. Moss, Lynn M. Paltrow, and Judy Crockett, representing the American Civil Liberties Union, a public-interest group committed to the protection of civil liberties, speak out against the imposition of criminal sanctions on pregnant women who use alcohol and drugs. Testifying before the House Select Committee on Children, Youth, and Families, they argue:

1. Criminal punishment of these women violates constitutional privacy and liberty guarantees that protect the right to decide whether to bear or beget a child.
2. Prosecutions deter women from getting health care.
3. They undermine doctor-patient trust.
4. People who are addicted to drugs and alcohol do not demonstrate willful behavior but rather show that they are ill.

# ☑ YES

---

## Should Legal Sanctions Be Imposed to Protect Fetal Rights?

---

### BRUCE FEIN AND WILLIAM BRADFORD REYNOLDS
### Addicts, Their Babies, and Their Liability

In the company of the casualties of gang warfare, drug abuse, and needle-transmitted AIDS stands—lies, really—a group of victims more innocent than all others ravaged by the drug scourge. We speak of the newborn infants whose mothers, in reckless indifference to their children's health and welfare, abused drugs or alcohol during pregnancy. The tragic consequences are devastating and growing worse:

- Approximately 375,000 infants are born annually with physical or mental handicaps likely caused by maternal substance abuse.
- Cocaine ingested during pregnancy increases the risk of crib death tenfold and may increase the risk of fetal stroke.
- Pregnant women who consume drugs or alcohol expose their babies to the almost certain dangers of mental retardation, growth deficiency, facial malformation, and nervous system dysfunction.
- The incidence of drug-abusing mothers in New York City alone has mushroomed by 3,000 percent over the past decade.

These horrifying facts will not disappear at the drop of a law. Like those of most other social evils, the causes of maternal irresponsibility are multiple and spring from resilient infirmities of human nature. Laws can promise only marginal alleviation until wholesale changes take place in public sentiment and attitude.

But legal rules carry some weight and should be seriously considered, at least as one possible response to the devastation. The questions need to be asked: How should the law respond? Should it respond at all?

Tort law already acknowledges the strong community interest in safeguarding the fetus from unreasonable risks. In every state and the District of Columbia, a child is endowed with a tort claim against any person, except the mother, for proximately causing prenatal injury. If the child dies of such injury after birth, the child's estate possesses a cause of action for wrongful death.

The reasons for a legal shield protecting the unborn are at least threefold: It deters dangerous conduct of no social utility. Preventable prenatal harms should not be permitted to set back a child's natural starting point. And our nation's educational, physical, and economic strength suffers when newborns are mentally or physically impaired.

None of these reasons justifies an exemption from liability for mothers whose negligence or recklessness causes prenatal injury. Perhaps existing tort law should be expanded, either by judicial decree or statute, to make a woman who becomes pregnant by choice liable in damages to a disabled newborn whose handicaps were proximately caused by substance abuse during pregnancy—where medical science knows, and the mother should reasonably have known, that the abuse created a significant risk of fetal harm. (Only one jurisdiction, Michigan, has explicitly recognized a tort of maternal prenatal negligence.)

Another question is the culpability of the father. Should he be held jointly and severally liable under tort law? A venerable principle holds individuals liable for unreasonably failing to guard against the foreseeable negligence of others. This suggests that a father could also be answerable to his child in damages, if he made the mother pregnant despite knowing that she might injure the fetus by substance abuse.

Criminal sanctions, too, might be considered for mothers who acted with knowledge of or reckless indifference to fetal danger. Some may plead the mother's case on grounds of addiction—that her uncontrollable appetite for drugs should legally excuse a battery on the fetus. But addiction alone does not disprove a culpable state of mind. An alcoholic enjoys no immunity from a vehicular-homicide charge if he or she succumbs to addiction before inflicting death on the highway. Why should there be greater leniency for the woman who voluntarily chooses pregnancy knowing the grave risks her addiction will pose for the fetus?

In a comparable context, Massachusetts has already initiated a vehicular-homicide prosecution against a woman whose miscarriage of her eight-and-one-half-month-old fetus was caused by her drunk driving. In Florida, a woman was found criminally culpable for delivery of illicit drugs through the umbilical cord to her fetus, which was later born alive.

So the idea is not without precedent. One could contemplate bringing a felony charge, punishable by up to 25 years in prison (perhaps for a second offense), against a mother who knowingly indulged in drugs, alcohol, or other dangerous substances that caused substantial mental or physical impairment to her child.

Nor should criminal punishment be considered only with reference to the mother. When the father is involved in, encourages, and helps provide the drugs for the habit during pregnancy, he, too, is a legitimate candidate for 25-years imprisonment for prenatal injuries.

These observations are admittedly tentative. The types of substance abuse giving rise to civil or criminal liability would have to be narrowly defined to include only activities that are regarded by society as morally reprehensible. Eating too much sugar and drinking a few glasses of wine during pregnancy, for example, are not the dangerous indulgences we have in mind—even though medical science may suggest that abstinence is preferable.

The question of the criminal culpability of at least some addicts is sure to be controversial. There would, however, be exemptions under our proposal for pregnancies that were not voluntary, i.e., the result of rape, incest, duress, or other coercive circumstances.

And, admittedly, this proposal could backfire. Civil or criminal sanctions for maternal substance abuse causing prenatal injury might aggravate the problem or yield other evils more severe. They might have the undesirable side effect of pushing some expectant mothers toward choosing abortion over childbirth if the woman believes the latter may bring civil or criminal penalties. The penalty provisions could additionally discourage some women, upon learning of pregnancy, from seeking drug or alcohol counseling for fear that doing so might later serve as evidence against them in a lawsuit or prosecution.

There is as well the harsh reality that a number of addicted parents would likely be judgment-proof. But is that reason to abandon all legal sanctions, or should it be no more relevant than the typical collection problem one faces with a civil claim against a common thief?

This only begins the discussion—yet it must begin. Drug treatment programs, at present, are no solace to mentally and physically injured newborns.

Perhaps legal initiatives along the lines suggested, if they treat female drug addicts as mature adults capable of controlling their own behavior during pregnancy, might encourage corresponding responsibility. That they would provide public expression of worthy moral sentiments also argues for such legislation.

Those whose inclination is to resist a move toward parental legal sanctions, when hundreds of thousands of babies are impaired annually by knowing or grossly negligent maternal substance abuse, seem to us to bear the far greater burden of persuasion on their shoulders.

☑ *NO*

*Should Legal Sanctions Be Imposed to Protect Fetal Rights?*

## KARY L. MOSS, LYNN M. PALTROW, AND JUDY CROCKETT

*No Criminal Prosecution of Alcohol- or Drug-Dependent Women Who Choose to Continue Their Pregnancies*

The federal government should take steps to stop the recent trend to subject alcohol and drug dependent women to criminal prosecution for their alcohol or drug use during pregnancy. To date, at least fifty women have been charged with crimes for their behavior during pregnancy. . . . The American Civil Liberties Union has been involved as counsel or advisor in most of these cases. Our national survey of these prosecutions confirm that women of color,[1] poor women, and battered women[2] are the primary victims. In none of these cases have the men whose violence threatened the health of the fetus been charged with child endangerment.

None of the women arrested were charged with the crime of possession of illegal drugs. Instead, they were arrested for a new and independent crime: continuing their pregnancy while addicted to drugs. Because women are discriminated against in drug treatment programs, and because it is virtually impossible to stop using drugs without help, these prosecutions, in effect, punish women for their decision to continue a pregnancy.[3] These prosecutions thus violate constitutional privacy and liberty guarantees that protect the right to decide "whether to bear or beget a child."[4]

Prosecutions also deter pregnant women from getting what little health care is available. As Senator Herbert Kohl stated at Congressional hearings on perinatal substance abuse, "[m]others—afraid of criminal prosecution—fail to seek the very prenatal care that could help their babies and them."[5] Women are also discouraged from seeking help because of the fear that they will lose custody of their children. According to Ricardo Quiroga, who is helping to set up an alcohol recovery house for Hispanic women with children in Massachusetts, women "don't want to seek help for fear they will lose their children."[6]

Prosecutions also undermine doctor-patient trust. Those women who seek medical care are often too frightened to speak openly to their doctors about their alcohol or drug dependency problems. In Florida, for example, after "[u]niformed officers wearing guns entered Bayfront Medical Center . . . to investigate new mothers suspected of cocaine abuse," doctors reported that they could no longer "depend on the mothers to tell them the truth about their drug use . . . because the word ha[d] gotten around that the police will have to be notified."[7] Without honest communication between doctor and patient, it will be impossible to provide pregnant women with the medical care they need to ensure the health of the mothers and babies.[8]

Criminal prosecution for the "crime" of being alcohol or drug dependent and pregnant reflects a lack of understanding that drug and alcohol dependency is not demonstrative of "willful" behavior but rather is an illness whose cure has confounded generations of doctors and psychologists.[9] We do not suggest that a woman cannot be prosecuted for a crime, such as possession of illegal drugs, simply because she is pregnant. Rather it is the focus on the drug use during pregnancy, as the basis for the prosecution, that is contrary to well-established principles of constitutional law.

Criminal prosecution is also ultimately premised on the assumption that pregnant addicts are indifferent to the health of their fetuses, or that the women willfully seek to cause their fetuses harm. These assumptions are incorrect: real resource constraints may prevent women from securing treatment or proper care during their pregnancies. Even when women can secure treatment, recovery may be constrained by the very nature of the addiction. Addiction typically involves loss of control over use of a drug and continued involvement with a drug even when there are serious consequences.[10] To treat alcohol and drug dependent pregnant women as indifferent and deliberate wrongdoers is to misunderstand the nature of addiction.

For all of these reasons, the American Civil Liberties Union opposes criminal prosecutions of alcohol or drug dependent women whose only "crime" is choosing to continue a pregnancy. We support a woman's constitutional right to decide whether or not to terminate a pregnancy free of governmental interference or coercion.

Yet, in several states it may become even easier to criminally prosecute these women. Bills that would make drug use during pregnancy a felony have been introduced in Ohio,[11] Georgia,[12] Louisiana,[13] and Rhode Island,[14] and perhaps other states as well. The bill pending in Ohio, for example, would actually mandate forced sterilization of women who are not able to overcome their dependency on drugs. Any woman who uses drugs while pregnant, causing a child to be addicted at birth, would be prosecuted as a felon. In addition to the prison term ordinarily authorized as punishment for felony offenses, the legislation authorizes several alternative sentences: a court could sentence any woman who pleads guilty to or was convicted of the offense to "elect" to "successfully complete a drug addiction program," to "undergo a tubal ligation," or to "participate in a five year program of monitored contraceptive use approved by the court . . . and during the five year period abstain from the addictive use of drugs of abuse." The proposed legislation gives a repeat offender only two "choices": she may "undergo a tubal ligation" or participate in the monitored contraceptive program described above.

The federal government should discourage states from enacting laws that would punish alcohol or drug dependent women who continue their pregnancies.

---

*NOTES*

1. Eighty percent of the forty-seven cases in which the race of the woman could be identified involve a woman of color.

2. A significant number of women arrested for their actions during pregnancy were in abusive relationships. Newspaper and court reports have documented that four of the white women prosecuted were beaten by their boyfriends; the actual number is likely higher. *State of Alaska v. Grubbs*, No. 4FA S89 415 Criminal (Sup. Ct. Aug. 25, 1989); *State of Wyoming v. Pfannensteil*, No. 1-90-8CR (Laramie County Ct. complaint filed Jan. 5, 1990); Charles Levendosky, "Turning Women into 2-Legged Petri Dishes," Sunday *Star Tribune*, Jan. 21, 1990 at A8; *Commonwealth of Mass. v. Pelligrini*, No. 87970 (Mass. Super. Ct. filed Aug. 21, 1989); Tom Coakley, "Suspect Is Said to Be Battered, Frightened," *Boston Globe*, Aug. 23, 1989 at 22; *State of California v. Stewart*, No. M508197 (San Diego Mun. Ct., Feb. 26, 1987).

3. Statements by the prosecutor in one criminal case illustrate: "When she delivered that baby, she broke the law in the state." The court agreed, noting that the defendant "made a choice to become pregnant and to allow those pregnancies to come to term." *State v. Johnson*, No. E89-890-CFA. Although there have been nearly fifty arrests and prosecutions of women for their behavior during pregnancy, Johnson was the first to be convicted after trial.

4. *Eisenstadt v. Baird*, 405 U.S. 438, 453 (1972); *Cleveland Bd. of Educ. v. LaFleur*, 414 U.S. 632, 640 (1973).

5. *Missing Links: Coordinating Federal Drug Policy for Women, Infants and Children*, Hearing before Senate Committee on Governmental Affairs, 101st Cong., 1st Sess. (July 31, 1989) (Opening statement of Senator Herb Kohl) at 5.

6. Malaspina, "Clean Living," *Globe Magazine*, Nov. 5, 1989 at 20.

7. "Angry Doctors Cut Drug Tests after Police Interview Moms," *St. Petersburg Times*, May 13, 1989 at 1B.

8. Physician failure to maintain patient confidentiality has been identified as one of the barriers to pregnant women seeking prenatal care. Curry, "Nonfinancial Barriers to Prenatal Care," 15 *Women & Health* 85, 92 (1989). Health care workers in localities in which women who used drugs during pregnancy have been prosecuted have repeatedly testified that pregnant women were driven away from their programs. *See* Declaration of Lydia Roper, L.C.S.W., *State v. Stewart*, M508197 (San Diego Mun. Ct.); Declaration of Cathy Hauer, M.S., *State v. Stewart*, M508196 (San Diego Mun. Ct.); Affidavit of Ira Chasnoff, M.D., *State v. Hardy*, 89-2931-FY (Muskegon County Dist. Ct. Mich.)

9. *See Robinson v. California*, 370 U.S. 660 (1962).

10. Cohen, S., M.D., *The Chemistry of Addiction* 59 (Care Institute, 1988). Drug dependency and alcoholism include tolerance development and are influenced by genetic predispositions and environmental factors outside the addicts' control. *Id.*

11. SB 324, 118th General Assembly, Regular Session 1989–90 (Ohio), introduced by Senator Cooper Snyder.

12. In Georgia, a bill was recently defeated that would have provided that any woman who uses a controlled substance or dangerous drug while pregnant, and who as a result gives birth to a child

who "tests positive for addiction," is guilty of the criminal offense of distributing a controlled substance to an unborn child—a crime subject to imprisonment of not less than one nor more than ten years. HB 1146.

13. H.B. 603.

14. H.B. 9320 would have expanded the definition of manslaughter to include death of a child resulting from ingestion of drugs by a pregnant woman.

## Questions for Discussion

1. What should the state do about pregnant women who are crack addicts and who do not want an abortion? What are the reasons for your answer?
2. Are fetal rights a feminist issue? Why?
3. What would be the consequences of imposing heavy criminal sanctions on drug-abusing pregnant women?
4. What (if any) criminal penalties should be directed at the male partners of drug-addicted pregnant women?
5. In assessing criminal penalties, would you distinguish among users of narcotics, alcohol, and tobacco? What distinctions would you make? On what basis?
6. What are the legal consequences of fetal rights for the abortion controversy?

## Suggested Readings

Blumberg, Lisa. "Why Fetal Rights Must Be Opposed." *Social Policy*, 18, no. 2 (Fall 1987), 40–41.

Chasnoff, Ira J., ed. *Drugs, Alcohol, Pregnancy, and Parenting*. Boston, Mass.: Kluwer Academic Publisher, 1988.

Feinberg, Joel. "Comment: Wrongful Conception and the Right Not to Be Harmed." *Harvard Journal of Law and Public Policy*, 8 (Winter 1985), 57–77.

Gallagher, Janet. "Prenatal Invasions and Interventions: What's Wrong with Fetal Rights." *Harvard Women's Law Journal*, 10 (Spring 1987), 9–58.

Jost, Kenneth. "Mother versus Child." *American Bar Association Journal*, 75 (April 1989), 84–88.

Krauthammer, Charles. "Children of Cocaine." *Washington Post*, July 30, 1989, p. C7.

Losco, Joseph. "Fetal Abuse: An Exploration of Emerging Philosophic, Legal, and Policy Issues." *Western Political Quarterly*, 42, no. 2 (June 1989), 265–286.

Mathieu, Deborah. "Respecting Liberty and Preventing Harm: Limits of State Intervention in Prenatal Choice." *Harvard Journal of Law and Public Policy*, 8 (Winter 1985), 19–55.

Pollitt, Katha. "A New Assault on Feminism: 'Fetal Rights.' " *Nation*, 250 (March 26, 1990), 409–411, 414–416, 418.

Thompson, Elizabeth L. "The Criminalization of Maternal Conduct during Pregnancy: A Decisionmaking Model for Lawmakers." *Indiana Law Journal*, 64, no. 2 (1988–1989), 357–374.

U.S. Cong., House of Representatives. *Cocaine Babies*. Hearing before the Select Committee on Narcotics Abuse and Control, 101st Cong., 1st Sess., 1987.

# Chapter 9

## *Does Freedom of Speech Include the Right to Make Racist Statements?*

The First Amendment to the Constitution provides that Congress can pass no law prohibiting the freedom of speech, the press, and assembly or the free exercise of religion. The Supreme Court has used the Fourteenth Amendment to expand these prohibitions to state governments as well.

In contemporary democracies these freedoms allow individuals and groups to influence government officials as well as their fellow citizens. Democracy is often distinguished from dictatorship, in fact, by the extent to which individual citizens enjoy these freedoms.

As with all First Amendment freedoms, however, freedom of speech is not an absolute. Supreme Court Justice Oliver Wendell Holmes once observed that it does not include the right to falsely shout "fire" in a crowded theater. And the Supreme Court has often been at the center of controversy when it considers cases that define limits on the freedom of speech.

In the past decade a number of issues involving the limits of speech have attracted attention. In 1989 the burning of the American flag provoked Congress into passing a law making such an act a crime, but the Supreme Court decided that the law was an unconstitutional limitation of freedom of speech. In 1990 a proposed constitutional amendment allowing the states to make desecrating the flag a crime failed in Congress.

Pornography has been linked to freedom of expression, and recent controversies have arisen over the display of so-called obscene materials in museums, theaters, and art galleries and the sale of recordings with obscene lyrics, as well as continued federal support of art that some say is pornographic. In the past the principal critics of pornography have come from conservative elements of society, such as religious fundamentalists. Today, however, the fundamentalists have found new allies with some liberals on this issue. Feminists see pornography as demeaning to women, and some feminists have tried to prevent works of this sort from being displayed or sold.

Racism, too, has provoked sensitive issues of drawing limits on freedom of speech. In the 1970s the right of American Nazis to march in a peaceful demonstration in Skokie, Illinois, was upheld by the Supreme Court. To many who experienced or remembered the atrocities committed by Nazi Germany against Jews, the granting of such a right to American Nazis was beyond comprehension.

More recently, university campuses in the United States have experienced an increase in racism, including the making of derogatory racial remarks to students of African American and other ethnic heritages. Some university administrations and faculty governing units adopted regulations forbidding offensive and bigoted remarks about race, religion, or gender.

Whether such limitations are proper on civil liberties grounds is a subject of great contention. Even the American Civil Liberties Union (ACLU), which often defends unpopular causes in the name of free speech, is divided on the issue of limiting bigoted speech. Although the national ACLU opposes such restrictions, some individual state chapters approve.

In the debate below, writer Nat Hentoff argues that free speech includes the right to make racist statements. He provides examples of campus administrations that have acted to suppress speech thought to be racist or sexist. He quotes Justice Oliver Wendell Holmes that the highest principle of the Constitution is "the principle of free thought—not free only for those who agree with us, but freedom for the thought we hate."

Attorney Bruce Fein takes an opposing viewpoint. In his opinion, the paramount purpose of speech in a civilized society is to trigger contemplation, reason, and tolerance for competing ideas as the moving force for private and political action. But racially or religiously bigoted speech seeks to arouse unthinking hatred, violence, and intolerance. Society, consequently, has a right to punish such speech. Other Western countries prohibit racially or religiously derogatory speech without undermining democracy, and the United States should act similarly, Fein argues.

## ☑ *YES*

*Does Freedom of Speech Include the Right to Make Racist Statements?*

### NAT HENTOFF

### *Free Speech on the Campus*

A flier distributed at the University of Michigan some months ago proclaimed that blacks "don't belong in classrooms, they belong hanging from trees."

At other campuses around the country, manifestations of racism are becoming commonplace. At Yale, a swastika and the words WHITE POWER! were painted on the building housing the University's Afro-American Cultural Center. At Temple University, a White Students Union has been formed with some 130 members.

Swastikas are not directed only at black students. The Nazi symbol has been spray-painted on the Jewish Student Union at Memphis State University. And on a number of campuses, women have been singled out as targets of wounding and sometimes frightening speech. At the law school of the State University of New York at Buffalo, several women students have received anonymous letters characterized by one professor as venomously sexist.

These and many more such signs of the resurgence of bigotry and know-nothingism throughout the society—as well as on campus—have to do solely with speech, including symbolic speech. There have also been physical assaults on black students and on black, white, and Asian women students, but the way to deal with physical attacks is clear: Call the police and file a criminal complaint. What is to be done, however, about speech alone—however disgusting, inflammatory, and rawly divisive that speech may be?

At more and more colleges, administrators—with the enthusiastic support of black students, women students, and liberal students—have been answering that question by preventing or punishing speech. In public universities, this is a clear violation of the First Amendment. In private colleges and universities, suppression of speech mocks the secular religion of academic freedom and free inquiry.

The Student Press Law Center in Washington, D.C.—a vital source of legal support for student editors around the country—reports, for example, that at the University of Kansas, the student host and producer of a radio news program was forbidden by school officials from interviewing a leader of the Ku Klux Klan. So much for free inquiry on that campus.

In Madison, Wisconsin, the *Capital Times* ran a story in January about Chancellor Sheila Kaplan of the University of Wisconsin branch at Parkside, who ordered her campus to be scoured of "some anonymously placed white supremacist hate literature." Sounding like the legendary Mayor Frank ("I am the law") Hague of Jersey City, who booted "bad speech" out of town, Chancellor Kaplan said, "This institution is not a lamppost standing on the street corner. It doesn't belong to everyone."

Who decides what speech can be heard or read by everyone? Why, the Chancellor, of course. That's what George III used to say, too.

University of Wisconsin political science professor Carol Tebben thinks otherwise. She believes university administrators "are getting confused when they are acting as censors and trying to protect students from bad ideas. I don't think students need to be protected from bad ideas. I think they can determine for themselves what ideas are bad."

After all, if students are to be "protected" from bad ideas, how are they going to learn to identify and cope with them? Sending such ideas underground simply makes them stronger and more dangerous.

Professor Tebben's conviction that free speech means just that has become a decidedly minority view on many campuses. At the University of Buffalo Law

School, the faculty unanimously adopted a "Statement Regarding Intellectual Freedom, Tolerance, and Political Harassment." Its title implies support of intellectual freedom, but the statement warned students that once they enter "this legal community," their right to free speech must become tempered "by the responsibility to promote equality and justice."

Accordingly, swift condemnation will befall anyone who engages in "remarks directed at another's race, sex, religion, national origin, age, or sex preference." Also forbidden are "other remarks based on prejudice and group stereotype."

This ukase is so broad that enforcement has to be alarmingly subjective. Yet the University of Buffalo Law School provides no due-process procedures for a student booked for making any of these prohibited remarks. Conceivably, a student caught playing a Lenny Bruce, Richard Pryor, or Sam Kinison album in his room could be tried for aggravated insensitivity by association.

When I looked into this wholesale cleansing of bad speech at Buffalo, I found it had encountered scant opposition. One protester was David Gerald Jay, a graduate of the law school and cooperating attorney for the New York Civil Liberties Union. Said the appalled graduate: "Content-based prohibitions constitute prior restraint and should not be tolerated."

You would think that the law professors and administration at this public university might have known that. But hardly any professors dissented, and among the students only members of the conservative Federalist Society spoke up for free speech. The fifty-strong chapter of the National Lawyers Guild was on the other side. After all, it was more important to go on record as vigorously opposing racism and sexism than to expose oneself to charges of insensitivity to these malignancies.

The pressures to have the "right" attitude—as proved by having the "right" language in and out of class—can be stifling. A student who opposes affirmative action, for instance, can be branded a racist.

At the University of California at Los Angeles, the student newspaper ran an editorial cartoon satirizing affirmative action. (A student stops a rooster on campus and asks how the rooster got into UCLA. "Affirmative action," is the answer.) After outraged complaints from various minority groups, the editor was suspended for violating a publications policy against running "articles that perpetuate derogatory or cultural stereotypes." The art director was also suspended.

When the opinion editor of the student newspaper at California State University at Northridge wrote an article asserting that the sanctions against the editor and art director at UCLA amounted to censorship, he was suspended too.

At New York University Law School, a student was so disturbed by the pall of orthodoxy at that prestigious institution that he wrote to the school newspaper even though, as he said, he expected his letter to make him a pariah among his fellow students.

Barry Endick described the atmosphere at NYU created by "a host of watchdog committees and a generally hostile classroom reception regarding any student comment right of center." This "can be arguably viewed as symptomatic of a prevailing spirit of academic and social intolerance of . . . any idea which is not 'politically correct.' "

He went on to say something that might well be posted on campus bulletin boards around the country, though it would probably be torn down at many of them: "We ought to examine why students, so anxious to wield the Fourteenth Amendment, give short shrift to the First. Yes, Virginia, there are racist assholes. And you know what, the Constitution protects them, too."

Not when they engage in violence or vandalism. But when they speak or write, racist assholes fall right into this Oliver Wendell Holmes definition—highly unpopular among bigots, liberals, radicals, feminists, sexists, and college administrators: "If there is any principle of the Constitution that more imperatively calls for attachment than any other, it is the principle of free thought—not free only for those who agree with us, but freedom for the thought we hate."

The language sounds like a pietistic Sunday sermon, but if it ever falls wholly into disuse, neither this publication nor any other journal of opinion—Right or Left—will survive.

Sometimes, college presidents and administrators sound as if they fully understand what Holmes was saying. Last year, for example, when the *Daily Pennsylvanian*—speaking for many at the University of Pennsylvania—urged that a speaking invitation to Louis Farrakhan be withdrawn, University President Sheldon Hackney disagreed.

"Open expression," said Hackney, "is the fundamental principle of a university." Yet consider what the same Sheldon Hackney did to the free-speech rights of a teacher at his own university. If any story distills the essence of the current decline of free speech on college campuses, it is the Ballad of Murray Dolfman.

For twenty-two years, Dolfman, a practicing lawyer in Philadelphia, had been a part-time lecturer in the Legal Studies Department of the University of Pennsylvania's Wharton School. For twenty-two years, no complaint had ever been made against him; indeed, his student course-evaluations had been outstanding. Each year students competed to get into his class.

On a November afternoon in 1984, Dolfman was lecturing about personal-service contracts. His style somewhat resembles that of Professor Charles Kingsfield in *The Paper Chase*. Dolfman insists that students he calls on be prepared—or suffer the consequences. He treats all students this way—regardless of race, creed, or sex.

This day, Dolfman was pointing out that no one can be forced to work against his or her will—even if a contract has been signed. A court may prevent the resister from working for someone else so long as the contract is in effect but, Dolfman said, there can "be nothing that smacks of involuntary servitude."

Where does this concept come from? Dolfman looked around the room. Finally, a cautious hand was raised: "The Constitution?"

"Where in the Constitution?" No hands. "The Thirteenth Amendment," said the teacher. So, what does *it* say? The students were looking everywhere but at Dolfman.

"We will lose our liberties," Dolfman often told his classes, "if we don't know what they are."

On this occasion, he told them that he and other Jews, as ex-slaves, spoke at Passover of the time when they were slaves under the Pharaohs so that they would remember every year what it was like not to be free.

"We have ex-slaves here," Dolfman continued, "who should know about the Thirteenth Amendment." He asked black students in the class if they could tell him what was in that amendment.

"I wanted them to really think about it," Dolfman told me recently, "and know its history. You're better equipped to fight racism if you know all about those post–Civil War amendments and civil-rights laws."

The Thirteenth Amendment provides that "neither slavery nor involuntary servitude . . . shall exist within the United States."

The black students in his class did not know what was in that amendment, and Dolfman had them read it aloud. Later, they complained to university officials that they had been hurt and humiliated by having been referred to as ex-slaves. Moreover, they said, they had no reason to be grateful for a constitutional amendment which gave them rights which should never have been denied them—and gave them precious little else. They had not made these points in class, although Dolfman—unlike Professor Kingsfield—encourages rebuttal.

Informed of the complaint, Dolfman told the black students he had intended no offense, and he apologized if they had been offended.

That would not do—either for the black students or for the administration. Furthermore, there were mounting black-Jewish tensions on campus, and someone had to be sacrificed. Who better than a part-time Jewish teacher with no contract and no union? He was sentenced by—George Orwell would have loved this—the Committee on Academic Freedom and Responsibility.

On his way to the stocks, Dolfman told President Sheldon Hackney that if a part-time instructor "can be punished on this kind of charge, a tenured professor can eventually be booted out, then a dean, and then a president."

Hackney was unmoved. Dolfman was banished from the campus for what came to be a year. But first he was forced to make a public apology to the entire university and then he was compelled to attend a "sensitivity and racial awareness" session. Sort of like a Vietnamese reeducation camp.

A few conservative professors objected to the stigmatization of Murray Dolfman. I know of no student dissent. Indeed, those students most concerned with making the campus more "sensitive" to diversity exulted in Dolfman's humiliation. So did most liberals on the faculty.

If my children were still of college age and wanted to attend the University of Pennsylvania, I would tell them this story. But where else could I encourage them to go?

## Does Freedom of Speech Include the Right to Make Racist Statements?

### BRUCE FEIN

### *Shunning Racial, Religious Bigotry*

Should speech intended to ignite racial or religious animosity be prohibited?

Let the answer speak from the weeping cemeteries around the world overflowing with victims of racial and religious prejudice. The timeline of history records Auschwitz, the Atlanta race riots, Mahatma Ghandi's assassination, Soweto, Tomas de Torquemada and Armenian massacres as solemn dirges occasioned by racial or religious bigots who merchandized their lethal vilifications in goose step with Adolf Hitler's *Mein Kampf.*

Those who would defend verbal frenzy so productive of evil surely must shoulder a heavy burden. It would seem a mocking gesture to the targets of Kristallnacht to pronounce with eloquence à la Brutus that it was not that Jews were loved less but that the right of Hitler to thunder anti-Semitic malignities was loved more!

If I may borrow without plagiarism from Jeanne Manon Roland at the guillotine during the French Revolution: O Free Speech! O Free Speech! What crimes are committed in thy name!

What is the paramount purpose of speech in a civilized society? It is to trigger contemplation, reason and tolerance for competing ideas as the moving force for private and political action. As Justice Louis Brandeis recognized in *Whitney* vs. *California,* a free and liberal democracy will die unless the deliberative forces of man prevail over the arbitrary. A nation riddled with bigotry and prejudice is a nation unfit for self-government, a political axiom verified by the Third Reich.

What is the purpose of racially or religiously bigoted speech? It is to arouse unthinking hatred, violence and intolerance in the audience. It is intended to appeal to human nature's instinct to find scapegoats for personal unhappiness, dissatisfaction or misfortune.

The fraudulent *Protocols of the Elders of Zion* and blood libel against Jews are not intended to elicit contemplation in the listeners about the Jewish religion or the aspiration of Zionists. When Jim Keegstia, a Canadian high-school teacher, instructed his students that Jews are evil, that the Holocaust was a hoax, that a camarilla of Jewish magnates was plotting to control the world, and that Jews had manipulated the course of history and had designs on Christianity's destruction, his purpose was not reasoned response from his pupils.

When white racist Joseph Beauharnais of the White Circle League vituperated in Chicago, Ill., that "[i]f persuasion and the need to prevent the white race from becoming mongrelized by the Negro will not unite us, then the aggressions . . . rapes, robberies, knives, guns and marijuana of the Negro surely will," he was seeking to close the minds of his audience with vicelike prejudice, not open them to the fresh air of reason.

In sum, the invectives of the racial or religious bigot are no more free speech than is the vulgar pornographic undulations of Annie Sprinkle a cousin of the Bolshoi Ballet. If the law supposes otherwise, as Mr. Bumble observed, "the law is a ass, a idiot." If racially or religiously bigoted speech were innocuous, then it might be ignored by governments. But it is not. The ugliest marks in the history of the United States have stemmed from the incitements to racial prejudice practiced by Theodore Bilbo, Orville Faubus, the Ku Klux Klan, and the producers of *The Birth of a Nation*. Diatribes of these types create an explosive social nitroglycerin waiting for an epithet or racial incident to spark violence.

Should free speech be a suicide pact? Should a country play Russian roulette with the innocent targets of racially or religiously prejudiced speech intended by the speaker to exploit the human temptation to let hatred trump rumination? Should the law protect gratification of verbal spite when spite fences are prohibited? Any sensible legal doctrine must be informed by human nature. It cannot be repealed by edict or decree. And all of human history shows that individuals must be consistently trained, cajoled and encouraged in the discipline of sober, reflective and undoctrinaire living to safeguard against the degeneration of democracy into an instrument of racial or religious oppression.

Enlightened self-government demands citizens steeled to resist easy gratification of prejudice and with humble and questioning minds that guide action in the ballot box or otherwise.

But what does law teach when it places on a par racial or religious calumnies and the Lincoln-Douglas debates? It teaches that appeals to reason are no more to be preferred than are appeals to fanaticism, that the arts of thinking and of group slander are in the eyes of the community equally commendable. In that instruction lies the end of free speech for all.

It is said that proving a malignant intent of the author of racially or religiously bigoted speech is unworkable. But proof of intent is a legal commonplace; it is an element of most crimes, libel suits, litigation addressing claims of racial or religious discrimination and free-speech challenges to removal of books from public-school libraries.

Even a dog knows the difference between a kick and an unwitting bump from his master!

It is said that if racially or religiously bigoted speech is squelched, there will be no stopping point to prevention of genuine free speech. Nonsense! The progress of civilization has been the progress of making refinements and differentiations in the law. Prohibitions on racially or religiously derogatory speech have existed in the United States, Canada, Great Britain, West Germany and elsewhere without undermining democracy, political dissent or debate. As

Justice Oliver Wendell Holmes observed, all law depends on matters of degrees "as soon as it is civilized."

It is said that citizens will lose their ability to understand and confront the evils of racial or religiously bigoted speech absent recurring exposures. But those evils can be taught by debating the wisdom and need to prohibit such verbal violence.

If that is insufficient tutelage, visits to graves from Beirut to Bergen-Belsen to Belfast ought to make up the shortfall.

Prohibiting racially and religiously bigoted speech is praiseworthy because it seeks to elevate, not to degrade, because it draws from human experience, not from woolly dogmas or academic slogans, because it salutes reason as the backbone of freedom and tolerance.

Those who doubt the vicious cycle of hatred derived from verbal assaults against a race or religion should ponder the words of Shylock in *The Merchant of Venice:* "If a Jew wrong a Christian, what is his humility? Revenge. If a Christian wrong a Jew, what should his sufferance be by Christian example? Why, revenge. The villainy you teach me, I will execute; and it will go hard but I will better the instruction."

## Questions for Discussion

1. What limitations can legitimately be placed on freedom of speech? What are the reasons for your answer?
2. What criteria would you use to judge remarks as racist or sexist?
3. What is the difference between racist acts and racist speech?
4. What is the proper role of speech in a free society?
5. What should university administrations and faculty do about racist speech? What are the reasons for your answer?
6. Who on a campus should decide whether speech is racist and should be punished?
7. Excluding racially offensive speech, what other kinds of speech should be restricted? Why?

## Suggested Readings

Cohen, Carl. "Free Speech and Political Extremism: How Nasty Are We Free to Be?" *Law and Philosophy,* 7, no. 3 (1988–1989), 263–279.

Dent, David J. "Campus Racism: Reassessing the Roots." *Playboy,* 36, no. 6 (June 1989), 74, 155–156.

Edelman, Peter. "Punishing Perpetrators of Racist Speech." *Legal Times*, 11, no. 49 (May 15, 1989), 20–21.

Ellis, Trey. "Campus Racism: Disillusioned in the Promised Land." *Playboy*, 36, no. 6 (June 1989), 74–75, 84, 157–161.

Farrell, Walter C., Jr., and Cloyzelle K. Jones. "Recent Racial Incidents in Higher Education: A Preliminary Perspective." *Urban Review*, 20, no. 3 (Spring 1988), 211–226.

Greenawalt, Kent. "Free Speech Justifications." *Columbia Law Review*, 89, no. 1 (January 1989), 119–155.

Lawrence, Charles R., III. "The Debates over Placing Limits on Racist Speech Must Not Ignore the Damage It Does Its Victims." *Chronicle of Higher Education*, 36, no. 8 (October 25, 1989), B1–B3.

Magner, Denise K. "Blacks and Whites on the Campuses: Behind Ugly Racist Incidents, Student Isolation and Insensitivity." *Chronicle of Higher Education*, 35, no. 33 (April 26, 1989), A1, A28–A31.

Metz, Holly. "Bad Apples, Evil Deeds: How Law Students Deface Free Speech." *Student Lawyer*, 18, no. 6 (February 1990), 32–38.

Steele, Shelby. "The Recoloring of Campus Life." *Harper's*, 278, no. 1665 (February 1989), 47–55.

Wiener, Jon. "Free Speech for Campus Bigots?" *Nation*, 250, no. 8 (February 26, 1990), 272–276.

———. "Racial Hatred on Campus." *Nation*, 248, no. 8 (February 27, 1989), 260–262, 264.

# *Is the Civil Rights Agenda Beneficial to Blacks?*

The civil rights revolution of the 1950s and 1960s was first and foremost a political upheaval. Supreme Court decisions, decisions by lower courts, and federal, state, and local government legislation removed the formal barriers against voting and established penalties for discrimination in accommodations, housing, education, and employment.

For many African Americans the changes in the law provided opportunities previously denied. Many blacks were subsequently elected to government offices, appointed to high-level government executive positions, and admitted into corporate and educational institutions. But many black people did not benefit from the civil rights laws and court decisions. Those concentrated in urban ghettos found that unemployment remained high and crime endemic, schools were not succeeding in their task of educating, and slum conditions stifled initiative. A black underclass emerged, with large numbers unemployed and dependent on government support for daily maintenance. Drug abuse became a major problem, and with drug abuse came more criminal activity. To be sure, problems of unemployment, dependency, and drug abuse affected white people and other minorities, too, but the problems became particularly severe for African Americans in ghetto areas.

Civil rights groups focused on problems of poverty and the underclass. In a speech before the National Urban League, a leading civil rights organization, John E. Jacob sets forth an agenda for the African-American community that is generally associated with most civil rights organizations. He calls for a comprehensive national policy designed to bring racial parity to the United States, a shifting of government resources to invest in people, and new government initiatives to deal with the issues of poverty, jobs, health, and education. He recommends affirmative action—efforts by government and private groups to recruit and promote women and members of racial or ethnic groups that had previously experienced discrimination in employment, education, and professional advancement. He also calls upon the community to help through private efforts.

J. A. Parker, editor of *Lincoln Review*, argues that the civil rights movement is irrelevant to the problems of blacks. He contends:

1. The civil rights movement has won its major battle against segregation and racial discrimination.
2. If black Americans remain, as a group, behind economically and educationally, it may not be because of bigotry in the larger U.S.

society but because the breakdown of the black family, the influence of drugs and teenage pregnancy, and the erosion of the work ethic have kept young black men and women from taking advantage of opportunities.

3. Other groups discriminated against, such as Jews, Japanese, and Chinese, have been able to surmount discrimination, and blacks should be able to make similar achievements.

4. The majority of black people have made considerable progress in income and employment.

5. Government welfare policies have made blacks dependent, and while more and more blacks are rejecting this path to permanent dependency, the civil rights establishment continues to favor such programs.

## ☑ YES

### Is the Civil Rights Agenda Beneficial to Blacks?

### JOHN E. JACOB

### Major Issues Facing African Americans: Drugs and Supreme Court Decisions

Every four years, we of the National Urban League bring our annual conference to Washington . . . to the capital of our nation . . . to the seat of power in America. We come to press on a new Administration the urgency of our mission and the justice of our cause.

The last time we met here, the new Administration was President Reagan's second—an Administration that tried to gut every important social program . . . an Administration that featured Ed Meese at the Justice Department and Brad Reynolds as the Assistant Attorney General for Civil Rights.

So perhaps you have noticed this year what I have noticed—Washington seems a kinder, gentler place.

We have disagreed with the new Bush Administration on a number of important policy issues. But we welcome the fresh winds of openness it has brought to our government.

We welcome the significant appointments it has made of African Americans.

We welcome the presence in the Cabinet of Department Secretaries who really care about African American progress . . . who share many of our concerns . . . and who don't spend their energy looking for ways to throw up new barriers on top of the mountain of old ones.

Some of them will join us this week, along with key Congressional leaders. And on Tuesday, President Bush will address our Conference.

We are hopeful that the President and our other distinguished speakers will take the opportunity afforded by this—to the nation's largest and most prestigious race relations forum—to present bold new initiatives that help America's poor people and put us back on the path of racial progress.

Our relations with this Administration will be based on honesty and candor. We will differ with it at times, but we will also be good partners with it whenever and wherever we can.

For the Iron Curtain of Reaganism has been lifted and today's leaders understand that they must lead all of the people of our nation, and not exclude minority Americans.

But while the atmosphere has greatly improved, honesty compels me to say that we expect more from this new Administration.

We look to this Administration to begin framing a comprehensive national policy designed to bring racial parity to America by the year 2000.

We look to this new Administration to reassess America's priorities and shift resources to invest in our people.

And we look to this new Administration for new initiatives to deal with the crucial issues of poverty, jobs, health and education.

I understand the problems this Administration faces—the legacy of the Reagan deficits . . . the clamor of contending national and international concerns . . . and the tensions within the governing party between those who want to do the right thing and those who do not.

But those are political problems that leaders always face—it comes with the territory.

Our expectations are high because this Administration encourages high expectations. When it tells people who have been brutalized by years of hostility that it seeks a kinder, gentler nation . . . we believe its words and demand actions to back up those words.

Our concern is with the problems of people in America today who are poor, who don't have enough to eat, who can't get jobs, who are discriminated against by an indifferent majority and preyed upon by a callous minority.

Our concern is with winning racial parity so that being black in America no longer means you're twice as likely to be a dropout and to be out of work.

. . . no longer means you're twice as likely to be homeless or without health insurance

. . . no longer means you're three times as likely to be poor

. . . no longer means that black infants are twice as likely to die in their first year and black adults live six fewer years than whites.

Some people get scared when they hear talk of parity. They say you can't guarantee outcomes.

You can't. But you *can* guarantee that everybody has an equal opportunity . . . you *can* remove race and class barriers to those opportunities . . . and you *can* come out in a place where roughly the same proportion of whites and blacks succeed and the same proportion fail.

Parity is the opposite of the gross inequality we have today, when every statistic that matters shows that African Americans lag far behind the white majority.

Even poverty isn't equal. The black poor have less income than the white poor. Black single women with children have lower incomes than white single women with children.

All across the board—in every category—African Americans are far from achieving the rough parity which we seek and for which this nation stands.

"All Men Are Created Equal," says our Declaration of Independence. But the slaveholders who passed the Constitution two centuries ago defined black people as three-fifths of other people.

And to this day, African American family income is three-fifths of white family income.

That Constitution was amended and African Americans won full legal rights that took a century of struggle to implement. And even today, those rights are seriously compromised and diluted in the context of an America that has yet to overcome its heritage of race.

We have to ask about America what Justice Blackmun asked about his colleagues on the Supreme Court—and I quote: "One wonders whether the majority still believes that race discrimination—or, more accurately, race discrimination against non-whites—is a problem in this society or even remembers that it ever was."

America suffers from racial amnesia.

It forgets that it was built on slavery.

It forgets that slavery was followed by a century of segregation and oppression.

It forgets that it was only 25 years ago that the Civil Rights Act was passed.

It forgets that it has the most unequal society in the western industrialized world and that it's become more unequal over the past decade.

We've got to help America to remember.

We've got to help America remember the time when a national consensus formed behind greater equality and racial justice.

We've got to help America remember that the vast white middle class was created by federal education, housing and job programs and that it can create a new black middle class the same way.

We've got to help America remember that race is still a factor in people's lives and that racial justice is as much a moral issue today as it was 25 years ago.

Instead of the races moving forward together, we have been forced onto the defensive . . . forced to re-educate Americans to lessons learned and forgotten . . . forced to hold on to the slim gains we've won.

The best example of that is on the legal front—in the struggle to keep Reagan's Supreme Court from doing to our legal and constitutional rights what Reagan's Administration did to our social and economic ones.

This Supreme Court has been highjacked by the Reaganites. The Court we once looked to as the protector of minority rights has itself become a threat to our rights.

Just this past term: it ruled against setasides to remedy past discrimination against black business

—said white males could upset court ordered affirmative action programs but that minorities and women can't challenge standing seniority systems

—limited the use of statistics in proving patterns of discrimination

—and made it easier to defend against discrimination charges by putting greater burdens of proof on the victims.

As if that wasn't enough, the Court said it's O.K. to execute retarded people and minors, and that it's O.K. for states to limit poor women's rights to abortion while allowing affluent women to have abortions.

Whatever your personal attitude toward abortion, current law as defined by *Roe* v. *Wade* strikes a balance between a woman's right to control her own body and the state's interest in preserving life.

But when you refuse to let public hospitals do otherwise legal procedures, you're denying to the poor what the affluent take for granted. Two sets of laws . . . two sets of medicine . . . one set for the poor; one for the wealthy.

And when the Court goes on the warpath against reasonable affirmative action decrees that remedy past discrimination, it says that African Americans, women and minorities won't be allowed to play catchup. They'll be stuck with the effects of past discrimination.

The Court is playing dice with the lives of America's minorities, and it's loading the dice against them.

We expected that from Rehnquist and the Reaganites. But the irony is that the swing vote on this Court—the vote that tips the balance to the reactionary majority—is the vote of Justice O'Connor.

Her role is ironic. She graduated from one of the nation's top law schools but leading law firms wouldn't even interview her because they didn't hire women.

And it's ironic, because she is on the bench today—not simply because of her brilliance or her outstanding achievement—but because President Reagan wanted a woman on the Supreme Court for political reasons.

So the victim of discrimination today votes against other victims of discrimination. The beneficiary of affirmative action today votes against affirmative action for others.

We must condemn this court for its callous misreading of the law and for betraying its role as protector of minority rights.

As we do so, we must also recognize and honor the fearless four justices who have been firm in their support for affirmative action, for privacy rights, for preservation of minority rights.

Their personal beliefs range from liberal to conservative. But they share a belief in the Constitution as the shield protecting our freedoms. They light the lamp of fairness and justice at a time when their colleagues are switching off the lights of hope.

Let me call their names because we of the National Urban League honor them: Justice Harry Blackmun . . . Justice William Brennan . . . Justice Thurgood Marshall . . . Justice John Paul Stevens.

Remember those names. Remember those names and tell your children about them. Note well that these brave men stood up for us and stood by us in a time of trouble.

Tonight, I call on the President and the Congress to stand by them . . . to carefully review the Court's recent anti–civil rights decisions and to frame legislation that will overrule those decisions.

Congress did it before—when it passed the Civil Rights Restoration Act to correct the Court's misreading of the law in the *Grove City* case.

It should do it again to roll back the shameful assault on affirmative action and fairness.

Congress has to act for two reasons.

First, because it's right for America.

Second, because the African American community will be watching very carefully to see if its representatives have enough respect for us to act on our concerns.

Today's battleground is the polling place and the halls of Congress.

The black vote is going to decide whether Congress acts and how it will act.

We've got to march to the ballot box and reward our friends and punish those who choose to be our enemies on civil rights.

We've got to demonstrate in the offices of Congressmen that we have the power and the political clout to have our needs considered.

It was through the political process that the Bork nomination was beaten and the *Grove City* case reversed.

It will be through the political process that these Supreme Court decisions will be overturned—through intensive legislative advocacy . . . working the halls of Congress . . . mobilizing local political clout . . . pressuring our Congressional representatives.

And the President and the Congress have to go beyond patching holes drilled by the Reagan Court. They've got to address long delayed economic and political issues that impact so heavily on the minority poor.

We need to improve our schools, and that's going to take federal investments in the shools that serve poor children.

We need to ensure equal access to health care, and that's going to take federal action to bring the 37 million Americans without any health insurance into a system of quality health care for all.

We need to house the homeless and provide affordable housing for moderate income families priced out of today's housing market. And that's going to take federal action to get back into the business of building affordable housing and encouraging the private sector to do it too.

We need to address what business is coming to understand as the most critical economic issue for the future—educating and training a workforce that's competitive with the best in the world.

The economy has changed and America needs a workforce that can read safety instructions . . . operate computerized factories . . . interact and communicate with suppliers and customers.

Tomorrow's workforce is in school today. It's going to need technical and communications skills our kids are just not getting now.

A third of tomorrow's workforce will be minority, and half of those children are growing up poor. A fourth drop out. Most won't have the skills to survive in an advanced economy.

But America's future depends on educating and training those children.

That's the real issue behind social programs that give kids a head start . . . that feed poor children . . . that provide job training for young workers.

When government nickel-and-dimes those programs it subverts the nation's economic future.

Without investment in bringing minority people into the mainstream, America won't have a competitive workforce . . . it won't have the productivity to raise everybody's living standards . . . it won't have enough people on the payrolls to support the expanding population of older people on Social Security.

If anything is certain in this uncertain world, it is that unless we change course and start developing our human resources, America is going to become an economic colony of Japan and Europe.

Congress and the Administration will have to stop the budget games that cut a few dollars out of this program and add it to that one.

They need to do whatever is necessary to put the job, education, health and housing needs of our people first.

I can't believe that a trillion dollar budget can't accommodate the programs America needs.

I can't believe there's no money for housing—not when Secretary Jack Kemp tells us that the bill for HUD's past mismanagement will be over $2 billion, and when we give people tax writeoffs for vacation home mortgages.

I can't believe there's no money to train everyone without skills—not when the General Accounting Office says the Pentagon has $30 billion in excess unusable spare parts all over the world. And that's just spare parts—we're not even talking about billion dollar bombers and $100 billion Star Wars fantasies.

And I can't believe that we can't assure poor women and their infants access to food and health care—not when Congress found over $100 billion to bail out the savings and loan industry.

Somehow the money is always there and can always be found—unless it's for poor people or for programs to get poor people into the mainstream.

We've got to be about the business of helping people to understand that the issue today is not inadequate resources but inadequate will and inadequate priorities.

Those priorities can change now because there's a little secret that's being kept in this town, a secret people are just beginning to catch on to.

And that secret is: the Cold War is over.

Well over a third of the federal budget is for the military and for interest on debt incurred by the military. And a lot of that money is going to be freed up when it finally sinks in that we've got to plan for peace and not war.

Gorbachev is running around the world telling people he's cutting back on Soviet military spending. He's switching their strategy to defensive formations instead of offense. He's frantically trying to reach agreements to cut back nuclear weapons and conventional armed forces. And he's changing his country to become more democratic and less threatening to the rest of us.

He's not doing that because he's a nice man. He's doing it because their economy is on the ropes . . . because a real war would destroy the planet . . . and because the Cold War is bankrupting both of us.

It's sensible to keep your guard up and be careful—but it's just plain stupid not to take advantage of this opportunity to close down the Cold War that's draining our economy.

We'll be able to safely put the Pentagon on a diet and beef up the civilian economy through programs that have everybody working and consuming American goods.

The grounds of world leadership and world competition are shifting. Tomorrow's world leader won't be the country with the most bombs, but the country with the most advanced workers and the most stable social system.

If Congress and the Administration use our strengths and resources wisely that world leader will be America.

The National Urban League is working to help make that happen. We are working to expand opportunities for minorities and to develop America's untapped human resources.

We were the first national organization to focus on the educational needs of minority children. We were the ones who said that the school reform movement wasn't even talking about the forgotten children of the poor . . . wasn't concerned with the aspirations of African American families.

It was the National Urban League that helped focus the spotlight on the schools our kids go to.

And it was the National Urban League—with few resources and an overburdened staff, but with a willing army of volunteers—that launched an Education Initiative to help prepare our children to succeed in this changing world.

Over 100,000 children and their parents have taken part in some 300 Education Initiative programs conducted in our local Urban Leagues.

They're being tutored in science and math . . . counseled on college admissions . . . enrolled in dropout prevention programs . . . given the support they need to excel in school.

One example—in Lansing, Michigan the black dropout rate is now lower than the white rate, thanks in large part to our efforts.

In some cities, the Urban League was the catalyst for systemic change in the school system.

In others, we worked closely with educators to involve parents in their kids' education.

In still others, we mobilized coalitions that are making changes in the way the schools serve our children.

The success of the Education Initiative shows what our nationwide network of affiliates and volunteers can do.

The Education Initiative is going to have even more of an impact as we move up the learning curve. We have a panel of distinguished social scientists studying and assessing our efforts.

We'll use their study to report to the nation, and then to go forward with improved programs that reach more of our kids and have even more of an impact on their schools.

Education is just one piece of the workforce puzzle. There's more to developing a trained workforce.

Today, I want to announce a new National Urban League effort—our National Workforce Development Program.

The biggest need in the African American community is jobs. The biggest need in the business community is a trained workforce.

Many of our constituents can't get jobs without intensive social services and training. And many of our business constituents can't get the workforce they need without the services of community-based organizations that counsel, recruit and train people.

The National Urban League's Workforce Development Program will serve both the disadvantaged worker and the employer by providing the services each needs.

People have to be prepared for the world of work . . . helped in the transition from school or the home to the workplace . . . equipped with training and skills.

America's employers need help in locating qualified people, and in providing the counseling and training to make people qualifiable.

And thanks to the computerization of the entire Urban League movement through the grant of computers by Digital Equipment Corporation, we will develop a nationwide skills bank that locates qualified minority individuals for any job, anywhere.

Through the Skills Bank and other elements of the Workforce Development Program, the Urban League movement will be better able to serve all employers—large or small—to help them secure a diverse workforce.

We will be able to help corporate America include minorities in all of its operations—from the factory floor to the executive suites.

And frankly, corporate America needs all the help it can get. The full import of the demographic revolution in the workforce hasn't really sunk in. Too many companies think it just means they'll have to recruit more women and make workplace changes to accommodate working mothers.

That should be instructive to the African American community for I remember learning at my old segregated school down in Houston, Texas, that Lincoln once said if he could save the Union without freeing the slaves, he would have done it.

So too, if America can solve its economic and workforce problems without blacks, it will do it.

But I want to tell you, America, you can't. We're here. We're here to stay.

Regardless of the Supreme Court, business will have to affirmatively recruit and train African American people, hire us for jobs, promote us to better jobs, and ultimately put us in the Chairman's seat of major corporations.

The National Urban League will help that process along through our new Workforce Development Program.

And corporate America will be a willing partner. I want to announce today that we have formed an NUL Workforce Development Program Council to advise and assist our program.

Coca-Cola, Continental Corporation, Digital Equipment, Honda North America, IBM, Merrill Lynch and Ryder System have joined the Council, and others will follow. These corporations have opted for a major partnership role with us in making America's workforce inclusive and our nation more competitive.

I want to announce another nationwide initiative by the National Urban League.

You know we have enough on our plate without taking on new priorities. You know we don't have the resources or the staff to deal with all the problems of our communities.

But you also know the Urban League goes the extra mile when it has to. You know that we leverage our resources by serving as a catalyst and by mobilizing community volunteers to help do what has to be done.

And we have to do something very important now—something that is absolutely crucial to the survival of our communities.

We have to mount a war against drugs.

That doesn't mean guarding the borders to stop the drug trade—although we will pressure our lawmakers to make that a major concern and not just a lot of rhetoric.

And it doesn't mean a "Just Say No" campaign, although we will teach our children to say no.

And it doesn't mean telling the nation that it won't stop drugs until it deals with the root causes of drug abuse and anti-social behavior. Even though it's true—we *can't wait* for that to happen.

Drugs are taking over our communities. They are destroying families and values. They are putting our neighborhoods under siege.

Our communities are held hostage by crack dealers. Gang wars are killing innocent people. Little children are out hustling for the pushers. Families are eating on their kitchen floors so bullets won't kill them at the table near the window. People can't leave their homes for fear of the drug gangs.

Drugs are everywhere. They're here in Washington, where some streets are open-air drug markets. They're in New York, where one out of five newborn infants last year was born addicted.

Think about that—one out of five newborns beginning life underweight, underdeveloped, and drug-infected.

And drugs are even in little Ozzie-and-Harriet middle class suburban and rural towns, where the crack invasion brings crime and drug dependency.

It's not a black problem. It's not a white problem. Drugs are a national problem, and if the nation isn't willing to wage war against it, we'll have to ourselves.

We've got to realize we're at war with the drug dealers—a war for control of our communities.

The pusher may drive a big car and have gold jewelry and kids may think he's cool—but he's a bigger threat to the African American community than this Supreme Court can ever be.

Drugs kill more blacks than the Klan ever did. They're destroying more children and more families than poverty ever did.

We can't be successful in our Education Initiative if our children get hooked on drugs and on dealing before they can get an education. We can't be successful in our Workforce Development Program if people are too drugged out to learn skills and hold a job.

When we went to Capitol Hill last Thursday, our Urban League executives told their members of Congress we want to see real action to stop drugs from coming into the country.

We told them Congress has to provide resources for treatment centers so that anyone on drugs can get off them.

There's no question that our government can and must do more, but we also have to do what we—and *only we*—can do to make our neighborhoods drug-free zones.

We have to confront this issue head-on—without becoming sentimental or forgiving. There's too much at stake. We don't help a drug abuser by making excuses for him.

There are no excuses for taking drugs.

And there are no excuses for selling them—for terrorizing our neighborhoods—or for corrupting African American values.

We can deal with the subtleties and the philosophical issues raised by drugs *after* they're out of our communities.

Right now there's only one priority—to make our neighborhoods drug-free.

We have to mobilize our communities to work closely with law enforcement authorities to identify dealers and to gather the evidence to convict them.

We've got to tell users that their drugs are not wanted in the community and they should either get off them or get out.

We've got to bring people together to take action against drug dealers and not be intimidated by them.

The Urban League—together with the organizations and community groups—will do that.

We'll document the drug problem in our communities—serve as a catalyst to bring the community together to reclaim our neighborhoods from the dealers—pressure the authorities to go after the pushers.

We'll fight for tough laws and penalties for drug offenses and support alternative prison sites to remove offenders from our communities.

And we'll organize a nationwide "Blacks against Drugs" movement to bring people together in the war on drugs and to keep our kids from getting hooked on drugs.

The Urban League's war on drugs is part of the broad movement in the African American community to control our own destiny . . . to reaffirm traditional African American values . . . and to take responsibility for our own fate.

Just as we've become tired of the excuses the larger community makes for not doing the right thing, we have to become impatient with the excuses within our own community for not doing the right thing.

There's a scene in Spike Lee's new movie where two street people are talking and one says he can never get anywhere because he's black in this white society and the other fellow says: "I'm getting tired of that excuse."

So am I. So are you. So are the brothers and the sisters all over the country.

Racism is real and it's deadly—but we can't let our kids be trapped into using it as an excuse. It's another barrier to leap over, or go under or around or through—but not to be stopped by.

Martin Luther King, Jr., used to say that "the only way to get ahead is to run faster than the man in front of you," and that's what we've always done.

To be black in America never meant making excuses for failure but working harder for success.

To be black in America meant clinging to values that enable us to overcome hardships . . . to family life that knits us together . . . to going to church to pray to God . . . and going to school and to work to fulfill our earthly needs.

Being black in America never meant crime and drugs and hopelessness.

 ☑ N O

*Is the Civil Rights Agenda Beneficial to Blacks?*

## J. A. PARKER

### *The Growing Irrelevance of the Civil Rights Movement*

On August 27, 1988, a crowd in Washington, D.C., marched to the Lincoln Memorial, 25 years after the Rev. Martin Luther King, Jr. spoke there of his dream of racial brotherhood, and were exhorted to work for "deferred dreams"—easing poverty and expanding opportunity.

The crowd was much smaller than that of the original 1963 March on Washington and a commemorative march held in 1983, both of which drew more than 200,000 people. Organizers of the 1988 march predicted a crowd of at least 500,000. The U.S. Park Police estimated the actual turnout at 55,000.

This is a time of reflection and re-evaluation of the status of the civil rights movement. Some civil rights leaders are pessimistic. The Rev. Joseph Lowery, the president of the Southern Christian Leadership Conference, which Dr. King founded, declared that, "Everything has changed and nothing has changed." By this, Mr. Lowery seems to mean that Congress in the 1960s passed legislation that fundamentally altered the lives of blacks by insuring the right to vote and access to public accommodations and fair housing. But, as Dr. King foresaw, the fight against poverty and social inequality has, in Mr. Lowery's words, "a long, long way to go." He states: "We won the battle to sit on the customer's side of the lunch counter but we are still fighting to get on the cash register side of the counter."

Civil rights spokesmen agree that there has been a great deal of progress since 1963 but, as Roger Wilkins, who is now professor of history at George Mason University, states, the recent progress "masks a hideous reality" in which the poorest of the black poor "are far more isolated."

Sociologists and economists have shown that the black middle class has also grown significantly and that the percentage of blacks living in poverty has declined, but civil rights spokesmen point to the explosive problem of hopelessness in the poorest of the poor. "In fact," said Mr. Wilkins, "a real revolution has occurred for many blacks, but the poor have in effect dropped off the political screens."

Other black participants in the August march on Washington were more hopeful. Rep. John Lewis (D-Ga.), who was a 23-year-old confidant of Dr. King when a sniper's bullet killed the civil rights leader in 1968, declared: "I may not be typical, but I feel very hopeful and very optimistic about the future. There are going to be some setbacks but we're going to move to the beloved community; we are going to make it as a nation and as a people."

Why did so few marchers participate in the much publicized 25th anniversary event? Columnist William Raspberry, who is black, writes that, "For those of us who remember August 28, 1963, what was missing was not crowd size or cadence, but context . . . The unrecapturable context of the original march was its admixture of hope and uncertainty, joy and fear, audacity and doubt. The only uncertainties this past weekend had to do with such things as crowd size or whether the speeches would be any good . . . And if we expected this re-enactment to reignite the feelings we had 25 years ago, we were bound to be disappointed . . . The history, it turned out, was almost solely in the minds of those who had been there in 1963. The re-enactment, lacking the essential context, was unable to re-create enough of the original feeling to satisfy the thirst of those who came hoping for it."

One reason the 25th anniversary march appears to have been a failure—the key reason—is that the civil rights movement has won its major battle against segregation and racial discrimination. Laws are now in place forbidding such discrimination and guaranteeing all Americans equal opportunity—for jobs, education, housing, voting, etc. If black Americans remain, as a group, behind economically and educationally, it may not be because of any form of bigotry on the part of the larger American society, but because of the breakdown of the black family, the influence of drugs and teenage pregnancy, the erosion of the work ethic, which have kept young black men and women from taking advantage of opportunities.

One who expounds this view is economist Thomas Sowell, a senior fellow at the Hoover Institution of Stanford University. In his book, *Civil Rights: Rhetoric or Reality?*, Dr. Sowell declares that,

> In reality, the crusade for civil rights ended years ago. The scramble for special privilege, turf, and for image is what continues on today under that banner and that rhetoric. . . . Risks must be taken for genuine civil rights. But the kinds of internal struggles that have torn other multi-ethnic societies apart must be for something more than the continuing viability of organizations or the continued employment of their lawyers. The dangers of the present course are both insidious and acute. Among the insidious dangers are the undermining of minority . . . self-confidences by incessant recitation of the themes of pervasive discrimination, hypocritical standards and shadowy but malign enemies relentlessly opposing their progress. However successful this vision may be in creating a sense of dependence on "civil rights" . . . it also obscures the urgency of acquiring economically meaningful skills or developing the attitudes to apply them with the best results. Pride of achievement is also undermined by the civil rights vision that assumes credit for minority advancement. This makes minority achievement suspect in their own eyes and in the eyes of the larger society.

The civil rights movement once called for equality of "opportunity," but now seeks equality of condition. Thus, if 10 percent of the workforce in a community is black, 10 percent of the factory workers or college faculty should also be black. If it is not, racial discrimination is claimed. In fact, Dr. Sowell argues, disparities in employment reflect long-standing cultural influences, not discrimination: "Blacks and whites are not just people with different skin colors. Nor is a history of slavery the only difference between them . . . blacks and whites have different cultures that affect how they live."

Black leaders have not served their constituency, Sowell declares, but only themselves. Instead of expressing concern over the decline of the black family, the increasing illegitimacy rate, the rise of inner-city crime—they instead speak only of "discrimination." Such civil rights leaders, Sowell argues, are feathering their own nests at the expense of those in whose name they speak. He states: ". . . evidence is increasingly evaded by those who speak in the name of civil rights. Whether it is low test scores or high crime rates, the first order of business is to dismiss the evidence and discredit those who ring it. Even good news—successful minority schools or the rise of a black middle class—is denounced when it does not fit the preconceived vision. Unvarnished facts are today more likely to arouse suspicion and hostility than any joyous anticipation of more ammunition for the good fight."

To argue that blacks are achieving at a lower level than others because of "discrimination" by the larger society ignores the experience of other groups which have met discrimination. Thus, in many parts of Europe, Jews suffered oppressive discrimination yet were "over-represented" in the highest-paying professions such as medicine and law. In Southeast Asia, Chinese suffer widespread discrimination yet are the most prosperous businessmen. In the U.S., Japanese and Chinese immigrants met a hostile and unfriendly welcome, yet now exceed whites in terms of education and income. Thomas Sowell concludes that, "Two key assumptions behind the civil rights vision do not stand up as general principles. The first is that discrimination leads to poverty and other adverse social consequences, and the second is the converse—that adverse statistical disparities imply discrimination."

Beyond this is the fact that, in recent years, there has been a growing dichotomy within black America—a growing and vibrant middle class and an underclass mired in poverty. For those able and willing to take advantage of the opportunities achieved by the civil rights movement, progress has been dramatic.

Black social scientist Bart Landry, a visiting scholar at the Joint Center for Political Studies, estimates that the upwardly mobile middle class of blacks has grown by a third in this decade to 4.8 million in 1988 from 3.6 million in 1980. In 1985, nearly a million black families claimed annual earnings of $40,000 or more; another 300,000 had earnings between $35,000 and $40,000. All told, the middle class now constitutes more than 40 percent of black households, and is larger than the black working class, or the black poor.

Between 1985 and 1986, median income for black families across the board rose by nearly 3 percent in real terms. The black employment rate has increased to record levels, from 49 percent in 1982 to 56 percent today. The U.S. Department of Education reports that the rate of college enrollment for 18-to-24-year-old blacks has increased to 28.6 percent from 26.1 percent a year earlier.

Joseph Perkins, an editorial writer for the Wall Street Journal, who is black, declares: "On balance, the majority of black Americans have made considerable progress in the 1980s. More blacks are staying in high school, graduating, and going to college. More blacks are working than ever before, in better jobs, and for higher wages. The black middle class has burgeoned . . . and black business has flourished."

Black unemployment exceeds white unemployment, states Walter Williams, professor of economics at George Mason University, not because of "racism" but because it "is part of a general pattern of carrots and sticks." He writes:

First, the carrots. Government programs—unemployment compensation, food stamps and welfare—make unemployment less painful. We all know that if something is subsidized, be it wheat, cheese, poverty or unemployment, we can expect more of it. Poor people are like the rest of us. They respond to incentives. Why give up $10,000 a year in nontaxable welfare benefits for a job paying $6,000 to $7,000 that's taxable?

Then there are sticks. The minimum wage law acts as an effective barrier to jobs and training prospects for low-skilled youths. Prior to minimum wage escalation that started in the 1950s, unemployment was lower for teenage blacks than teenage whites. This was before politicians did the bidding of labor unions who sought to restrict employment in order to get higher wages for union members. The quid pro quo is that black politicians get political backing from labor unions, and black people get the unemployment line.

Those who defend our increasingly generous welfare policies—including our leading civil rights organizations—do so on the basis of their concern for the poor and underprivileged. But, Dr. Williams asks, "How truly compassionate is it to have a system which encourages dependency and discourages people from achieving their potential?" In this connection, he writes: "What motivates a person to take a low-paying entry-level job? It used to be there were no other alternatives. Now there is welfare. But by taking a low-paying entry-level job, a person was not only learning work habits, getting some skills, and learning about other opportunities, he was establishing himself as a reliable worker and gaining the dignity of supporting himself."

Even among his own liberal friends, Williams declares,

I know of no one who would treat their children as we treat poor people. They would not provide incentives for their fourteen year old daughters to have babies. They stress to their children the importance of education. They often see to it that their children live with the unpleasant consequences of their behavior. Do they show the same compassion and common sense toward the poor? No, they take the position that the poor have a right to dependency.

Evidence indicates clearly that the continuing unemployment of the underclass in the nation's inner cities has little to do with the availability of work. In an article entitled "The Coming of Custodial Democracy" (Commentary, September, 1988), Charles Murray, Bradley Fellow at the Manhattan Institute for Policy Research, notes that,

For two, three, and four years now, some major American cities have been experiencing a full-employment job market. There is reason to believe, moreover, that those markets will remain tight over the next several years as (because of demographic factors) the number of new job entrants drop . . . the black-white ratio of unemployment has continued to rise even during the recovery, as it has tended to do now for more than thirty years, in good times and bad. But there is no question that blacks looking for jobs have done better during the recovery. In the period 1982–87, in all age groups and for both sexes, blacks in the labor market made large gains.

The underclass remains in its present status not because of a lack of opportunities within the American society for advancement, but because of the pathology of the inner city—broken families, crime, illegitimacy, drugs, a lack of work ethic and dependence on welfare—which prevents it from taking advantage of the real opportunities which exist in abundance.

Charles Murray writes that,

> The labor-market behavior of the men of the underclass is especially crucial, for only by changes in their behavior—in work and in marriage—can the size of the underclass be reduced. The reality that is going to become harder to evade as time goes by is that a large core of young black men is not in the labor market and the size of that core seems to be extremely resistant to improvements in the economy. The only sign of progress in the aggregate statistics is among black male teen-agers, where the proportion not in the labor market fell from 60 to 56 percent during the years 1982–87. But this can be considered progress only if one ignores the huge size of the base. In 1982, for the critical age period twenty-to-twenty-four, the years when experience and a work record are being (or need to be) established, 21 percent of black males were not in the labor market. In 1987, after five years of economic expansion and falling unemployment, that figure had *risen* to 22 percent. (The comparable white figures were 14 percent and 13 percent respectively.)

In Boston, which had reached nearly full employment for blacks by 1987 (the black unemployment rate was a remarkably low 4.1 percent), the proportion of blacks not in the labor market *increased,* from 35 percent in 1982 to 39 percent in 1987.

It is Charles Murray's view that,

> The argument that "there just aren't any jobs" . . . is becoming increasingly hollow, and at the same time a large and increasingly visible subpopulation of poor black young males is remaining out of the labor market. For many years, academics and policy-makers alike have found it convenient to dismiss reports of problems in the labor-market behavior of inner-city males as the product of racism or "structural" barriers. A different reality has been out there all along, it has been resolutely ignored, and it is finally beginning to intrude. . . .

Writing in *Time* (October 10, 1988), Richard Stengel refers to "the Seven Ages of Underclass Man and Woman." He describes them this way:

| | |
|---|---|
| Birth | More than half of all black infants are born out of wedlock—and in the inner cities, that figure can reach 90 percent. |
| Childhood | Two in five black children are dependent on public assistance—and at least 100,000 are homeless. |

| | |
|---|---|
| Adolescence | Nearly half of black females are pregnant by the age of 20. |
| School days | The high school dropout rate in many inner cities is well over 50 percent. |
| Adulthood | Only half of all black men in the ghetto have jobs. |
| Death | The leading cause of death for young black men is murder by another young black man. |

Liberals, together with the civil rights movement, once believed in equality of opportunity, and then moved toward advancing equality of condition through the advocacy of affirmative action programs. Now, a new consensus with regard to the black underclass may be emerging, one which is prepared to place them on a permanent dole.

In this connection, Charles Murray writes that,

By the mid-1990s, what is now a more or less hidden liberal condescension toward blacks in general, and toward the black underclass in particular, will have worked its way into a new consensus. The particular form the new liberal consensus will take depends on circumstances, but in general mainstream liberal intellectuals and policy-makers will have become comfortable believing something like this: (1) inner-city blacks are really quite different from you and me, and the rules that apply to us cannot be applied to them; (2) it is futile to seek solutions that aim at bringing them into participation in American life, because we have seen that it cannot be done; and (3) the humane course is therefore to provide generously, supplying medical care, food, housing and other social services—much as we currently do for American Indians who live on reservations. And so we will have arrived in the brave new world of custodial democracy, in which a substantial portion of our population, neither convicted as criminal nor adjudged to be insane, will in effect be treated as wards of the state.

The civil rights movement, rather than working to improve the lives of black Americans, to restore a healthy family life, to rid the inner city of crime and drugs, has preferred to make common cause with white liberals whose goal was an expanded welfare state rather than a society in which individuals could go as far as their abilities would take them.

Rather than providing incentives for academic achievement, civil rights groups prefer to demand more expensive government welfare programs, ignoring the fact that welfare simply breeds dependency and that we already have third and fourth generations of welfare recipients and an underclass created by such government programs. By blaming "white racism" for every difficulty within the black community, the NAACP [National Association for the Advancement of Colored People], the Urban League and the others have succeeded only in obscuring the real problems we face and making millions of black Americans little more than wards of the state. Freedom, not dependency, was the original goal of the civil rights movement, but is little discussed at the present time.

Fortunately, more and more black Americans are rejecting this path to permanent dependency. John Thompson, the respected basketball coach at Georgetown University, and coach of the U.S. Olympic basketball team, states:

> I talk about economics an awful lot. I think more change has come about because of economics, because people totally disregard color barriers if you have economic value. . . . I tell young people to put themselves in a position of power where you create a need for yourself that has an economic effect on somebody. The world is not black or white as much as it is green. And I think our kids have got to understand and learn that.

The key to advancement in society is attitude. William Raspberry contrasts the achievement level of the children of recently arrived Asian immigrants, and those of the black inner city:

> There are two intriguing things about these Asians. The first is that they see America, with its free education, free enterprise and rewards for exertion, as a land of unsurpassed opportunity. This group succeeds at a pace that eclipses that of privileged whites. Our native-born minorities, on the other hand, see America as the place that has treated them unfairly. . . . The second intriguing thing about the newly arrived minorities is they know that the key to success is hard work. They take as a given that anybody who works hard enough can achieve success.

How, Raspberry asks,

> has this attitude escaped our low-income black and Hispanic groups? Partly we have tended to view everything through the prism of the civil-rights assumptions that the absence of the good things is proof of discrimination. Sometimes this assumption is correct. . . . But for today's black underclass, school failure, joblessness, adolescent pregnancy, juvenile crime and drug abuse are due far less to discrimination than to inadequate exertion. . . . The way to include middle-class attitudes in the underclass is to teach their children what the middle class takes for granted: that their fate is in their own hands.

Perhaps the 1988 March on Washington attracted such a small crowd because today's civil rights movement has nothing more to say to black Americans. The battles have been won. The doors are open. What is needed now is individual initiative to walk through those doors to a better life.

## Questions for Discussion

1. How does affirmative action affect African Americans?
2. Who are the beneficiaries of government policies designed to help African Americans?
3. What role should the black community play in the problems of the ghetto? Why?
4. What role should government play in dealing with the problems of the inner city? Why?
5. What role does racism play in the condition of the underclass?

## Suggested Readings

Bell, Derrick. "White Supremacy in America: Its Legal Legacy, Its Economic Costs." *Villanova Law Review,* 33, no. 5 (September 1988), 767–779.

Dingle, Derek T. "Affirmative Action." *Black Enterprise,* 20, no. 2 (September 1989), 42–46, 48.

Graham, Hugh Davis. *The Civil Rights Era: Origins and Development of National Policy.* New York: Oxford Univ. Press, 1990.

Herrnstein, R. J. "Still an American Dilemma." *Public Interest,* no. 98 (Winter 1990), 3–17.

Huckfeldt, Robert, and Carol Weitzel Kohfeld. *Race and the Decline of Class in American Politics.* Urbana, Ill.: Univ. of Illinois Press, 1989.

Katz, Phyllis A., and Dalmas A. Taylor, eds. *Eliminating Racism: Profiles in Controversy.* New York: Plenum Press, 1988.

Kilson, Martin. "Problems of Black Politics: Some Progress, Many Difficulties." *Dissent,* 36, no. 4 (Fall 1989), 526–534.

Kosof, Anna. *The Civil Rights Movement and Its Legacy.* New York: Watts, 1989.

Pohlman, Marcus D. *Black Politics in Conservative America.* New York: Longman, 1990.

Sawhill, Isabel V. "The Underclass: An Overview." *Public Interest,* no. 96 (Summer 1989), 3–15.

Sowell, Thomas. " 'Affirmative Action': A Worldwide Disaster." *Commentary,* 88, no. 6 (December 1989), 21–41.

——. *Civil Rights: Rhetoric or Reality?* New York: William A. Morrow, 1984.

U.S. Cong. *The Underclass.* Hearing before the Joint Economic Committee, 101st Cong., 1st Sess., 1989.

Williams, Juan. *Eyes on the Prize: America's Civil Rights Years, 1954–1965.* New York: Viking, 1987.

Williams, Walter E. "Myth Making and Reality Testing." *Society,* 27, no. 4 (May–June 1990), 4–7.

# Government Policy Makers

A s indicated in Part I, the Framers of the Constitution established a system of separation of powers and checks and balances constituted in three branches of government—legislative, executive, and judicial. The Framers feared that the concentration of powers in the hands of one branch would be a danger to liberty.

The Constitution, as has so often been said, is a living document, and it has changed over time through formal constitutional amendment, statutes, political practices, and customs. In part because of the ambiguities in some provisions of the Constitution and in part because of historical developments, power has shifted in different eras from one branch to another.

Constitutional amendments have modified the major branches of government. For example, the Seventeenth Amendment, adopted in 1913, changed the method of choosing U.S. senators from election by the state legislatures, as provided in Article I of the Constitution, to direct popular election in each state. Statutes have also changed the Constitution. Congress has passed numerous laws in the nineteenth and twentieth centuries establishing new departments and government agencies. When the Constitution was adopted, the role of government in society was minimal, but through statutes passed, particularly in this century, Congress has given executive agencies—the bureaucracy—vast powers in both domestic and foreign policy.

The formal constitutional actors in the U.S. political system have had their own impact on constitutional development. The Constitution says nothing about the power of judicial review, but the Supreme Court, under John Marshall, asserted that power in *Marbury* v. *Madison* in 1803. Today the power of judicial review is an accepted principle of the U.S. political system. The Constitution, moreover, says nothing about the organization of Congress into committees, but congressional committees today play important roles in the enactment of legislation.

Custom, too, influences the Constitution. George Washington left office at the end of his second term, and a two-term tradition was widely accepted over time until Franklin D. Roosevelt was elected to a third term in 1940 and a fourth term in 1944. Adopted in 1951, however, the Twenty-second Amendment limited presidential terms to two, thus giving formal constitutional sanction to what had become a custom until Roosevelt's third term.

The power of the principal institutions of government depends, then, on a variety of factors. The Constitution and laws provide the basic structure and define the formal powers of the major actors in the political system. The relationship of policy makers over time, however, depends on the personalities of the policy makers, the ties between the president and influential members of Congress, the character of judicial decisions, the astuteness of top bureaucrats, and historical developments.

Part IV deals with some of the important issues about the power, role, and behavior of policy makers in the national government today. The debates consider the power of the president, the limitation of terms for members of Congress, the use of private organizations to serve public goals, the utility of the Central Intelligence Agency, and the philosophy of the Supreme Court.

# Chapter 11

## Is the President Too Powerful in Foreign Policy?

In May 1987 a special committee of members of both the Senate and the House of Representatives opened hearings to investigate the actions of President Ronald Reagan, other members of the executive branch, and private citizens in secretly selling arms to Iran and in using the profits illegally to aid the Contras, a group of anticommunist fighters at war against the Sandinista government in Nicaragua. With massive media coverage, the committee investigated in detail the activities of the principal actors in what has come to be called the Iran-Contra affair.

Congressional investigations such as these into the conduct of foreign policy derive from specific authority granted in the Constitution as well as historical developments involving war and peace. The Constitution gives roles in foreign policy to *both* the president and the Congress. Article I of the Constitution grants Congress the powers to declare war; raise and support armies; provide and maintain a navy; make rules for the government and regulation of the land and naval forces; provide for calling forth the militia to execute the laws of the Union; and provide for organizing, arming, and disciplining the militia. Other provisions add to Congress's constitutional role. Such provisions include the Necessary and Proper Clause of Article I, Section 8, allowing Congress broad scope to carry out the powers specifically enumerated in the Constitution and its general constitutional powers of taxation and appropriation.

The Senate is given specific foreign policy powers. The ratification of a treaty requires approval by two-thirds of the senators present and voting. The Senate also has the power to confirm most presidential appointments.

The president's constitutional powers are set forth in Article II. That article gives the president executive power and designates the holder of that office as commander in chief of the armed forces. In addition, the president is given power to make appointments and to make treaties, "with the Advice and Consent of the Senate." The president's oath of office includes a statement that the president agrees to "preserve, protect, and defend the Constitution."

Inherent in the Constitution itself are conflicts between the legislative and executive branches of government. Some of the principal issues that have developed over time have involved the president's right to send military forces in combat situations without the consent of Congress, the use of executive agreements instead of treaties, and the reliance on covert operations by the president and members of the agencies involved in the conduct of foreign policy.

One of the most important reasons for the growth of executive power anywhere is the existence, or the imminent prospect, of war among nations or war within a nation. Executive power tends to increase during wartime, sometimes because the legislature grants the president emergency powers and sometimes because the executive takes action without asking for the approval of Congress.

At the outbreak of the Civil War, President Abraham Lincoln took steps that, according to the Constitution, were illegal. These included spending money that had not been appropriated by Congress and blockading southern ports. Lincoln expanded the powers of the president as commander in chief beyond the intent of the Framers of the Constitution. In 1940, President Franklin Roosevelt transferred fifty ships to Great Britain in return for the leasing of some British bases in the Atlantic—without congressional authorization to take such actions. He also ordered U.S. ships to "shoot on sight" any foreign submarine in waters that he regarded were essential for the nation's defense. In giving such an order, he was making war between the United States and Germany more likely.

Since the end of World War II, the United States has become a principal actor in world politics—a status in the international community that will be discussed at greater length in Part V. Here it is only essential to state that as a major world power, the United States has had to concern itself with global security issues in a manner unprecedented in its history.

The permanent emphasis of foreign and national security considerations has plagued executive-legislative relations since 1945. President Harry Truman sent U.S. troops to Korea without a formal declaration of war. President Dwight Eisenhower approved actions by the Central Intelligence Agency (CIA) to help bring down one government in Guatemala and put the shah in power in Iran. John Kennedy authorized the CIA to assist a military operation planned by Cuban exiles against a communist regime in Cuba—an operation that turned out to be a foreign policy disaster for the young president. He also increased the number of military advisers to Vietnam from several hundred to about seventeen thousand.

The actions of Presidents Lyndon Johnson and Richard Nixon in the war in Indochina sparked an increasing involvement by Congress in the conduct of foreign policy. Johnson raised the number of U.S. troops to five hundred thousand. Nixon engaged in a "secret" air war in Cambodia in 1969 and sent U.S. troops into that country in 1970.

The 1970s were marked by massive congressional involvement in the conduct of foreign policy. In 1971 Congress adopted legislation forbidding the expenditures of funds to carry on the war in Cambodia. Overriding a veto by President Nixon, it passed a War Powers Act (1973) sharply limiting the president's ability to send troops. Under the act the president has the power on his own authority to send U.S. armed forces into an area for a period of sixty days but then must get the approval of Congress or else terminate the use of armed forces. The president is also required to consult with Congress, if possible, before military intervention is ordered. Every president since Nixon has taken the position that the War Powers Act is unconstitutional because a statute cannot take away powers that are traditionally the preserve of presidents in the conduct of foreign policy. But every president has complied with its provisions. If and when a time comes in which a president refuses to comply with the law, the Supreme Court will decide on the constitutionality of the act.

Throughout the 1970s Congress continued to impose restrictions on executive actions in the conduct of foreign policy. To restrict some arms transfers, Congress used the legislative veto, which under certain conditions allowed either one or both chambers to cancel a proposed executive action. (The legislative veto, which had originated under Herbert Hoover in 1932 and had been applied to both domestic and foreign policy matters, was struck down as unconstitutional by the Supreme Court in 1983.)

Congress took steps to limit the actions of the president in areas other than arms transfers. In 1973 and 1974 it linked improved trade status of the Soviet Union in its dealings with the United States to a liberalization of Soviet emigration practices. The Senate failed to approve the Strategic Arms Limitation Treaty, known as SALT II, in 1979 and 1980, so President Jimmy Carter withdrew the treaty from the Senate's consideration. In an attempt to undermine President Reagan's policy in Nicaragua, Congress adopted the Boland Amendments restricting aid to the Contras in a variety of ways from 1983 to 1985. In 1986, however, Congress authorized a resumption of aid to the Contras, but stipulated that it could not be used to purchase weapons or other military equipment. In 1987, Congress approved assistance to the Contras with few restrictions, and, consequently, the U.S. government was permitted to supply the Contras with weapons and other military equipment. But the Boland Amendments had been directly responsible for the most important crisis of the Reagan administration's second term—the Iran-Contra affair—an intensive investigation of the executive branch by both Congress and the media.

Is the president too powerful in foreign policy? Political scientist Daniel P. Franklin argues the affirmative. He contends:

1. The president exercises too much power in foreign affairs without having to account to Congress or directly to the public and the press.
2. There are a temptation and tendency in the Executive Office for the president and his foreign policy advisers to conduct foreign policy through illegal means.
3. Congress can and should be brought into consultation on most foreign policy matters, while decisions are being made instead of after the fact.

Political scientist Ryan J. Barilleaux argues the negative. He advances seven propositions designed to clarify the nature of presidential power in foreign affairs:

1. The United States needs a strong president for foreign affairs.
2. Presidential power, while substantial, is constrained by the Constitution, law, and public opinion.
3. Abuses of presidential power in foreign affairs are doomed to fail.
4. There is very little that a president can do in foreign affairs without congressional acquiescence or approval.
5. Attempts to inhibit presidential power through mechanical "solutions" are self-defeating.
6. The current level of presidential power in foreign affairs, however imperfect, is about the best that can reasonably be expected.
7. Realistic reforms that would not upset the basic structure of the U.S. government could help improve the situation.

Professors Franklin and Barilleaux comment on each other's selection in rejoinders.

 ☑ *YES*

## *Is the President Too Powerful in Foreign Policy?*

### DANIEL P. FRANKLIN

### *The President Is Too Powerful in Foreign Affairs*

In the nuclear age, presiding over the government of a superpower state, the president is in a position to determine not only the fate of our nation but, in some sense, the fate of the rest of the world. That sort of responsibility is much too important to be left to the haphazard, incoherent system of foreign policy decision making in the presidency that has become common since the end of World War II. Specifically, the presidency in its conduct of foreign affairs suffers from the absence of adequate democratic control. Democratic control is essential in the making of foreign policy not only because it is "right" in the philosophical sense, but because it is more likely to succeed.

The assertion that the president has too much power in foreign policy making involves two separate but related arguments. First, in the liberal democratic sense, the president is too powerful. The president exercises too much responsibility in foreign affairs without having to account to Congress or directly to the public and the press. According to this logic, presidents are too powerful because their actions violate the separation of powers doctrine.[1]

Second, because presidents often operate beyond the control of the other branches of government, there are a temptation and tendency in the Executive Office for presidents and their advisers to conduct foreign policy through illegal means. The Iran-Contra affair, in which the "Reagan White House" (President Ronald Reagan has always denied his direct involvement) delivered arms to Iran and funds to rebels fighting to topple a left-wing government in Nicaragua in direct contravention of the law, is simply one in a succession of scandals in the modern presidency that involve violations of the law in the pursuit of national security goals.[2]

To be fair, this lack of democratic control in foreign policy making is not merely the consequence of the exercise of unrestrained ambitions by unscrupulous presidents. Rather, three general factors account for this lack of control. First, the nature of modern warfare, airpower, and nuclear weapons dictates that the president be able to act quickly and without restraint in emergencies. Second, because of its parochial orientation, Congress does not always display a great deal of initiative or oversight in the conduct of foreign affairs, particularly in the review of covert operations and the use of force. After all, there is little electoral benefit to be gained for the member of Congress who is actively involved in all but a few foreign policy issues (two exceptions to this rule are foreign trade legislation and foreign aid appropriations). Finally, a tradition has developed, based on precedent, that legitimizes an expanded role for the modern presidency in foreign affairs. The courts, for their part, have either declined to intervene in preventing the expansion of presidential power in foreign policy or actively supported presidential claims in this regard. Thus the loss of democratic control has been a gradual process in which the ambitions of individual presidents have played only a partial role.

## THE PROBLEM OF DEMOCRATIC CONTROL

Most analysts agree that a democracy is a system of government characterized by the "rule of the people". Beyond this simple definition, however, there is tremendous disagreement about the other requisites of a democratic government. In fact, there is a broad variation in the structures of democratic regimes, but certain unifying characteristics seem to be common to all democracies. These basic conditions are popular consent, popular control, and freedom of speech and of the press. Furthermore, it is essential that all of these characteristics be present at the same time for a democracy to maintain its viability. In its conduct of foreign policy, however, the presidency does not always satisfy these conditions necessary for democratic control.

Popular consent in a democracy is facilitated through uncoerced participation. To the extent that the president is popularly, freely elected, the presidency is subject to popular consent. In the realm of foreign policy, however, where much of the decision making in the postwar era is carried out by the president's staff who are subject to neither the will of Congress nor the restraints of the professional bureaucracy, popular consent is limited. Activist, experienced presidents (Dwight Eisenhower, for example) are able to control rather than be controlled by their own foreign policy staffs. However, since there is no prior experience quite like the presidency, individuals chosen to serve as president are likely to have limited experience (and, perhaps, limited interest) in the conduct of foreign affairs as commander in chief. Consequently, in the administration of a president who is relatively inexperienced (as was John Kennedy at the time of the Bay of Pigs invasion, Jimmy Carter during the Iran hostage crisis, and Ronald Reagan during the Iran-Contra affair), foreign policy decision-making authority, by default, falls on the shoulders of the president's unelected staff. This situation is not only a violation of the notion of popular consent; it is a dangerous way to make policy.

Noted presidential scholar Thomas Cronin argues, "Perhaps the most disturbing aspect of the expansion of the presidential establishment is that it has become a powerful inner sanctum of government, isolated from traditional, constitutional checks and balances."[3] For presidents, there are very real problems associated with depending too heavily on their own staffs for foreign policy expertise. Specifically, a president may become isolated in the White House from the rest of the policy-making community.[4] For example, while President Lyndon Johnson was an active manager of his own Vietnam policy, he was also isolated from dissenting views by staffers who were either deferential to the president, in agreement with the president, or excluded because of their dissenting views.[5] This kind of decision-making arrangement calls into question the wisdom of making foreign policy in the White House without including, whenever possible, presidential consultation with officials and individuals from outside the Executive Office.

"Popular control" means that there must be some relationship in a democracy between what the public wants and what the government does. For the most part, popular control is maintained through periodic elections. Politicians will try to anticipate the desires of voters in their quest for reelection. In that sense, the president is subject to popular control. This control, however, has eroded. For one thing, pursuant to the Twenty-second Amendment, the president cannot run for a third term and therefore is a "lame duck" throughout the second term.

There is, in addition, a more subtle violation of the principle of popular control associated with presidential foreign policy making. The public is generally poorly informed and uninvolved in foreign affairs. There are, of course, exceptions to this rule. Certain ethnic and interest groups do have an intense interest; Jews, for instance, are often very concerned about U.S. policy toward Israel, as are American automobile manufacturers about the U.S. relationship with Japan. In the main, however, elected officials have very little popular guidance in these matters. In fact, the flow of influence tends to be in the other direction; public officials, and particularly the president, have a tremendous impact on public opinion in regard to foreign affairs. This influence gives the president a great deal of leeway in foreign policy making. However, just because the public may have no *opinion* on foreign affairs does not mean that the public has no *stake* in foreign affairs. It is incumbent upon public officials in this instance to seek out the public interest rather than strike out on their own. Freedom of action is not an unrestricted license for a public official in a democracy. Since there is really no such thing as a "unified" public interest but only an amalgam of many points of view, representation of the public interest entails the inclusion of actors from outside the presidency in the decision-making process (including members of Congress). Yet, this is not often the case. Foreign policy decision making in the Executive Office can be, and often is, carried out largely by fiat, even including those decisions that do not involve any time constraints. This pattern is an overall derogation of popular control over foreign policy decision making.

Finally, freedom of speech and of the press is an essential component of any democratic system. After all, public participation from a position of ignorance cannot really be considered democratic participation at all. However, behind the twin veils of "executive privilege"[6] and "national security," the president has managed to arrogate the flow of information regarding national security affairs. It is not that the press cannot print or the Congress cannot investigate foreign policy activities of the presidency; the problem is that in dealing with the obstacle of government secrecy, Congress and the press may not know which questions to ask or what information to request. As the House Foreign Affairs Committee once noted:

> Congress has repeatedly experienced difficulty in getting sufficient, accurate, and timely information. This was demonstrated in the Dominican Republic intervention in 1965, the *Mayaguez* incident in 1975, and the Iranian hostage rescue atttempt in 1980, to name only a few examples. Having little information beyond that available in the media, Members of Congress enter discussions with executive branch officials on an unequal footing.[7]

President George Bush, in the manner of this tradition, did not inform congressional leaders of his decision to invade Panama until the evening of December 20, 1989, when U.S. troops were beginning their assault.

Ostensibly, this barrier of secrecy is intended to protect the nation's security—to keep our enemies from sharing our most sensitive intelligence. While it is true that certain information must be protected, the classification of information for security purposes may have gone well beyond the limits of what is acceptable and necessary in a viable democracy. As one frustrated (anonymous) member of Congress stated, "The actions of the United States are not secret to other nations, only to Congress and the American people."[8] As this comment implies, much of what passes for classified information is labeled secret not because it should not be or is not known by our adversaries, but because that information is embarrassing to the administration and is not and should not be known (from the administration's perspective) by the people and the Congress of the United States.

White House officials will argue that this secrecy is necessary because Congress is incapable of protecting sensitive information. However, in the aftermath of a series of revelations concerning misconduct by the Central Intelligence Agency (CIA) in the 1970s, Congress set up an intelligence review structure that is designed specifically to prevent leaks. Intelligence committee staffs are screened and given security clearances, committee meeting rooms are "bug proofed," and access to sensitive information reported to the committees is restricted. Besides, members of Congress have plenty of options other than leaking information to the press when they object to a particular intelligence operation. Members can use their leverage with the president, who has, after all, an entire program to pass on the Hill. In any event, it is probably the case that most leaks originate in the permanent bureaucracy or in the Executive Office itself. Nevertheless, despite these congressional precautions and despite the legal requirement that the president "fully inform the intelligence committees in a timely fashion of intelligence operations in foreign countries,"[9] President Bush recently reiterated the Reagan administration view that "the 'timely fashion' language [of the law] should be read to leave the President with virtually unfettered discretion to choose the right moment for making the required notification."[10] In the absence of at least a congressional review, the executive's penchant for secrecy violates the third minimum standard for democratic control. How can the voters, or their representatives, pass judgment on presidential actions they know nothing about?

## CONSEQUENCES OF THE LOSS OF CONTROL

Since the earliest days of the Republic, the role and implications of a relatively unfettered executive branch have been debated. In 1795 Alexander Hamilton and James Madison engaged in a spirited public exchange over the foreign policy powers of the president. President George Washington had proclaimed U.S. neutrality in a conflict between Britain and France. Hamilton defended the president's action arguing, in part, that the executive powers of the president pursuant to Article II of the Constitution were "subject only to the exceptions and qualifications which are expressed in the instrument." Consequently, Hamilton argued, short of a declaration of war or some other action specifically authorized by Congress pursuant to its constitutional authorities, the president set the U.S. agenda in foreign affairs. For his part, Madison responded by warning that to allow the president to set the policy agenda without consulting Congress would impose on Congress an "obligation" that would constitute a violation of the legislative function. In other words, by acting without the participation of Congress, the president would by his actions present Congress a fait accompli.[11] For example, by invading Panama without properly consulting Congress, President Bush in effect presented the legislature with a bill for the cost of the invasion plus the obligation the United States has incurred to support the new Panamanian regime.[12]

While Hamilton's broad interpretation of the president's foreign policy authority has come to dominate, we would be well advised to heed Madison's warning. This disregard of the necessity of democratic control has very real consequences for the viability of policy execution. The strength of a democracy is in the public sense of involvement created by popular participation. A true democratic government is not only representative of the public, it *is* the public. Therefore, when a democratic regime makes a ruling or imposes a restriction, that policy is representative of the "general will" and is, for the public, a self-imposed restraint or obligation. In the absence of meaningful participation, the public feels no compulsion (nor is it morally bound) to live up to its legal obligations.[13]

For one thing, if the public and its representatives do not get a sense that they are being consulted in matters of foreign affairs, support for administration policies will be "shallow." Pollsters have identified the so-called rally-around-the-flag effect, or the tendency of the public to support the bold foreign policy moves of a president in the short term but not in the long term.[14] Political commentators interpret this effect to mean that the public does not have the "stomach" (anymore) for foreign involvement.[15] But what if this obvious distaste for interventionism is more a function of the feeling the public gets in a nondemocratic state that it has no investment (except for tax dollars, of course) in decisions made: no public involvement, no public support? If this is the case, this lack of public commitment robs us, as a democracy, of one of our primary sources of power—popular mobilization. The leader of a democratic state can count on popular support of a kind that can tap a nation's strength in no other, comparable way. With public support we fought the Second World War, helped rebuild Western Europe, defended South Korea, and sustained a war effort in Vietnam for many years. These examples are evidence of a tremendous public tolerance for the sacrifice associated with interventionism. The recent decline in support for an interventionist foreign policy only shows that there is a limit to that tolerance. The people of the United States had, and have, "what it takes" to support a superpower foreign policy.

At the same time, the administration that operates beyond democratic control will often behave with a certain arrogance. This "arrogance of power" is the tendency of unrestrained leaders "to equate power with virtue and major responsibilities with a universal mission."[16] In other words, the presidency that is beyond democratic control not only has the latitude to go beyond constitutional constraints; it has a mistaken sense of virtue in doing so. Corruption is a consequence of a lack of democratic control. It is not that all presidents are corrupt, but that an institution that is beyond control will at some point be corrupted.[17] In that event, citizens are viewed contemptuously by their leaders as "subjects" rather than as equals and participants. The administration that trades in arms in direct contravention to the law, as did the Reagan administration, is an administration that holds the public and its representatives in contempt. Only a president who agrees to and, indeed, is obliged to consult with the public's representatives from outside the Executive Office will overcome the arrogance of power.

## IMPLEMENTATION

To say that we need to impose a democratic structure on foreign policy decision making is not to say that we should run our foreign policy by plebiscite. The vast majority of voters are neither interested nor qualified to be involved with governmental decision making on a day-to-day basis. Rather, through our representatives, we can have a participatory foreign policy without having a plebiscitary one. In a representative democracy, voters designate elected officials who, as part of their job responsibility, develop an expertise in public affairs. Thus, while it is impractical to involve the general public in routine or emergency foreign policy making, there are plenty of foreign policy specialists on Capitol Hill who represent a component of the public interest and who can be tapped by the Executive Office. For example, as of 1990 Claiborne Pell (chair of the Senate Foreign Relations Committee) and Dante Fascell (chair of the House Foreign Affairs Committee) had served in Congress and specialized in foreign affairs for a combined total of sixty-eight years! There is no reason to believe that there is a monopoly of foreign policy expertise at the White House. Furthermore, not only does the president sacrifice policy expertise when members of Congress are excluded; the president also loses the political expertise and the opinions of actors who are not presidential sycophants. Members of Congress, even from the president's own party (had they been consulted), would have flagged former President Reagan's decision to approve an arms-for-hostage trade with Iran.

No one is going to argue that the president should be required to consult Congress (or other outsiders) in every situation. Sometimes there are circumstantial barriers (the principals may be out of town) or time constraints. After all, the president may have as little as ten or fifteen minutes to respond to a "bolt-out-of-the-blue" nuclear attack. No one expects the president confronted with this situation to convene and consult with Congress or even to call congressional leaders. However, these situations are so rare or unlikely as to be virtually nonexistent. The "time constraint" argument is more often used as an excuse to avoid congressional involvement or consultation *while* the decision is being made. Congress is thoroughly capable of acting quickly when the need arises. Congressional leaders can be summoned to the White House at a moment's notice. And, if in the course of being consulted, congressional leaders disagree with the president's proposals, perhaps the commander in chief would be well advised to listen seriously to and consider their objections.

Neither reform nor any amount of democratic involvement in foreign policy decision making is going to guarantee success. Mistakes will be made, the difference being that the responsibility for mistakes in a democracy is shared. In 1983, when President Reagan (under duress) negotiated an agreement with Congress to authorize the deployment of peacekeeping troops in Lebanon, the president took one of the most fateful steps of his administration. The subsequent deaths of 241 Marines in their Beirut barracks led not only to a shared sense of national grief but a shared sense of responsibility among decision makers in Washington. Would President Bush have been in the same position had the invasion of Panama failed? Will the president find, in making requests for assistance to the government he installed in Panama, that congressional support for economic assistance will be "soft"? Will members of Congress tend to disassociate themselves, because of the overall federal budget "crunch," from the costs and obligations incurred by a Panamanian invasion about which they were not consulted? Only time will tell what will be the final consequences of the invasion of Panama. But, if a democratic government is to be a responsible government, no political leader should have the right to control, or bear the sole responsibility of controlling, the fate of the nation. Such exclusive conduct of policy making is not only wrong in the philosophical sense; it is unlikely to succeed.

---

*NOTES*

1. The separation of powers doctrine was the Framers' way of preventing tyranny by ensuring the separateness of the different branches of government. The Framers recognized that the delay and conflict associated with the separation of powers were the necessary price of preventing one interest from dominating government. In particular, see John Jay, Alexander Hamilton, and James Madison, *The Federalist Papers,* ed. Clinton Rossiter (New York: New American Library, 1961), nos. 10, 48.

2. Other obvious examples include the secret bombing of Cambodia and White House–authorized covert activities of the Central Intelligence Agency (CIA) both inside and outside the United States, including CIA participation in the break-in at Daniel Ellsberg's psychiatrist's office during the Nixon administration. Ellsberg was a Department of Defense official who leaked the contents of a secret report about the Vietnam War to the *Washington Post* and *New York Times.*

3. Thomas Cronin, "The Swelling of the Presidency," in *Classic Readings in American Politics,* ed. Pietro S. Nivola and David H. Rosenbloom (New York: St. Martin's Press, 1986), p. 415.

4. For a discussion of the detrimental consequences of presidential isolation, see Irving L. Janis, *Groupthink: Psychological Studies of Policy Decisions and Fiascoes,* 2nd ed. (Boston: Houghton Mifflin, 1982).

5. For an excellent account of Vietnam War policy making in the Johnson White House, see James G. Thompson, "How Could Vietnam Happen? An Autopsy," *Atlantic Monthly,* 221, no. 4 (April 1968), 47–53.

6. Executive privilege is the principle, upheld by the courts, that permits presidents and their staffs to withhold certain information regarding national security matters (and other administrative responsibilities) from Congress. The limits of executive privilege are not well defined (criminal investigations are exempt), and presidents tend to be broad in their definition of what sort of information can be withheld. See Chief Justice Warren Burger's decision in *United States* v. *Nixon* 418 U.S. 683 (1974).

7. U.S. Congress, House of Representatives, Foreign Affairs Committee, *Strengthening Executive-Legislative Consultation on Foreign Policy,* Congress and Foreign Policy Series, no. 8 (October 1983), p. 65.

8. Quoted in *Congressional Quarterly Weekly Report,* vol. 34, no. 46 (November 13, 1976), p. 3170, and in Charles W. Kegley and Eugene R. Wittkopf, *American Foreign Policy: Pattern and Process,* 2nd ed. (New York: St. Martin's Press, 1982), p. 412.

9. National Security Act, as amended, Section 501 (b).

10. President George Bush to Senator David L. Boren, chair of the Senate Select Committee on Intelligence, October 30, 1989. A copy of this letter was made available to the author.

11. See the "Pacificus-Helvidius [Hamilton-Madison] Debates on the Nature of the Foreign

Relations Power 1793," reprinted from the *Gazette of the United States,* June 29, 1793, in Jean E. Smith, *The Constitution and American Foreign Policy* (St. Paul: West Publishing Co., 1989), pp. 49–58.

12. The estimated cost of economic assistance alone may be close to $2 billion in the short term. See John Felton, "Panama: Rebuilding Broken Economy Will Strain Purse Strings," *Congressional Quarterly Weekly Report,* 48, no. 1 (January 6, 1990), 43–44.

13. For a classic discussion of this justification for democracy, see Jean-Jacques Rousseau, *The Social Contract,* trans. Richard W. Crosby (Brunswick, Ohio: King's Court Press, 1978). (The book was originally published in 1762.) Rousseau ultimately came to the conclusion that a direct democracy was the only appropriate structure for a democratic state. The French Revolution and its aftermath eventually discredited Rousseau's view of democratic structure but did not necessarily discredit his overall moral and practical justifications for democracy in some form.

14. Jong R. Lee, "Rallying around the Flag: Foreign Policy Events and Presidential Popularity," *Presidential Studies Quarterly* 7, no. 4 (Fall 1977), 252–256.

15. Charles Krauthammer, "Divided Superpower: The Real Cause of the North Affair," *New Republic,* 195, no. 25 (December 22, 1986), 14–17.

16. The statement from which this definition is adapted is J. William Fulbright: "The Tendency of Great Nations to Equate Power with Virtue." *The Arrogance of Power* (New York: Random House, 1966), p. 9. Fulbright is former chair of the Senate Foreign Relations Committee.

17. This is precisely the point Madison was trying to make in Federalist no. 47 when he argued, "The accumulation of all powers, legislative, executive, and judiciary, in the same hands, whether of one, a few, or many, and whether hereditary, self-appointed, or elective, may justly be pronounced the very definition of tyranny." *Federalist Papers,* p. 301.

 ☑ NO

## Is the President Too Powerful in Foreign Policy?

### RYAN J. BARILLEAUX

### *Seeing Presidential Power Clearly*

The presidency has long been plagued by the question of whether it endows a single official with too much power. Before the office was created, many of the nation's political leaders feared the rule of a king and wanted to ensure that the chief executive of the United States could never become one. Their descendants criticized presidential power in the succeeding generations of U.S. history, from "King" Andrew Jackson to the "imperial" presidencies of Lyndon Johnson and Richard Nixon. Today, in an age of nuclear weapons and guerrilla war, there is even more concern about the possible excesses of executive power.

Is the president too powerful? The question is not merely a rhetorical one, because it reflects a long-standing U.S. fear of tyrants. Americans want a government that is strong, but not one so strong as to threaten liberties and the lives of citizens.

With regard to the presidency, the question essentially comes down to the issue of the president's powers in foreign affairs. Scholars have noted a distinction between presidential power in foreign affairs and domestic matters, with the former considerably outweighing the latter in its impact on the U.S. political system. As Aaron Wildavsky puts it: "The United States has one President, but it has two presidencies. . . . Presidents have had much greater success in controlling the nation's defense and foreign policies than in dominating its domestic policies."[1] In domestic policy, presidential power is understood to be "the power to persuade," because the president must convince Congress, the public, interest groups, and others to accept his policies. His actual ability to command is limited.

In foreign policy, however, the situation is different. The president has much greater ability to shape policy on his own: he is commander in chief of the armed forces, controller of all diplomacy, keeper of nuclear weapons, and leader of the western alliance. He decides when and on what terms the United States will negotiate with foreign nations. He controls the military might of the nation, even to the use of force in emergency situations. He can recognize foreign governments or refuse to do so. He alone speaks for the nation in world affairs and often speaks on behalf of all democracies. The president's prerogative power in foreign affairs, i.e., power to choose on his own, is extensive.

But is it too great? Many critics believe so. They argue that the president is far too powerful for his or the nation's good, because he can launch an invasion or start World War III on his own. Consequently, the nation finds itself caught in an endless series of military encounters—wars in Indochina in the 1960s and early 1970s, the invasion of Grenada in 1983, the toppling of Manuel Noriega's dictatorship in Panama in 1989, and the deployment of armed forces in the Persian Gulf after Iraq's invasion of Kuwait in 1990. The nation, moreover, finds that its leaders have engaged in embarrassing political intrigues, such as what has come to be known as the Iran-Contra affair—the events in 1985 and 1986 involving selling U.S. armaments to Iran in exchange for the release of U.S. citizens held captive in Lebanon and the illegal U.S. government funding of Nicaraguan rebel forces, known as Contras, who were resisting the Marxist Sandinista government in Nicaragua. All of these events, critics contend, add up to a presidency out of control.

These charges about excessive presidential power are wrong. Of course, there are legitimate grounds for criticism of presidential foreign policy conduct. There have been excesses committed by presidents, and room for reasonable reforms certainly exists. But it is too much to say that the president is too powerful in foreign affairs. What happens is that critics see certain problems and generalize them into flaws in the basic nature of the presidency. In doing so, they fail to see presidential power clearly.

A clear view of presidential power is exactly what we need. With such a view, the problems to which critics point can be seen in context and better understood. Therefore, this article advances seven propositions designed to clarify the nature of presidential power in foreign affairs.

# 1. THE UNITED STATES NEEDS A STRONG PRESIDENT FOR FOREIGN AFFAIRS

Alexander Hamilton noted government's need for a strong executive, particularly for the conduct of foreign policy. In his famous phrasing, Hamilton declared that "energy in the executive is a leading character in the definition of good government." He pointed to the virtues of "unity, secrecy, and dispatch" that executives embody, all of which are necessary in the international arena.[2] The speed with which international events move, in a world of nearly two hundred nations and a growing list of nuclear powers, demands decisiveness and action such as is beyond the reach of a legislative body. Without a strong president, the United States would soon be forced to isolate itself from the world or sit by while events overwhelmed us.

To that extent, the president's foreign policy power cannot be measured against some ideal of an unaggressive and "tame" executive. Rather, any charge of too much presidential power can be made only if his powers far exceed the rather great strength that the president needs to act at all in the world arena.

# 2. PRESIDENTIAL POWER, WHILE SUBSTANTIAL, IS CONSTRAINED BY THE CONSTITUTION, LAW, AND PUBLIC OPINION

Even as great as it must be, the president's foreign policy power is not unlimited. Chief executives are always mindful of the limits on their powers. Indeed, President Lyndon Johnson once complained that he had only one real power (i.e., to launch a nuclear attack), and it was one that he could not use.

How is the president limited? First, the Constitution sets a number of conditions under which he can conduct foreign affairs. Presidential appointments, whether to the position of secretary of defense or ambassadorships, require Senate confirmation. Thus the Senate is able to impose limits, albeit broad ones, on the kinds of individuals it will accept for office. President Jimmy Carter was forced to withdraw his first nominee for the position of director of the Central Intelligence Agency, Theodore Sorensen, because many senators considered the appointee unacceptable. Likewise, the Senate denied President George Bush his first choice for the job of secretary of defense, John Tower, because many senators had doubts about his personal character and fitness for the post. All treaties require Senate approval, and all money spent by the president, whether on weapons or foreign aid, must be appropriated by Congress. Congress also regulates the size of the armed forces and the number and kinds of weapons in the U.S. arsenal. In short, the president must play by the rules, and the rules already include extensive congressional participation in the foreign policy process.

Second, Congress has created a number of laws that further restrict the president. The Case Act (1974), for example, requires the president to inform Congress of all agreements other than treaties that he makes with foreign nations.[3] Congress can and does limit the purposes for which money may be spent, such as prohibiting a president to use federal funds to conduct a war in Southeast Asia.[4] The president must notify Congress of any use of U.S. forces in hostile situations and receive congressional approval for maintaining them in conflict for more than sixty days.[5] The president has extensive power of initiative in international affairs but limited power of fulfillment.

Third, a further constraint on the president is public opinion. Even when the president has unilateral power and/or the approval of Congress, public disapproval may cause him to reconsider his actions. Sensing a strong public antipathy to Vietnam-type conflicts, chief executives since the mid-1970s have been reluctant to engage the nation in any military actions that cannot be resolved quickly and with few American lives lost. Despite strong words about the nature of the threat that Nicaragua's Sandinista government posed to both its Central American neighbors and U.S. security, President Ronald Reagan was careful during his two terms never to call for the highly unpopular U.S. military involvement that his argument implied.

What this all means is that in reality presidential power in foreign affairs is more limited than it appears to be. It is not the unrestrained power that critics often suggest but is an extension of the "power to persuade" that is recognized in domestic matters. The difference between foreign and domestic policy is that Congress and the American people are willing to grant the president more latitude abroad than they do at home.

## 3. ABUSES OF PRESIDENTIAL POWER IN FOREIGN AFFAIRS ARE DOOMED TO FAIL

Critics of presidential power usually focus their attention on various real or alleged abuses of power by chief executives: Vietnam, the Iran-Contra affair, and so forth. Their argument is that abuses prove the disproportionate power of the president and warrant greater restraints on the chief executive. In other words, what these critics are saying is that it is better to have a president who is too weak than to risk abuses of power.

The problem with this argument is that it is both unrealistic and incorrect. It is unrealistic because there is no way to design political institutions that cannot be abused, and efforts to do so will probably only make things worse. Restraining presidential power to the degree necessary to prevent any abuse will yield an executive incapable of the kind of "unity, secrecy, and dispatch" that the nation needs. The nation must live with the risk of abuse and be vigilant against it.

Moreover, the argument is incorrect. Abuses of presidential foreign policy power are ultimately doomed to fail. Because the government of the United States is one of separate institutions sharing power, Congress can investigate abuses such as the Iran-Contra affair. Because the government historically has been unable to keep most things secret, problems such as Iran-Contra do not survive for long. The only "abuses" of presidential power that continue for any time are those, like the Vietnam War, in which Congress allows the president to act unilaterally.

There is no way to make the government foolproof against abuses and still maintain effective government. Perhaps that means that the United States will swing back and forth between too much presidential autonomy in foreign affairs and too little, but the alternative is a consistently weak executive.

## 4. THERE IS VERY LITTLE THAT A PRESIDENT CAN DO IN FOREIGN AFFAIRS WITHOUT CONGRESSIONAL ACQUIESCENCE OR APPROVAL

This point is even more important than the last for seeing presidential power clearly. In truth, the president's power in foreign affairs is that of initiation and persuasion: the president initiates actions, negotiations, diplomacy, policy changes, and commitments; then he attempts to persuade Congress to go along with him. Extended presidential war making, as in Vietnam and Korea, depends on congressional acquiescence. So do treaties, national commitments, defense expenditures, foreign aid, and all other significant foreign policy decisions.

This point does not mean that the president is weak but that many of the so-called abuses of presidential power in foreign affairs occurred with the full knowledge of Congress. For example, for six years the United States observed the nuclear arms limitation provisions it had concluded with the Soviet Union in a proposed Strategic Arms Limitation Treaty (SALT II) of 1979. It took action despite the absence of Senate approval of the agreement and in apparent violation of American law, because Congress was tacitly willing to let the president do so.[6] Moreover, although the president can commit American forces to hostile situations for a short time, as in bombing Libya or invading Grenada, he must inform Congress of what he is doing and obtain its approval of any extended actions. Thus presidents are careful about the kinds of situations in which they place themselves, for they will need Congress's support and the public's as well.

So, while the president has the upper hand in foreign policy making, he does not have absolute power. If Congress acquiesces in presidential actions or commitments, then the problem does not lie in the executive alone.

## 5. ATTEMPTS TO INHIBIT PRESIDENTIAL POWER THROUGH MECHANICAL "SOLUTIONS" ARE SELF-DEFEATING

Despite the fact that many presidential "abuses" of power occur with the acquiescence or even approval of Congress, the legislature occasionally objects to such actions and tries to prevent future problems by creating mechanical "solutions." The best example of this approach is the War Powers Resolution (1973), which creates a set of deadlines and requirements for the president to follow. The purpose of the resolution is to prevent a long-term, Vietnam-type commitment of U.S. forces without Congress's approval. But the War Powers Resolution has not solved the problem as intended. It has made presidents more careful about the use of force, but it has not produced a situation of legislative control over executive assertiveness in the use of force.[7]

The point here is that Congress, if it wants to restrain presidential power in foreign affairs, cannot do so by developing these mechanical "solutions." When it relies on such devices, it becomes complacent about controlling executive power or it impairs the president's ability to act effectively. If Congress wants to maintain an active role in foreign policy, it can do so only by actively pursuing its traditional rights, powers, and responsibilities in that area.

## 6. THE CURRENT LEVEL OF PRESIDENTIAL POWER IN FOREIGN AFFAIRS, HOWEVER IMPERFECT, IS ABOUT THE BEST THAT CAN REASONABLY BE EXPECTED

The United States could do much worse than having the current system for controlling foreign policy. It could have a system of weak executive power, which might prevent presidential abuses but cost the nation its ability to cope with a dangerous world. It could have a more powerful president, checked only by his conscience and the persuasiveness of advisers, but that situation would surely mean tyranny.

What the nation does have is a system with a strong, but restrained, executive who exercises his power within a system of checks and balances in which he is held accountable for his actions. The United States Constitution establishes a government of three branches, each checking and balancing the wielding of power by the other two. The president has great power, but it is not absolute power. This situation is not perfect, but it is a workable and reasonable one. It allows the president to exercise the leadership and decisiveness needed by the United States, but obligates him to pay attention to Congress and the public. It does not create perfect equilibrium, with presidential power waxing and waning over time as circumstances and congressional and public attitudes change, but in politics equilibrium often means paralysis. Attempts to alter the system significantly, as in removing the president's power to conclude executive agreements or employ U.S. forces abroad without congressional authorization, would not be worth whatever benefits they might bring.

## 7. REALISTIC REFORMS THAT WOULD NOT UPSET THE BASIC STRUCTURE OF AMERICAN GOVERNMENT COULD HELP IMPROVE THE SITUATION

For all that a clear view of presidential power reminds us of the excessiveness of critics, it is also true that the current situation is not perfect. There are realistic reforms that could make things better without damaging needed presidential powers. For example, the Case Act could be amended to require the president to report to Congress on all significant agreements he concludes with other nations, even informal ones. Without hampering the president, this action would give Congress better information about U.S. foreign policy. Similarly, Congress could enhance its ability to play an active and responsible role in foreign affairs by coordinating its oversight of executive actions and decisions in that area: it could create a joint intelligence committee, or even a joint national security committee, to simplify and thus improve executive-legislative consultation on foreign policy. At present, foreign affairs and intelligence matters in Congress are divided between the House and the Senate and within each chamber among committees on Foreign Affairs, Armed Services, and Intelligence. The result is a confusion that inhibits Congress's ability to oversee and respond to executive actions and decisions in foreign affairs. The president could also make a concerted effort to increase his consultation with congressional leaders, even if he did so only with members of his own party. In these ways, the chief executive could head off many potential problems.

## CONCLUSION

In the final analysis, the president will consult with Congress and restrain his power only to the extent he feels it necessary to do so. Therefore, critics of presidential power ought to look to Congress as well as to the executive. The legislature's interest in and involvement with foreign policy are determined largely on Capitol Hill and not in the White House. The president does not have too much power in foreign affairs, but neither does Congress have too little. What counts is what is done with power. Perhaps Congress needs to do more.

---

NOTES

1. Aaron Wildavsky, "The Two Presidencies," in *The Presidency,* ed. Aaron Wildavsky (Boston: Little, Brown, 1969), p. 230.

2. John Jay, Alexander Hamilton, and James Madison, *The Federalist Papers,* ed. Clinton Rossiter (New York: New American Library, 1961), no. 70, p. 423.

3. PL 92-403; 86 Stat. 619, August 22, 1972; 1 U.S.C. 112.

4. See Thomas M. Franck and Edward Weisband, *Foreign Policy by Congress* (New York: Oxford Univ. Press, 1979), pp. 13–57.

5. PL 93-148; 87 Stat. 555; 50 U.S.C. 1542, 1543.

6. Ryan J. Barilleaux, "Executive Non-Agreements and the Presidential-Congressional Struggle in Foreign Affairs," *World Affairs* 148 (Spring 1986), 217.

7. Daniel Paul Franklin, "War Powers in the Modern Context," *Congress and the Presidency* 14 (Spring 1987), 77–92.

---

## ☑ *Y E S*

---

## *Is the President Too Powerful in Foreign Policy?*

---

### DANIEL P. FRANKLIN
### *Rejoinder*

For the most part, Professor Barilleaux and I agree on the proper role of the president in the making of foreign policy. I agree that presidential abuses of power are doomed to failure. That is why I would like to see those abuses prevented before they take place. I agree that superficial, mechanical "solutions" are probably inadequate and possibly even counterproductive. Mere mechanical solutions are probably not going to be a sufficient remedy for the systematic problems of the foreign affairs presidency that have become particularly acute since World War II. I even agree that the United States needs a strong president in foreign affairs. It is over this last point, however, that our two positions begin to diverge. Both Professor Barilleaux and I believe that the United States should be a strong, flexible, and influential actor on the world scene. We simply do not, however, agree on the best way to achieve these goals.

Power, loosely defined, is the ability to make some individual, group, or nation do something that it would not ordinarily do. One major problem with this concept of power is that it is not entirely clear what a society needs to do to enhance its own national power. It is too simple to say that all a nation needs is more weapons or more troops to maximize its strength. If that were the case, the United States would have won the Vietnam War, Israel would have long since disappeared, and the shah of Iran would still be on the Peacock Throne. In each of these instances, there was a distinct imbalance in military power; the United States had nuclear weapons, the North Vietnamese did not; the combined strength of the Arab nations' military forces did and does outnumber Israeli military forces by a large factor; the shah had a strong, modernized military that was easily defeated by largely unarmed mobs in the street. Thus the concept of national power is much more complex than it seems to be. All kinds of factors beside military strength go into the calculation of national power, including natural resources, location, climate, culture, and, of course, "national will." I argued in my essay that democracy, as a political system, enhances national power. Professor Barilleaux, while he clearly does not discount the need for democratic control, sees democratic participation as much more a constraint than an opportunity. Therein lies the major difference between our two positions: we disagree as to the value of democratic participation in the maximization of national power.

Professor Barilleaux assumes that the presidency, because of its advantages in speed, secrecy, and expertise, is more suited as an institution for the conduct of foreign policy. With this I agree. What I disagree with is Barilleaux's tendency to assume that "making" foreign policy and "conducting" foreign policy are the same thing. Conducting foreign policy, or making the day-to-day decisions of how to implement policy, is properly (and constitutionally) an executive function. I am not going to dispute the proposition that as "commander in chief" or as "chief executive" the president should have a certain amount of flexibility in the conduct of foreign affairs. The creation of foreign policy, however, as with making any other kind of national policy, is a legislative function. To the extent that Congress is invested with the legislative power, it is the responsibility of Congress to help determine foreign policy goals. Even so, as a practical matter (and constitutional by-product), the president has a tremendous input into the legislative process. Also, as a practical matter, it is not always going to be possible for the president to consult with Congress in emergency situations under severe time constraints. Nevertheless, this dominance of the presidency in even the making of policy should not be interpreted to mean that Congress need be excluded from the decision-making process in foreign affairs.

Congress has a varying degree of input into the foreign policy decision-making process. On foreign trade or foreign aid issues, or even the expenditure side of military operations, Congress is an active participant. In matters of military policy outside the budget (the so-called war powers) and intelligence concerns, Congress has much less of an impact. And yet it is precisely this kind of decision—the decision to commit U.S. armed forces to combat or to embark on some kind of covert adventure—that determines long-term U.S. commitments, military and otherwise. Professor Barilleaux "blames the victim" when he suggests that Congress acquiesces in presidential actions or commitments. In some cases this may be true. However, Congress cannot be considered a full participant in foreign policy decision making when it is not properly consulted or informed. The absence of congressional opposition to the Panama invasion cannot be read as acquiescence but simply as silence for the lack of a better response. Congress was presented by President George Bush with a fait accompli. Once operation "Just Cause" (the code name for the invasion) was under way, it was too late for Congress to become meaningfully involved.

It is all well and good for Professor Barilleaux to suggest that Congress actively pursue its traditional rights to be, for example, fully informed of a presidential decision to go to war or to conduct a covert operation. But when a president refuses to live up to his responsibilities under the Constitution, what then is Congress to do? It is impossible for Congress to act upon events it knows nothing about. In other words, in some of the most important areas of foreign policy decision making, congressional oversight is more form than substance. If this is, indeed, the case, we again return to the question of the value of congressional involvement. Should we be disturbed that congressional participation in some areas of foreign policy making is little more than veneer?

The answer is yes. To exclude Congress from some of the most sensitive areas of foreign policy decision making, either through secrecy or by ensuring that Congress does not get involved until after the fact (until, for example, troops are already committed), is to weaken our national power. First, to bypass Congress is to lose an important independent perspective on the issue. Members of Congress represent a constituency different from that of the president. Members of Congress have a different point of view, different levels of expertise (sometimes superior to those of the president's staff), and even, at times, greater political experience—all of which is lost when Congress is excluded. Professor Barilleaux does seem to acknowledge this problem when he makes some limited suggestions for facilitating congressional participation, which are, it seems, a step in the right direction. Second, excluding Congress from what are policy and, therefore, legislative decisions is a violation of the separation of powers. When this is the case, the nation will experience the kinds of problems the Framers were trying to prevent by applying the separation of powers structure to our government. Specifically, a branch of government unrestrained by the separation of powers may become dominated by, to use James Madison's term, a "faction," and that faction will be tempted, if it is beyond control, to violate individual rights and the Constitution. Illegality is a consequence of the violation of the separation of powers. Finally, in the absence of democratic inclusion, we lose one of the most important sources of power in a democracy—sustained popular mobilization in support of foreign policy goals. Paradoxically, therefore, because the president is too powerful in foreign affairs, the foreign policy of the United States is weak.

---

*Is the President Too Powerful in Foreign Policy?*

---

## RYAN J. BARILLEAUX
### *Rejoinder*

The United States system of government is far from perfect, but it was created by a group of leaders who understood that perfect political institutions are unachievable. That is why the only fair way to judge the performance of U.S. political institutions is to compare them to realistic alternatives, not against visions of political perfection.

In his essay, Professor Franklin brushes dangerously close to an unrealistic criticism of presidential power in foreign affairs. He tries to develop a set of criteria for evaluating the power of the presidency but ends up comparing existing politics to a vision of how he would wish government to be. Unfortunately, the best of all imaginable worlds is beyond our grasp: politics is the art of the possible.

Nevertheless, Professor Franklin presents a serious critique of the presidency and one that deserves some serious answers. His argument is that presidential conduct of foreign affairs is beyond democratic control because it violates all three requirements for democratic government: popular consent, popular control, and freedom of speech and of the press. Consequently the nation does not get the foreign policy it deserves, and U.S. citizens are too vulnerable to the decisions and actions of a single officeholder.

Does the United States really have a presidency that is out of control? The evidence for that view is not convincing. Yes, there are many problems and there have been excesses, but one cannot conclude from events such as the Vietnam War, the Iran-Contra affair, and the invasion of Panama that there are structural flaws in the nation's leadership that threaten it with ruin. After all, time and again, events have demonstrated the power of Congress and the courts to restrain or punish the presidency. A few examples will make this point:

- During the Korean War, an attempt by President Harry Truman to force U.S. steel mills to remain open during a strike was stopped by the Supreme Court. Truman, commander in chief of a large military establishment, gave in to a court of nine elderly judges who possess no police force.
- When Congress decided that it wanted to end the Vietnam War in 1975, it voted to do so. As a result, the war ended. President Gerald Ford had no discretion regarding how or when to end the war: it ended.

193

- In 1975, Congress prevented President Ford from intervening in a civil war in the African nation of Angola. Despite the very real threat of a communist victory there—a victory that ultimately occurred—the United States did not intervene.
- In the 1970s, Congress investigated and restrained the power of the Central Intelligence Agency, cutting through layers of secrecy and diminishing the power of this presidential agency to conduct intelligence and espionage activities without congressional knowledge.
- In 1979 and 1980, congressional resistance to President Jimmy Carter's Strategic Arms Limitation Treaty (SALT II) with the Soviet Union stopped the president from winning acceptance of his most-desired foreign policy initiative. Although Congress tacitly accepted observance of the treaty without ratification, it handed the president a serious defeat as leader of foreign affairs.
- In 1986 and 1987, Congress investigated the Iran-Contra affair, moving right to the heart of presidential conduct of foreign affairs, uncovering a number of closely held secrets, and holding accountable the government officials and private individuals involved. In court, top presidential assistants, including two presidential national security advisers, were found guilty of violating the law and punished.
- After the 1989 invasion of Panama that deposed and captured dictator Manuel Noriega, President George Bush turned his prey over to the legal system for punishment. Noriega's fate would be determined by the U.S. judicial system, not by the chief executive.

These examples belie Professor Franklin's points about the presidency being out of control. Popular consent and popular control certainly exist, because Congress and public opinion can and do restrain presidents. Moreover, for all the illusion of impenetrable secrecy in the White House, there have been too many investigations of executive activities for that illusion to survive.

As my original seven propositions demonstrated, we must see presidential power clearly if we are to truly understand our government. The criticisms of Professor Franklin remind us of the problems that we face in trying to make our system work and the limitations of the system, but they do not prove that we have a presidency that thwarts the purposes of democracy.

Consequently, it is inaccurate to portray the presidency as out of control. If that were indeed the case, then the events listed above would never have occurred. But they did because the U.S. system is one of checks and balances. It is not perfect, but it works. As long as each of the three branches of government vigilantly guards against abuses of power by the others, the system will continue to function effectively into the future.

## Questions for Discussion

1. What are the constitutional powers of Congress in foreign policy?
2. How should the United States go about requiring and implementing "meaningful" consultation between the president and Congress, particularly in emergency situations?
3. What effect would the adoption by the United States of a parliamentary-type government have on legislative power in foreign policy?
4. How does the war against international terrorism affect the debate over presidential powers?
5. How would the Framers of the Constitution have viewed presidential power in foreign policy since the administration of Franklin Roosevelt?
6. Does George Bush's handling of the Persian Gulf crisis of 1990-1991 demonstrate presidential strength or weakness? What are the reasons for your answer?

## Suggested Readings

Allison, Graham. *Essence of Decision.* Boston, Mass.: Little, Brown, 1971.

Barilleaux, Ryan J. *The President and Foreign Affairs.* New York: Praeger, 1985.

Bell, Coral. *The Reagan Paradox.* New Brunswick, N.J.: Rutgers Univ. Press, 1989.

Buchanan, Bruce. *The Citizen's Presidency.* Washington, D.C.: Congressional Quarterly Press, 1988.

Fisher, Louis. *The Politics of Shared Power: Congress and the Executive.* 2nd ed. Washington, D.C.: Congressional Quarterly Press, 1987.

Franklin, Daniel P. *Extraordinary Measures: The Exercise of Prerogative Powers in the United States.* Pittsburgh, Pa.: Univ. of Pittsburgh Press, 1991.

George, Alexander L. "The Case for Multiple Advocacy in Making Foreign Policy." *American Political Science Review,* 66, no. 3 (September 1972), 751–785.

Hamilton, Alexander, James Madison, and John Jay. *The Federalist Papers,* edited by Clinton Rossiter. New York: New American Library, 1961.

Inderfurth, Karl F., and Loch K. Johnson. *Decisions of the Highest Order: Perspectives on the National Security Council.* Pacific Grove, Calif.: Brooks/Cole, 1988.

Kellerman, Barbara, and Ryan J. Barilleaux. *The President as World Leader.* New York: St. Martin's Press, 1991.

Krauthammer, Charles. "Divided Superpower: The Real Cause of the North Affair." *New Republic,* 195, no. 25 (December 22, 1986), 14–17.

Morris, Bernard S. "Presidential Accountability in Foreign Policy: Some Recurring Problems." *Congress and the Presidency,* 13, no. 2 (Autumn 1986), 157–176.

Rousseau, Jean-Jacques. *The Social Contract* (1762), translated by Richard W. Crosby. Brunswick, Ohio: King's Court Press, 1978.

Schlesinger, Arthur M., Jr. *The Imperial Presidency,* with a new epilogue by the author. New York: Houghton Mifflin, 1989.

U.S. Cong., Senate. *The War Powers after 200 Years: Congress and the President at a Constitutional Impasse.* Hearings before the Special Subcommittee on War Powers of the Committee on Foreign Relations, 100th Cong., 2nd Sess., 1988.

The Constitution specifies the duration of the terms of office for members of Congress: two years for representatives and six years for senators. Although the Framers considered limiting the number of terms that a person may hold congressional office, they abandoned the idea. They did not limit the number of presidential terms either.

George Washington established a precedent for the presidency when he voluntarily stepped down at the end of his second term. Franklin D. Roosevelt upset the tradition of a two-term presidency when he won reelection to third and fourth terms. Roosevelt's experience may never be duplicated because in 1951 the Twenty-second Amendment, limiting the number of presidential terms to two, was adopted. Though spearheaded by Republicans, it may have adversely affected two Republican presidents, Dwight D. Eisenhower and Ronald Reagan, who would have been strong contenders for third terms had they chosen to run again.

From time to time, proposals for limiting congressional terms have been put forward. The idea has won the support of Presidents Abraham Lincoln, Harry S. Truman, Dwight D. Eisenhower, and John F. Kennedy. In 1990 new proposals were made, most notably by a group composed largely of Republicans—Americans to Limit Congressional Terms. Currently, the proposed constitutional amendment is this:

Section 1. No person shall be elected to the Senate for more than two full terms. No person shall be elected to the House of Representatives for more than six full terms.

Section 2. Notwithstanding section 1, a person may serve not more than fourteen years as a Senator and not more than thirteen years as a Representative.

Section 3. For purposes of determining eligibility for election under section 1, no election occurring before the date on which this article is ratified shall be taken into account. For purposes of determining years of service under section 2, no service of any part of a term of office of a Senator or Representative elected to such term before the date this article is ratified shall be taken into account.

It is not difficult to understand why Republican support for limiting congressional terms is strong. The Democratic party has been in continuous control of the House of Representatives since 1955 and has been the majority party in the Senate for most of those years. Democrats have benefited most from incumbency, since incumbents tend to get reelected.

Since 1974, more than 90 percent of the incumbents who have run have been reelected.

Democrats have also been helped by the fact that more members of Congress run for reelection than ever before. In the nineteenth century the number fluctuated between 40 and 70 percent, but it is generally more than 90 percent now.

In proposing a constitutional amendment to limit the number of congressional terms, former senator Gordon Humphrey (R-N.H.) presents his arguments on the subject:

1. Congressional incumbents who seek reelection usually are successful; consequently, elections are meaningless.
2. Incumbents have unfair advantages with franking privileges (for free mail), staff help, support from special interests, and the benefits of seniority.
3. Term limitations would end the problem of pay raises to maintain a comfortable standard of living, for there would no longer be career legislators.

Journalist Albert R. Hunt contends that the current system of unlimited terms is fine as it is. He argues:

1. The real purpose of the proposal is to break the Democratic hold on Congress.
2. Term limitation would increase the power of the permanent bureaucracy and the special interests.
3. Republicans are mistaken to think that they would actually gain from the change.
4. The notion that Congress is permanently embedded is an exaggeration.

 **YES**

## Should the Number of Congressional Terms Be Limited?

### GORDON HUMPHREY

### Limit Congressional Terms

On behalf of Senator DeConcini and on my own behalf, I introduce a joint resolution proposing an amendment to the Constitution limiting the number of terms one may serve in Congress. Although this measure may not be welcomed with open arms by some in this body, I believe it presents a sound and serious remedy for the fundamental flaws which have developed in our system of representative democracy. A recent Gallup poll shows that 70 percent of the American public favor a term limitation, and I believe we in Congress must give careful consideration to this strong popular sentiment. . . .

The proposed amendment to the Constitution would limit Senators to two full terms and Members of the House to six full 2-year terms. . . . This proposed amendment would authorize an additional period of service beyond the term limitation to accommodate the situation of Members who are elected or appointed to complete an unfulfilled term. It would thus limit future Senators to 14 years total service and future House members to 13 years total service, where the circumstance of appointment or election to fill an unfulfilled term arises.

I also stress that both measures exclude the past and current terms served by current Members of Congress from the limitations imposed. In other words, no matter how many terms have been served by a current Member at the time the amendment might be adopted, he or she could still serve two additional Senate terms and six additional House terms under this measure. I hope this provision will make the proposal more palatable.

Frankly, I prefer not to include that provision. It is, after all, a grandfathering provision, and in the case of more than a few Members a grandmothering provision. But I feel that the measure has no hope whatsoever without that provision in it. Thus I included it.

Mr. President, near-guaranteed incumbency has rendered elections nearly meaningless. Members of Congress have increasingly become creatures of the Washington establishment. Both the House and the Senate need more new Members who are willing and able to isolate themselves from this narrow, self-contained culture. This can only be achieved by greater turnover and greater diversity in both Houses of Congress.

Institutionalization of incumbency makes it nearly impossible for a challenger to defeat an incumbent. Franking privileges, legions of eager staffers, and lavish financial and in-kind support from special interest groups often make it all but impossible for well-qualified new candidates to mount a meaningful challenge to sitting Members of Congress. For example, in the 1988 elections, over 98 percent of House Members seeking reelection were successful. By comparison, only 79 percent of the House Members were successful some 40 years ago.

This system of entrenched incumbency is reenforced by the special advantages of accumulated seniority. Seniority leads to key chairmanships, additional platoons of staff, and even greater power to command the financial support of the business and interest groups which are most affected by the committee where the Member wields power.

Because of these circumstances, few elections today are really decided on the relative merits of the opposing candidates. Instead, the outcome is generally predetermined by the institutional and financial advantages of the incumbent. This is nothing less than a malfunctioning of representative democracy.

Some will suggest, no doubt, the remedy for this real problem is to provide for public financing of elections. Whatever the merits of that idea may be, it will not help, because all other things being equal, incumbency will still predominate in most situations.

In fact, I think the argument can be made that public funding of elections is an incumbent protection scheme itself. Others may not think so, but many do.

The fact is that incumbents have always found . . . ways to protect and enhance the advantages of incumbency, and they always will because it is human nature to do so.

The reasonable term limitations proposed by this resolution will go a long way toward restoring a more truly representative Congress. No longer would seats in the House and the Senate be the equivalent of personal fiefdoms, as they are today. No longer would meritorious new candidates be effectively barred from seeking to represent their States or districts by the unassailable advantages of a perpetually entrenched incumbent.

Term limitations would have another beneficial effect. The recurring debates over the need for congressional pay raises largely result from the fact that so many Members of Congress are now career legislators. Since these Members expect to spend their entire active careers in Congress, they claim that recurring pay raises are the only way they can maintain a comfortable standard of living for their families.

And it is true. I do not deny the economics. I have argued that very case. But the point is one should not make a career of serving in Congress.

Mr. President, I am convinced that the term limitations contained in this proposal will produce a more responsible Congress. I urge the Judiciary Committee to hold hearings on this proposal in the near future, and I ask my colleagues for their support.

Mr. President, in their consideration of this resolution, I would ask each Member to ask himself this question: Would it not work an enormous change in attitudes in this institution of Congress if Members knew upon the first day of their first term that no matter how clever they were in enhancing and using the advantages of incumbency, no matter how clever they were in marshaling the support of special interest groups, there would be no possible way to make a career of serving in Congress?

The answer to that question is surely yes; if Members knew on day 1 that no matter what they did, they could not make a lifetime career of serving in Congress, I believe to the depth of my soul that we would see an enormous change in this institution, that we would begin to see the kind of intellectual honesty and political courage that are so sorely needed in dealing with the difficult issues of our time and which are so sorely absent on most occasions in this body.

*Should the Number of Congressional Terms Be Limited?*

## ALBERT R. HUNT

### *Congress's Terms: Just Fine As They Are*

The Democrats have few peers when it comes to rationalizing their inability to win the presidency: one time it's their clinker candidate, another it's the superficial television appeal of Ronald Reagan or the "unfair" hardball tactics of GOP [Republican party] strategist Lee Atwater.

These are exercises in self-delusion. The Democrats lost five of the past six presidential races because most Americans have more confidence in the Republicans on the broad issues of the economy and peace and war.

Yet, during those same two decades, the Republicans' strength actually declined at every other political level, including Congress. Today [1990] the Democrats enjoy the same 55-to-45 advantage in the Senate that they had 20 years ago. They have 15 more House members. The GOP, like the Democrats on the presidential level, offer all manner of rationalizations: redistricting, the campaign financing system and the generous perquisites of incumbency.

Now there's a new GOP-inspired initiative to do something about it: constitutionally limiting congressional terms to 12 years. Former Republican office holders and some GOP political consultants, together with a sprinkling of disgruntled or "populist" Democrats, have banded together to form Americans to Limit Congressional Terms. The idea commands majority support among the public.

The objective, they claim, is to return to the "citizen legislators" that the Founding Fathers envisioned. The real goal, however, is to break the decades-old Democratic lock on Congress.

There's nothing wrong with posturing for political advantage, but the term-limitation proposal is a bad idea that likely would have unintended consequences. It's another of those schemes to take politics out of politics. We don't want to take businessmen out of business or athletes out of sports or doctors out of medicine. Nor should we try to limit the role of politicians in politics.

Term limitation, by removing years of expertise from Capitol Hill, would increase the power of the permanent bureaucracy. "Power would flow from elected to unelected officials," says Thomas Mann of the Brookings Institution.

It would enhance too the power of special interests. Instead of fresh-faced citizen legislators we'd end up with men and women who knew that after 12 years they had to seek a new line of work, most probably with the very interests that are lobbying them. "Most members today don't think about what they're going to do next until their last term," notes Rep. Vin Weber, a conservative Minnesota Republican. "But with a term limitation, the clock would start ticking right away with members thinking, 'What am I going to do when I get out of here in 12 years?' For many, the obvious answer would be to cultivate a relationship with those who can help you later."

Moreover, the premise that this would enhance GOP prospects is dubious. In the 1980s, while Ronald Reagan was riding high, there were 147 wide-open contests for House seats—elections in which there was no incumbent because of either retirement or death; there was a net Democratic gain in those contests of 1.

For years Republicans have been insisting they would dominate politics in the South as soon as the old-time Democrats retired. In 1981, at the dawn of the Reagan era, Virginia seemed the model, with Republicans controlling nine of the 10 House seats; eight years later the Democrats had won back half of the House seats.

But this isn't simply a Southern phenomenon. Going back to 1972, Republicans eyed the third congressional district on the New Jersey shore with its relatively affluent retirees. When incumbent Democrat Jim Howard died in 1988, the GOP saw a golden opportunity, particularly in a year in which George Bush would carry the district by more than 60,000 votes. The result: Frank Pallone, Jr., a Democrat, won by 10,000 votes.

The notion of a permanently embedded Congress is an exaggeration; two-thirds of the current members have been there for less than 12 years. To be sure, there are some extraordinary advantages of incumbency: campaign finance laws and mailing privileges are major assets. And since the Democrats control most state legislatures, gerrymandering of congressional districts probably adds between a half dozen and a dozen seats to the Democratic majority in the House.

But far more importantly, Democrats dominate congressional elections for the same reasons that Republicans dominate presidential elections: The voters think they're better suited.

That was dramatically evident in a Wall Street Journal-NBC News survey in November. On the broad national challenges pertaining to presidential leadership, the Republicans win in a walk: a 43 percent to 13 percent edge on dealing with the Russians, 40 percent to 26 percent on dealing with the economy, and 31 percent to 17 percent on keeping world peace. But when it came to the day-to-day quality-of-life issues, voters are just as decidedly pro-Democratic: 36 percent to 15 percent on protecting the environment, 30 percent to 15 percent on education, and 44 percent to 21 percent on helping the middle class.

"Just as Democrats have not gotten their act together in speaking coherently about broad national interests, neither have the Republicans gotten our act together about how government responds to personal and local needs," says Rep. Vin Weber. "That is much more our problem than incumbency." Republicans like Rep. Weber—and Jack Kemp and Newt Gingrich—have been trying to fashion responsive Republican alternatives, but they still have a ways to go.

Republicans also would do well to remember 40 years ago when they used term limitations to do what they never could do to the late Franklin Roosevelt in life; enact the 22nd Amendment limiting presidents to two terms. Since then it has affected two presidents: Dwight Eisenhower and Ronald Reagan.

## Questions for Discussion

1. Are term limitations for members of Congress democratic? Why or why not?
2. Why do incumbents have an advantage in getting reelected?
3. What effect would public financing of congressional campaigns have on incumbent reelection prospects?
4. Who would benefit and who would be hurt by the adoption of Senator Humphrey's proposal? Explain why.
5. What effect would the amendment have on the power of the special interests?
6. What effect would the amendment have on voting turnout?

## Suggested Readings

Broder, David S. "The Mirage of Term Limits." *Washington Post,* June 13, 1990, p. A23.

Crovitz, L. Gordon. "The Least Responsive Branch." *Commentary,* 87, no. 3 (March 1989), 38–41.

Foundation for the Study of Presidential and Congressional Terms. *Presidential and Congressional Term Limitation: The Issue That Stays Alive.* Washington, D.C.: Foundation for the Study of Presidential and Congressional Terms, 1980.

Hertzberg, Hendrik. "Twelve Is Enough." *New Republic,* 202, no. 20 (May 14, 1990), 22, 24, 26.

Kinsley, Michael. "In Defense of Congress." *Time,* 133, no. 16 (April 17, 1989), 84.

———. "Voters in Chains." *New Republic,* 202, no. 14 (April 2, 1990), 4, 41.

O'Connor, Alice, and Mary L. Henzel. *"The Root of Republican Government": Terms of Office in the Legislative Branch—A Guide for Discussion of Proposals to Change Congressional Terms.* Washington, D.C.: Jefferson Foundation, 1984.

Shields, Mark. "Limit Everybody's Term!" *Washington Post,* March 17, 1989, p. A19.

Will, George F. "Is 18 Years on the Hill Enough?" *Washington Post,* January 7, 1990, p. B7.

# Chapter 13

## *Is Privatization a Preferred Way to Deliver Public Services?*

When the Constitution was adopted in the late eighteenth century, only a few hundred people were employed by government at the national level. Today, however, there are about 3.1 million civilian federal government employees. Millions of other public employees serve in the armed forces and the agencies of state and local governments. About one out of every six employed people in the United States works for government at the national, state, or local level.

Government has grown remarkably in this century because of its increased activity in areas such as foreign policy, the economy, and welfare. In the late eighteenth century the United States was a small power on the periphery of the world's major powers of Europe. Today it is a superpower with great military and economic strength. In meeting the challenges of the post–World War II period, the United States has adopted a policy of internationalism, rejecting the isolationism of its past history. Today millions of people are employed by the federal government to manage its foreign policy needs. These have required the services of large numbers of people in the armed forces. Government, moreover, has been engaged in dispensing foreign aid, gathering intelligence information, assisting individuals and groups abroad, and helping to promote international trade.

In addition to the growth of foreign policy activities, domestic factors are responsible for government expansion. Business has asked for government assistance to build highways, improve railroads, construct dams, widen waterways, and administer tariffs. It has also requested government support for research in energy, transportation, and military technology. The demands of labor have also increased government involvement in the economy. Labor has asked for government inspection involving safety at work sites, government supervision of minimum wage laws, and government employment of those who cannot find jobs in the market economy. Labor has sought government protection of unions against the strong power of business.

At all levels of government, a public bureaucracy plays a vital role in providing government services. Government units deliver mail; run hospitals; operate police, fire, and sanitation departments; teach students from elementary school through college; and dispense welfare services. In all of these activities, the private sector plays some role. For example, the United States Postal Service purchases trucks from private corporations, and boards of education buy textbooks from private publishers.

Since the 1980s the idea of privatization—the transfer of government assets or activities to the private sector—has sparked lively controversy. As the first article in this chapter indicates, privatization can take many forms, such as the sale of government assets, deregulation, government contracting with private firms, and vouchers that can be used to obtain services from the private sector. Some cities and states have even hired private contractors to handle fire protection services and the supervision of prisons.

Advocates of privatization contend that it offers one solution to the federal government's deficit problem. The federal government built up a huge debt burden in the 1980s as it spent more money than it was willing or able to collect. In an attempt to reduce the deficit, Congress passed the Gramm-Rudman Act (named after Senators Phil Gramm of Texas and Warren Rudman of New Hampshire) in 1985. The act sets annual deficit reduction targets that would ultimately eliminate the deficit. It also requires automatic cuts in defense and domestic spending if the targets are not reached.

Is privatization a preferred way to deliver public services? Writing for the conservative think-tank the Heritage Foundation, Stuart M. Butler makes the case for privatization. He contends:

1. Privatization enables the deficit to be reduced without cutting necessary services.
2. The private sector uses resources more efficiently than the government.
3. Privatization has proven to be successful at the state and local level and should be equally successful at the federal level.

Robert Kuttner, economics editor of *New Republic,* makes a case against what he regards as the excessive claims of advocates of privatization. He contends:

1. Privatization does not result in greater efficiency in providing expenditure for public services; a national system is not only more efficient but more equitable.
2. The supposed ability of the government or the consumer to "shop around" among competing suppliers quickly erodes when the vendor gains a monopoly on knowledge specific to the task.
3. The nominal budgetary savings of privatization are often illusory.
4. The goal of most U.S. advocates of privatization is not just making government more effective, but rather enlarging the market and shrinking the polity.
5. Privatization undermines the ethic of public service that is vital to the democratic system of government and can do irreparable harm to the culture of voluntarism.

# ☑ YES

## Is Privatization a Preferred Way to Deliver Public Services?

### STUART M. BUTLER
### *Privatizing Federal Services: A Primer*

## INTRODUCTION

A new word—*privatization*—has entered the lexicon of federal budget making. Put simply, privatization means the transference of federal assets or activities to the private sector. That can take many forms. Facilities owned by the federal government can be sold to the private sector; these same facilities can be kept in federal hands but managed by private firms or groups; federal services can be provided, under contract, by private firms; or low-income Americans can be given the means to obtain services in the private sector. These forms of privatization enable the deficit to be reduced without cutting necessary services. The reason: by turning over functions to the private sector, bureaucratic decision-making is replaced by competitive private management incentives. So resources are used more efficiently, to the benefit of both the taxpayer and service recipients.

Ronald Reagan's FY 1987 budget draws heavily on privatization to meet the deficit reduction targets required under the Gramm-Rudman legislation. This makes good political and economic sense. Privatization offers politicians the attractive alternative of cutting spending without necessarily eliminating programs; all that is changed is the mechanism by which programs are delivered. And privatization revenues obtained from the sale of federal assets, such as power generating facilities or the student and farm loan portfolios, provide a substantial inflow of immediate revenue. This gives Congress breathing space to find sensible ways to reform and restructure programs to meet the deficit reduction targets, rather than resorting to disruptive across-the-board cuts.

While privatization may be new to many Washington policy makers, it is practiced extensively at the state and local level, and by many foreign governments. Their experience proves that privatization can bring relief to budget heartburn, and that it can be very popular with voters. As Congress explores ways to cut the deficit within the Washington political climate, privatization should become increasingly attractive to lawmakers.

## WHAT IS PRIVATIZATION?

Privatization can take many forms. Each has different economic and political effects.

### The Sale of Assets

The most complete form of privatization, obviously, is to sell government-owned assets to private buyers. This removes government entirely from any involvement in the activity and the sale provides revenue to the Treasury. Example: The Reagan Administration's budget proposal to sell the federal Power Marketing Administrations, which generate and distribute electricity. Britain has done this by selling several government-owned firms and nearly one million public housing units to the public, earning $20 billion for the Exchequer.

Asset sales are particularly attractive because they can provide a considerable amount of revenue to the government in a very short time. Other forms of privatization, where the private sector involvement enhances the efficiency of performance, often take time to yield substantial savings.

The potential for the sale of federal assets is enormous. The federal government, for instance, has a portfolio of outstanding loans in excess of $200 billion. This includes loans to students, small businessmen, and farmers. The federal government also owns over 700 million acres of land—the majority of which long has been in commercial use for timber or grazing land—valued at hundreds of billions of dollars. Uncle Sam owns many other assets of significant value, including two of Washington's airports, over one million public housing units, and many valuable lots in the nation's cities.

By selling assets, the federal government "cashes out" the future income they generate—just as an investor will sell a stock certificate for a price based on its anticipated income. Predictably, this has led critics of this form of privatization to claim that the strategy is a shortsighted and inefficient response to the deficit problem—like selling the furniture to pay the rent.

But every successful businessman knows that it is often prudent to liquidate assets during a crisis to provide a cushion to permit essential restructuring of the firm. The federal government is in a financial crisis. It must meet strict deficit reduction targets required by the Gramm-Rudman law. The up-front revenue from asset sales would make it easier for Congress to meet the Gramm-Rudman ceilings for the next couple of years. It could use this breathing space to make sensible, structural reforms in federal programs. This would avoid the meat ax of across-the-board cuts mandated by Gramm-Rudman if the ceilings otherwise are not met.

Privatization, moreover, does far more than merely allow the government to cash out its future income. Such sales are likely to yield a better price than the present value of the government's probable income from the asset. The reason is that managers of publicly owned assets are subject to constant political and budget constraints. They also lack the positive incentives influencing private sector managers. This is why the Forest Service manages to lose money in managing millions of acres of valuable timberland, and why the Postal Service is constantly outgunned in those areas where it faces competition, such as overnight package delivery.

The price a private buyer of a federal asset is willing to pay reflects the income the buyer estimates he can make—not the lower expectations of the public managers. Selling federal assets, therefore, means the full value of the asset is realized. As important to the economy, the resources would be used more wisely. In private hands, the rangeland would not be overgrazed, delinquent student loans would tend to be collected, and Washington's airports would run more smoothly because private owners have the incentive to manage these valuable assets more carefully and efficiently.

## Deregulation

A second form of privatization involves simply allowing the private sector to provide a service now monopolized by the government. Take the Postal Service. Private carriers compete with the Postal Service for the delivery of parcels; the result is that 70 percent of that business is now in the hands of the United Parcel Service [UPS]. It is a different story when it comes to the letters sent by American individuals and businesses. A federal law, the Private Express Statutes, makes it illegal for anyone to compete with the Postal Service in the handling of first class mail. Deregulation would allow private carriers to compete for first class mail business. These new entrants would succeed or fail solely on their ability to serve the public. The federal Treasury would gain both from the contract fees paid by the new private mail delivery services, and from corporate taxes the private firms would pay. And the consumer would gain enormously if first class mail were handled as efficiently as UPS and Federal Express deliver packages.

The Social Security system also could be improved by privatization. American workers and employers are forced to save for their retirement through the government-run pension system. Benefits under the program are a political football, while studies indicate that few younger workers can expect a return on their Social Security contributions comparable with the yield on private pension plans.[1] Giving workers the option to put their Social Security contributions into a private plan would privatize the system by allowing private firms to offer better pension plans.[2]

In this form of privatization, deregulation breaks a government-sponsored monopoly. This leads to more competition and choice, to the benefit of the consumer, and it cuts the budget by reducing the need for government provision of a service.

## Contracting Out

In this form of privatization, the government still funds the service, but invites private firms to bid for the right to provide the service under contract. The cost of the service is reduced because the successful contractor must outbid his rivals.

Hundreds of American cities routinely use private contractors to supply basic municipal services, such as garbage collection, maintenance work and even, in some instances, fire protection. At the federal level, the so-called A-76 program enacted in 1955 requires agencies to compare the in-house cost of routine commercial services with those obtainable from private suppliers. In theory, each agency is supposed to use the least expensive supplier of the appropriate quality of service.

In practice, there is little contracting out at the federal level.[3] One reason is that Congress buckles to pressure from the public employee unions, and places obstacles in the path of privatization. Spurious national security considerations, for instance, have been used to rule privatization out of bounds in many programs. Example: Congress has blocked cost-saving contracting out of much supply, maintenance and repair work despite requests from the Pentagon. Agencies have also been instructed not to even consider a private bidder unless the saving is at least 10 percent of the in-house cost.

Another factor inhibiting federal contracting out is the mechanism used to compare costs. Instead of an independent commission making these comparisons, each agency determines whether it or a private bidder is more economical. Needless to say, employees of the agency have the incentive to use every possible accounting trick to minimize their own stated costs. Until a truly independent method of cost comparison is used in the A-76 program, the deck will be stacked against the private contractor—and hence the taxpayer.

The savings from contracting out are likely to be greatest when the degree of competition within the private sector is most intense. Tough competition means the government knows that the contractor will keep on his toes, for fear of losing the contract.

## Vouchers

In this form of privatization, the government also continues to fund the service. But instead of a federal agency giving a contract to a specific firm to provide a service, the agency gives the users of the service the means—probably a voucher—to purchase a specific service in the open market. In this way the government provides individuals with the power to become consumers. This approach is most appropriate in cases where a healthy market for a service exists, but where households have insufficient income to obtain an adequate supply.

The first widespread use of vouchers has been the Food Stamp program. Low-income families were provided with stamps of a certain value, which they could use only to purchase food. Recipients had the incentive to shop around to obtain the best value for their stamps—and supermarkets had to compete for their business, ensuring efficient provision of food to the poor.

Vouchers could provide low-income Americans with other basic requirements as service providers compete for the consumer's dollar. Rather than continuing a system of expensive public housing and subsidies for landlords, for instance, a housing voucher could be given to the poor. It would empower them as consumers and thus open the competitive private rental market to low-income families. The Administration's FY 1987 budget requests Congress to create 50,000 such housing vouchers, to replace part of the spending on other housing programs.

Similarly, a medical voucher for low-income and elderly Americans would provide them with the incentive to seek the most efficient health insurance available, or the lowest cost subscription to an adequate health maintenance organization.

As with contracting out, vouchers do not reduce the federal government's commitment to provide the service involved. But by encouraging voucher holders to seek the most efficient provider, privatization enables the government to keep the cost of the service as low as possible.

## THE RECORD

Privatization is under way in over 50 countries.[4] Canada is looking into the sale of several "crown corporations," and Mexico has earmarked over 200 state firms for sale to the private sector. Even Cuba is busily transferring the ownership of public housing stock to the tenants.

Several Asian countries are turning to privatization to help state finances and resuscitate stagnant government corporations. In South Korea, for instance, the government has divested itself of several major banks, an oil company, and several other enterprises. Malaysia intends to privatize the telephone system, its national airline, and various government facilities. Other Asian countries are taking similar steps. Perhaps most important of all, Japan will soon be selling stock in the state-owned Nippon Telegraph and Telephone, the country's telephone company, and is planning to restructure and partly privatize its heavily money-losing government railroad system.

Privatization is also becoming a trend in Europe. Turkey has already sold stock in the Bosphorus Bridge and the Keban Dam, and is drawing up plans to sell two dozen other government concerns. In West Germany, many municipalities contract out such services as public housing management and health clinics. Even in socialist-ruled France, the government of François Mitterand is taking steps toward returning to the private sector many of the corporations it hastily nationalized during the past four years.

By far the most extensive privatization is occurring in Britain. Since Margaret Thatcher became prime minister in 1979, there has been widespread contracting out at all levels of government, approximately $20 billion worth of government assets has been sold to private buyers, and over 400,000 government workers have been moved to private payrolls. Over 800,000 public housing units have been sold to tenants, while various commercial firms and the entire telephone system have been sold to the public.[5]

## The American Experience

Privatization is not new to the U.S., even though the term itself has only recently become familiar to most Americans. At the state and local level, governments are increasingly turning to privatization to reduce the cost of services. A recent survey by the National Center for Policy Analysis found that approximately 35 percent of local governments now have private firms to collect residential garbage, 42 percent use private firms to operate and maintain their bus systems, and 80 percent contract out vehicle towing and parking.

Other functions routinely undertaken by the private sector in U.S. towns and cities include street repair work, traffic signal maintenance, tree trimming, utility billing, ambulance services, health and welfare programs, park landscaping and maintenance, and legal services.[6] Even fire departments and prison facilities are operated by private firms in many cities. A study by the International City Management Association found a 50 percent rise in the number of cities privatizing one or more of the services during the past ten years.[7] The use of private firms to collect garbage has more than doubled during the decade, private street repair operations have risen 600 percent, and the use of private firms to manage parks has skyrocketed 2,700 percent.[8]

The overriding factor leading local officials to privatization is cost: the competitive private market generally provides routine services much cheaper than a government department. Study after study confirms the significant cost savings when private contractors are used.[9] A recent study of the Los Angeles area, for instance, reveals that street cleaning by city employees typically costs 43 percent more than the equivalent service provided by a private firm; janitorial services cost 73 percent more than the private alternative; and road resurfacing 96 percent more. Of the eight services analyzed, only in payroll preparation were public sector costs comparable with those in the private sector.[10]

As a sizeable bonus, of course, the private firms that win contracts to perform public services pay local taxes. The municipal bureaucracy pays nothing to the town treasurer.

At the federal level, there have been relatively few privatization initiatives, even under Ronald Reagan. One reason is that many government activities in other countries are already delivered by the private sector in America. Another reason is that the Reagan Administration's political experiences with privatization have not been pleasant—mainly because it has failed to profit from the tactical lessons learned the hard way by foreign governments. Margaret Thatcher, for instance, carefully builds coalitions of those who have or will have a vested interest in privatization. The Reagan Administration has not. It thus ran into a political buzz saw when it attempted to sell the weather satellite system and a small portion of federal land holdings to the private sector.[11]

Even contracting out routine services to the private sector has not been expanded to the degree that might be expected of a conservative administration. The Administration has done almost nothing to remove the obstacles to the fulfillment of the A-76 program by which federal agencies are required to compare the in-house cost of providing commercial services with bids from private firms, and to choose the lowest cost option.

## THE POLITICS OF PRIVATIZATION

The Reagan Administration has set bold privatization goals for the FY 1987 budget. It has proposed selling such assets as the Power Marketing Administrations, the Naval Petroleum Reserve, and a part of the federal loan portfolio. In addition, it is pressing for a full voucher program for low-income housing and compensatory education. These and other privatization initiatives, says the Administration, could cut the deficit by $7 billion in FY 1987, and many billions more in later years.

The outlook for these initiatives has been improving dramatically. The passage of balanced budget legislation, and the mounting wealth of tactical experience from abroad, suggests that privatization could be the key to bringing federal spending under control.

### The Impact of Gramm-Rudman

The Gramm-Rudman-Hollings deficit reduction timetable marks a turning point in the debate over federal spending. Even if the Supreme Court upholds the lower court ruling invalidating part of Gramm-Rudman, Congress is committed to reducing the deficit. Reagan's determination to veto any tax increases leaves lawmakers with only one deficit reducing option—cut spending. This could be stingingly painful for Congressmen. What could spare them this pain, while meeting deficit reduction guidelines, is privatization.

As a model, Congressmen need only examine recent state and local experiences. Trapped between the rock of voter resistance to tax increases and the hard place of reduced assistance from Washington, the country's mayors have found that through privatization they can maintain the quality of services at lower cost. This already makes for good politics at the local level.

It would make good politics at the national level. Instead of slashing services to meet spending targets, as traditional budget cutting requires, privatization allows lawmakers to continue supplying the services. The only difference is that a new sign will hang over the programs proclaiming: "Under New Management."

It should not take long for Congressmen, like their local counterparts, to recognize privatization's attractiveness.

## Privatization Coalitions

A major reason why even the most wasteful or redundant federal program can be impervious to budget cutting efforts is that a tight coalition forms around it. This coalition consists of program beneficiaries, those who serve these beneficiaries, and the political and bureaucratic constituencies whose careers depend on the program's existence. When the program's budget is challenged, this coalition has a strong vested interest to wage a ferocious campaign to preserve it. As the Reagan Administration has discovered, it may be possible to dent programs supported by these coalitions, but is usually impossible to eliminate them.

These coalitions win because it is difficult to find congressional and grassroots allies who will support budget cutting with tenacity. The average taxpayers will denounce spending in principle, but in practice will rarely join in an all-out effort to trim or eliminate a particular program.

Privatization changes these dynamics. The creation of a private mechanism spawns groups of beneficiaries and supporters which create a "mirror image" coalition to that defending the existing programs. Like the coalitions supporting government programs, the mirror image coalitions consist of individuals who will receive services and the providers of those services—in this case private firms and groups. And these private coalitions have the incentive to campaign hard for stepped-up privatization.

Privatization at the local level has produced a multitude of private sector organizations that have lobbied intensively and successfully against "public sector coalitions." These coalitions can often draw strength from the groups that once supported the government provision. In Britain, for instance, giving public housing tenants the right to buy their units at a discount turned one-time advocates of public housing subsidies into cost-conscious homeowners. Similarly, giving British public sector workers free stock in the privatized companies that replaced their public agency converted privatization's fiercest opponents into some of its strongest supporters.

   While these privatization coalitions quickly and almost automatically form when privatization takes place, they need to be mobilized in advance if privatization proposals are to gain the support they need to become law. Thatcher's government has taken careful steps to build a constituency for privatization, primarily by giving key groups, such as employees, management, and customers, an ownership stake in the designated privatized firm.[12] So far the Reagan Administration has ignored this lesson. It is this that has caused its privatization initiatives to be delayed or abandoned.

## CREATING THE POLITICAL CLIMATE FOR AMERICAN PRIVATIZATION

The Reagan Administration must create a political environment conducive to privatization and design initiatives to win the support of key constituencies. To accomplish this, several steps should be taken. Among them:

### 1. Organize Coalitions

Even before announcing a privatization initiative, officials should identify and mobilize those constituencies likely to gain directly or indirectly. In some cases this may involve helping organize such constituencies into an effective political force to counter the established constituencies favoring government delivery of services. Example: the greatest beneficiaries of an education voucher program would be low-income parents and the small neighborhood private schools that cater to lower-income parents. Helping these groups form national networks and recognizing leaders of these networks as legitimate spokesmen on education issues would strengthen the voucher movement.

### 2. Attempt to Erode Anti-privatization Coalitions

Public employees understandably are concerned that privatization may endanger their jobs. This concern, and the opposition to privatization that it produces, may be reduced in a number of ways. The pace of contracting out, for instance, can be limited such that the number of jobs lost in the private sector corresponds to the usual rate of attrition. In that way the existing workforce is not threatened—there is simply a freeze on new hiring. Or the employees may be given an ownership stake, even outright ownership, of a privatized asset.

When the British government privatized the government-owned National Freight Corporation in 1982, the employees were allowed to purchase 85 percent of the trucking company. With the incentive of ownership, the workers became advocates rather than opponents of the privatization. Private ownership, meanwhile, has turned the money-losing drain on the taxpayer into a highly profitable, taxpaying company.

Steps may be needed to quell the public's fear about private ownership of government assets. It is a fear often fanned by the opponents of privatization. For instance, when the Reagan Administration sought in 1982 to sell five million acres of commercial range and timberland—a tiny fraction of the 750 million acre federal inventory—it faced a crippling barrage of criticism. The argument in effect was that it was selling the national parks to developers, desecrating the memory of Smokey the Bear. Public outcry stymied the sale.

Such a reaction could be averted in the future. The management of parks and wilderness areas, for example, could be given, under contract, to environmental organizations. This should reassure the public that these lands will not be part of any sale policy.[13] Similarly, any proposal to introduce an element of privatization into the Social Security system should be preceded with an iron-clad guarantee that existing retirees and those nearing retirement would not be affected.

## 3. Spread Ownership Widely

A key lesson of the British experience with asset sales is that spreading the private ownership widely, especially among groups that might otherwise be hostile to the sale, helps win political support for privatization. It is now almost routine for Britain to structure sales of government enterprises as stock offerings to the public. But preference is given to purchasers who are employees, users of the asset, and small investors. Sometimes even free stock is given to these groups. When Britain's telephone system was privatized in 1984, 96 percent of the employees and two million Britons bought stock in a tidal wave of enthusiasm for the sale.

The Reagan Administration should heed this lesson. Its sale of the federally owned freight railroad, Conrail, to the Norfolk-Southern Railroad, for instance, would be an excellent deal for the taxpayer. But the sale has been slowed, perhaps fatally, by opposition from key beneficiaries of federal ownership of the freight railway system. Yet these key constituencies might have been converted to supporters of Conrail's privatization if attractively priced blocks of stock had been reserved for employees, shippers and other groups. When the Administration attempts to win congressional support of its plan to sell the five huge Power Marketing Administrations, it will have a better chance of success if it adopts a stock sale strategy favoring employees and customers.[14]

## 4. Recognize the Importance of Tax Incentives

A tax incentive can provide the focus around which a privatization coalition can develop. Favorable tax treatment of sale-leasebacks, for instance, encouraged construction firms to press municipalities to explore innovative, lower cost wastewater treatment plants. The deduction for Individual Retirement Accounts has stimulated the growth of a powerful new constituency for private pensions.

The powerful stimulus to privatization provided by tax incentives should be part of the effort to simplify the tax code. The purpose of raising taxes is to pay for government spending. Privatization reduces the need for government spending. But eliminating certain tax incentives would reduce the level of privatization, because deductions stimulate charitable contributions, private pension plans, and other alternatives to government programs. Ending such tax incentives would discourage these private options, and that may result simply in more demands for spending—and ultimately higher taxes.

## 5. Adopt an Independent Method of Comparing Costs

The current method of comparing the bid of a private contractor with an in-house cost estimate is heavily biased against the contractor. This could be rectified, leading to more privatization, if the role of comparing costs and deciding when to contract out were transferred to an independent commission staffed by government and private sector accountants.

## CONCLUSION

Privatization allows federal spending to be reduced without denying services that Congress agreed to provide. And by using vouchers, private contractors, or asset sales, services can be provided more efficiently. Replacing direct government spending on low-income housing with a system of housing vouchers does not cut the housing budget by providing less shelter—it does so by giving tenants the incentive to seeking better housing for fewer voucher dollars. And selling the Bonneville Power Administration to the private sector does not mean that generators will fall silent—it means that the utility's management will have to pay closer attention to the needs of their customers.

Privatization recognizes that it is possible to reduce the cost of government by changing the role of government. Government is not very good at running railroads, or building housing, or picking up garbage. By recognizing this simple fact, and drawing on the competitive private sector to perform such functions, Congress can cut the deficit by ensuring that more efficient services, not fewer services, are provided to the American people.

---

*NOTES*

1. Peter Ferrara, "Rebuilding Social Security, Part 1: The Crisis Continues," Heritage Foundation *Backgrounder* No. 345, April 25, 1984.

2. Peter Ferrara, "Rebuilding Social Security, Part 2: Toward Lasting Reform," Heritage Foundation *Backgrounder* No. 346, April 25, 1984.

3. See Stuart M. Butler, *Privatizing Federal Spending* (New York: Universe Books, 1985), pp. 53–56.

4. See "Privatization—Everybody's Doing It Differently," *The Economist*, December 21, 1985; *Privatization around the Globe*, Policy Report #120 (Dallas, Texas: National Center for Policy Analysis, January 1986).

5. See Butler, *op. cit.;* Madsen Pirie, *Dismantling the State* (Dallas, Texas: National Center for Policy Analysis, 1985).

6. *Privatization in the U.S.*, Policy Report #116 (Dallas, Texas: National Center for Policy Analysis, June 1985).

7. E. S. Savas, "The Efficiency of the Private Sector," in Stuart M. Butler, ed., "The Privatization Option," Heritage Foundation *Lecture Series* No. 42, 1985.

8. *Privatization in the U.S., op. cit.* See also Robert Benenson, "Privatizing Public Services," *Editorial Research Report*, Vol. II, No. 4, *Congressional Quarterly*, 1985.

9. Savas, *op. cit.;* see also E. S. Savas, *Privatizing the Public Sector* (Chatham, New Jersey: Chatham House, 1982).

10. Barbara Stephens, "Company Public and Private Sector Efficiency," *National Productivity Review*, Autumn 1984.

11. Butler, *op. cit.*, pp. 82–91.

12. Butler, *op. cit.*, Chapter 2.

13. John Baden, "Let Environmentalists Manage Wilderness Lands," Heritage Foundation *Backgrounder* No. 461, October 8, 1985.

14. Milton R. Copulos, "Cutting the Deficit by Selling Federal Power Marketing Administrations," Heritage Foundation *Backgrounder* No. 485, February 13, 1986.

 ☑ N O

---

## *Is Privatization a Preferred Way to Deliver Public Services?*

---

### ROBERT KUTTNER

### *False Profit: The Perils of Privatization*

Next month the libertarian Cato Institute is holding a conference to discuss the privatization of money. As Milton Friedman says in a conference brochure, "Money is too important to be left to central bankers." Although even most conservatives would probably balk at taking coin out of the public realm, the idea of privatization is much in vogue in conservative circles. Supposedly, almost everything that the government does could work better if left to the private market, and no function, no matter how sovereign, is sacred. The Reagan administration sold billions of dollars worth of federal assets and introduced a variety of voucher and government-by-contract schemes. At the state and local level, fiscal pressures made it attractive to privatize a range of services, from ambulances to prison administration to garbage collection. The March 1988 report of the President's Commission on Privatization (slyly subtitled "Towards More Effective Government") called for stepped-up privatization of everything from air traffic control to Amtrak. Privatization appeals to the Bush administration, too, though more for budgetary reasons than ideological ones.

The case for privatization invites careful scrutiny. At bottom, the idea is based on the laissez-faire proposition that the market must be more efficient than the state. Yet liberals, perhaps even more than conservatives, share a strong interest in efficient, accountable government, since they rely on it to a greater degree. If the private sector can indeed deliver public services with greater efficiency, accountability, and choice, then privatization is worth considering.

One must begin by sorting out the several uses of the word. Most literally, privatization simply means turning over public enterprises to private industry. But this is a much bigger issue in Western Europe and South America, where direct government ownership of commercial enterprises has been more widespread than in the United States. For the most part, American privatization seeks to bring the private sector into public services. In their heart of hearts, the more libertarian of the privatizers also want government out of the business of providing health services, education, housing, retirement income, and so on. But obviously, pure privatization of such public responsibilities would not only introduce greater choice and competitiveness. It would simply place health and educational services beyond the reach of those without the resources to pay for them. Few privatizers are prepared to argue that case. As a result, the big push for privatization, U.S.-style, has been a drive for vouchers and contracts as substitutes for direct government services.

The Heritage Foundation's Stuart Butler has argued that privatization not only shrinks the state directly, by shedding government functions, but dismantles the constituency for government spending and substitutes a "mirror image coalition" made up of prospective contractors who have "the incentive to campaign hard for stepped-up privatization." Following his own advice, Butler has been featured at events sponsored by something called the Privatization Council, a lobbying group underwritten by contractors seeking more government business. The co-chairman of this body is Prescott Bush, Jr., the president's brother.

The privatizers rely heavily on "public choice" theory, which holds that the polity can be best understood as just another marketplace, in which self-interested individuals maximize their satisfactions by demanding government spending. Ostensibly civic or public values are said to conceal narrow private interests. In public choice theory, government agencies are merely monopoly providers whose main goal is the enlargement of turf and the extraction of "monopoly rents," whose narrow interests overwhelm the general interest in keeping spending under reasonable control. As Harvard's Steven Kelman recently wrote in a convincing critique of public choice theory, "Common to all public choice writing is the conclusion that, while the pursuit of self-interest in the marketplace maximizes social welfare, pursuit of self-interest in the political marketplace produces catastrophe."

Even if one accepts this sanguine view of the market and the corollary pessimism about the competence of the polity, the obvious logical fallacy is the touching assumption that contractors are innocent of political influence. Contractors, however private, join the coalition not just for spending per se, but for inefficient spending. In practice, this turns out to be the weak link in the privatization argument. Privatization only changes the venue, not the public responsibility. And if government pays the freight, government necessarily has to police the contractor. Yet the more reach contractors have under a privatized system, the less capacity government is likely to retain. The claim of hopeless government incompetence becomes a convenient self-fulfilling prophesy. Pentagon weapons procurement is surely the longest-running refutation of the hypothesis that government supervision of contractors is efficient.

To examine the major cases of government by voucher and contract is to appreciate why privatization is no panacea. Take the Medicare program, which in effect uses both vouchers and contracts. Under Medicare, the citizen is free to shop around for a doctor or a hospital. The provider is then reimbursed by the government. Presumably, this enhances choice and puts medical providers under competitive discipline. But in order to damp down the inevitable inflation that results when government foots the bill for a commodity—health—whose demand is nearly infinite, a bewildering proliferation of regulations is necessary. The regulations attempt to contain costs by stipulating what the government will pay for particular procedures. But the dialectic of cost containment is anything but technical or politically neutral. It is in the financial self-interest of the medical industry to exert its considerable political power to minimize regulatory restraints, not to maximize efficiency. Public choice theory has it exactly backward. Under Medicare, the force for cost containment has been the public officials—and they are no match for a private sector bent on expansion of outlays.

Even worse, the current system diverts scarce medical resources from areas of genuine medical need to ones that can command reimbursement. This outcome is not the fruit of bad regulation, but the natural consequence of the dynamic tension between for-profit providers and government paymasters. Universal systems of health care that are less privatized turn out to be more efficient, in two respects. They have less wasteful administrative and regulatory overhead. And since foreign hospitals under universal health systems typically have annual budgets based on a given population rather than case-by-case reimbursement, they have no artificial incentive to deploy resources based on what is reimbursable. A comprehensive national system is not only more equitable, but more efficient, as well.

A second general problem with government-by-contract is that the supposed ability of the government or the consumer to "shop around" among competing suppliers quickly erodes when the vendor gains a monopoly on knowledge specific to the task. In an extensive report titled "Purchase of Services: Can State Government Gain Control?" the Massachusetts Taxpayers Foundation, a conservative business-funded fiscal watchdog, lamented the fact that the political and technical power of vendors made effective supervision and cost containment all but impossible. State "agencies did not have the structural capacity to establish standards and expectations for programs, much less to monitor and evaluate them." The report went on to describe how large providers become oligopolies because government agencies grow dependent on them. If the vendor can restrain its greed, it can extract moderate monopoly rents indefinitely.

Vouchers, though they offer a wider choice of providers, often present similar problems. One delicate hypocrisy in the conservative argument for vouchers is the failure to acknowledge just how expensive a generalized voucher system would be. This is a kind of good cop/bad cop game: the conservatives touting the superiority of vouchers are never the same ones responsible for writing actual budgets. The Reagan administration was very high on housing vouchers, for the usual free market reasons—but funded them only at a fraction of the cost of the direct government housing programs that they were supposed to replace.

Moreover, voucher advocates have a naive view of the market power of consumers. Vouchers may work well enough in areas where there is an almost infinite supply of vendors and an abundance of the product—the best example here is food stamps, which is the rare voucher with buying power as good as cash. But in health, or education, or housing, the low-income buyer armed with a government voucher is typically in a hopelessly unequal bargaining position vis-à-vis the seller. In large cities with housing shortages, the family carrying a government housing voucher is a tenant of last resort. The landlord is doing the government a favor to take the voucher at all. In practice, such tenants do not end up with the same freedom of choice as other consumers; the government ends up subsidizing astronomical rents for poor quality housing; and the voucher, far from adding to the housing supply, only serves to tighten markets further and drive up costs. In some large cities, more than half of the voucher recipients could not find any suitable housing that would accept the voucher.

Proprietary trade schools offer another case against the alleged superiority of vouchers. Ironically, the most "entrepreneurial" sector of postsecondary education today is financed almost entirely by government funds. Fly-by-night technical schools can make a quick buck because federal law permits low-income students to use higher education grants to buy education at for-profit trade and technical schools. A $2,000 Pell Grant pays only a fraction of the tuition of a university, but all of the tuition of a storefront school of cosmetology or data entry. Government is not equipped to police all of these schools, nor is there the well-developed system of accreditation that exists at the university level. The result is that private entrepreneurs financed by vouchers profit from an immense waste of public funds.

The third basic problem with government by contract or voucher is that the normal budgetary savings are often illusory. Take ambulances. Many suburban towns have "saved money" by shifting from tax-supported ambulances to private, contract ambulance companies. Big cities, with a much needier population, still typically run their own ambulances, generally at a substantial loss. The reason, however, has nothing to do with the greater efficiency of private ambulances. The suburbs can slough off ambulance service onto contractors because most of their residents have private health insurance or Medicare, which reimburses ambulance vendors at profitable rates. In big cities, many ambulance customers have only Medicaid, which reimburses at a far lower rate, or are too disorganized to have any insurance and the city agency must absorb the entire cost. Not surprisingly, private ambulance companies avoid large cities. The greater "efficiency" of suburban ambulance privatization is mainly an accounting artifact.

Prisons also turn out to be disappointing candidates for privatization. Even aside from the issue of whether something as inherently public as coercive custody should be placed in private hands, there is little evidence that private persons produce durable savings to the public purse. John Donahue, of Harvard's Kennedy School, reviewed the evidence on privatized prisons and concluded that prison administration does not lend itself to genuine competition for prison management contracts, because incumbent operators are "likely to become entrenched," and because "the enterprise of incarcerating people has relatively little scope for technical progress in trimming costs." In general, privatized prisons have demonstrated cost savings only by skimming the easier inmate populations, leaving the more difficult ones to the state.

Prisons, of course, suggest the more fundamental problem with privatization as a philosophy. As Paul Starr has written, "Privatization calls upon motives of private gain, weakening the grounds of authority and capacity to assert collective interests over more narrow ones." In a political democracy that is also a market economy, the polity offers a realm of choice based on one person/one vote, a criterion fundamentally different from that of the market economy. But democratic choice is no less a form of individual liberty than choice based on purchases in the marketplace. And when government, as the agent of the polity, offers all citizens the use of parks and schools, or prosecutes law breakers, it also signals membership in a political community with common public values that would be diminished by privatization.

To be sure, it is reasonable to debate where the boundaries of market and polity lie. As Starr suggests, the instruments that were essential to bind together a polity in 1790 are not necessarily the same ones needed in the 1990s. The postal service, Starr observes, "no longer has the same practical and symbolic importance in knitting together the nation that it once did." Some elements of postal service are fair game for privatization, yet the pure market criterion of requiring all postal services to pay their own way would force a postal system to withdraw cheap universal service from small towns and rural areas. To that extent, a partial rationale for postal service as a function of the polity rather than the market remains.

As society changes, government should be able to add some functions, and shed others. For example, contract garbage collection, a great favorite of privatizers, often seems to save money without diminishing service (though fee-for-service trash pickup could erode universal sanitation in poor neighborhoods). In principle, one could imagine the careful introduction of market measures to improve the capacity and competence of the polity. Unfortunately, most of the American privatizers have as their ideological agenda not just "more effective government," but the goal of enlarging the market and shrinking the polity. In Sweden the social democratic government is in the process of introducing a variety of marketlike devices into public agencies. For example, the state labor market board, which provides grants for worker retraining, now offers localities a choice of either hiring the state to retrain workers or hiring private vendors. But this reform was undertaken as part of a program to enhance the public worker training service, not diminish it.

Possibly the worst single contribution of the economics profession to the understanding of political society is the tautological and straitened attempt to reduce all public-spiritedness or altruism to merely an odd, masochistic special case of egoistic utility-maximization. As Steven Kelman has observed, an ethic of public service is vital to a democratic system of government. When everything is reduced to a private, profit-maximizing transaction, that ethic is diminished. Government, certainly, does not have to conduct every piece of public business itself. The large non-profit sector, much of which today operates on public subsidy, is a crucial agent of public service. But like the polity, its ethic is service, community, and altruism, rather than private gain. The savings and loan industry used to be part of that sector. Today it has become part of the market sector, and the fire-sale disposition of savings and loan assets suggests just how inefficient a government bent on privatizing can be.

Libertarians find it convenient to invoke Tocqueville and to insist that government flourishes at the expense of community and voluntarism. But in truth, voluntary associations have often existed in cooperative symbiosis with government. The PTA [Parent-Teacher Association] is perhaps the supreme example of private voluntary energies working in close coordination with a public institution, the local school system. Almost every free public library has its adjunct association of volunteers. Hospital volunteers work to support institutions that today get close to half their income from the government. Ceding all of this activity to private profit-making institutions would do irreparable harm to the culture of volunteerism. The logic of service and the logic of profit are largely at odds. Why volunteer your time to an organization whose entire purpose is making a buck?

In a political society, the efficiency test is not the only test that matters. Even if the privatizers were right that government by contract and voucher were invariably more efficient and conducive to greater choice, there would still be a persuasive case for a strong and vital public realm. That case, of course, would be far more difficult to argue if one had to accept the claim that an effective polity required some sacrifice of economic well-being. But, happily, the privatizers are substantially wrong even on their own chosen ground of debate.

## Questions for Discussion

1. Are there some areas in which privatization is more applicable than others? Which areas? Explain why.
2. What effect does privatization have on government spending?
3. What effect does privatization have on efficiency in delivering public services?
4. Should Social Security be privatized? Why or why not?
5. What effect would vouchers have on education? What are the reasons for your answer?

## Suggested Readings

Bandow, Doug. "Private Cures for Postal Ills." *Reason*, 20 (December 1988), 24–27.

Butler, Stuart M. *Privatizing Federal Spending*. New York: Universe Books, 1985.

Carver, Robert H. "Examining the Premises of Contracting Out." *Public Productivity and Management Review*, 13 (Fall 1989), 27–40.

Donahue, John D. *The Privatization Decision: Public Ends, Private Means*. New York: Basic Books, 1989.

Henig, Jeffrey R. "Privatization in the United States: Theory and Practice." *Political Science Quarterly*, 104 (Winter 1989–1990), 649–670.

Kamerman, Sheila B., and Alfred J. Kahn, eds. *Privatization and the Welfare State*. Princeton, N.J.: Princeton Univ. Press, 1989.

McClenahen, John S. "Should Government Run Like a Business?" *Government Executive*, 22, no. 1 (January 1990), 12–14, 16.

McDonald, Douglas C., ed. *Private Prisons and the Public Interest*. New Brunswick, N.J.: Rutgers Univ. Press, 1990.

"Overview: Perspectives on Privatization and the Public Interest." *Yale Law & Policy Review*, 6, no. 1 (1988), 1–108.

Savas, Emanuel S. "False Prophet: The Faulty Reasoning of a Privatization Foe." *Privatization Review*, 4, no. 2 (Spring 1989), 23–27.

———. *Privatization: The Key to Better Government*. Chatham, N.J.: Chatham House, 1987.

U.S., Cong. *Privatization of the Federal Government*. Hearings before the Subcommittee on Monetary and Fiscal Policy of the Joint Economic Committee, 98th Cong., 1st Sess., 1983. Pts. 1, 2.

Wilson, James Q. *Bureaucracy: What Government Agencies Do and Why They Do It*. New York: Basic Books, 1989.

# Chapter 14

## Is the Central Intelligence Agency an Anachronism?

Democracy requires openness rather than secrecy. The citizens of a democracy must know what their government is doing so they will be able to evaluate both issues and the quality of leadership. In the United States, a free press and legislative oversight of the executive branch help to provide information about what government is doing to the benefit of an informed electorate.

While democracy requires openness, the requirements of foreign policy often demand secrecy. An enemy of the United States reads the same newspapers and watches the same television programs as Americans. If every plan and move of the United States in foreign policy were made public, the country's enemies would have advantages that would harm its security.

There is an inevitable tension between the government's need to maintain secrets and the people's right to know. Perhaps nowhere in U.S. foreign policy activities is the conflict between secrecy and openness more focused than in the Central Intelligence Agency (CIA).

The CIA was formed in 1947 as part of the reorganization of the national security agencies in light of the cold war between the United States and the Soviet Union. The CIA was an outgrowth of the Office of Strategic Services, which had been established during World War II to gather strategic information and engage in secret operations against the wartime enemies of the United States.

Today the CIA is one of twelve intelligence agencies responsible for national security. Its objective is to provide intelligence information of interest to the security of the United States. But it has also acted to implement policy. It has intervened in the internal affairs of many foreign governments, most notably to support governments friendly to the United States and opposed to the Soviet Union. At times the CIA has allied with foreign democratic forces, but it has also supported regimes that have violated human rights.

The CIA has received criticism for its involvement in Vietnam, its support in toppling a government in Guatemala, and its role in assassination attempts of foreign leaders. Since "The Agency," as the CIA is sometimes called, is shrouded in secrecy, it is often unable to publicize its successes lest it divulge its sources to U.S. enemies.

As the CIA's major role has been to provide intelligence for the United States in its relations with the Soviet Union, its mission has recently been called into question. By 1990, most people believed that the cold war, with its strong ideological, political, and economic conflict between the United States and the Soviet Union, was over. Soviet forces had withdrawn from Afghanistan. East Germany, which had been under the domination of the Soviet Union, was united with the Federal Republic of Germany under noncommunist leadership. Communist governments in Eastern Europe, once loyal to Moscow, were independent and in most cases free and democratic. The Soviet Union, moreover, was reducing its military forces and was approving arms control agreements.

In view of these changes, is the CIA now an anachronism? The former National Security Council staff member Roger Morris argues that it is. He contends:

1. The new dangers that the CIA emphasizes to justify its budget dollars are international narcotics, terrorism, and industrial espionage, but the CIA's performance in dealing with these dangers is poor.
2. The notion that the CIA is needed to cope with increased Soviet intelligence activities is unfounded.
3. The CIA has engaged in shady operations with failed financial institutions and organized crime and has also been involved in extraconstitutional activities.
4. The agency has supported corrupt and brutal regimes that violate fundamental human rights and its interventions have often paved the way for such regimes.
5. The CIA has been unable to assess Soviet developments accurately.

Morris calls for a shifting of intelligence activities from the CIA to other agencies.

Senator David L. Boren (D-Okla.) defends the CIA and says it is needed to acquire new and different kinds of information. He argues:

1. Espionage against the United States has not diminished.
2. The Soviet Union remains capable of using nuclear weapons against the United States and so needs constant watching. Moreover, the United States needs to observe the Soviet Union's compliance with arms control agreements.
3. The United States can never be certain who will control nuclear weapons in the Soviet Union.
4. The United States still faces dangers posed by the proliferation of chemical and biological weapons, regional conflicts, terrorism, nuclear war between other nuclear powers, and a possible cutoff of supplies of vital resources, especially oil.
5. The post–cold war world requires a reorientation of U.S. intelligence priorities and not a dismantling of the CIA.

*Is the Central Intelligence Agency an Anachronism?*

## ROGER MORRIS

### *CIA—Costly, Inept, Anachronistic*

Of all the rusting relics of the cold war, none lingers on with more irony, more resistance to its growing anachronism than the Central Intelligence Agency [CIA].

Born in the crucible of the great postwar U.S.-Soviet rivalry and some of its worst expedients, with often no apparent vision save conflict, no abiding purpose save bureaucratic justification or aggrandizement, America's ministry of espionage should be facing questions about its mission and ethic, its practical and constitutional role in the international relations and security of a democratic society. Yet there seems little evidence that either the CIA or the Bush Administration has begun to ponder a more relevant concept of an intelligence service in a radically changed world.

Not surprisingly, the CIA has resorted to the hoary but dependable politics of the past 45 years. It has trotted out suitably new, old or simply hidden dangers, asked for more money and scrambled to protect bureaucratic flanks.

Along with its 11 related institutions in the U.S. espionage community—including the Defense Intelligence Agency and the electronic eavesdroppers and code breakers of the National Security Agency—the CIA dined well on the flush national security spending of the 1980s. Intelligence budgets tripled over the decade to reach nearly $30 billion in fiscal 1990. Money for CIA operations and analyses has continued to grow throughout the past five years, even as Pentagon appropriations have peaked and declined.

To preserve and extend that expanding domain while much of its rationale disappears, the CIA has begun to advertise new perils of the post–cold-war period—international narcotics, terrorism, industrial espionage, even the spread of chemical weapons. In each field, however, the agency's own performance has been inept if not worse.

From hostage-taking to airline bombing, U.S. intelligence on terrorist attacks has been notoriously flawed, and little better on the humming commerce and intrigue that built chemical warfare arsenals in the Middle East. As for policing the narcotics trade, the CIA itself stands shrouded in a long history of alleged, still unresolved complicity with drug traffickers—from mountain tribesmen and corrupt colonels of Southeast Asia in the 1960s to Gen. Manuel Noriega and the contras of Central America in the 1980s.

As if aware of the vulnerability of these newer projects, CIA lobbyists have summoned an old ally in the budget wars—the agency's major foreign counterpart and in some disturbing ways its mirror image, the Soviet KGB [secret police]. Thus the predictable speeches, leaks and briefings in which the CIA Director, William H. Webster, sees what he calls "more aggressive, more robust" Soviet intelligence efforts, lavishly funded and cunningly effective despite the veritable bankruptcy, political chaos and disintegration within the USSR [Union of Soviet Socialist Republics].

The Russians somehow retain their secret police control in Eastern Europe even as the bloc crumbles, Mr. Webster told one audience last winter [1989]. The now-acknowledged backwardness and disarray of the Soviet economy, he maintained, only means even greater KGB zeal in industrial and technological espionage.

Moreover, there are the imminent new U.S.-Soviet arms agreements, the intelligence demands of on-site monitoring and verification, the inspectors who are spies and thus the spies to watch the inspectors. Nor can it all be done safely with a mere $10 billion to $15 billion more for new radar-imaging satellites, part of a major investment in reconnaissance and listening posts already committed by Congress and the White House last year.

In its perennial rivalry with electronic intelligence, the CIA will require added "humint"—human-collected intelligence—and thus more manpower. As Mr. Webster told the National Press Club last November, his needs are "staggering." Peace, it turns out, is going to be even more expensive than the cold war, and by all odds a growth industry for the intelligence community.

It is symptomatic of our plight, of our gagged dialogue in national security, that there has been in Congress or the media so little challenge to this campaign, however transparent or contrived. As usual, hard edges of issues and money have been softened by settling on personality, in this case on the somewhat bland and dutiful Mr. Webster.

A U.S. Court of Appeals judge from St. Louis and the FBI [Federal Bureau of Investigation] Director for nine years, Mr. Webster came to the agency in 1987 to calm everyone after the swift exit and death of William Casey amid the Iran-contra affair—still another scandal in which the CIA was deeply embroiled yet escaped virtually free of consequence.

Mr. Webster was hardly a reformer. He had left behind at the FBI an unsavory record of surveillance of dissident groups as well as charges of racial discrimination. His anemic response to the constitutional atrocity of Iran-contra was to dismiss a pair of lesser officials and demote or reprimand five others, moves widely interpreted in Washington as essential immunity for the agency at large.

The new Director went on to oppose the creation of a quasi-independent CIA inspector general, legislation that became law late last year despite Administration opposition, and to date the only potentially significant new oversight measure to emerge from the Iran-contra revelations.

For his loyalty, Mr. Webster has been rewarded with fattening budgets and only occasional sniping of the sort reserved by the intelligence bureaucracy for exogenous directors. (In acid comparison with William "Wild Bill" Donovan, the legendary head of U.S. wartime intelligence and godfather of the CIA, agency veterans reportedly call the current Director "Mild Bill.")

Rather more ominous are the first accounts this spring [1990] by a *Houston Post* reporter, Pete Brewton, of extensive ties between failed financial institutions and the CIA—more than 20 savings and loan institutions and at least two banks with agency connections or relationships with organized crime figures with links themselves to the CIA.

Money-laundering, looting of thrifts to finance forbidden covert actions, manipulation of markets, Mafia alliances—hovering over the *Post* stories and an inquiry by the House Select Committee on Intelligence are too-familiar, too-believable ghosts. These are all too consistent with the shady, seamy margin on which the agency has operated for so long, and which now threatens to mock Mr. Webster's rectitude and hands-off management.

The Central Intelligence Agency has been at the core of America's cold-war Faustian bargain: by one count, at least 900 major projects and several thousand secondary actions over more than four decades, often deliberate decisions to enlist or engage evil in the service of perceived good, often to match in kind an enemy whose values we deplored.

It will not be necessary for scholars of the next century to seize upon the agency's relatively rare renegade departures from Presidential edict. The record of proposing, organizing, executing, rationalizing and then concealing authorized policy will be enough for the most extraordinary chapter in the history of American foreign relations.

The proof, as they like to say at CIA headquarters, is in results. Off only the briefest roll call—Iran, Guatemala, Indonesia, Zaire, Ecuador, Ethiopia, Chile, Somalia, Brazil, Angola, Libya, Nicaragua, Vietnam, El Salvador, Cambodia, Panama, Lebanon, Korea—some conclusions are already plain. Whatever the presumed alternative, most CIA interventions have consigned or left countries to repression and prolonged suffering. Despite billions in secret subsidies of U.S. tax dollars, several of our most favored clients fell of their own savagery and corruption, leading to violently anti-American successor regimes. Many of our secret police proxies and protégés have displayed an amazingly consistent penchant for torture.

Yet history may not judge so harshly, after all, the seedy bag men or sleepy watch officers counting off the moments to a faraway coup d'état. Far worse than any covert action, however wrong or misshapen, is an intelligence agency's intellectual dishonesty, the ideological, political or bureaucratic corruption of the information that is the essence of the art. Expected to deceive everyone else, it must never willfully or by incompetence lie to itself.

That the CIA has done just that so often, and especially vis-à-vis the Soviet Union, its most vital object of study, should now raise the gravest doubts about its future role and funding. The agency's bafflement at the process loosed by glasnost, its stuffy, orthodox ignorance of the volcanic forces so close beneath the surface of Soviet society, is only the latest and most spectacular failure.

There is, too, what one scholar has called "politics and guesswork," the systematic overstatement of Soviet military expenditures since 1948, distorted estimates that in the eerie cold-war twilight of the past decade came to look somehow moderate beside the wildly tendentious and budget-plumping analyses of the Defense Intelligence Agency. Without a discourse of integrity, the CIA could not accurately gauge the old Soviet threat, or honestly inform U.S. policy in response. Now, with little sense at home or abroad of a politics of the left, it sees clearly neither the present nor the future of a new Soviet Union that is still the most important power in Europe or Asia.

Reconversion is as essential to the CIA as to so much of the bloated weapons industry it helped feed. In a Washington no longer in thrall to the old myths of ideology and power, most political intelligence could be vested in a revitalized foreign ministry and diplomatic service, where it belongs. Military intelligence, much too important and tempting to be left to the generals, should be shifted entirely to a broader new National Security Agency with no stake in either the Pentagon budget or old bureaucratic quarrels.

Left—with open budgets, openly arrived at—would be a truly new CIA for an obviously new world, a select and streamlined agency shorn of its operational folly and extraconstitutional means. The new agency would be dedicated unequivocally to analyses of cultural sensibility and socioeconomic developments. One might hope that these would inform a new relevance in government decision-making, from development aid to control of the arms or drug traffic, from combating AIDS [acquired immune deficiency syndrome] to fostering human rights. The peace dividend of that CIA, of course, would not only be billions in savings and genuine national security but also a fresh generation of talented and idealistic young officials for whom intelligence was once again a public service.

Like high priests railing at an end to superstition, the professionals will call such a plan heresy, impossible. If only they could tell us that the danger were really gone, they have always said. Only then could we change this obese, tunnel-vision relic, slouching toward Capitol Hill for still more money, still more ominous briefings on a world already past.

---

*Is the Central Intelligence Agency an Anachronism?*

---

## DAVID L. BOREN
### New World, New CIA

The cold war is over. And some now argue that in this dramatically changed world, intelligence services like the CIA [Central Intelligence Agency] are costly anachronisms that should be sharply reduced. In fact these changes have increased, not decreased, the need for the right kind of intelligence. What's called for is not less intelligence activity but the acquisition of new and different kinds of information.

For years, the Soviet military threat was the driving force behind intelligence budgets. Today, the Warsaw Pact is no longer a viable military threat, although the Soviet Union remains highly armed. Now we must begin to confront the question of how to relate to a democratic Soviet Union and how to contend with the explosion of information about that country and Eastern Europe.

We must have a strategy, vision and discipline to guide U.S. intelligence in the future. This is particularly so because budgets will not be as large, and bureaucracies accustomed to unprecedented growth in resources cannot be allowed to sanctify the present and ignore the future.

Despite world trends toward democracy, caution is required. Our evidence shows that espionage against the United States has not diminished. Emerging East European democracies are struggling to control intelligence and security services that remain loyal to their KGB [Soviet secret police] masters. The Soviet Union, while moving toward cooperation with us in many areas, remains the only nation in the world capable of destroying us with nuclear weapons. As the USSR [Union of Soviet Socialist Republics] experiences its own internal power struggles and moves through a radical transformation, we can never be certain whose hand will be on the nuclear trigger.

U.S. intelligence must be able to monitor Soviet military deployments and developments as well as the intentions of Soviet political and military leaders. We also must have the means to verify new and complicated arms control agreements and protect against technological breakouts.

While superpower tensions are easing, the world is not completely at peace. The proliferation of chemical, nuclear and biological weapons—especially in less responsible nations—threatens the entire world. Regional conflicts show no sign of abating. The political instability that feeds terrorism has not waned. Dangers of war between India and Pakistan present the world with the possibility of nuclear confrontation. The West's dependence on oil imported from the Persian Gulf continues to grow.

These are not new problems. But we should now focus on them more of our resources that were once consumed by the Soviet military threat.

230

The strategy to guide U.S. intelligence must be based on a number of factors. First, we have to re-emphasize classic human-source intelligence. We are weakest at determining the intentions of our adversaries and friends. Better human intelligence is critical to meeting the threats of the next century: penetrating terrorist cells, breaking the money-laundering activities of narco-traffickers and combating the spread of weapons technology.

The Congressional oversight committees are working with the CIA to develop an innovative, long-term strategy that sheds cold war priorities and focuses on language and cultural skills and economic expertise.

Even in the most sensitive relationships, we must now align ourselves with the forces of change in the world. Anti-Communism can no longer justify cozy relationships with foreign intelligence services that commit or condone human rights abuses or prop up authoritarian regimes.

Second, we must understand that future American influence will depend more upon our economic strength and less upon our military strength. Nations previously followed our lead because they needed our protection. Now our influence will have to come more from economic strength and the strength of the example of our political and social systems.

The fastest growing area of espionage activities by foreign governments against the U.S. is not the theft of military secrets, but the theft of commercial secrets from private American companies to further national economic interests. This confronts the United States with serious questions of policy. How do we protect against government-conducted commercial espionage? Should we retaliate by collecting such information ourselves? If we did collect it, how could it be appropriately used by a free enterprise system with many competing producers of the same goods?

One thing is certain: Future intelligence officers will need a high level of ability to understand and evaluate economic data on subjects as diverse as currency, trade policy and new commercial technologies.

Third, the U.S. military presence abroad will be reduced. Thus the projection of U.S. forces will be much more difficult in the future, and we will need earlier warning of hostile intentions. Information must be timely and complete and in a form useful to our military commanders.

Intelligence excesses are largely behind us. We now have a body of laws and a process of Congressional intelligence oversight that aggressively seeks to insure that the CIA operates in a manner consistent with the fundamental values of the American people. Critics should not ignore the fact that the intelligence community today is led by a man, Judge William Webster, who is committed to telling the truth and obeying the law.

Now is not the time to think about dismantling our intelligence service or calling for mindless budget slashing. The men and women of the intelligence community provide us with real accomplishments about which there can be little public discussion.

The transformation of our intelligence priorities is beginning. The oversight committees and the leadership of the intelligence community have begun the dialogue. The members of the Senate Intelligence Committee understand all too well that we will place our nation at risk if we do not change our thinking to reflect the changes in the world around us.

## Questions for Discussion

1. What role should the CIA play in the post–cold war era?
2. Are covert operations ever justified in a democracy? Justify your answer.
3. What role should Congress play in overseeing the CIA?
4. Should the United States ever support governments that violate fundamental human rights? Justify your answer.
5. What criteria should be used in evaluating the effectiveness of the CIA's work?

## Suggested Readings

Jeffreys-Jones, Rhodri. *The CIA and American Democracy.* New Haven, Conn.: Yale Univ. Press, 1989.

Johnson, Loch K. *America's Secret Power: The CIA in a Democratic Society.* New York: Oxford Univ. Press, 1989.

Mitgang, Herbert. *Dangerous Dossiers: Exposing the Secret War against America's Greatest Authors.* New York: D.I. Fine, 1988.

Moyers, Bill. *The Secret Government: The Constitution in Crisis.* Cabin John, Md.: Seven Locks Press, 1988.

Prados, John. *President's Secret Wars: CIA and Pentagon Covert Operations from World War II through Iranscam.* New York: W. Morrow, 1988.

Ranelagh, John. *The Rise and Decline of the CIA.* Rev. ed. New York: Simon & Schuster, 1987.

Roosevelt, Archibald. *For Lust of Knowing: Memoirs of an Intelligence Officer.* Boston, Mass.: Little, Brown, 1988.

Smith, Russell J. *The Unknown CIA: My Three Decades with the Agency.* Washington, D.C.: Pergamon-Brassey's, 1989.

Treverton, Gregory F. *Covert Action: The Limits of Intervention in the Postwar World.* New York: Basic Books, 1987.

Woodward, Bob. *Veil: The Secret Wars of the CIA, 1981–1987.* New York: Simon & Schuster, 1987.

# Chapter 15

## Should the Supreme Court Abide by a Strict Constructionist Philosophy?

Of the three branches of the federal government—president, Congress, and the Supreme Court—the last is the least democratic. Although representative democracy requires periodic elections, the members of the Supreme Court are appointed, never run for office in popular elections, and once on the Court, usually remain there for life or until they retire. Presidents, senators, and representatives may envy the justices' luxury of not having to run for public office.

The Supreme Court's power of judicial review is—at least on the surface—another undemocratic feature of this arm of government. Judicial review is the power of the Supreme Court to examine state and federal laws and the acts of state and federal public officials to determine whether they are in conflict with the Constitution. If these laws and acts are in conflict, then the Court may declare them invalid. The fact that a majority of nine unelected members of the Court may declare null and void the laws enacted by the representatives of the majority of the people who vote seems to be a limitation on the principle of majority rule. The argument is often made, however, that the specific content of court decisions has strengthened rather than weakened democracy.

Judicial review is not the practice in all representative democracies. The British system of government, for example, permits the courts to interpret the laws but not to declare an act of Parliament void. Judicial review is not specifically mentioned in the Constitution of the United States. Debate surrounds the question of whether the Framers intended the Supreme Court to have this power over the laws of the federal government. There is general agreement, however, that the Framers understood that judicial review is applicable to acts of state legislatures in conflict with the Constitution. The Supreme Court first declared an act of Congress unconstitutional in *Marbury* v. *Madison* (1803). In this case the court found the Judiciary Act of 1789 to be in conflict with Article III of the Constitution. Today the Supreme Court's authority to declare a statute unconstitutional is unchallenged.

Over the past century the Supreme Court has exercised its power of judicial review in a variety of cases. Those who have benefited from the Court's decisions have hailed the wisdom of the Court. The "losers" have called for a variety of responses, including limiting the jurisdiction of the Court, amending the Constitution, enlarging the size of the Court, or impeaching the chief justice.

Court decisions have not supported one group of people exclusively. In the early part of the twentieth century, for example, Court decisions were more favorable to big business, states' rights advocates, and segregationists. Since the days of the Warren Court (for former Chief Justice Earl Warren) in the mid-1950s, however, Court decisions have been more favorable to groups demanding extension of civil rights and civil liberties. The changing character of Supreme Court decisions is a reflection of such factors as the composition of the Court, legal precedents, and the political environment. One other factor that has received much attention, however, is the philosophical outlook of the judges.

Two principal philosophical outlooks have guided judicial decision making, and they are always in conflict. As we saw in Chapter 1, William Bradford Reynolds held the intentions of the Framers of the Constitution in the highest regard, while Thurgood Marshall argued that the wisdom of the Constitution lies in its adaptability to changing social needs. Strict constructionists, like Reynolds, believe that the Supreme Court should be bound by the intent of the Framers and the language in the document itself. Loose constructionists argue that strict constructionism is misconceived, impossible, or even fraudulent. At various times in U.S. history, conservatives have supported strict constructionism, but liberals, too, at times, have taken a similar philosophical approach.

The debate below elicits the main arguments of the contending schools. Federal appeals court judge J. Clifford Wallace makes a case for interpretivism—the principle that judges, in resolving constitutional questions, should rely on the express provisions of the Constitution or upon those norms that are clearly implicit in its text. He contends:

1. The Constitution itself envisions and requires interpretivist review.
2. Interpretivist review promotes the stability and predictability essential to the rule of law.
3. Judges are not particularly well suited to make judgments of broad social policy.
4. The argument put forward by noninterpretivists that certain constitutional provisions invite justices to use value judgments outside the Constitution is invalid.
5. Although the Framers' intent cannot be ascertained on every issue, interpretivism will exclude from consideration entire ranges of improper judicial responses.
6. The Fourteenth Amendment did not produce so fundamental a revision in the nature of U.S. government that the intentions of the Framers are scarcely relevant any longer.
7. The Constitution can still be changed by the only legitimate means for which it provides: formal amendment.

8. When noninterpretivists justify their actions on the basis of "doing justice," they act improperly because they are incapable of deciding what is just.
9. An activist judiciary undermines the very principles of democracy.
10. An interpretivist view shows respect for precedent.

Law professor Jeffrey M. Shaman takes the negative position on the issue. He contends:

1. History shows that whenever the Supreme Court makes a decision that someone does not like, the justices are accused of holding to their own personal views and not to the words of the Constitution or the intent of the Framers.
2. From its early history, the Supreme Court has had to go outside the written Constitution and the intent of the Framers in making some decisions.
3. The Court often must create meaning for the Constitution because the document is rife with general and abstract language.
4. There is no reason to pay greater attention to the intent of the Framers than to that of the people who ratified the Constitution or to the succeeding generations who retain it.
5. The intent of the Framers is difficult to discern.
6. The conditions that shaped the Framers' attitudes have changed in two centuries of constitutional experience.
7. The Constitution provides only the bare bones; its meaning must be augmented by the justices.
8. The Court is subject to popular constraints that keep its power limited.

*Should the Supreme Court Abide by a Strict Constructionist Philosophy?*

## J. CLIFFORD WALLACE
### *The Case for Judicial Restraint*

This year we celebrate the 200th anniversary of our Constitution. This remarkable document has structured our government and secured our liberty as we have developed from 13 fledgling colonies into a mature and strong democracy. Without doubt, the Constitution is one of the grandest political achievements of the modern world.

In spite of this marvelous record, we will celebrate our nation's charter in the midst of a hotly contested debate on the continuing role that it should have in our society. Two schools of constitutional jurisprudence are engaged in a long-running battle. Some contend that the outcome of this conflict may well determine whether the Constitution remains our vital organic document or whether it instead becomes a curious historical relic. The competing positions in this constitutional battle are often summarized by a variety of labels: judicial restraint versus judicial activism, strict construction versus loose construction, positivism versus natural law, conservative versus liberal, interpretivism versus noninterpretivism.

In large measure, these labels alone are of little assistance in analyzing a complex problem. Ultimately, what is at stake is what Constitution will govern this country. Will it be the written document drafted by the Framers, ratified by the people, and passed down, with amendments, to us? Or will it be an illusive parchment upon which modern-day judges may freely engrave their own political and sociological preferences?

In this article, I intend to outline and defend a constitutional jurisprudence of judicial restraint.[1] My primary thesis is that a key principle of judicial restraint—namely, interpretivism—is required by our constitutional plan. I will also explore how practitioners of judicial restraint should resolve the tension that can arise in our current state of constitutional law between interpretivism and a second important principle, respect for judicial precedent.

## INTERPRETIVISM VS. NONINTERPRETIVISM

What is the difference between "interpretivism" and "noninterpretivism"? This question is important because I believe interpretivism to be the cornerstone of a constitutional jurisprudence of judicial restraint. By "interpretivism," I mean the principle that judges, in resolving constitutional questions, should rely on the express provisions of the Constitution or upon those norms that are clearly implicit in its text.[2] Under an interpretivist approach, the original intention of the Framers is the controlling guide for constitutional interpretation. This does not mean, of course, that judges may apply a constitutional provision only to situations specifically contemplated by the Framers. Rather, it simply requires that when considering whether to invalidate the work of the political branches, the judges do so from a starting point fairly discoverable in the Constitution.[3] By contrast, under noninterpretive review, judges may freely rest their decisions on value judgments that admittedly are not supported by, and may even contravene, the text of the Constitution and the intent of the Framers.[4]

## INTERPRETIVIST REVIEW

I believe that the Constitution itself envisions and requires interpretivist review. To explore this thesis, we should first examine the Constitution as a political and historical document.

As people read the Constitution, many are struck by how procedural and technical its provisions are. Perhaps on first reading it may be something of a disappointment. In contrast to the fiery eloquence of the Declaration of Independence, the Constitution may seem dry or even dull. This difference in style, of course, reflects the very different functions of the two documents. The Declaration of Independence is an indictment of the reign of King George III. In a flamboyant tone, it is brilliantly crafted to persuade the world of the justice of our fight for independence. The Constitution, by contrast, establishes the basic set of rules for the nation. Its genius lies deeper, in its skillful design of a government structure that would best ensure liberty and democracy.

The primary mechanism by which the Constitution aims to protect liberty and democracy is the dispersion of government power. Recognizing that concentrated power poses the threat of tyranny, the Framers divided authority between the states and the federal government. In addition, they created three separate and co-equal branches of the federal government in a system of checks and balances.

The Framers were also aware, of course, that liberty and democracy can come into conflict. The Constitution, therefore, strikes a careful balance between democratic rule and minority rights. Its republican, representative features are designed to channel and refine cruder majoritarian impulses. In addition, the Constitution's specific individual protections, particularly in the Bill of Rights, guarantee against certain majority intrusions. Beyond these guarantees, the Constitution places its trust in the democratic process—the voice of the people expressed through their freely elected representatives.

Raoul Berger argues persuasively in *Government by Judiciary* that the Constitution "was written against a background of interpretive presuppositions that assured the Framers their design would be effectuated."[5] The importance of that statement may escape us today, when it is easy to take for granted that the Constitution is a written document. But for the Framers, the fact that the Constitution was in writing was not merely incidental. They recognized that a written constitution provides the most stable basis for the rule of law, upon which liberty and justice ultimately depend.

As Thomas Jefferson observed, "Our peculiar security is in the possession of a written constitution. Let us not make it a blank paper by construction."[6] Chief Justice John Marshall, in *Marbury* v. *Madison,* the very case establishing the power of judicial review, emphasized the constraints imposed by the written text and the judicial duty to respect these constraints in all cases raising constitutional questions.[7]

Moreover, the Framers recognized the importance of interpreting the Constitution according to their original intent. In Madison's words, if "the sense in which the Constitution was accepted and ratified by the Nation . . . be not the guide in expounding it, there can be no security for a consistent and stable government, [nor] for a faithful exercise of its powers."[8] Similarly, Jefferson as President acknowledged his duty to administer the Constitution "according to the safe and honest meaning contemplated by the plain understanding of the people at the time of its adoption—a meaning to be found in the explanations of those who advocated . . . it."[9] It seems clear, therefore, that the leading Framers were interpretivists and believed that constitutional questions should be reviewed by that approach.

Next, I would like to consider whether interpretivism is necessary to effectuate the constitutional plan. The essential starting point is that the Constitution established a separation of powers to protect our freedom. Because freedom is fundamental, so too is the separation of powers. But separation of powers becomes a meaningless slogan if judges may confer constitutional status on whichever rights they happen to deem important, regardless of textual basis. In effect, under noninterpretive review, the judiciary functions as a superlegislature beyond the check of the other two branches. Noninterpretivist review also disregards the Constitution's careful allocation of most decisions to the democratic process, allowing the legislature to make decisions deemed best for society. Ultimately, noninterpretivist review reduces our written Constitution to insignificance and threatens to impose a tyranny of the judiciary.

## PRUDENTIAL CONSIDERATIONS

Important prudential considerations also weigh heavily in favor of interpretivist review. The rule of law is fundamental in our society. To be effective, it cannot be tossed to and fro by each new sociological wind. Because it is rooted in written text, interpretivist review promotes the stability and predictability essential to the rule of the law. By contrast, noninterpretivist review presents an infinitely variable array of possibilities. The Constitution would vary with each judge's conception of what is important. To demonstrate the wide variety of tests that could be applied, let us briefly look at the writings of legal academics who advocate noninterpretivism.

Assume each is a judge deciding the same constitutional issue. One professor seeks to "cement a union between the distributional patterns of the modern welfare state and the federal constitution." Another "would guarantee a whole range of nontextually based rights against government to ensure 'the dignity of full membership in society.' " A third argues that the courts should give a "concrete meaning and application" to those values that "give our society an identity and inner coherence [and] its distinctive public morality." Yet another professor sees the court as having a "prophetic" role in developing moral standards in a "dialectical relationship" with Congress, from which he sees emerging a "more mature" political morality. One professor even urges that the court apply the contractarian moral theory of Professor Rawls' A Theory of Justice to constitutional questions.[10] One can easily see the fatal vagueness and subjectivity of this approach: each judge would apply his or her own separate and diverse personal values in interpreting the same constitutional question. Without anchor, we drift at sea.

Another prudential argument against noninterpretivism is that judges are not particularly well-suited to make judgments of broad social policy. We judges decide cases on the basis of a limited record that largely represents the efforts of the parties to the litigation. Legislators, with their committees, hearings, and more direct role in the political process, are much better equipped institutionally to decide what is best for society.


## NONINTERPRETIVIST ARGUMENTS

But are there arguments in favor of noninterpretivism? Let us consider several assertions commonly put forth by proponents. One argument asserts that certain constitutional provisions invite judges to import into the constitutional decision process value judgments derived from outside the Constitution. Most commonly, advocates of this view rely on the due process clause of the Fifth and Fourteenth Amendments. It is true that courts have interpreted the due process clause to authorize broad review of the substantive merits of legislation. But is that what the draftsmen had in mind? Some constitutional scholars make a strong argument that the clause, consistent with its plain language, was intended to have a limited procedural meaning.[11]

A second argument asserts that the meaning of the constitutional text and the intention of the Framers cannot be ascertained with sufficient precision to guide constitutional decisionmaking. I readily acknowledge that interpretivism will not always provide easy answers to difficult constitutional questions. The judicial role will always involve the exercise of discretion. The strength of interpretivism is that it channels and constrains this discretion in a manner consistent with the Constitution. While it does not necessarily ensure a correct result, it does exclude from consideration entire ranges of improper judicial responses.

Third, some have suggested that the Fourteenth Amendment effected such a fundamental revision in the nature of our government that the intentions of the original Framers are scarcely relevant any longer. It is, of course, true that federal judges have seized upon the Fourteenth Amendment as a vehicle to restructure federal/state relations. The argument, however, is not one-sided. Berger, for example, persuasively demonstrates that the framers of the Fourteenth Amendment sought much more limited objectives.[12] In addition, one reasonable interpretation of the history of the amendment demonstrates that its framers, rather than intending an expanded role for the federal courts, meant for Congress (under section 5 of the amendment) to play the primary role in enforcing its provisions.[13] Thus, it can be argued that to the extent that the Fourteenth Amendment represented an innovation in the constitutional role of the judiciary, it was by limiting the courts' traditional role in enforcing constitutional rights and by providing added responsibility for the Congress.

Advocates of noninterpretivism also contend that we should have a "living Constitution" rather than be bound by "the dead hand of the Framers." These slogans prove nothing. An interpretivist approach would not constrict government processes; on the contrary, it would ensure that issues are freely subject to the workings of the democratic process. Moreover, to the extent that the Constitution might profit from revision, the amendment process of Article V provides the only constitutional means. Judicial amendment under a noninterpretivist approach is simply an unconstitutional usurpation.

Almost certainly, the greatest support for a noninterpretive approach derives from its perceived capacity to achieve just results. Why quibble over the Constitution, after all, if judges who disregard it nevertheless "do justice"? Such a view is dangerously shortsighted and naive. In the first place, one has no cause to believe that the results of noninterpretivism will generally be "right." Individual judges have widely varying conceptions of what values are important. Noninterpretists spawned the "conservative" substantive economic due process of the 1930s as well as the "liberal" decisions of the Warren Court. There is no principled result in noninterpretivism.

But even if the judge would always be right, the process would be wrong. A benevolent judicial tyranny is nonetheless a tyranny. Our Constitution rests on the faith that democracy is intrinsically valuable. From an instrumental perspective, democracy might at times produce results that are not as desirable as platonic guardians might produce. But the democratic process—our participation in a system of self-government—has transcendental value. Moreover, one must consider the very real danger that an activist judiciary stunts the development of a responsible democracy by removing from it the duty to make difficult decisions. If we are to remain faithful to the values of democracy and liberty, we must insist that courts respect the Constitution's allocation of social decisionmaking to the political branches.

## RESPECT FOR PRECEDENT

I emphasized earlier the importance of stability to the rule of law. I return to that theme now to consider a second principle of judicial restraint: respect for precedent. Respect for precedent is a principle widely accepted, even if not always faithfully followed. It requires simply that a judge follow prior case law in deciding legal questions. Respect for precedent promotes predictability and uniformity. It constrains a judge's discretion and satisfies the reasonable expectations of the parties. Through its application, citizens can have a better understanding of what the law is and act accordingly.

Unfortunately, in the present state of constitutional law, the two principles of judicial restraint that I have outlined can come into conflict. While much of constitutional law is consistent with the principle of interpretivism, a significant portion is not. This raises the question how a practitioner of judicial restraint should act in circumstances where respecting precedent would require acceptance of law developed under a noninterpretivist approach.

The answer is easy for a judge in my position, and, indeed, for any judge below the United States Supreme Court. As a judge on the Ninth Circuit Court of Appeals, I am bound to follow Supreme Court and Ninth Circuit precedent even when I believe it to be wrong. There is a distinction, however, between following precedent and extending it. Where existing precedent does not fairly govern a legal question, the principle of interpretivism should guide a judge.

For Supreme Court justices, the issue is more complex. The Supreme Court obviously is not infallible. Throughout its history, the Court has at times rejected its own precedents. Because the Supreme Court has the ultimate judicial say on what the Constitution means, its justices have a special responsibility to ensure that they are properly expounding constitutional law as well as fostering stability and predictability.

Must Supreme Court advocates of judicial restraint passively accept the errors of activist predecessors? There is little rational basis for doing so. Periodic activist inroads could emasculate fundamental doctrines and undermine the separation of powers. Nevertheless, the values of predictability and uniformity that respect for precedent promotes demand caution in overturning precedent. In my view, a justice should consider overturning a prior decision only when the decision is clearly wrong, has significant effects, and would otherwise be difficult to remedy.

Significantly, constitutional decisions based on a noninterpretivist approach may satisfy these three criteria. When judges confer constitutional status on their own value judgments without support in the language of the Constitution and the original intention of the Framers, they commit clear error. Because constitutional errors frequently affect the institutional structure of government and the allocation of decisions to the democratic process, they are likely to have important effects. And because constitutional decisions, unlike statutory decisions, cannot be set aside through normal political channels, they will generally meet the third requirement. In sum, then, despite the prudential interests furthered by respect for precedent, advocates of judicial restraint may be justified in seeking to overturn noninterpretivist precedent.


## CONCLUSION

It is obvious that courts employing interpretivist review cannot solve many of the social and political problems facing America, indeed, even some very important problems. The interpretivist would respond that the Constitution did not place the responsibility for solving those problems with the courts. The courts were not meant to govern the core of our political and social life— Article I gave that duty, for national issues, to the Congress. It is through our democratically elected representatives that we legitimately develop this fabric of our life. Interpretivism encourages that process. It is, therefore, closer to the constitutional plan of governance than is noninterpretivist review.

After 200 years, the Constitution is not "broke"—we need not fix it—just apply it.

---

*NOTES*

This article is adapted from an address given at Hillsdale College, Hillsdale, Michigan, on March 5, 1986.

1. I have elsewhere presented various aspects of this jurisprudence. See, e.g., Wallace, "A Two Hundred Year Old Constitution in Modern Society." 61 *Texas Law Review,* 1575 (1983); Wallace, "The Jurisprudence of Judicial Restraint: A Return to the Moorings." *George Washington Law Review* 1 (1981).

2. Wallace, "A Two Hundred Year Old Constitution," *supra* n. 1; Ely, *Democracy and Distrust* 1 (Cambridge, MA: Harvard University Press, 1980).

3. Ely, *supra* n. 2, at 2.

4. *See id.* at 43–72.

5. Berger, *Government by Judiciary* 366 (Cambridge, MA: Harvard University Press, 1977).

6. *Id.* at 364, *quoting* Letter to Wilson Cary Nicholas (Sept. 7, 1803).

7. *Marbury v. Madison,* 5 U.S. (1 Cranch) 137, 176–80 (1803).

8. Berger, *supra* n. 5, at 364, quoting *The Writings of James Madison* 191 (G. Hunt ed. 1900–1910).

9. *Id.* at 366–67, citing 4 Elliot, *Debates in the Several State Conventions on the Adoption of the Federal Constitution* 446 (1836).

10. Monaghan, "Our Perfect Constitution," 56 *New York University Law Review,* 353, 358–60 (1981) (summarizing theories of noninterpretivists).

11. *See, e.g.,* Berger, *supra* n. 5, at 193–220.

12. *See id.*

13. *See id.* at 220–29.

## Should the Supreme Court Abide by a Strict Constructionist Philosophy?

### JEFFREY M. SHAMAN

### The Supreme Court's Proper and Historic Function

Considerable criticism, frequently quite sharp, has recently been directed at the Supreme Court for the way it has gone about its historic function of interpreting the Constitution. In particular, Edwin Meese, the current Attorney General of the United States, has accused the Court of exceeding its lawful authority by failing to adhere strictly to the words of the Constitution and the intentions of the Framers who drafted those words.[1]

The Attorney General's attack upon the Court echoes a similar one made by Richard Nixon, who, campaigning for the Presidency in 1968, denounced Supreme Court Justices who, he claimed, twisted and bent the Constitution according to their personal predilections. If elected President, Nixon promised to appoint to the Court strict constructionists whose decisions would conform to the text of the Constitution and the intent of the Framers. (Ironically, it is some of the Nixon appointees to the Court that Meese now accuses of twisting and bending the Constitution.)

I hasten to add that it is not only politicians who sing the praises of strict constructionism; there are judges and lawyers, as well as some scholars, who join the song. Among legal scholars, though, the response to strict constructionism has been overwhelmingly negative. There are legal scholars, for instance, who describe strict constructionism as a "misconceived quest,"[2] an "impossibility,"[3] and even a "fraud."[4]

Those who criticize the Court point to rulings during the tenure of Chief Justice Burger, most notably the decision in *Roe* v. *Wade*[5] legalizing abortion, as examples of illegitimate revision or amendment of the Constitution based upon the personal beliefs of the justices. Some years ago, similar charges were leveled at the Warren Court for its ruling requiring reapportionment along the lines of one person-one vote,[6] its decision striking down school prayer,[7] and other rulings, even including the one in *Brown* v. *Board of Education* outlawing school segregation.[8]

It should not be supposed, however, that strict constructionism is always on the side of conservative political values. In the 1930s it was the liberals who claimed that the Supreme Court was not strictly construing the Constitution when the justices repeatedly held that minimum wage, maximum hour, and other protective legislation violated the Fourteenth Amendment.[9] As the liberals then saw it, the conservative justices on the Court were illegitimately incorporating their personal values into the Fourteenth Amendment, which had

243

been meant to abolish racial discrimination, not to protect the prerogatives of employers.

## HISTORY LESSONS

The lesson of this bit of history seems to be that, whether liberal or conservative or somewhere in between, whoever has an ox that is being gored at the time has a tendency to yell "foul." Whenever the Supreme Court renders a decision that someone doesn't like, apparently it is not enough to disagree with the decision; there also has to be an accusation that the Court's decision was illegitimate, being based upon the justice's personal views and not the words of the Constitution or the intent of the Framers.

We can go back much further in history than the 1930s to find the Supreme Court being accused of illegitimacy. In 1810, for instance, Thomas Jefferson condemned Chief Justice John Marshall for "twistifying" the Constitution according to his "personal biases."[10]

History also reveals something else extremely significant about the Court, which is that from its earliest days, the Court has found it necessary in interpreting the Constitution to look beyond the language of the document and the intent of the Framers. In the words of Stanford Law Professor Thomas Grey, it is "a matter of unarguable historical fact" that over the years the Court has developed a large body of constitutional law that derives neither from the text of the document nor the intent of the Framers.[11]

Moreover, this has been so from the Court's very beginning. Consider, for example, a case entitled *Hylton v. United States*,[12] which was decided in 1796 during the term of the Court's first Chief Justice, John Jay. The *Hylton* case involved a tax ranging from $1.00 to $10.00 that had been levied by Congress on carriages. Mr. Hylton, who was in the carriage trade and owned 125 carriages, understandably was unhappy about the tax, and went to court to challenge it. He claimed that the tax violated section 2 of Article I of the Constitution, which provides that direct taxes shall be apportioned among the several states according to their populations. Hylton argued that this tax was a direct one, and therefore unconstitutional because it had not been apportioned among the states by population. This, of course, was years before the enactment of the Sixteenth Amendment in 1913, authorizing a federal income tax. Prior to that, Article I prohibited a federal income tax, but what about a tax on the use or ownership of carriages—was that the sort of "direct" tax that was only permissible under Article I if apportioned among the states by population?

The Supreme Court, with several justices filing separate opinions in the case (which was customary at that time), upheld the tax as constitutional on the ground that it was not direct, and therefore not required to be apportioned. What is most significant about the *Hylton* case is how the Court went about making its decision. As described by Professor David Currie of the University of

Chicago Law School, the Court in *Hylton* "paid little heed to the Constitution's words," and "policy considerations dominated all three opinions" filed by the Justices.[13] In fact, each of the opinions asserted that apportioning a carriage tax among the states would be unfair, because a person in a state with fewer carriages would have to pay a higher tax. While this may or may not be unfair, the justices pointed to nothing in the Constitution itself or the intent of the Framers to support their personal views of fairness. Moreover, one of the justices, Justice Patterson, went so far in his opinion as to assert that the constitutional requirement of apportioning direct taxes was "radically wrong," and therefore should not be extended to this case. In other words, he based his decision, at least in part, upon his antipathy to a constitutional provision.

While Justice Patterson went too far in that respect, he and his colleagues on the court could hardly have made a decision in the case by looking to the text of the Constitution or the intent of the Framers. The language of the document simply does not provide an answer to the constitutional issue raised by the situation in *Hylton*. The text of the document merely refers to "direct" taxes and provides no definition of what is meant by a direct tax. Furthermore, as Professor Currie points out, the records of the debates at the Constitutional Convention show that "the Framers had no clear idea of what they meant by direct taxes."[14] Thus, to fulfill their responsibility to decide the case and interpret the law, the justices found it necessary to create meaning for the Constitution.

## CREATING MEANING

Indeed, it is often necessary for the Supreme Court to create meaning for the Constitution. This is so because the Constitution, being a document designed (in the words of John Marshall) to "endure for ages,"[15] is rife with general and abstract language. Those two great sources of liberty in the Constitution, the due process and equal protection clauses, are obviously examples of abstract constitutional language that must be invested with meaning. The Fourth Amendment uses extremely general language in prohibiting "unreasonable" searches and seizures, and the Eighth Amendment is similarly general in disallowing "cruel and unusual" punishment.

Even many of the more specific provisions of the Constitution need to be supplied with meaning that simply cannot be found within the four corners of the document. The First Amendment, for instance, states that Congress shall not abridge freedom of speech—but does that mean that the government may not regulate obscene, slanderous, or deceptive speech? The First Amendment also says that Congress shall not abridge the free exercise of religion—does that mean that the government may not prohibit polygamy or child labor when dictated by religious belief? These questions—which, by the way, all arose in actual cases—and, in fact, the vast majority of constitutional questions presented to the Supreme Court, cannot be resolved by mere linguistic analysis of the Constitution. In reality there is no choice but to look beyond the text of the document to provide meaning for the Constitution.

There are those, such as Attorney General Meese, who would hope to find meaning for the Constitution from its authors, the beloved and hallowed Framers of the sacred text. By reputation, these fellows are considered saints and geniuses; in actuality, they were politicians motivated significantly by self-interest.

## THEORETICAL DRAWBACKS

But even if the Framers do deserve the awe that they inspire, reliance on their intentions to find meaning for the Constitution still has serious theoretical drawbacks. In the first place, why should we be concerned only with the intentions of the 55 individuals who drafted the Constitution and not the intentions of the people throughout the nation who ratified it, not to mention the intentions of the succeeding generations who retain the Constitution? After all, even when finally framed, the Constitution remained a legal nullity until ratified by the people, and would be a legal nullity again if revoked by the people. The Framers wrote the Constitution, but it is the people who enacted and retain the Constitution; so if anything, it is the people's intent about the document that would seem to be the relevant inquiry.

Moreover, there are considerable difficulties in discerning what in fact the Framers intended. The journal of the Constitutional Convention, which is the primary record of the Framers' intent, is neither complete nor entirely accurate. The notes for the journal were carelessly kept, and have been shown to contain several mistakes.[16]

Even when the record cannot be faulted, it is not always possible to ascertain the Framers' intent. As might be expected, the Framers did not express an intention about every constitutional issue that would arise after the document was drafted and adopted. No group of people, regardless of its members' ability, enjoys that sort of prescience. When the Framers did address particular problems, often only a few of them spoke out. What frequently is taken to be the intent of the Framers as a group turns out to be the intent of merely a few or even only one of the Framers.

There are also constitutional issues about which the Framers expressed conflicting intentions. A collective body of 55 individuals, the Framers embraced a widely diverse and frequently inconsistent set of views. The two principal architects of the Constitution, James Madison and Alexander Hamilton, for instance, had extremely divergent political views. Madison also on occasion differed with George Washington over the meaning of the Constitution. When Washington, who had presided over the Constitutional Convention, became President, he claimed that the underlying intent of the Constitution gave him the sole authority as President to proclaim neutrality and to withhold treaty papers from Congress. Madison, who had been a leader at the Constitutional Convention, disagreed vehemently. And so, the man who would come to be known as the father of this nation and the man who would come to be known as the father of the Constitution had opposing views of what the Framers intended.[17]

These examples demonstrate that it simply makes no sense to suppose that a multi-member group of human beings such as the Framers shared a unitary intent about the kind of controversial political issues addressed in our Constitution. We can see, then, that, at best, the so-called Framers' intent is inadequately documented, ambiguous, and inconclusive; at worst, it is nonexistent, an illusion.

Even if these insurmountable obstacles could be surmounted, there are other serious problems with trying to follow the path laid down by the Framers. The Framers formed their intentions in the context of a past reality and in accordance with past attitudes, both of which have changed considerably since the days when the Constitution was drafted. To transfer those intentions, fashioned as they were under past conditions and views, to contemporary situations may produce sorry consequences that even the Framers would have abhorred had they been able to foresee them. Blindly following intentions formulated in response to past conditions and attitudes is not likely to be an effective means of dealing with the needs of contemporary society.

## LOCKED TO THE PAST

Some scholars take this line of reasoning one step further by maintaining that the Framers' intent is inextricably locked to the past and has no meaning at all for the present.[18] In other words, because the Framers formed their intentions with reference to a reality and attitudes that no longer exist, their intentions cannot be transplanted to the present day. What the Framers intended for their times is not what they may have intended for ours. Life constantly changes, and the reality and ideas that surrounded the Framers are long since gone.

The futility of looking to the Framers' intent to resolve modern constitutional issues can be illustrated by several cases that have arisen under the Fourth and Fifth Amendments. The Fourth Amendment prohibits unreasonable searches and seizures, and further requires that no search warrants be issued unless there is probable cause that a crime has been committed. Are bugging and other electronic surveillance devices "unreasonable searches"? May they be used by the police without a warrant based on probable cause? What about the current practice of some law enforcement agencies of using airplanes to fly over a suspect's property to take pictures with a telescopic camera—is that an "unreasonable search"? The Fifth Amendment states that no person shall be compelled to be a witness against himself. What about forcing a suspect to take a breathalyzer test, or a blood test, or to have his or her stomach pumped—do those procedures amount to self-incrimination that violates the Fifth Amendment?

Whatever you may think should be the answers to these questions, you cannot find the answers by looking to the Framers' intent. The Framers had no intent at all about electronic surveillance, airplanes, telescopic cameras, breathalyzer tests, blood tests, or stomach pumping, for the simple reason that none of those things existed until well after the days of the Framers. Not even Benjamin Franklin, for all his inventiveness, was able to foresee that in the 20th century constables would zip around in flying machines taking snapshots of criminal suspects through a telescopic lens.

Many of the difficulties in attempting to resolve constitutional issues by turning to the Framers are illustrated by the school prayer cases.[19] The religious beliefs of the Framers ranged from theism to atheism, and among even the more devout Framers there was a wide diversity of opinion concerning the proper relationship between church and state. Moreover, as often happens when human beings ponder complex issues, the views of individual Framers about church and state did not remain the same over time. As a member of Congress, James Madison, for example, once voted to approve a chaplain for the House of Representatives, but later decided that the appointment of the chaplain had been unconstitutional.[20] Insofar as school prayer specifically was concerned, the Framers expressed virtually no opinion on the matter, for the simple reason that at the time public schools were extremely rare. Thus, the Framers had no intention, either pro or con, about prayer in public schools.

Given the theoretical deficiencies of trying to decide constitutional questions by looking to the Framers' intent, it should come as no surprise that this approach has been a failure when attempted by the Supreme Court. Scholars who have closely studied the Court's use of this approach commonly agree that it has not been a satisfactory method of constitutional decisionmaking, because the Court ends up manipulating, revising, or even creating history under the guise of following the Framers' intent.[21] The fact of the matter is that neither the Framers' intent nor the words of the document are capable of providing much constitutional meaning.

## BARE BONES

What we are left with, then, are the bare bones of a Constitution, the meaning of which must be augmented by the justices of the Supreme Court. And that is exactly what the justices have been doing since the Court was first established. The overwhelming evidence of history shows that the meaning of the Constitution has undergone constant change and evolution at the hands of the Supreme Court. Through the continual interpretation and reinterpretation of the text of the document, the Court perpetually creates new meaning for the document.

Although it is formally correct that we, unlike the citizens of Great Britain, have a written Constitution, its words have been defined and redefined to the extent that for the most part we, like the citizens of Great Britain, have an unwritten Constitution, the meaning of which originates with the Supreme Court.

Strict constructionists argue that it is undemocratic for Supreme Court Justices—unelected officials who are unaccountable to the populace—to create meaning for the Constitution. Of course, using the Framers' intent to interpret the Constitution also is undemocratic; following the will of the 55 persons who supposedly framed the Constitution or the smaller group of them who actually participated in the framing is hardly an exercise in democracy.

When strict constructionists cry that the Court is undemocratic, they are ignoring that our government is not (and was not intended by the Framers) to be a pure democracy. Rather, it is a limited or constitutional democracy. What this means is that there are constitutional limits to what the majority may do. The majority may not, for example, engage in racial discrimination, even if it votes to do so in overwhelming numbers. The majority may not abridge freedom of speech or the free exercise of religion or other constitutional rights guaranteed to every individual.

Article III of the Constitution states that there shall be a Supreme Court, and in combination with Article II, decrees the Court's independence from the electorate. By its very terms, the Constitution establishes a counter-majoritarian branch of government, the Supreme Court, in juxtaposition to the more democratic executive and legislative branches. This scheme reflects one of the guiding principles that underlies the Constitution—the principle of separate powers that check and balance one another. The Supreme Court's constitutionally mandated independence functions as a check and balance upon the more majoritarian branches of federal and state governments. It thereby provides a means of maintaining constitutional boundaries on majoritarian rule.

The role of the Supreme Court is to enforce constitutional requirements upon the majoritarian branches of government, which otherwise would be completely unbridled. As dictated by the Constitution, majority control should be the predominant feature of our government, but subject to constitutional limits.

Moreover, the Supreme Court is not quite as undemocratic as the strict constructionists sometimes like to portray it to be. While it is true that the justices who sit on the Court are appointed rather than elected and that they may be removed from office only for improper behavior, it is also true that they are appointed by a popularly elected president, and their appointment must be confirmed by a popularly elected Senate. Turnover of the Court's personnel, which sometimes occurs frequently, enhances popular control of the Court. Additionally, the Court's constitutional rulings may be overruled by the people through constitutional amendment, which, though a difficult procedure, has been accomplished on four occasions.[22] Thus, while the Court is not directly answerable to the public, it is not entirely immune from popular control.

## THE ULTIMATE AUTHORITY

The people also have the ultimate authority to abolish the Supreme Court. That they have not done so during our two centuries of experience indicates popular acceptance of the Court's role. Admittedly, there are particular decisions rendered by the Court that have aroused considerable public outcry, but given the many controversial issues that the Court must decide, this is inevitable. More telling about the public attitude toward the Court is that the people have taken no action to curtail the Court's authority to interpret the Constitution. Indeed, the public has shown little, if any, inclination toward abolishing the Court or even restricting its powers. Despite Franklin Delano Roosevelt's overwhelming popularity, his "court-packing plan" was a dismal failure;[23] the proposal to establish a "Court of the Union" composed of state court justices which would have the power to overrule the Supreme Court evoked such widespread public disapproval that it was quickly abandoned;[24] the campaigns to impeach Justices Earl Warren and William O. Douglas never got off the ground;[25] and although various members of Congress often propose bills threatening to restrict the Court's jurisdiction, the full Congress always rebuffs those threats.[26] These experiences suggest that even in the face of controversial constitutional decisions, there has been abiding public consent to the role of the Supreme Court in our scheme of government.

The Court's role, when all is said and done, is to create meaning for a Constitution that otherwise would be a hollow document. It is perfectly appropriate for anyone to disagree with Supreme Court decisions, and to criticize the Court on that basis. But it is not appropriate to attack the Court's decisions as illegitimate on the ground that they do not follow the Framers' intent. Pretending to use the Framers' intent to impugn the legitimacy of the Supreme Court is a spurious enterprise. The Court's legitimate function is, and always has been, to provide meaning for the Constitution.

---

NOTES

1. Address by Attorney General Edwin Meese, III, before the American Bar Association, Washington, DC (July 9, 1985); "Q and A with the Attorney General," 81 *American Bar Association Journal* 44 (July 1985).

2. Brest, "The Misconceived Quest for the Original Understanding," 60 *Boston University Law Review* 204 (1980).

3. Ely, "Constitutional Interpretation: Its Allure and Impossibility," 53 *Indiana Law Journal* 399 (1978).

4. Nowak, "Realism, Nihilism, and the Supreme Court: Do the Emperors Have Nothing But Robes?" 22 *Washburn Law Journal* 246, 257 (1983).

5. 410 U.S. 113 (1973).

6. *Reynolds* v. *Sims*, 377 U.S. 533 (1964).

7. *Engle* v. *Vitale*, 370 U.S. 421 (1962); *Abington School Dist.* v. *Schempp*, 374 U.S. 203 (1963).

8. 347 U.S. 483 (1954).

9. See, e.g., Boudin, *Government by Judiciary* 433–43 (New York: W. Goodwin, 1932);

Haines, *The American Doctrine of Judicial Supremacy* (Berkeley, CA: University of California Press, 1932).

10. Ford (ed.) 9 *Writings of Thomas Jefferson* 275–76 (1902).

11. Grey, "Origins of the Unwritten Constitution: Fundamental Law in American Revolutionary Thought," 30 *Stanford Law Review* 843, 844 (1978).

12. 3 U.S. (3 Dall.) 171 (1796).

13. Currie, *The Constitution in the Supreme Court, 1789–1888* 34 (Chicago: University of Chicago Press, 1985).

14. *Id.* at 36.

15. *McCulloch* v. *Maryland,* 17 U.S. (4 Wheat.) 316, 414 (1819).

16. See, Rohde & Spaeth, *Supreme Court Decision Making* 41 (1976); 1 *The Records of the Federal Convention of 1787* xii–xiv (Farrand ed. San Francisco: W.H. Freeman, 1937).

17. Burns, *The Vineyard of Liberty* 101–04 (New York: Knopf, 1982).

18. Wofford, "The Blinding Light: The Uses of History in Constitutional Interpretation," 21 *University of Chicago Law Review* 502 (1964).

19. *Supra* n. 7.

20. Stokes & Pfeffer, *Church and State in the United States* 181–82 (Colorado Springs: Shepard's 1975).

21. See, e.g., tenBroek, "Uses by the United States Supreme Court of Extrinsic Aids in Constitutional Construction," 27 *California Law Review* 399, 404 (1939); Kelly, "Clio and the Court: An Illicit Love Affair," 1965 *Supreme Court Review* 119, 122–25; Alfange, "On Judicial Policymaking and Constitutional Change: Another Look at the 'Original Intent' Theory of Constitutional Interpretation," 5 *Hastings Constitutional Law Quarterly* 603, 617 (1978).

22. The Eleventh Amendment overruled the holding of *Chisholm* v. *Georgia,* 2 U.S. (2 Dall.) 419 (1793); the Fourteenth Amendment nullified, in part, the decision in *Dred Scott* v. *Sandford,* 60 U.S. (19 How.) 393 (1857); the Sixteenth Amendment nullified the holding of *Pollack* v. *Farmers' Loan and Trust, Co.,* 157 U.S. 429 (1895); the Twenty-sixth Amendment neutralized *Oregon* v. *Mitchell,* 400 U.S. 112 (1970).

23. "Not all the influence of a master politician in the prime of his popularity was quite enough to carry a program that would impair judicial review," McCloskey, *The American Supreme Court* 177 (Chicago: University of Chicago Press, 1960). The plan was rejected vehemently by the Senate Judiciary Committee. See *Senate Comm. on the Judiciary, Reorganization of the Fed. Judiciary Adverse Report,* S. Rep. No. 711, 75th Cong., 1st Sess. 23 (1937).

24. Pfeffer, *This Honorable Court* 424–25 (Boston: Beacon Press, 1965).

25. Those who campaigned for Chief Justice Warren's impeachment were unable to have impeachment proceedings initiated against him. While impeachment proceedings were instituted against Justice Douglas, they never got beyond the subcommittee stage and were eventually forsaken. See *Special Subcomm. on H. Res., 920 of the House Comm. on the Judiciary,* 91 Cong., 2d Sess., Final Report, Associate Justice William O. Douglas (Comm. Print 1970).

26. "In the fifteen years between 1953 and 1968, over sixty bills were introduced in Congress to eliminate the jurisdiction of the federal courts over a variety of specific subjects; none of these became law." Bator, Mishkin, Shapiro & Wechsler, *Hart & Wechsler's the Federal Courts and the Federal System* 360 (Mineola, NY: Foundation Press, 2d ed. 1973).

## *Questions for Discussion*

1. What kinds of contemporary issues would the Framers have never contemplated?

2. What consequences about strict interpretivism can be drawn from your answer to Question 1?
3. How should you evaluate the qualifications of a person nominated to the Supreme Court who accepts the strict constructionist viewpoint?
4. Can the nonconstructionist view be reconciled with the U.S. system of democratic rule? What are the reasons for your answer?
5. Does the Constitution as written require the judiciary to follow the principle of judicial restraint? What are the reasons for your answer?

## Suggested Readings

Berger, Raoul. "Justice Brennan vs. the Constitution." *Boston College Law Review,* 29 (September 1988), 787–801.

Eaton, William. *Who Killed the Constitution? The Judges v. The Law.* Washington, D.C.: Regnery Gateway, 1988.

Farber, Daniel A. "The Originalism Debate: A Guide for the Perplexed." *Ohio State Law Journal,* 49, no. 4 (1989), 1085–1106.

Finkelman, Paul. "The Constitution and the Intentions of the Framers: The Limits of Historical Analysis." *University of Pittsburgh Law Review,* 50, no. 2 (Winter 1989), 349–398.

Graglia, Lino A. "Judicial Activism: Even on the Right, It's Wrong." *Public Interest,* no. 95 (Spring 1989), 57–74.

Larisa, Joseph S., Jr. "Popular Mythology: The Framers' Intent, the Constitution, and Ideological Review of Supreme Court Nominees." *Boston College Law Review,* 30 (July 1989), 969–986.

Lewis, Anthony. "Preserving the System: The Role of Judges." *Hastings Constitutional Law Quarterly,* 14 (Fall 1987), 1–19.

Lively, Donald E. "The Imperial Judiciary: Occupational Hazards of a Constitutional Society." *Villanova Law Review,* 34, no. 1 (February 1989), 1–23.

Maltz, Earl. "Foreword: The Appeal of Originalism." *Utah Law Review,* 1987, no. 4, 773–805.

Meese, Edwin, III. "The Attorney General's View of the Supreme Court: Toward a Jurisprudence of Original Intention." *Public Administration Review,* 45, no. 6 (November 1985), 701–704.

# Public Policy

**P** olitical democracy involves a contest over public policy. An element of that contest includes convincing individuals, private groups, and political leaders that particular policies are wise and just. An underlying theme of democratic rule is that conflicts should be resolved peacefully through discussion, freedom of association, and agreed-upon procedures for determining policy outcomes.

People who choose sides on different issues of public policy do so for many reasons. Sometimes, the choice is based on self-interest, as when a manufacturer or trade union favors protectionism so as to reduce competition from abroad. At other times, the choice is based on a perception of justice, as in issues relating to the elimination of racism or the protection of the environment. Often, choices derive from a combination of self-interested and altruistic impulses.

This part deals with some contemporary issues in domestic and foreign policy matters of concern to the people of the United States. Specifically, the debate questions consider the legalization of drugs, the role of housing shortages in causing homelessness, the relationship between government and artists, the nature of threats to the environment, statehood for Puerto Rico, and U.S. national interest.

# Chapter 16

## Should Drugs Be Legalized?

In the 1960s the culture of drugs won some popular approval—particularly among the young. In the minds of some advocates of drugs at that time, rational decision making had brought U.S. involvement in the Vietnam War, a high military budget when other national priorities were neglected, and the rigidities of a conformist society. Timothy Leary, a former Harvard instructor, supplied the drug culture with its motto: Turn on, tune in, drop out.

The drug culture of the 1960s was in the spotlight with Haight-Ashbury, a section of San Francisco where "hippies" pursued their way of life, and Woodstock, a small town in New York State that hosted a huge rock concert, with much drug use. But drugs began to take their toll. In the 1960s and the years that followed many performers, including some who performed at Woodstock, died of overdoses and addictions: John Belushi, Jimi Hendrix, Janis Joplin, Elvis Presley. Hundreds of thousands of men and women from all social strata suffered death and physical and mental disabilities.

By the 1980s drug use was no longer a subject of comic quips by entertainment figures anxious to get quick laughs, and Americans were overwhelmingly hostile to drug abuse and drug pushers—the people who sold drugs. Elected public officials declared wars on drugs, and funding to fight against drug use was provided at all levels of government.

Although the term "drugs" is used here to mean illegal drugs, it is important to remember that not all drugs are illegal. People who are ill use drugs prescribed by physicians that otherwise would be illegal, although these are also given to abuse. And alcohol and tobacco are drugs that are legal and available to most adults. But the major drugs of most concern are cocaine (and its derivative "crack") and heroin. Marijuana, too, has been increasingly considered to be unsafe because today's variety of that substance is many times more powerful than the "grass" hippies smoked in the 1960s.

As public awareness and government action have increased, actual drug use declined. Even use of alcohol and tobacco is declining as Americans become increasingly concerned about good health and physical fitness. From a health point of view, tobacco and alcohol take a greater toll on the lives and health of the American people than do the major illegal drugs.

Still, the problem of drug use—and the criminal activities and street deaths it spawns—remains serious, and there is no agreement on a solution. One approach is to intensify criminal punishment. Some would do so by increasing police budgets, working with governments of foreign countries where drugs are produced, and imposing the death penalty on drug dealers. Another approach is to provide increased public assistance for treatment.

In the past few years, however, a number of observers have argued in favor of legalization or decriminalization of hard drugs. This approach has won the support of some eminent public figures who span the political spectrum. These figures include Kurt Schmoke, the mayor of Baltimore; Robert Sweet, a New York judge and former New York City police commissioner; William F. Buckley, Jr., the conservative columnist; and George Shultz, secretary of state in the Reagan administration.

The debate below pits David Boaz against former New York City Mayor Ed Koch. David Boaz is vice-president of the Cato Institute, a public policy research foundation in Washington, D.C. Boaz favors decriminalization. He contends:

1. Drug prohibition causes high crime rates.
2. It encourages corruption.
3. It brings users into contact with criminals and gets them involved in a criminal culture.
4. It results in the creation of more potent drugs.
5. It destroys civil liberties.
6. It is futile.

Boaz calls for decriminalization of all recreational drugs, including marijuana, cocaine, and heroin.

Koch opposes legalization. He contends:

1. Drug legalization would mean that we have surrendered in the war on drugs.
2. More than 90 percent of the American public reject decriminalizing all illegal drugs.
3. Legalization would not reduce drug abuse and crime but increase them.
4. The cost of legalization would be higher than the cost of retaining the present system.
5. Greater resources for the war on drugs will help to solve the problem.

## Should Drugs Be Legalized?

### DAVID BOAZ
### The Case for Legalizing Drugs

Let me start my discussion of drug prohibition with the following quotation:

> For thirteen years federal law enforcement officials fought the illegal traf-
> fic. State and local reinforcements were called up to help. The fight was
> always frustrating and too often futile. The enemy used guerrilla tactics,
> seldom came into the open to fight, blended easily into the general popu-
> lation, and when finally subdued turned to the United States Constitution
> for protection. His numbers were legion, his resources unlimited, his
> tactics imaginative. Men of high resolve and determination were sum-
> moned to Washington to direct the federal forces. The enemy was pur-
> sued relentlessly on land and sea and in the air. There were an alarming
> number of casualties on both sides, and, as in all wars, innocent bystand-
> ers fell in the crossfire.

That passage wasn't written recently. It was written about the prohibition of
alcohol in the 1920s, and it illustrates a very simple point: Alcohol didn't cause
the high crime rates of the 1920s, prohibition did. Drugs don't cause today's
alarming crime rates, drug prohibition does.

What are the effects of prohibition? (Specifically I'm considering drug prohibition here, but the analysis applies to almost any prohibition of a substance or
activity people want.) The first effect is crime. This is a very simple matter of
economics. Drug laws reduce the number of suppliers and therefore reduce the
supply of the substance, driving up the price. The danger of arrest for the seller
adds a risk premium to the price. The higher price means that users often have
to commit crimes to pay for a habit that would be easily affordable if it was
legal. Heroin, cocaine, and other drugs would cost much less if they were
legal. Experts estimate that at least half of the violent crime in major U.S. cities
is a result of drug prohibition.

Crime also results from another factor, the fact that dealers have no way to
settle disputes with each other except by shooting each other. We don't see
shoot-outs in the automobile business or even in the liquor or the tobacco
business. But if a drug dealer has a dispute with another dealer, he can't sue, he
can't go to court, he can't do anything except use violence.

And then the very illegality of the drug business draws in criminals. As
conservatives always say about guns, if drugs are outlawed, only outlaws will
sell drugs. The decent people who would like to be selling drugs the way they

might otherwise sell liquor will get squeezed out of an increasingly violent business.

The second effect of prohibition is corruption. Prohibition raises prices, which leads to extraordinary profits, which are an irresistible temptation to policemen, customs officers, Latin American officials, and so on. We should be shocked not that there are Miami policemen on the take, but that there are some Miami policemen not on the take. Policemen make $35,000 a year and have to arrest people who are driving cars worth several times that. Should we be surprised that some of this money trickles down into the pockets of these policemen?

A third effect, and one that is often underestimated, is bringing buyers into contact with criminals. If you buy alcohol you don't have to deal with criminals. If a student buys marijuana on a college campus, he may not have to deal with criminals, but the person he buys it from probably does deal with criminals. And if a high school student buys drugs, there is a very good chance that the people he's buying drugs from—the people who are bringing drugs right to his doorstep, to his housing project, to his schoolyard—are really criminals; not just in the sense that they are selling drugs, but people who have gone into the drug business precisely because it's illegal. One of the strongest arguments for legalization is to divorce the process of using drugs from the process of getting involved in a criminal culture.

A fourth effect is the creation of stronger drugs. Richard Cowan in *National Review* has promulgated what he calls the iron law of prohibition: The more intense the law enforcement, the more potent the drugs will become. If a dealer can only smuggle one suitcase full of drugs into the United States or if he can only drive one car full of drugs into Baltimore, which would he rather be carrying—marijuana, coca leaves, cocaine, or crack? He gets more dollars for the bulk if he carries more potent drugs. An early example of that is that a lot of people turned to marijuana when alcohol became more difficult to get during Prohibition. A few years after Prohibition began in the 1920s there began to be pressures for laws against marijuana. When one advocates drug legalization, one of the standard questions is, "Well, marijuana is one thing, maybe even cocaine, but are you seriously saying you would legalize crack?" And the answer is that crack is almost entirely a product of prohibition. It probably would not have existed if drugs had been legal for the past 20 years.

The fifth effect of prohibition is civil liberties abuses. We have heard a lot recently about Zero Tolerance and the seizure of cars and boats because a small amount of marijuana or cocaine is allegedly found. I recall a time in this country when the government was only allowed to punish someone after he got convicted in a court of law. It now appears that the drug authorities can punish an American citizen by seizing his car or his boat, not even after an indictment—much less a conviction—but after a mere allegation by a police officer. Whatever happened to the presumption of innocence?

There is an inherent problem of civil liberties abuses in victimless crimes. Randy Barnett wrote about this in the Pacific Research Institute book *Dealing with Drugs;* the problem is that with victimless crimes, such as buying drugs, there is no complaining witness. In most crimes, say robbery or rape, there is a person who in our legal system is called the complaining witness: the person who was robbed or raped, who goes to the police and complains that somebody has done something to him or her. In a drug purchase, neither party to the transaction complains. Now what does this mean? It means there are no eyewitnesses complaining about the problem so the police have to get the evidence some other way. The policemen have to start going undercover, and that leads to entrapment, wiretapping, and all sorts of things that border on civil liberties abuses—and usually end up crossing the border.

The sixth effect of prohibition is futility. The drug war simply isn't working. Some say that much of today's support for legalization that we're seeing from politicians and others is merely a sign of frustration. Well, frustration is a rational response to futility. It's quite understandable why people have gotten frustrated with the continuing failure of new enforcement policies.

If a government is involved in a war and it isn't winning, it has two basic choices. The first is escalation, and we've seen a lot of proposals for that.

New York Mayor Ed Koch has proposed to strip-search every person entering the United States from South America or Southeast Asia. Members of the D.C. City Council have called for the National Guard to occupy the capital city of the United States. Congress has bravely called for the death penalty for drug sellers.

Jesse Jackson wants to bring the troops home from Europe and use them to ring our southern border. The police chief of Los Angeles wants to invade Colombia.

The White House drug adviser and the usually sensible *Wall Street Journal* editorial page have called for arresting small-time users. The *Journal,* with its usual spirit, urged the government to "crush the users"; that's 23 million Americans.

The Justice Department wants to double our prison capacity even though we already have far more people in prison as a percentage of our population than any other industrialized country except South Africa. Former attorney general Edwin Meese III and others want to drug test all workers.

The Customs Service has asked for authorization to "use appropriate force" to compel planes suspected of carrying drugs to land. It has clarified, in case there was any doubt, that yes, it means that if it can't find out what a plane is up to, it wants the authority to shoot the plane down and then find out if it's carrying drugs.

These rather frightening ideas represent one response to the futility of the drug war.

The more sensible response, it seems to me, is to decriminalize—to de-escalate, to realize that trying to wage war on 23 million Americans who are obviously very committed to certain recreational activities is not going to be any more successful than Prohibition was. A lot of people use drugs recreationally and peacefully and safely and are not going to go along with Zero

Tolerance. They're going to keep trying to get drugs. The problems caused by prohibition are not going to be solved by stepped-up enforcement.

So how exactly would we legalize drugs? Defenders of drug prohibition apparently consider that a devastating question, but it doesn't strike me as being particularly difficult. Our society has had a lot of experience with legal dangerous drugs, particularly alcohol and tobacco, and we can draw on that experience when we legalize marijuana, cocaine, and heroin—as we will, fairly soon, when more Americans come to understand the cost of prohibiting them.

Some critics of prohibition would legalize only "soft" drugs—just marijuana in many cases. That policy would not eliminate the tremendous problems that prohibition has created. As long as drugs that people very much want remain illegal, a black market will exist. If our goal is to rid our cities of crime and corruption, it would make more sense to legalize cocaine and heroin while leaving marijuana illegal than vice versa. The lesson of alcohol prohibition in the 1920s and the prohibition of other drugs today is that prohibition creates more problems than it solves. We should legalize all recreational drugs.

Then what? When we legalize drugs, we will likely apply the alcohol model. That is, marijuana, cocaine, and heroin would be sold only in specially licensed stores—perhaps in liquor stores, perhaps in a new kind of drugstore. Warning labels would be posted in the stores and on the packages. It would be illegal to sell drugs to minors, now defined as anyone under 21. It would be illegal to advertise drugs on television and possibly even in print. Committing a crime or driving under the influence of drugs would be illegal, as with alcohol.

It is quite possible that such a system would be *less* effective in attracting young people to drug use than the current system of schoolyard pushers offering free samples. Teenagers today can get liquor if they try, and we shouldn't assume that a minimum purchasing age would keep other drugs out of their hands. But we don't see many liquor pushers peddling their wares on playgrounds. Getting the drug business out of our schoolyards and streets is an important benefit of legalization.

It is likely that drug use would initially increase. Prices would be much lower, and drugs would be more readily available to adults who prefer not to break the law. But those drugs would be safer—when's the last time you heard of a liquor store selling gin cut with formaldehyde?—and people would be able to regulate their intake more carefully.

In the long run, however, I foresee declining drug use and weaker drugs. Consider the divergent trends in legal and illegal drugs today. Illegal drugs keep getting stronger—crack, PCP, ecstasy, designer drugs—as a result of the Iron Law of Prohibition. But legal drugs are getting weaker—low-tar cigarettes, light beer, wine coolers. About 41 million Americans have quit smoking, and sales of spirits are declining; beer and wine keep the alcohol industry stable. As Americans become more health-conscious, they are turning away from drugs. Drug education could do more to encourage this trend if it was separated from law enforcement.

By reducing crime, drug legalization would greatly increase our sense of safety in our neighborhoods. It would take the astronomical profits out of the drug trade, and the Colombian cartel would collapse like a punctured balloon. Drugs would be sold by Fortune 500 companies and friendly corner merchants, not by Mafiosi and 16-year-olds with BMWs and guns. Legalization would put an end to the corruption that has engulfed so many Latin American countries and tainted the Miami police and U.S. soldiers in Central America.

Legalization would not solve all of America's drug problems, but it would make our cities safer, make drug use healthier, eliminate a major source of revenue for organized crime, reduce corruption here and abroad, and make honest work more attractive to inner-city youth—pretty good results for any reform.

 *N O*

## Should Drugs Be Legalized?

### EDWARD I. KOCH

### The Case against Legalizing Drugs

I would normally preface my remarks by saying that I'm glad to be here, but today that is not the case. Given the devastation that drugs have wrought on our communities and nation, particularly over the last few years, I find it astounding that I am here to discuss a notion that seems to me to be the equivalent of extinguishing a raging fire with napalm—a fire that at this very moment is frying the brains of thousands of Americans.

Mr. Chairman, this committee, along with the very active support of the vast majority of America's mayors, has made valiant efforts in the past few years to devise ways to combat the drug scourge that continues to tear at our nation. Today, a small, small, number in these ranks are unwittingly impeding our progress by suggesting that we wave the white flag in the war on drugs and succumb to the enemy. Is their vision for the future of this country nothing better than one of its becoming a banana republic?! I hope not, but surely that is where their proposition would lead us.

I am far from alone in feeling this way. The September 15th *New York Times* reported that an ABC news poll found that more than 90 percent of the American public *reject* decriminalizing all illicit drugs. They also believe, by a 2 to 1 ratio, that the legalization of drugs would lead to an increase in crime.

And yet, in part because of the frustration some have had with the difficult task of addressing the drug problem, the idea of legalization has been elevated, undeservedly, to a place within the realm of debatable, if not potential, policy alternatives. Now that it is there, it may in fact be necessary to put the question of legalization on the table, but only to put it to rest, so that we can move forward with the strategies that *will* have an impact.

Before I continue, let me cite some statistics which reveal the dimension and impact of the drug problem.

There are over 500,000 heroin abusers in this country and six million people who have a serious cocaine or crack abuse problem. Even more troubling is the increasing numbers of our youth who are abusing certain drugs. Although no one knows for certain the number of juveniles using drugs, surveys of high school students have shown dramatic increases in their use of cocaine over the last ten years.

The devastating effects of drug abuse and the drug trafficking that supplies the abusers with their poison are quite clear. Reliable studies have concluded that drug abuse and drug traffickers are responsible for much of the violent crime in our nation.

These assertions are supported by data from the National Institute of Justice's drug forecasting survey, which recently showed that in New York City, 79 percent of the surveyed arrestees tested positive for at least one drug (including marijuana), 63 percent tested positive for cocaine, including crack, and 25 percent tested positive for heroin.

Indeed, the New York City Police Department has arrested almost 150,000 people for drug related crime over the last two years—up 17 percent from 1986 to 1987 and 11 percent in the first five months of 1988. This data clearly underscores the relationship between drug abuse and crime.

It is undeniable that, if we do not reduce drug abuse, its resulting crime and other destructive physiological consequences will continue to escalate and will result in a national tragedy of much greater proportions than it is today.

The suggestion that we should legalize drugs is therefore all the more shocking. How would legalization reduce drug abuse and its resulting devastation and crime? Let's analyze the legalization arguments.

To start with, some would have us believe that the laws against drug use and drug trafficking are prohibitions against a manner of personal conduct or style and that they are the imposition of society's moral values on the individual. This is just not the case. Rather, they are laws that prohibit conduct which destroys not only the individual users, but their families, the innocent victims of their crimes and the very foundation of a productive society.

The proponents of legalization are weak on the specifics of the implementation of a policy of "drugs for all." Some suggest that government should play a "big brother" role, providing fixed doses to addicts, and thereby limiting drug use. Their lack of understanding of drug abuse is startling, since there is no such thing as a fixed dose that will satisfy a drug addict's appetite for greater and greater quantities. Accordingly, the black market that legalizers say will be eliminated, would, of necessity, exist to provide an additional avenue of obtaining that which is not available from "legitimate" sources.

Piggy-backing on the assertion that legalization will eliminate the high profit margins on drug sales and therefore the black market, proponents say that crime associated with drug trafficking will diminish once drugs become an acceptable commodity. They ignore history and the facts.

Cheap drugs won't reduce crime and they never have.

In fact, given England's desperate failure to relieve its heroin addiction problem through heroin distribution programs during the 1960s and 1970s, the opposite is closer to the truth.

Until 1970, heroin was freely prescribed in Britain by private doctors. But over-prescription led to a doubling of the addicted population between 1970 and 1980. Then it took off.

Cheap heroin from Pakistan, which sold for $5 a fix on the street, began flooding the black market. Not only was it super cheap, it was more potent than what the government was handing out and came without bureaucratic restrictions. Cheap, potent and hassle free, the new street heroin *quadrupled the number of addicts in five years.* By 1986 the British Home Office estimated that there were 50,000 to 60,000 heroin addicts in the country. Some unofficial estimates were three times greater.

How was crime in Britain affected by legalization? In one 1978 study, 50 percent of the addicts in government programs were convicted of crimes in their first year of participation. Unemployment among addicts remained chronic too, as did other kinds of drug use—84 percent of the addicts registered with the government were found to use other illicit drugs as well. All told, the government program was a disaster.

Another facet of the crime problem associated with drugs that is frequently overlooked is that a number of drugs, and crack in particular, have been shown to have behavioral effects that result in violent criminal conduct not limited to theft to obtain money to purchase drugs. I don't think that we would be too far from the mark by assuming that the emerging "designer" drugs would have similar effects as the drug sellers search for a product that gives quicker and more intense highs. Should the government distribute or condone these crime-inducing drugs too?

Permitting drug use and encouraging even greater drug use by legalization would perpetuate and *expand* the devastating effects of drug abuse and its resulting crime.

Another erroneous argument for legalization is based on the economic rationale that it would be cheaper to provide drugs to addicts than it is to enforce the laws and pursue anti-drug strategies. It would not be cheaper. As the drug using population increases, the costs to society for the crime and other detrimental health effects of drug abuse would be far greater than they are now. We would still require the police, courts, prosecutors and jails to deal with drug related crime. We would need to dramatically increase treatment programs for those who, once on drugs, want to get off. And we would still have the economic impact on business, not only in terms of lost productivity, but in terms of increased health care insurance, worker safety and unemployment benefits.

Even if it is more expensive to do what we are doing to eradicate this problem, can government's obligation to protect the public safety be abdicated because it is expensive? Clearly not.

Two weeks ago on a nationwide television broadcast on this same topic, it was suggested that anti-drug law enforcement efforts, now estimated at $8 billion nationwide, could be cut to $2 billion if drugs were legalized. How can we say that $8 billion is too much to spend? How much is too much? Earlier this year I read in the *Washington Post* that leaders of the infamous Medellin drug cartel offered to pay off Colombia's estimated $15 *billion* national debt in return for immunity from prosecution and the scrapping of the country's extradition treaty with the U.S. This handful of individuals were willing to spend almost twice as much to stay in the game than we, at 240 million strong, are to keep them out. I think that it is all too painfully obvious that $8 billion is not nearly enough and we need to commit more—in the right places.

Part of our problem has been a lack of national commitment—not on the part of the average American, but by those who are representing them. The tough choices that have to be made are not being made. While the 1986 Omnibus Drug Bill authorized $230 million for drug law enforcement, only $70 million was actually appropriated. Why? The most common excuse is that there's no more money for anything since Gramm-Rudman. Let's face it, unless we find a new revenue stream for funding anti-narcotics efforts, we may never be able to adequately address our needs.

On a number of occasions over the past year I have suggested a three year federal income tax surcharge dedicated *solely* to eliminating the drug problem. I believe that the American public would support such a tax if it were proposed in this context. However, in this election year [1988], everyone in Washington is loath to mention that "T" word for any purpose. I believe that that is terribly shortsighted.

Now I'm not throwing the entire burden in the lap of the federal government, but I think you'll agree that whether it's Los Angeles, New York, Utica or Topeka, on its own, a city can't win the war on drugs. Washington must do its job too.

The cities are already doing their part. New York City, in particular, is dedicated to do whatever it can in terms of fighting the drug war. With 1,400 officers dedicated solely to narcotics interdiction, we are spending *nearly half a billion dollars* in city money to address all aspects of drug control.

But I plan to do more. Building on the success of a special police unit we organized last spring, the "Tactical Narcotics Team" (TNT), which was used to clean up a particularly drug infested area of Queens, I am in the process of expanding its efforts citywide with close to 650 additional officers.

This huge expansion of our drug enforcement efforts will obviously put pressure on our criminal justice system. It will necessitate an increase in jail beds over and above the 3,800 in my current capital plan and the 4,700 added in the last two years. It will increase the caseloads of district attorneys and the Legal Aid Society who will receive $9.5 million more than previously planned over the next two years.

The total price tag for this expansion: $110 million. How will I fund it? By making some tough decisions—raise taxes on cigarettes and alcohol, temporarily increase local property taxes or, if neither of these alternatives are successful, cut some city services. However we do it, it must be done.

The reaction of some people to my proposal has been that perhaps I should wait and hope the next president and the new Congress will be able to do more to fight drugs. But those of us out there on the front lines, those who deal on a daily basis with the ravages of this war simply can't afford to wait.

Mr. Chairman, what it comes down to is this. When people say that we should legalize drugs because law enforcement efforts have failed, they ignore the fact that a truly effective war has yet to be launched against drugs. What we really need to do is more, not less. A real war on drugs must include interdiction of illicit drugs by the armed forces at the borders, in the air and on the high seas. It must include more federal funding for education and treatment on demand. It must include "federalization" of drug prosecution and incarceration. These are all ideas I've laid out in detail in previous forums. I will continue to strive to see that they become part of the arsenal in the war on drugs.

It is time to raise the battle flag, not wave the white one.

## Questions for Discussion

1. What effect would legalization of drugs have on crime?
2. What effect would legalization of drugs have on solving the drug problem?
3. What relevance does U.S. experience with the prohibition of alcohol between 1920 and 1933 have on the issue of legalization of drugs today?
4. What is the best method to reduce the use of illegal drugs?
5. Is drug abuse a victimless crime? What are the reasons for your answer?

## Suggested Readings

Abadinsky, Howard. *Drug Abuse: An Introduction.* Chicago: Nelson-Hall, 1989.

Fingarette, Herbert. "Alcoholism: The Mythical Disease." *Public Interest,* no. 91 (Spring 1988), 3–22.

Gazzaniga, Michael S. "The Federal Drugstore." *National Review,* 42, no. 2 (February 5, 1990), 34, 36–41.

Holden, Constance. "Is Alcoholism Treatment Effective?" *Science,* 236, no. 4797 (April 3, 1987), 20–22.

Kaplan, John. "Taking Drugs Seriously." *Public Interest,* no. 92 (Summer 1988), 32–50.

Lapham, Lewis H. "A Political Opiate: The War on Drugs Is a Folly and a Menace." *Harper's*, 279, no. 1675 (December 1989), 43–48.

Macdonald, Donald I. *Drugs, Drinking, and Adolescents.* 2nd ed. Chicago: Year Book Medical Publishers, 1989.

Musto, David F. *The American Disease: Origins of Narcotic Control.* Enlarged ed. New York: Oxford Univ. Press, 1988.

Nadelman, Ethan A. "The Case for Legalization." *Public Interest*, no. 92 (Summer 1988), 3–31.

U.S. Cong., House of Representatives. *Drug Legalization—Catastrophe for Black Americans.* Hearing before the Select Committee on Narcotics Abuse and Control, 100th Cong., 2nd Sess., 1988.

———. *The Federal Drug Strategy: What Does It Mean for Black America?* Hearing before the Select Committee on Narcotics Abuse and Control, 101st Cong., 1st Sess., 1989.

———. *Legalization of Illicit Drugs.* Hearing before the Select Committee on Narcotics Abuse and Control, 100th Cong., 2nd Sess., 1988. Pts. 1, 2.

White House. *National Drug Control Strategy.* Washington, D.C.: Government Printing Office, 1989.

Wilson, James Q. "Against the Legalization of Drugs." *Commentary*, 89, no. 2 (February 1990), 21–28.

# Chapter 17

## *Is Housing the Principal Solution for Homelessness?*

The homeless are everywhere in the United States—in cities and in rural areas. They sleep in subway stations, alleys, parks, and building entrances. They line up at public and private shelters for a night of temporary housing. They live in single-room occupancy (SROs) dwellings in unclean and unsafe motels and form lines at soup kitchens. They receive public assistance, yet they beg the public for money.

To some extent, the problem of homelessness is not new. Even during earlier periods of prosperity the United States had homeless people, but because the police often would make certain that there was no begging or sleeping in public places, the homeless were less visible. Today, however, there are increasing numbers of homeless people. Their plight has received attention from homeless advocates and the media, and court decisions have extended their constitutional rights.

Although homelessness has made the national agenda, not much is known about it. There is uncertainty, for example, about the very number of people who are homeless, with estimates varying from 250,000 to 3 million. The Census Bureau's efforts to count the homeless in 1990 were hampered by the fact that few homeless people have fixed addresses and were opposed by homeless advocates who feared that the information would be used to curtail government programs aiding the homeless. Also unknown with any precision are the reasons why people become homeless and how long they remain homeless.

Some facts are accepted about the homeless, however. Most homeless people are single, but some family members—many from single-parent households—have become homeless, too. Some homeless people have fallen on hard times outside their control, such as physical illness or unemployment. The homeless population includes large numbers of alcoholics, drug addicts, and the mentally ill.

The debate below considers housing as a principal solution to the homeless problem. Homeless advocate David W. Crosland asserts that the solution to homelessness is the provision of permanent affordable housing to the poor. He points out that:

1. In the 1980s low-rent dwellings virtually evaporated, single-room occupancy units were reduced by half, and public and subsidized programs cut back. The lack of housing the poor can afford has reached crisis proportions.
2. It is difficult to tell if mental illness is a cause or consequence of

homelessness, but with housing guaranteed, the anxieties of the people who would otherwise be homeless would be lessened.

3. Many full-time working parents cannot afford to house their families.
4. Shelters are not the best permanent solution because they are often unsanitary.

Law professor Robert C. Ellickson says that housing is not the solution for the homeless. He contends:

1. Field surveys of the homeless turn up thankfully few families—meaning one or more parental figures accompanied by one or more minor children—sleeping in places not designed for residential living.
2. Many people who are counted as homeless are not street people but rather leave the homes they are using for available shelters.
3. Federal spending on low-income housing programs actually increased sharply in the 1980s in contrast to claims made by homeless advocates.
4. The connection between homelessness and changes in housing markets is uncertain.
5. The claim made by some advocates of the homeless—that the stress of being on the streets *causes* the high incidence of mental illness and substance abuse—is unsupportable.

In sum, Ellickson concludes, "The great majority of homeless people are not random victims of a housing-market squeeze, but rather deeply troubled individuals and families who, when deserving of government aid, should be given tailored financial assistance and help in managing their lives more successfully."

 YES

*Is Housing the Principal Solution for Homelessness?*

## DAVID W. CROSLAND
### Housing and Homelessness

I am pleased to have the opportunity to testify today and to express to you the [American Bar] Association's [ABA] support of legislation that will increase the number of permanent housing units for homeless persons and for those individuals most at risk of becoming homeless.

The American Bar Association has long been committed to laws and programs that would lessen the impact of poverty. It has supported legislation implementing legal services for the poor and, through its membership, is involved in over 600 organized bar projects providing legal representation free or at substantially reduced rates to those who cannot afford to pay.

The ABA first addressed the issue of homelessness as a problem separate and distinct from poverty in 1986. In August of that year, through its policy-making House of Delegates, the ABA resolved to support legislative efforts to ameliorate the plight of homeless people in our nation. Specifically, the ABA resolved to support enactment of federal, state and local legislation that would:

1. Prohibit discrimination on the basis of transient or homeless status in government assistance programs . . . and prohibit interference with the exercise of civil rights solely on the basis of transient or homeless status;
2. Address the pressing need for emergency relief to individuals and families now without permanent shelter and other basic necessities;
3. Encourage public and private initiatives to increase the supply of habitable low-cost housing in the United States; and
4. Adopt public policies and programs that will contribute to the ability of homeless people to become productive citizens.

At the same time, the House of Delegates further resolved that the ABA, in cooperation with state and local bar associations, would encourage lawyers to assist the homeless and to implement its recommendations. To carry out this portion of the resolution, the ABA during the following fiscal year, allocated funds for a staff person who would help lawyers and local bar associations carry out the 1986 resolution by working with members to establish pro bono bar homeless programs.

The ABA's Representation of the Homeless Project began in March, 1988. It has the dual responsibility of educating lawyers about homelessness and of stimulating the activation of bar programs to help homeless persons. Since 1986, and at a faster pace since the Project began, lawyers around the country have begun organizing bar programs through which they and their colleagues work to ameliorate the plight of homeless individuals. There are now over 20 bar programs designed to serve the legal needs of homeless persons. Recently, approximately three dozen additional bar associations and law schools have taken steps to develop their own homeless programs.

Although there is a dispute about the exact number of persons who are now without safe, adequate and affordable shelter, no one argues that the number is expanding at a frightening pace. Volunteer attorneys representing homeless clients have noticed the increased population and changing demographics. The homeless community now includes many, many more women and children. A volunteer lawyer who coordinates the Kansas City Bar pro bono homeless program said that over 50 percent of the homeless persons the attorneys assist are children. And the New York Times recently reported that the average

age of a homeless individual is four years old. Moreover, families are becoming homeless with ever-increasing frequency as are working people.

It is now undisputed that the increasing scarcity of low- and moderate-income housing is a major cause of homelessness. Over the past decade, low-rent dwellings have virtually evaporated, replaced by luxury apartments, co-operatives and condominiums. During the 1970s, almost 50 percent of the nation's single room occupancy (SRO) units, traditionally a major source of low-rent housing, were demolished. At the same time, public and subsidized housing programs have been severely cut back. The lack of housing affordable by the poorest in our nation has reached crisis proportions.

The single most important cause of homelessness—lack of permanent housing—is true for all groups within the homeless community. Experts estimate that as much as 30 percent of the homeless population is mentally ill. They believe that providing permanent housing for their clients is the number one priority. In the Spring 1986 edition of *Human Rights Annual*, published by New York Law School, a member of the Project's Steering Committee wrote:

> For many homeless mentally ill people their most pressing need is not for mental health services, but for a decent place to live. . . . Like all people who are homeless, those who are mentally ill need, more than anything else, a home. . . . [A]ny real solution to the problem of mentally ill people who are homeless must be part of the solution needed by all homeless people, an expansion of affordable housing.

Often it is difficult to determine to what extent a client's mental illness is a cause rather than the consequence of living on the streets or in shelters; with housing guaranteed, other anxieties are lessened or abated. And certainly, for the severely mentally ill, it is necessary to develop appropriate housing with community and mental health services available.

It has long been part of the American dream that if wage earners work hard and well, they can feed, clothe and house their families. This is no longer true. Full-time minimum wage workers earn less than $7,000 a year. Rising housing costs coupled with a pullout by the federal government from the subsidized low-income housing market have combined to place the opportunity to own or rent housing beyond the reach of most of them. It is now the American nightmare that many full-time working parents can no longer expect to house their families and in fact must regularly choose between shelter and food.

For example, a family of eight—six children ranging in age from 4 to 15, and their parents are now living in a shelter. The father works full-time in a hotel kitchen in Santa Rosa, California, clearing less than $600 a month. The mother was recently laid off her job. As a result, the family could no longer pay rent and voluntarily left the apartment rather than be evicted. Even though the mother now receives welfare payments, the family still does not have enough money to get back into the housing market.

In Los Angeles, a family of four—parents and two small children—relied on the father's income to provide their basic necessities including housing. While the father did not earn enough to pay for housing for the family, they were able to afford sharing an apartment with another family. When the father lost his job, the family had to leave the apartment and now are living in a garage, in one parking space. The father is looking for employment, and hopes to find another sharing arrangement in an apartment when he finds another job. This example is unfortunately not isolated. The *Los Angeles Times* reports that in that area alone, over 40,000 garages are rented out to people to use as housing. These are not garages converted into apartments; these are garages which now protect humans not cars from the elements.

The most innocent victims of homelessness are not making it. Twenty-five out of every thousand babies born to homeless mothers die. Of the survivors more than half exhibit clinical anxiety and depression during early childhood. Dr. Ellen Bassuk, of Harvard Medical School, works with homeless children. Her studies and professional observations reveal that homeless children exhibit developmental lags far worse than what one finds in comparable children from even the poor population. Among the clinical histories she cites are

- a three month old baby who was listless and unresponsive;
- a nineteen month old homeless infant who stopped eating and sleeping due to nightmares;
- a ten year old homeless boy who manifested his anxiety by pulling out three of his permanent teeth.

Homeless youngsters who can get through early childhood have a tremendous burden to carry on their small shoulders as they set off to elementary school. With no place to call home, and often no school to call their own, they are transferred as their parents are forced to move from shelter to shelter. Some children are tormented for being homeless, others are isolated for the same reason. Almost half never even get to school.

Our volunteer lawyers working here in D.C. [District of Columbia] report that in one case where a family was moved to three separate shelters in as many days, the parents were afraid to let their child attend school because the youngster would not know which shelter the family would be in at night, and would not know where to go after school.

In the 1989 U.S. Conference of Mayors *Status Report on Hunger and Homelessness in America's Cities: 1988,* Detroit described the effects of homelessness on its smallest citizens.

Homeless children receive inadequate nutrition, inadequate health care, have their schooling disrupted and do not have the normal opportunities to develop socialization skills. Life is looked upon as a "one day at a time" situation. There are few dreams and few plans and sharply reduced expectations about the future. There is despair, a loss of hope.

And from Kansas City:

> Homelessness is producing a generation of insecure, unmotivated and dependent children. They lack positive and stable role models. When living in crowded shelter situations they are surrounded by all types of people, most of whom they do not trust or have confidence in. Often times if they attend school, developing friendships is very tough, and in most cases they tell very little about being homeless because of the shame.

It is time for the federal government to step in. The majority of low-income renters receive no housing subsidies. In 1985, two-thirds of renters with incomes below $5,000 and three-quarters of those with incomes between $5,000 and $10,000 lived in unsubsidized housing. In that year, too, over one household in ten really could not afford anything for housing, according to government figures for "modest family budgets."

Within recent years, federal government decisions have resulted in more financial subsidies for the wealthy than for the poor. Cumulative federal housing spending for all U.S. Department of Housing and Urban Development low- and moderate-income housing was five billion dollars less than homeowner tax benefits in 1986 and 1987. An analysis of 1988 household income data and housing expenditures, including tax expenditures, indicates that the bottom fifth of all households received about 16 percent of all housing subsidies, while the top 27 percent got 62 percent of all subsidies. The average per household subsidy per month for households with incomes below $10,000 annually was $49, while the average monthly subsidy for households with incomes above $50,000 was $187 a month.[1] The National Low-Income Housing Coalition estimates that in 1989 approximately fifty-two percent of all federal housing expenditures (including spending and revenue losses) will go to the 17 percent of all American households earning more than $50,000 a year.[2] A more equitable arrangement must address both the needs of homeowners and those of the poor and homeless.

Speaking to members of the Association at the ABA's annual meeting in 1987, Frances Werner of the National Housing Law Project described homeowner deduction provisions of the tax code as the "single-most important housing policy operative today . . . a federal housing policy that redounds to the benefit of those at the upper end of the income scale." To achieve parity, she advocated a massive renewal of the new construction and rehabilitation programs for low-income families and the elderly with subsidies adequate enough to ensure the long-term economic viability of the housing and the stabilizing of costs for residents at an affordable level.

It is not necessary for the federal government to create a host of new programs to deal with housing and homelessness. Instead, what is essential is the tailoring of available assistance to meet the new needs created by homelessness, along with funding to begin to redress the devastation wrought by cuts in existing programs. In other words, the federal government must assume the responsibility of creating and maintaining affordable housing for poor people no matter what their circumstances, housing that will not be permitted to deteriorate [beyond] the point of inhabitability, housing from which the poor cannot be evicted at the whim of a landlord.

The following illustrates a situation that needs federal government attention. Last year, a Community Action Agency in one of our southern states reported this problem to the Housing Assistance Council, a report which was echoed by other agencies in other locales.

> [This County's] Section 8 Existing Payments Program is limited to serving only 68 families countywide, while maintaining a four (4) year waiting list for assistance. Recent families determined eligible for this type of assistance have found it impossible to locate affordable decent housing using the HUD [Department of Housing and Urban Development] Fair Market Rents. . . . In addition, the program has documented the loss of what has been traditionally considered the program's housing stock at 29 percent in one (1) year. This housing stock has been traditionally reserved by its owners for the Section 8 program to aid low-income families. The owners have withdrawn these units from service to be better able to reap the benefits of the tight housing market. . . . What [are] considered low-income neighborhoods [are] becoming more and more occupied by families with higher incomes. Owners are not required to give proper notice and sometimes just refuse rent payments to remove renters prior to sale to developers. . . . Because rents are so high, low-income families find themselves in critical need of emergency housing following displacement. . . . Families have been found to take up residence in tents, barns, cars, anywhere they can get out of the weather.[3]

While not as apparent or dramatic, rural homelessness and housing problems are as serious as those in our metropolitan areas. Rural housing funding has been cut by 50 percent in absolute terms—the number of units assisted has been reduced by two-thirds. Homeless people in the country do not have urban support systems such as welfare hotels and soup kitchens to rely on. When they are homeless, they must find shelter in severely dilapidated or overcrowded housing, or in inappropriate places such as cars or caves. A study in West Virginia found that

> [s]ubstandard housing conditions can be used as a reason to remove children from a home . . . but not to provide aid . . . for the homeless. Nor is overcrowding recognized as a condition of homelessness—even in instances . . . of 15 persons living in a five-room house.[4]

On the same subject, the National Coalition for the Homeless stated

> [w]hile in the worst neighborhood in New York, 11.6 percent of the housing is dilapidated, 49 percent of the rental housing in some rural counties of the South fits the same label, lacking any plumbing facilities

whatever. And the rate of overcrowding in the Bronx is less than the 20–25 percent rate estimated for countless poor rural parts of the country.[5]

*Taking Stock,* the Housing Assistance Council's study of rural poverty, described two counties in the Arkansas Ozarks where over half of the houses lack complete bathrooms and residents dispose of their wastewater without benefit of public sewer, septic tank or cesspool. Most houses lack even basic windows. Half to three-fourths of the residents use wood for heat. Some people live in barns papered inside with newspapers.

In West Feliciana Parish, Louisiana, 55 percent of the occupied housing units have no plumbing. Another study, this one of Clay County, West Virginia, reported that thirty-one families live in houses, ten live in trailers (of which only one is less than twenty years old), two families live in campers, one lives in a camper top, and one family lives in a shed. Less than half of the households have hot and cold running water, and fifteen have no running water. More than half of the families heat with wood or coal; one family has no heat source.

The Rural Homelessness Project in West Virginia charged that the U.S. Department of Housing and Urban Development contributes to homelessness by subsidizing substandard and dangerous housing. It urged that "the definition of homeless be expanded to include those who live in structurally unsound dwellings without safe water and sewage disposal; . . ." that rural solutions to homelessness and poverty include systems "which allow rural people to remain in rural areas in single unit housing with enough land for gardens and play space for children."[6]

For the homeless, shelters are not the solution. In *Atkikson v. Barry,* Case No. CA 11976 88, filed by one of our volunteer lawyers on behalf of homeless clients here in Washington, Superior Court Judge Harriet Taylor described two of the city's three permanent shelters as "virtual hell-holes." Last month she set out her reasons.

Some of the life and health-threatening perils confronting the homeless at those facilities have already been described, but that list is far from complete. For example, the toilet facilities at Blair and Pierce usually do not function and are infrequently cleaned; urinals and toilets are stuffed up and overflowing, so that men sleeping on hall floors often wake up to find themselves lying in urine; those toilets which do work are often covered with feces for days at a time; the stench throughout the facilities is overpowering.

Windows in Blair and Pierce have been broken for months.

The shower facilities in Blair and Pierce have been unuseable within recent memory. . . .

The intended sleeping facilities . . . are cots, or beds with mattresses; there are blankets but no sheets. No attempt is made to clean the mattresses, cots *or* blankets between residents or at any reasonable intervals. Last year, for example, the blankets were washed one time or not at all. The results are predictable. Cots or mattresses and blankets retain blood and pus from open and festering wounds, or vomit, phlegm, sputum and the like from those with illnesses of short or long duration. They also become home to mites . . . , lice, and other parasites.

Even the best of shelters, which are clean, warm and safe, are still not suitable. Often they do not permit adolescent boys to stay with their mothers and younger siblings, or husbands to stay with wives and children. Frequently, they do not have cribs and other facilities for newborns and infants. There is not enough room and children must go outside to find quiet places to do school-work, read or be alone.

The following examples are typical of and not exceptions to city shelter practices. In Boston, many family shelters cannot accept males over the age of twelve years old, while in Chicago, transitional shelters will not house males over the age of fourteen. In Los Angeles, Saint Paul and New Orleans, males over twelve years of age cannot stay in family shelters. In Norfolk, Virginia, some shelters do not allow family members of the same sex to stay together; boys over the age of seven must stay in the facility's all-male ward.

It is not unusual for shelters to close down during the day, sending residents once more into the streets. Portland, Oregon's response in the U.S. Conference of Mayors *Status Report* is descriptive of the lot of homeless parents and children nationwide.

Most of the shelters for homeless families are operated by churches, and they are night shelters only. There is one family resource center, but it cannot provide day shelter to all who need it. Other families seek shelter in their cars, the libraries, shopping malls, laundromats and under bridges.

Here, in the District of Columbia, one of our volunteer lawyers worked with a family of three—a father, a seven months pregnant mother and a three year old daughter. The father, a construction worker, was laid off this winter. Unemployment compensation was insufficient for the family to continue paying rent in the private sector. Although the family was eligible for federal housing, none was available. Evicted, the three went to a shelter. Because they could not produce a marriage certificate, the father was not permitted to stay with his wife and child. He slept in his truck on that bitterly cold night, while the mother and baby stayed in the shelter. As the shelter was an "overnight" facility, mother and daughter were put out the next morning. They spent the next few days in the family truck and the nights at the shelter, while the father spent days and nights in the truck. In a few weeks he found employment. Unfortunately, it required that he take his truck to the worksite. This left the mother and three year old without a place to stay during the day. Anxiety, long days cooped up in a truck and the difficulties of shelter life caused an already high-risk pregnancy to become worse. The mother was hospitalized. The father then had to keep his three year old in the truck during the day so that he could continue working. He could not stay at a shelter in the evenings with his daughter because single adult males are not permitted in shelters for women and children.

Most families choose emergency shelters as a last resort. Studies indicate that before surfacing as homeless, families have lived doubled or tripled up with relatives or acquaintances until discovered by a landlord or until the over-crowded situation becomes intolerable. Many parents are fearful of alerting welfare workers to their homelessness because they may then lose their children to charges of neglect or be pressured into "voluntarily" placing their little ones in foster care. Once separation occurs, it is very difficult to reunite the family and almost impossible to eradicate the effects of the double trauma— loss of home and family.

The solution to homelessness is the provision of permanent affordable housing to the poor. The federal government has a particular responsibility to address the acute need for affordable housing. In part, the national crisis in housing we are now experiencing is the result of government action or inaction over the past decade. The supply of rental housing that is available and affordable to poor people is shrinking. At the same time, a greater portion of our population is falling below the poverty line. To meet this situation, existing federally assisted units must be retained and upgraded, when necessary; new units must be developed. Residents must be guaranteed safe and secure housing. The national goal first enunciated by Congress in 1949 must continue to be one we strive for: "a decent home and a suitable living environment for every American family."

---

*NOTES*

1. *Background Data on Low Income Housing*, Cushing N. Dolbeare, Washington, D.C. (November 1988); "Affluent Get Thousands in Subsidies," *The Washington Post*, October 15, 1988.

2. *A Vision for the Future*, Children's Defense Fund, Washington, D.C. (1989), p. 33.

3. *The Homeless Crisis from a Rural Perspective*, Housing Assistance Council, Washington, D.C. (1987), p. A–18.

4. *"It Ain't Much, but It's All I Got": A Study of Living Conditions in Two Rural West Virginia Counties*, Covenant House, Inc., Charleston, West Virginia (1988), p. 7.

5. *Rural Homelessness in America: Appalachia and the South*, National Coalition for the Homeless, Washington, D.C. (November 1987), pp. 7–8.

6. *Op. cit.*, *"It Ain't Much . . .,"* at 70–71.

## Is Housing the Principal Solution for Homelessness?

### ROBERT C. ELLICKSON
### The Homelessness Muddle

During the past decade, homelessness has emerged as a major social problem; yet our attempts to combat it seem only to have worsened things. Although the number of shelter beds in the United States almost tripled between 1983 and 1988 (going from 98,000 to 275,000), beggars now frequent downtown sidewalks and parks in ever-growing numbers. To understand why this has happened—in particular, why increases in government shelter programs have increased the count of homeless people as they are currently defined—one must realize that the view of homelessness proffered by activists like Robert Hayes, Jonathan Kozol, and Mitch Snyder is fundamentally flawed. Although these advocates deserve credit for bringing attention to the human tragedy of homelessness, their central policy proposal—more government-funded housing projects—is as wrongheaded as their assessment of the current situation. Instead of providing unconditional shelter to all who apply for it, policymakers should devise aid programs that better reflect the diversity of the homeless population and that do more to discourage dependency.

The current confusions in homelessness policy start with semantics. The term "homeless" is now used to describe people in two quite different situations on a given night. First, it applies to the street homeless—people who sleep in vehicles, parks, bus stations, and other places not designed as residences. Second, it includes the sheltered homeless—those who obtain temporary housing either in shelters that local governments or charities operate, or in rooms that can be rented with emergency housing vouchers supplied by welfare agencies. Unlike the street homeless, the sheltered homeless sleep in places designed for residential living; members of both groups, however, almost invariably lack permanent homes.

This bundled definition of homelessness leads to the paradoxical result that greater governmental spending on shelter programs increases the reported number of homeless people. New beds in free shelters draw not only people from the streets, but also those who are housed. Shelters are often used by poor people who have been doubled up with friends or relatives, living in cheap rented rooms, or confined in hospitals, detox centers, or other institutions.

To see how the bundled definition of homelessness misleads, suppose (not unrealistically) that a new hundred-bed shelter draws forty people from the street and sixty who would otherwise have slept in housing or institutions. The street homeless population would fall by forty, and the sheltered homeless population would rise by a hundred—which would increase the total reported homeless population by the sixty who were drawn from their previous housing. Semantic imprecision is thus a major reason why recent bursts in aid to the homeless have been widely regarded as inadequate and ineffectual. To improve the quality of public debate, policymakers and journalists should distinguish between street and sheltered homeless, and should strive to report separate tallies of each. Emphasis on this distinction would help reveal the successes (or failures) of new shelters in reducing street populations; it would also reveal that about half of homeless individuals—and the vast majority of homeless families—are in shelters, not on the streets.

## HOMELESS FAMILIES

Field surveys of the homeless turn up thankfully few families—meaning one or more parental figures accompanied by one or more minor children—sleeping in places not designed for residential living. In 1985–1986 Peter Rossi and his associates supervised a pioneering middle-of-the-night canvass of Chicago's abandoned buildings, vehicles, and public places where street homeless might be found sleeping. Rossi's investigators turned up no unsheltered children. In 1986 a different team applied Rossi's techniques in the skid-row area of Los Angeles and also found no families outside. Similarly, Martha Burt and Barbara Cohen of the Urban Institute conducted a nationwide survey in 1987 that located no children in a sample of outdoor places where homeless people congregate.[1]

These findings hardly mean that minors always are sheltered. Some homeless parents using soup kitchens, for example, have told investigators that they sleep with their children in vehicles or other places not designed as housing. Based on reports of this sort, Burt and Cohen estimated that 2–5 percent of homeless children nationwide are unsheltered. In 1988 the Colorado Coalition for the Homeless conducted a warm-weather survey in the Denver area that suggested a somewhat higher percentage. It is nevertheless clear that, in part because child-welfare agencies intervene to prevent abuse and neglect of children, on any given night the vast majority of homeless families are in places designed for residential living.

Families arriving at shelters are overwhelmingly drawn from housing, not from the street. A 1988 survey of New York City, directed by James Knickman and Beth Weitzman, found that 90 percent of arriving families were currently receiving Aid to Families with Dependent Children (AFDC).[2] Seventy-one percent of these families had been doubled up with family or friends during the previous night. Another 18 percent had been living in their own places.

A further indication that family shelters draw mainly from housing is that the number of families receiving emergency shelter varies dramatically over place and time. It is improbable that changes in the neediness of local families would be nearly so abrupt, and indeed the shifts correspond closely to changes in the content of family-aid programs. The experience of New York City is instructive. During the 1970s, when the city was willing to decline some families' applications for emergency shelter, the best available data indicate that it provided emergency housing assistance to fewer than a thousand families per night. In the early 1980s, under pressure of litigation, New York began to provide free shelter to all families that showed up at its intake points; by August 1987 it was providing emergency housing to 5,200 families a night. The city then began revising its program, partly because federal officials had threatened to stop sharing the huge cost of housing families for long periods in horrendous welfare hotels. Over the next two years the total number of families that New York City was aiding in hotels and shelters declined by 25 percent, to 3,900. This drop almost certainly stemmed from the city's policy changes, not from a sudden decline in need.

The fact that tallies of homeless families are highest in the localities that offer the most generous aid supports the proposition that family shelters mostly substitute for other forms of housing. In 1987, according to Burt and Cohen's estimate, American cities with populations above 100,000 had a combined total of roughly 40,000 people in homeless families. In that same year New York City alone was aiding 17,000 people in homeless families, or about 40 percent of Burt and Cohen's national big-city total. New York's per capita incidence of family homelessness was five times the average for other big cities. The most obvious explanation for this discrepancy is that during the 1980s New York City had become one of the few cities to offer free shelter, with no questions asked, to all families that showed up at emergency intake sites.

Statistics from other areas in the Northeast strongly support the proposition that providing poorly tailored aid increases family homelessness. In September 1989 Westchester County (north of New York City) was giving emergency housing aid to about eight hundred families, three-fourths of which it was putting up in motels and providing with cash food allowances; at the same time, Nassau County (east of the city), whose population is half-again larger than Westchester's, was giving emergency aid to fewer than fifty families, none of them in motels. Differing county policies account for most of this disparity: Westchester County typically grants families that apply for emergency housing a free stay in a motel, while Nassau County refers them first to small nonprofit shelters and sends them to motels only as a last resort. Similarly, in New Haven, where families are placed in motels, the rate of family homelessness is six times higher than in Hartford and Bridgeport, two comparably sized and comparably poor Connecticut cities where homeless families are sent to congregate shelters.

Survey data also indicate that heads of homeless families are responsive to differences in aid programs. In 1985 Richard Towber interviewed families applying for emergency shelter in New York City. In his sample 61 percent of the family heads stated that they would turn down some types of emergency housing aid, and 89 percent of this subgroup said that they would decline placement in a congregate shelter. One can infer that many applicants for emergency shelter have other housing options, such as doubling up with friends or using part of their AFDC stipend to pay rent.

Cities obviously need a system of temporary emergency aid to house families victimized by fires, intrafamily violence, and other sudden emergencies. Many governments, however, have come to define homelessness so broadly that they offer emergency aid to households turned out by primary tenants (friends or relatives) or evicted for nonpayment of rent. To avoid creating perverse incentives, a government that broadly identifies the families eligible for emergency aid must be wary of providing significant financial benefits to applicants. Unfortunately, some governments have not learned this lesson. To clear homeless families from its costly emergency shelters and hotels, for example, New York City has at various times jumped these families to the top of the waiting list for the city's subsidized housing projects. To relocate homeless families from motel rooms, Connecticut administrators have granted them rental assistance payments (RAPs), covering most of the rent in their subsequent dwellings; the present value to a family of a stream of RAP benefits runs in the tens of thousands of dollars. Many poor families, of course, are not aware of specific program details; still, as welfare officials have found, prospective beneficiaries tend to understand the general picture. Partly because it is desirable to shield children from the chaos of temporary housing, governments should be wary of making indigent parents welcome eviction.


## *HOMELESS INDIVIDUALS*

Burt and Cohen estimated that the homeless singles population outnumbers the homeless family population by about three to one. Homeless individuals are somewhat more likely than homeless families to sleep in places not designed as dwellings. Nevertheless, particularly during harsh weather, many fewer homeless individuals sleep outside than is generally supposed. In his sweeps during the Chicago winter of 1986, for example, Rossi found 74 percent of the homeless sleeping in shelters; 25 percent in stations, theaters, and other public-access places; and only 1 percent in unheated venues such as abandoned buildings or parked cars.

Irving Piliavin and Michael Sosin found in their study of Minneapolis that the typical homeless individual cycles between street and residential settings within the space of a year.[3] A thirty-year-old alcoholic, for example, might sometimes stay with friends or family, sometimes have a place of his own, sometimes live on the streets, and sometimes be in a jail or detox facility. The establishment of an emergency shelter inserts another possible landing place into this cycle. Although a city that opens a new shelter usually intends to serve the street homeless, in practice a shelter substitutes for locations both on the street and in the housing stock.

It is easy to imagine circumstances under which the opening of a new emergency shelter would draw in individuals who otherwise would live in housing. Suppose, for example, that the alcoholic had been staying with a friend or relative who had increasingly found him to be difficult company. Upon learning that a new shelter had opened, the primary tenant might become more willing to tell the roomer that he had overstayed his welcome. Or suppose that a worker with a low-wage job and a cocaine addiction were living alone in a rented room. If a tolerable shelter were to open, this worker might consider moving from the rented room in order to free up funds for drugs. Conversely, a jobless person who had been staying for months in a round-the-clock, full-service shelter might see little cause to find a job that would enable him to rent a room.

Regrettably, we do not really know to what extent beds in new shelters for individuals substitute for the street and to what extent for beds in housing and institutions. The most pertinent evidence at hand, all of it from New York City, comes from interviews with homeless individuals themselves. In 1982 Stephen Crystal found that 38 percent of the new arrivals at New York shelters had spent the prior night on the street; 47 percent had been in housing and 16 percent had been in a hospital, a jail, or another institution. Subsequent studies in New York also found that fewer than half of the new arrivals at shelters had come directly from living on the street.

Evidence of how singles-shelter populations have varied according to time and place also suggests that new shelter beds for singles largely substitute for housing. During the 1980s, New Haven, Westchester County, and New York City all began to offer a free bed to anyone who asked for it (and was willing to obey rules against alcohol, drugs, and bad behavior). The singles-shelter populations in all three places promptly leapt upward, quadrupling in New York, for example, between 1981 and 1987. It is possible, of course, that the political leaders of the three jurisdictions correctly anticipated large bursts in latent homelessness—the amount of street homelessness that would exist in the absence of any social programs; by providing shelters, they may have staved off large increases in their street populations. A city that opens up shelters may also attract migrants from the streets of other cities. Nevertheless, the best explanation for the prevalence of homelessness in, say, Westchester County (which assists ten times more homeless individuals than Nassau County) is that its unusually generous homeless-aid programs have pulled in many people from its own housing stock.

On the whole, it seems highly probable that singles shelters substitute in significant part for housing. If accepted for purposes of policy analysis, this proposition would have two important implications. First, it would carry the welcome news that latent homelessness has not been escalating to the degree that many people think. Second, it would call attention to the fact that shelters significantly aid two other groups besides street people: impoverished individuals who choose a free shelter bed over other housing options, and primary tenants who, because of the availability of shelters, are emboldened to evict difficult housemates. Whether members of these two groups should be aided in this way, or indeed specially aided at all, are debatable questions. One can imagine the relief that shelter programs have sometimes provided to families and friends who have lost patience with housemates. On the other hand, the wretched social environment in many shelters may aggravate underclass pathologies of dependence, unemployment, and substance abuse. If so, Peter Rossi's suggestion of a program of Aid to Families with Dependent Adults—that is, public-assistance payments that would help families house and feed adult members incapable of supporting themselves—would seem more sensible than a program of building more shelters. The point, however, is that policymakers cannot even begin to debate these alternatives until they come to recognize that singles shelters apparently draw significantly, perhaps even primarily, from housing.

## THE NATIONAL NUMBERS DEBATE

In light of the political volatility of the homelessness issue, it is hardly surprising that estimates of the growth and size of the homeless population have varied widely. Predictably, those who advocate spending more on homelessness programs have produced some of the most inflated estimates. For example, Mitch Snyder's advocacy organization, the Community for Creative Nonviolence (CCNV), currently asserts that America has three to four million homeless people. As scholars of homelessness have often pointed out, the CCNV's national estimates have never rested on any credible factual foundation. Indeed, Snyder himself has never seriously tried to defend the CCNV figures, and for good reason.

In 1984 the Department of Housing and Urban Development (HUD) made the first systematic attempt to count the national homeless population, and arrived at a figure of 250,000 to 350,000—about one-tenth the CCNV's number. The most careful recent field studies, such as Rossi's, Burt and Cohen's, and Georges Vernez's, indicate that HUD was not far from the mark. Estimating the homeless population is obviously a Herculean task, particularly because of the difficulty of counting the street homeless. To overcome this problem, Rossi pioneered the use of intensive field sweeps, while Burt and Cohen interviewed patrons of soup kitchens about where they had recently slept.

These scholars' findings suggest that the national homeless population—both street and sheltered—on any given night is between 0.1 percent and 0.2 percent of the total population. Thus their counts correspond closely with HUD's 1984 estimate. Rossi, for example, estimated the total Chicago homeless at around 2,300 per night during the fall of 1985, or a bit under 0.1 percent of the city's population. In his 1989 book, Rossi indicated that his "best estimate" of the national homeless population was 250,000 to 350,000—the same estimate that HUD had made five years earlier.

By 1989, however, HUD officials had begun to rely on a national estimate of

600,000, a number derived from calculations made by Martha Burt in a memorandum dated September 11, 1988. Burt herself has made clear that this figure is probably too generous. Most of Burt's estimates aim at fixing the number of different people who would be on the street or in a shelter on at least one night during a one-week period. Previously, HUD had estimated the homeless population for a single night; given the fluidity of the homeless population, this number is considerably smaller. Burt did make some one-day estimates as well, but she based them on a street-shelter ratio of two to one. This ratio is almost certainly too high for several reasons. First, Burt applied the ratio to families, who are almost all sheltered, as well as to individuals. Second, there were far more shelter beds in 1987, the year of Burt's estimate, than in 1984, when HUD judged the street-shelter ratio to be less than two to one; by 1987 a one-to-one basis was more realistic. Lastly, Burt assumed without explanation that the rate of homelessness in suburban and rural areas is about three times higher than her supporting studies would indicate. Stripped of all these upward biases, Burt's one-day estimates of the 1987 homeless population probably would have come out slightly above HUD's 1984 estimate of 250,000 to 350,000.

## WHY LATENT HOMELESSNESS IS ON THE RISE

Although most of the advocates' figures appear to be inflated, the nation's homeless population undoubtedly did grow during the 1980s. Even if we account for the fact that the addition of some 177,000 shelter beds between 1983 and 1988 pulled significant numbers of people out of housing and institutions, most observers believe that latent homelessness has been increasing.

The rise nevertheless has been smaller than most people who frequent downtowns might think. Such observers fail to reckon with the near demise of skid rows, where many destitute people used to live in relative isolation. In 1986 the New York Times reported, for example, that there were only one-fourth as many flophouse beds in New York's Bowery section as there had been twenty years earlier. Significantly, in most cities new skid rows have not arisen to replace the ones that have been gentrified. The dispersion of skid-row populations has done much to increase public awareness of the destitute and homeless.

One reason for the continuing decline of skid rows is that Social Security and federal disability benefits have increased greatly over the past two decades. Many older people who would otherwise have spent their autumn years in skid-row neighborhoods can now afford to live elsewhere. In addition, since the 1960s the legal system has extended much more protection to down-and-out people. Before these reforms, an unspoken mission of the police in many cities was to keep "bums" out of the nicer parts of town. A police officer could perform this task with vagrancy arrests, mass roundups of street drunks, and commands—backed by a nightstick—to move along. Such tactics have now been blocked. Judicial decisions have struck down vagrancy laws, curbed the mass arrests of drunks, and assessed damages against police departments that have been too aggressive with street people. These legal innovations, coupled with greater police and citizen solicitude for the down and out, have allowed skid-row residents to escape their old confines. Advocates also seem to have learned that situating soup kitchens in conspicuous locations yields political benefits. The rise in homelessness, although real, is thus less than meets the middle-class eye.

Homeless advocates such as Jonathan Kozol offer a simple explanation for the increase in latent homelessness during the 1980s: Reagan administration cuts in the federal housing budget. But the premise of this argument is false. During the late 1970s the Carter administration's HUD mapped out an ambitious expansion of federally subsidized housing projects, concentrating on public-housing projects built and managed by local authorities. Beginning in 1981, Reagan's HUD drastically cut back on these plans for future projects and instead redirected new federal spending to Section 8 housing allowances, which help low-income householders pay the rent due private landlords. Under federal accounting rules, Congress must provide forty years of "budget authority" when it approves a new public-housing dwelling unit, but only five years when it approves a new Section 8 allowance. This discrepancy arises because the unavoidable federal financial commitment is more long-lived in the case of public housing. As a result, the Reagan administration's decision to shift future initiatives from public housing to Section 8 assistance reduced by 87.5 percent the budget authority that HUD needed to aid an additional low-income household. When the specialists involved in the production of subsidized housing projects bemoan federal cuts, they usually trot out figures based on these paper cuts in budget authority, a highly misleading measure.

Much more relevant to low-income families are the trends in how much HUD is spending and how many households it is aiding. Federal spending on low-income housing programs actually increased sharply during the 1980s. According to computations by University of Virginia economist Edgar Olsen, federal housing subsidies for low-income families went from $5.8 billion in fiscal 1980 to $13.8 billion in fiscal 1988. Adjusting for rent inflation, this represented a real spending increase of over 50 percent. Between 1980 and 1987 (the last year reported in the *Statistical Abstract*), the stock of public-housing units increased from 1.2 million to 1.4 million, as projects that Carter's HUD had put into the production pipeline were completed. More significantly, during the same years the number of low-income households receiving Section 8 assistance doubled to 2.2 million. Thus from 1980 to 1987, the federal government came to provide housing aid to an additional 1.3 million low-income households—more households than the entire public-housing program had assisted in 1980.

Advocates also frequently assert that decreases in the number of single-room occupancy units (SROs) have reduced vacancies, raised rents, and spurred latent homelessness. This is plausible in some cities, notably New York, where municipal housing codes, rent controls, and slum-clearance programs have often impeded the creation and maintenance of these low-cost forms of housing. Still, the connection between homelessness and changes in housing markets is uncertain. Because most anti-SRO policies predated the 1980s, it is unclear why the SRO market would suddenly have started to function poorly in that decade. Although many SROs have been demolished in recent years, many replacement dwelling units may also have been supplied by landlords who reconfigured their buildings to meet the demand for cheap rooms. Little is known about these matters, because in most cities data on abandonments and conversions are poor. Information on trends in rent levels *is* available, and it shows that during the 1980s residential rents generally did rise appreciably faster than inflation in the Northeast and West. If real rent increases were an important cause of the rise in latent homelessness, however, the South and Midwest, where real rents have not risen, should be relatively free of street people. Significant regional variations in homelessness have yet to be detected.

Other explanations for the recent increase in latent homelessness are more compelling. First, most homeless individuals are between twenty-five and forty-five. This age cohort, the baby-boom generation, is currently unusually large; in addition, it came of age when norms against substance abuse were unusually weak. The crack and cocaine epidemics of the 1980s undoubtedly boosted latent homelessness. Addictions lessen capacities to pay rent and to keep a job; in addition, primary tenants are no doubt more likely to evict addicted housemates than unaddicted ones.

It is furthermore well known that many of the most forlorn of the homeless are on the streets because of the emptying of mental hospitals, prompted in part by changes in treatment policies and in part by a sharp increase in the constitutional and statutory rights of the mentally ill. Today, a person cannot be committed involuntarily without a judicial finding—reached through protective procedures that include a right to counsel—that the person is dangerous to self or others. A physician, hospital, or police officer who violates these legal protections can be held liable for substantial damages to the wrongly confined patient. Half a million fewer people are in institutions today than would be the case if the rate of institutionalization were what it was in the 1950s. Indeed, between 1960 and 1975 the average daily population of state and county mental hospitals dropped by 60 percent. And, despite continuing increases in the adult population, the number of patients in state and county mental hospitals has continued to drop, going from 193,000 to 107,000 between 1975 and 1987. Because the last people to be released would tend to be least able to take care of themselves, the emptying of hospitals explains much of the rise in homelessness. There are now many more troubled people on the streets; in New York City between 1980 and 1988, for example, the number of emergency calls reporting emotionally disturbed people rose from 21,000 to 47,000.

Finally, the rise in latent homelessness seems linked to the increasing social isolation of the underclass—that is, poor people who grew up in poor neighborhoods in single-parent or no-parent households that were highly dependent on public assistance. During the 1970s the central-city poor became more and more concentrated in poor neighborhoods. The connection between homelessness and the deepening of underclass cultures remains somewhat speculative, however, because interviewers have rarely asked homeless individuals about their cultural backgrounds. Nevertheless, the evidence does suggest that the homeless have disproportionately grown up in underclass households. In 1985 Harvard psychiatrist Ellen Bassuk conducted detailed interviews of families in Massachusetts shelters;[4] she found that one-third of homeless mothers never knew their own fathers. Similarly, Piliavin and Sosin reported that 38 percent of homeless individuals had received out-of-home care during childhood. The increasing fragility of poor families heightens susceptibility to homelessness in a number of ways. People without appropriate family role models have more difficulty entering the world of work; children who grow up in fragile families (not to mention foster homes) typically have fewer helpers to fall back on when adversity strikes them as adults.

## REALISM ABOUT THE HOMELESS

These explanations for the rise in latent homelessness highlight a key issue in the current policy debate. Activists for the homeless often suggest that the only thing that distinguishes the homeless from the rest of the population is the lack of a home. For example, Kozol begins *Rachel and Her Children,* a book on the plight of homeless families in a squalid and dispiriting welfare hotel in New York, with a chapter entitled "Ordinary People." But the families that he describes are far from ordinary in important respects. For example, Kozol profiles Laura, a young unmarried mother who, partly because she is illiterate, fails to obtain medical treatment for an infant with scabies and later abandons her children to become a prostitute.

Most homeless families are not random victims of a recent run of bad luck, and it is highly misleading to suggest otherwise. In their study of New York, Knickman and Weitzman found that a major cause of family homelessness was the relative inability of heads of homeless families to function independently— a theme missing in the *New York Times* story on the study, which focused instead on the city's tight housing market. Similarly, Bassuk found that the homeless families she interviewed were overwhelmingly headed by young unmarried women, a majority of whom had never had a job and more than half of whom had first given birth in their teens. Some 91 percent of these families were currently receiving AFDC payments; a majority had been receiving them for over two years. One-third of these mothers had never known their own fathers and one-third had been physically abused as children.

Like homeless families, few homeless individuals were leading ordinary lives before slipping into homelessness. Most homeless individuals suffer from either mental illness or substance abuse, or from both. Findings from dozens of careful field studies suggest that about 25 percent of homeless individuals have been patients in mental hospitals and that an overlapping one-third currently show signs of a psychosis or an affective disorder. Georges Vernez, who supervised a far-flung field study in California, reported that 69 percent of homeless individuals interviewed were abusing either drugs or alcohol; over half of this subgroup abused both substances. Even more distressingly, Vernez found that three-quarters of the homeless with serious mental illnesses were also substance abusers. Only 23 percent of the homeless individuals in Vernez's sample were free from both major mental illness and substance abuse.[5]

Many homeless individuals have histories of multiple stays in institutions other than mental hospitals. Rossi found that one-third of the Chicago homeless had been in a detoxification unit for alcohol or drug abuse. Average findings in a dozen studies indicate that 21 percent of the homeless have served time in prison and an additional 21 percent have spent time in jail.

The claim made by some advocates of the homeless—that the stress of being on the streets *causes* the high incidence of mental illness and substance abuse—is unsupportable. Thus Piliavin and Sosin found in their study of Minneapolis that 70 percent of the homeless who had been patients in mental hospitals had been there before their first episode of homelessness.

## WHAT IS TO BE DONE?

No magic sword will slay homelessness. In a society committed to individual liberty, the ravages of substance abuse and mental illness cannot and should not always be hidden from view. Social-service programs designed to put down-and-out people back on their feet are of course appropriate in many contexts, but they are unlikely to enjoy high rates of success. Nonetheless, while my main purpose has been to describe the present situation, it is appropriate to close with a few suggestions.

First, all involved—particularly the media—should work to dispel the fog of misinformation that surrounds the homelessness issue. Hayes, Kozol, Snyder, and other advocates for the homeless have misled the public by exaggerating the size of the homeless population, asserting the ordinariness of homeless people, and misrepresenting recent trends in spending on low-income housing. If not corrected, these distortions may result in ill-advised policies.

Second and relatedly, policymakers should reject the policy proposals that stem from the assumption that the homeless are ordinary people down on their luck. Many advocates refer to the housing market as a game of musical chairs. This invalid assumption underlies Robert Hayes's frequent assertion that the solution to homelessness can be stated in three words: "Housing, housing, housing."

Hayes's view is flawed because homelessness is not mainly attributable to breakdowns on the supply side of the housing market, any more than hunger in the United States can be blamed on inadequacies in food production. Instead, homelessness in most cities stems primarily (if not entirely) from the demand side of the market—that is, from the condition of the homeless people themselves. The great majority of homeless people are not random victims of a housing-market squeeze, but rather deeply troubled individuals and families who, when deserving of government aid, should be given tailored financial assistance and help in managing their lives more successfully. The construction of nonprofit and public housing projects is a slow and highly roundabout way of serving those ends.

Opening more all-purpose shelters also makes no sense. As officials in New York City have learned, mass shelters that serve all comers not only make it difficult to deliver social services, but also foster a subculture of dependence and deviance. A faster, more economical, and less destructive way to house homeless people is to give them vouchers. Voucher programs, however, must be narrowly and carefully designed. Connecticut's experience with RAPs shows that a poorly structured program may induce households to get themselves into jams in order to receive vouchers.

Vouchers hold particular promise for the one-third of homeless individuals with serious mental problems. Once identified, individuals with such problems could be given specialized housing vouchers that could be cashed only in small board-and-care facilities equipped to serve people with their ailments. Rossi's proposal for in-home cash assistance to families with dependent adults is even more decentralized and family-oriented.

Perhaps as many as a third of homeless singles are presently employable (or indeed already employed), and more could work if they were to take appropriate medication. Many of these people are in their thirties (a prime working age) and must be encouraged to enter the job market. A policy that New York City recently adopted may help to achieve this goal. New York now "segments" homeless individuals among specialty shelters, such as facilities for the elderly and the mentally ill. This innovation will make it easier for the city to encourage those staying in its general shelters to reenter the labor and housing markets. Many nonprofit shelters have found it desirable to set a ceiling on the period during which able-bodied people can receive their services. Some limit maximum stays to perhaps two weeks at a time; others intentionally close during daylight hours, rather than staying open around the clock. To adopt policies along these lines, New York City would have to succeed in modifying the consent decrees that it signed to settle lawsuits brought by Hayes and others. If the city could implement these policies, it would both interrupt dependencies and signal that it expects able-bodied persons to reenter the work force.

For homeless families, another sort of reform seems promising. About 90 percent of the heads of homeless families are already receiving AFDC benefits when they apply for emergency housing aid; Knickman and Weitzman found that these mothers are much less able than other AFDC mothers to manage an independent household, and that many of them turn repeatedly to emergency shelters within the course of a year. A paternalistic concern for the welfare of the children in these chaotic families should override the mothers' claims to autonomy. For the sake of these children, legislatures should amend welfare laws to let state agencies pay rent directly to the landlord of a family that has previously made significant use of emergency shelters. Both by deterring the repeat use of emergency shelters and by encouraging lasting post-shelter placements, this reform could bring a bit more stability to the lives of children growing up under the most trying of circumstances.

In sum, government and charities should make distinctions among the homeless instead of muddling together a highly diverse group of people. Such distinctions would enable service providers to extend aid to, say, the casualties of deinstitutionalization, and to cease providing unlimited and unconditional aid to the able-bodied. The current shelter policies of many cities mire young adults in the dependent and antisocial culture of the underclass. By now we should know better than to provide cures that simply make things worse.

*NOTES*

1. See Peter H. Rossi, *Down and Out in America* (University of Chicago Press, 1989); Hamilton, Rabinowitz and Alschuler, Inc., "The 1986 Los Angeles Skid Row Demographic Survey"; Martha R. Burt and Barbara E. Cohen, "Feeding the Homeless" (Urban Institute, 1988).

2. James R. Knickman and Beth C. Weitzman, "A Study of Homeless Families in New York City" (NYU Graduate School of Public Administration, 1989).

3. Irving Piliavin and Michael Sosin, "Tracking the Homeless," *Focus*, vol. 10, no. 4 (1987– 1988), p. 20.

4. Bassuk reports her findings in "Characteristics of Sheltered Homeless Families," *American Journal of Public Health*, vol. 76 (1986), p. 1097.

5. See Georges Vernez, *et al.*, "Review of California's Program for the Homeless Mentally Disabled" (Rand Corporation, 1988).

## Questions for Discussion

1. Who are the homeless?
2. What causes homelessness?
3. What constitutional rights should the homeless have?
4. What is the best solution for the problem of homelessness? Justify your answer.
5. What is the worst solution for the problem of homelessness? Justify your answer.

## Suggested Readings

Atlas, John, and Peter Dreier. "The Phony Case against Rent Control." *Progressive*, 53, no. 4 (April 1989), 26–31.

Barbieri, Robert A., and Dennis W. Fricke. "The Crisis in Affordable Housing." *GAO Journal,* no. 5 (Spring 1989), 28–33.

Burt, Martha R., and Barbara E. Cohen. "Who Is Helping the Homeless? Local, State, and Federal Responses." *Publius,* 19, no. 3 (Summer 1989), 111–128.

Hilfiker, David. "Are We Comfortable with Homelessness?" *Journal of the American Medical Association,* 262, no. 10 (September 8, 1989), 1375–1376.

Horowitz, Carl F. "Mitch Snyder's Phoney Numbers: The Fiction of Three Million Homeless." *Policy Review,* no. 49 (Summer 1989), 66–69.

Kozol, Jonathan. *Rachel and Her Children: Homeless Families in America.* New York: Crown, 1988.

Rossi, Peter H. "The Family, Welfare and Homelessness." *Notre Dame Journal of Law, Ethics & Public Policy,* 4, no. 2 (1989), 281–300.

Schiff, Laurence. "Would They Be Better Off in a Home?" *National Review,* 42, no. 4 (March 5, 1990), 33–35.

Shuger, Scott. "Who Are the Homeless?" *Washington Monthly,* 22, no. 2 (March 1990), 38–46, 48–49.

Torrey, E. Fuller. "Thirty Years of Shame: The Scandalous Neglect of the Mentally Ill Homeless." *Policy Review,* no. 48 (Spring 1989), 10–15.

Tucker, William. "The Economics of Public Housing." *American Spectator,* 22, no. 11 (November 1989), 26–29.

U.S. Cong., House of Representatives. *Homelessness in America: The Need for Permanent Housing.* Hearings before the Subcommittee on Housing and Community Development of the Committee on Banking, Finance and Urban Affairs, 100th Cong., 1st Sess., 1989.

———. *Homelessness in America—1988.* Hearing before the Subcommittee on Housing and Community Development of the Committee on Banking, Finance and Urban Affairs, 100th Cong., 2nd Sess., 1988.

———. *Homelessness and Housing: A Human Tragedy, A Moral Challenge.* Hearing before the Subcommittee on Housing and Community Development of the Committee on Banking, Finance and Urban Affairs, 100th Cong., 2nd Sess., 1988.

———. *Homelessness in the 1990s.* Hearing before the Task Force on the Budget, 100th Cong., 1st Sess., 1989.

Whitman, David. "Hope for the Homeless." *U.S. News & World Report,* 104 (February 29, 1988), 25–28, 31, 34–35.

Wright, James D. "Address Unknown: Homelessness in Contemporary America." *Society,* 26, no. 6 (September–October 1989), 45–53.

# Chapter 18

## Should Government Give Direct Support to Artists and Writers?

In 1989 the Corcoran Gallery of Art in Washington, D.C., prepared to exhibit photographs of Robert Mapplethorpe, a U.S. artist of some renown who had died of AIDS (acquired immune deficiency syndrome). The presentation contained photographs of a homoerotic nature. What made the show controversial was not so much that these pictures would be displayed but that the program was funded by the National Endowment for the Arts (NEA), a federal government unit.

For a quarter of a century, the NEA and its counterpart in the humanities, the National Endowment for the Humanities (NEH), have provided grants for artists, writers, musicians, ballet companies, and museums in the cause of promoting the arts and the humanities. But with the Mapplethorpe exhibition, members of Congress became incensed that taxpayers were funding works deemed offensive by members of Congress as well as by large numbers of taxpayers themselves. Of equal notoriety was federal support to the artist Andres Serrano, who had created a sculpture depicting Christ on the cross submerged in the artist's urine.

Critics of NEA practices, such as Senator Jesse Helms (R-N.C.), introduced legislation to prevent the NEA from funding works that were pornographic. Artists differed with Helms and his supporters about what constitutes pornography. Nevertheless, the NEA soon felt pressure to police itself lest its funding be curtailed and, worse yet, the unit be abolished. A few artists turned down grants by refusing to sign affidavits that the grants would not be used for work that was pornographic. When faced with the prospect of not getting funding, however, most grant recipients complied with the law.

Supporters of the congressional action contended that it was not censorship. The issue, they said, was not the right of artists to exhibit their work no matter how controversial. Some of the opponents of NEA practices even sided with a gallery in Cincinnati when local officials sought to prevent the exhibition of the Mapplethorpe photographs on the grounds that the works were pornography rather than art. That exhibition was not supported by federal money. Cincinnati courts relied on a Supreme Court decision that community standards can be a factor to prevent pornography from being displayed. In a much publicized trial, the director of the gallery was acquitted of the obscenity charges.

The relationship between artist and government is often strained not only in the United States but in other countries as well. Dictators are concerned with what people think and, consequently, persecute writers and artists who do not abide by approved doctrine. In 1989, for example, the Ayatollah Khomeini, the late leader of Iran, put writer Salman Rushdie on a death list, offering a heavenly reward for anyone who killed him because Rushdie's *Satanic Verses* was considered blasphemous. Rushdie, who was living in Great Britain, went into hiding and continued to remain in hiding even after Khomeini's death.

But in democracies, too, there has often been an uneasy relationship between government and the arts. On the one hand, artists are hailed for their accomplishments. On the other hand, their works are sometimes banned. Offensive books and magazines are removed from libraries and bookstores. Laws against obscenity and racism also regulate the creativity of artists and writers.

Criticism of the artists and writers comes from many sources. Fundamentalist religious leaders are sometimes principal advocates of restrictions against the arts. But groups generally associated with liberal views have also favored restrictions. Some feminists, for example, call for city ordinances punishing pornographers. Civil rights advocates have sought to suppress works that they feel depict blacks in a derogatory manner.

In the debate below, the issue of direct government support to the arts is considered by two prominent U.S. writers: Garrison Keillor and John Updike. In an appearance before a Senate committee considering reauthorization of the NEA, Keillor contends:

1. The creation of the NEA helped to promote the arts throughout the United States.
2. The NEA aided him and other writers in achieving professional success at early stages of their careers when they lacked the credentials of popular success.
3. The NEA has contributed mightily to the creative genius of the United States.

Testifying in 1978 before joint congressional committees considering House Joint Resolution 639, which calls for a White House Conference on the Humanities, Updike argues against government support. He contends:

1. The essence of government is concern for the widest possible public interest; the essence of the humanities is private study.
2. As an artist, Updike would prefer to please private citizens who purchase his work rather than government officials administering government funds.
3. Better than providing direct grants to artists, government should reduce inflation so artistic enterprises can be self-supporting.
4. "How can legislators, asked to vote tax money away," Updike asks, "not begin to think of guidelines that insidiously edge toward censorship?"

## Should Government Give Direct Support to Artists and Writers?

### GARRISON KEILLOR
### *The Case for Government Support*

I'm grateful to those who have so ably attacked the [National] Endowment [for the Arts, NEA] over the past year or so for making it necessary to defend it. I enjoy controversy and I recognize the adversary, they are us. My ancestors were Puritans from England. They arrived here in 1648 in the hope of finding greater restrictions than were permissible under English law at that time. But over the years, we Puritans have learned something about repression, and it's as true today as when my people arrived: man's interest in the forbidden is sharp and constant. If Congress doesn't do something about obscene art, we'll have to build galleries twice as big to hold the people who want to see it. And if Congress does do something about obscene art, the galleries will need to be even bigger than that.

All governments have honored artists when they are old and saintly and successful and almost dead, but twenty-five years ago Congress decided to boldly and blindly support the arts—support the act of creation itself—and to encourage artists who are young and dangerous and unknown and very much alive. This courageous legislation has changed American life.

Today, in every city and state, when Americans talk up their home town, when the Chamber of Commerce puts out a brochure, invariably, they mention the arts—a local orchestra or theater or museum or all three. It didn't used to be this way. Forty years ago, if an American man or woman meant to have an artistic career, you got on the train to New York. Today, you can be a violinist in North Carolina, a writer in Iowa, a painter in Utah. This is a small and lovely revolution that the National Endowment has helped to bring about. The Endowment has fostered thousands and thousands of artistic works—many of which will outlive you and me—but even more important, the Endowment has changed how we think about the arts. Today, no American family can be secure against the danger that one of its children may decide to become an artist.

I grew up in a family who never attended concerts or museums, never bought books. I never imagined that a person could be a writer.

Twice in my life, at crucial times, grants from the Endowment made it possible for me to be a writer. The first, in 1969, arrived when I was young, broke, married with a baby, living on very little cash and a big vegetable garden. I was writing for the *New Yorker* at the time but they weren't aware of it. I wrote every morning and every night. I often had fantasies of finding a patron—a beggar would appear at my door one day, I'd give him an egg salad sandwich, and suddenly he'd turn into a man in a pinstripe suit, Prince Bob from the Guggenheim Foundation. But instead of him, I got a letter offering me a job for one month in the Writers in the Schools program in Minneapolis, funded by the NEA, directed by Molly LaBerge, which sent young writers into the schools to read and teach. In 1969, there were three such programs, in New York, California, and Minnesota; today, there's at least one in every state.

In 1974, a grant from the NEA enabled me and my colleagues at Minnesota Public Radio to start "A Prairie Home Companion." The help of the Endowment was crucial because the show wasn't that great to begin with. For our first broadcast, we had a crowd of twelve persons, and then we made the mistake of having an intermission and we lost half of them. The show wasn't obscene, just slow, and it took us a few years to figure out how to do a live radio show with folk music and comedy and stories about my home town of Lake Wobegon. By the time the show became popular and Lake Wobegon became so well-known that people thought it was real, the Endowment had vanished from the credits, its job done.

When you're starting out, it seems like nobody wants to give you a dime, and then, when you have a big success and have everything you could ever want, people can't do enough for you. The Endowment is there at the beginning, and that's the beauty of it.

When I was a young writer, I looked down on best-sellers as trash, but gradually over the years they improved and then suddenly one of them was mine. First, *Lake Wobegon Days* and then *Leaving Home,* and my desk filled up with offers to speak, to write, to appear, to endorse, which I've thoroughly enjoyed, but I remember very well when nobody else but my mother and the National Endowment was interested, and I'm grateful for this chance to express my thanks.

When I graduated from college, the degrees were given out in reverse order of merit, so I got mine early and had a chance to watch the others, and I remember the last graduate, the summest cum laude, a tall shy boy who walked up the stairs to the platform and en route stepped on the hem of his own gown and walked right up the inside of it. Like him, the Endowment has succeeded in embarrassing itself from time to time—to the considerable entertainment of us all—and like him, the Endowment keeps on going. It has contributed mightily to the creative genius of America—to the art and music and literature and theater and dance which, to my wife and other foreigners, is the most gorgeous aspect of this country. Long may it wave.

## Should Government Give Direct Support to Artists and Writers?

### JOHN UPDIKE
### The Case against Government Support

I am honored to have been asked to testify at this hearing on a bill calling for a White House Conference on the Humanities. This is the first piece of testimony I have to offer. We in the humanities, whether we call ourselves men of letters or men of scholarships are fascinated and charmed by power and anxious to please it.

The week after I accepted the invitation to speak here for 5 minutes today I received from the National Endowment for the Humanities in a succession of envelopes at least 2 pounds of xeroxed material, ranging from biographies of Chairman [Joseph D.] Duffey to appreciations of the paintings of Paul Cézanne, much of this material duplicatory or even triplicatory, but all of it testifying to the resources of the Secretary of Labor and photocopying equipment.

A freelance writer, working in a corner of his own home, producing his manuscripts on his own manual typewriter works on a Lilliputian scale and must view even this measure of interest in his work with a combination of gratitude and alarm as of a wren whose nest is being appraised by an eagle.

The essence of government is concern for the widest possible public interest. The essence of the humanities, it seems to me, is private study. Publicity is as essential to the one as privacy is to the other. Can these two realms then be joined without distortion? Is it true, as H.J. Res. 639 states, that the development and encouragement of national strength in the humanities is of the utmost importance to the life and heritage of the United States? And is it appropriate to encourage maximum participation by citizens?

I was educated in public schools. When my interests ranged beyond the curriculum there I found material for exploration in the surprisingly well-stocked public library of the nearby city. When I was a young writer I applied for and received a grant given by a private foundation, whose tax-exempt status represented an indirect Government investment in the humanities.

As an older writer I have been blessed with Government-sponsored memberships, invitations and travels. My friendship with writers and critics, including those in Communist and Third World countries, has made me emphatically appreciative of the freedoms and opportunities I enjoyed as an American.

I love my country's Government for its attempt in a precarious world to sustain a peaceful order in which work can be done and happiness can be pursued not for the good of the State but in a State that exists for our good.

I love my Government not least for the extent to which it leaves me alone. My personal ambition has been simply to live by the work of my pen. This is not a very fastidious ambition. If I were aware of large amounts of Federal money available to purveyors of the written words I would attempt to gain access to it and hope to please the administrators of this fund as I hope to please magazine editors and bookbuyers.

But I would rather have as my patron a host of anonymous citizens digging into their own pockets for the price of a book or a magazine than a small body of enlightened and responsible men administering public funds. I would rather chance my personal vision of the truth striking home here and there in the chaos of publication that exists than attempt to filter it through a few sets of official, honorable, public-spirited scrutinizers.

Rather than Government subsidies to ballet companies, I would rather see the Government reduce inflation so that these enterprises could again become self-supporting.

It can be said that the actual achievement of the National Endowment for the Humanities has been to expand the public exposure of privately produced works. When it was decided to dramatize a television series supported by a grant I was of course flattered that one of my stories was presented. But my own television set failed on the night of its screening. The text of the story was unchanged by the experience. But I had not written the story with broadcasting in mind.

The realms of scientific research are now inextricably involved with Government funding. Can we fear that the humanities might become similarly dependent? If I try to think of who in the last century has most brilliantly illuminated our sense of humanity, which I take to be the end purpose of the humanities, I think of Freud and Kafka, of Proust and Joyce, of Whitman, Henry James. I wonder how many of these brave, strange, stubborn spirits would have wanted subsidies from their governments.

How can public salaried men not think in terms of respectability, of social optimism, of broad and uncontroversial appeal? How can legislators, asked to vote tax money away, not begin to think of guidelines that insidiously edge toward censorship?

If Government money becomes an increasingly important presence in the financing of the humanities, is there a danger, I respectfully ask, of humanists becoming politicians?

## Questions for Discussion

1. What is pornography?
2. What role should government play in promoting the arts and the humanities?
3. Should government impose any restrictions on grants to artists and writers? What are the reasons for your answer?

4. Does government aid to the arts inevitably lead to censorship?
5. Should a museum, which receives general government support, be prevented from exhibiting controversial works? What are the reasons for your answer?
6. Should the same standard for government grants be applied to artists whose works deal with sexually explicit themes as to those whose works promote antisemitism or racism? Justify your answer.

## Suggested Readings

Corn-Revere, Robert. "The New Assault on Artistic Freedom." *Student Lawyer,* 18, no. 6 (February 1990), 18–23.

Danto, Arthur C. "Art and the Taxpayers." *Nation,* 249, no. 6 (August 21–28, 1989), 192–193.

Hochfield, Sylvia. "Art and the NEA: Caught in the Crossfire." *Art News,* 89, no. 1 (January 1990), 146–149.

Kramer, Hilton, "Is Art above the Laws of Decency?" *New York Times,* July 2, 1989, sec. II, pp. 1, 7.

Posner, Richard A. "Art for Law's Sake." *American Scholar,* 58, no. 4 (Autumn 1989), 513–520.

U.S. Cong., House of Representatives. *Hearing on the Rights of Artists and Scholars to Freedom of Expression and the Rights of Taxpayers to Determine the Use of Public Funds.* Hearing before the Subcommittee on Postsecondary Education of the Committee on Education and Labor, 101st Cong., 1st Sess., 1989.

U.S. Cong., Senate. *Reauthorization of the National Foundation on the Arts and Humanities Act: National Endowment for the Arts.* Hearings before the Subcommittee on Education, Arts and Humanities of the Committee on Labor and Human Resources, 101st Cong., 2nd Sess., 1990.

Vance, Carole S. "The War on Culture." *Art in America,* 77, no. 9 (September 1989), 39, 41, 43, 45.

Yardley, Jonathan. "The NEA Debate, Derailed by Drama." *Washington Post,* April 9, 1990, p. C2.

# Chapter 19

# *Do We Need a Massive Program to Improve the Environment?*

In campaigning for the presidency in 1988, candidate George Bush said that he wanted to be known as the "environmental president." He drew attention to his life as an outdoorsman to show that he was at one with the environment. And when he became president, he placed a portrait of Theodore Roosevelt in a prominent position in the White House. Roosevelt was a conservationist and left a legislative record of accomplishment in environmental matters.

Bush recognized that the environment had become a matter of great concern to many Americans. To be sure, such concerns had been expressed over the course of decades; they did not appear suddenly in 1988. Americans had become increasingly aware of the pollution of rivers and lakes, the poisoning of water supplies, the dangers of pesticides to health, and the hazards of nuclear radiation. Some events at home and abroad highlighted these concerns: the toxic chemical contamination of Love Canal in New York, which required many families in the area to evacuate their homes; the explosion of nuclear reactors in Chernobyl in the Soviet Union, which had enormous consequences to life and food not only in the Soviet Union but in neighboring and distant countries as well; the spilling of millions of gallons of oil from the *Exxon Valdez* off the Alaskan coast, which seriously damaged the ecology. Even population increases, with their potential for increases in demands on natural resources and for consumer goods, are considered ecological threats.

A current focus of concern is global warming. The excessive burning of fossil fuels by industrial societies and the destruction of tropical forests for timber and agricultural development threaten the ozone layer around the earth that protects life. It is possible, scientists say, that with thinning ozone, warming temperatures will generate a "greenhouse effect," seriously altering the earth's ability to provide sufficient food and water for its human population. Such an environmental disaster, and the wars and social disruption it will spawn, will threaten life itself.

Scientist Peter H. Raven takes up the environmentalists' cause in the selection below. He contends:

1. Whole ecosystems are being disrupted to an unprecedented degree.
2. We are using too much of the earth's resources, and, given the growth of global population, we will use even more in future decades.

3. Deforestation in the tropics can contribute to the prospects of global warming.
4. Entire species of plant life, animals, and microorganisms, necessary to sustain the life of human beings, may become extinct in the next few decades.
5. The United States should join with other nations of the world to deal with these great environmental problems.

Nicolas S. Martin, executive director of a consumer education association, claims that environmentalists are perpetuating myths and hoaxes. He argues:

1. Prophesies about environmental dangers have proven wrong, including scares about asbestos, pesticides, dioxin, and radiation.
2. Overpopulation is not a cause of poverty.
3. Many scientists argue that there is no global warming or greenhouse effect.

 YES

## Do We Need a Massive Program to Improve the Environment?

### PETER H. RAVEN

### A World in Crisis

Even though we live in a world where far more people are well-fed, clothed, and housed than ever before, more than 10,000 people starve to death every day, we consume well over a third of the total biological productivity on Earth, and our activities are threatening up to a quarter of all other kinds of organisms with extinction in the near future. The global human population, having passed the 5,000,000,000 mark for the first time in 1987 and growing at an annual rate estimated at 1.7 percent—adding the equivalent of a new Mexico every year— is a dominant ecological force without precedent. Our numbers have *doubled* since 1950 and will double again in about 40 years if present trends continue. How will we respond to these threats, and why should those of us who live in the relative comfort of countries like the U.S. even care?

Many of our most serious problems are centered in the tropics, where biological diversity is concentrated and being lost most rapidly and whole ecosystems are being disrupted. As recently as 1950, about 1,100,000,000 people, out of a global population of 2,500,000,000, lived in wholly or partly tropical countries (excluding China). Today, there are 2,700,000,000 there; by 2020, there will be 5,000,000,000. At the same time, the proportion of the world's people living in industrial countries is falling drastically. For each person living in countries like the U.S. in 1950, there were approximately two other people living elsewhere; by 2020, there will be five. These relationships indicate that the world is changing rapidly and should inspire us to try to do something about it for everyone's benefit.

The rapidly growing populations of tropical countries include large numbers of poor people. In 1987, for example, the average per capita income in the U.S. was estimated at $16,400, whereas neighboring Mexico's amounted to $2,080 and Honduras' was $730. Over all, the industrial nations, with less than a quarter of the global population, control about 82 percent of the world's wealth, while the largely tropical developing countries, including China, with about three-quarters of the world's population, support their standard of living with the remaining 18 percent. Meanwhile, in both Africa and Latin America, the standard of living has declined through the 1980s and is projected to continue its downward trend.

Within countries that are wholly or partly tropical, about 44 percent of the estimated 2,700,000,000 people live in absolute poverty, unable to count on adequate food, shelter, and clothing from one day to the next. Of these, about 400,000,000 people consumed an average amount of food that was less than 80 percent of the U.N. [United Nations]-recommended minimum dietary standard, a diet insufficient to prevent "stunted growth and serious health risks." UNICEF [United Nations Children's Fund] estimates that about 14,000,000 children under the age of five starve to death or die of associated diseases each year in tropical and subtropical countries; some 40,000 young children die from such causes every day. These deaths constitute nearly a third of the world total of *all* fatalities. Worse, many millions of additional children exist only in a state of lethargy, their mental capacities often permanently impaired by their lack of access to adequate amounts of food.

In addition to large populations and extensive poverty, tropical countries generally suffer from insufficient information about how to achieve productive agriculture and forestry, and a lack of governmental and private action in this area even when the facts are known. Many tropical soils are relatively infertile or poor in other ways, requiring careful handling. In the natural ecosystems that develop on such soils, most of the nutrients, especially phosphorous and nitrogen—which often are scarce—are held in the vegetation itself. Cutting and burning trees releases these nutrients to the soil, fertilizing it and allowing the cultivation of crops for a few years. When the excess nutrients are exhausted, the forests must be given time to recover—typically, decades or even centuries. Agricultural practices of this sort succeed when there are relatively few people involved. Given the large and explosively growing numbers who live in tropical countries now, coupled with the fact that some 1,500,000,000 people depend on firewood as their primary source of energy, recovery tends to be a rare event.

Based on 1981 Food and Agriculture Organization estimates, projected to date, about 2,200,000 square miles of tropical evergreen forest probably remain now—an area about two-thirds the size of the 48 contiguous states of the U.S. Ten years ago, about 2 percent of the remaining forest was being cut or deeply disturbed each year—an area about equal to the state of Kansas. Even if there were no population growth, all of this forest would be gone within 50 years. Since the numbers of people are soaring and the forest destruction is distributed unequally, most of the forests will be gone within a few decades. This matters greatly because, in general, they will not be replaced with productive agriculture and forestry, but simply will become exhausted, cut-over fields. About a quarter of the total forest loss goes to supply the hardwood demands of industrialized countries, with reforestation minimal in most areas.

One of the simplest ways to evaluate human pressure on the biosphere is to calculate the proportion of the total biological productivity that we consume directly, waste, or co-opt (as in clearing pastures). Like all organisms that lack the ability to capture energy from the sun directly (as do plants or algae), we depend directly on this energy for our survival. Although we are just one of the estimated 5–10,000,000 species on Earth, our use of world resources now amounts to some 40 percent of the total. As our numbers double by the middle of the next century, will we be able to use the world's productivity even more extensively and in a stable manner? Moreover, can individual and national standards of living be increased?

The destruction of natural resources in the tropics and subtropics is related intimately to the global economy, driving the production of cash crops such as cacao, bananas, and oil palm in many regions rapidly upward, often displacing additional poor, rural farmers in the process and contributing to the short-term destruction of additional forests. The export earnings clearly are needed, but if they are not applied in part to the benefit of the poor people in their countries, the destruction will continue, with its attendant social, political, and economic instability.

In addition, efforts to repay the international debt, which Willy Brandt has characterized as "a blood transfusion from the sick to the healthy," further are destabilizing developing countries throughout the world. The existence of the debt encourages many Third World countries to overexploit their natural resources without the creation of stable, productive alternatives. Logging restrictions are eased, poor farmers are displaced to regions that will not support them over the long term, and the production of foods that people consume directly is decreased. Impoverished unstable countries are poor markets for our products, but good prospects for competitive political and military intervention from all sides and excellent sources for millions of refugees and emigrants.

Yet another major problem linked with deforestation in the tropics is its effect on global climates. The warmest year in recent history was 1987, and many scientists believe that it signaled the start of the greenhouse effect, which will result in a long-term increase in global temperatures. Destroying forests on a major scale contributes to this effect, which cries out for a global response similar to that for ozone depletion. In addition, regional climates often are altered demonstrably by the effects of the deforestation, with negative impacts on agriculture.

The most serious, long-term global problem that results from the destruction of forests and natural resources generally in the tropics, however, is the extinction of a large proportion of species of plants, animals, and microorganisms in the world within a few decades. The loss of biological diversity, which is proceeding at a rate that has not occurred since the end of the age of dinosaurs some 65,000,000 years ago, is extremely important to human prospects for the future. For example, only about 150, out of the 250,000 species of plants, are used widely as crops at present; many thousands of the additional ones could be used if we found and saved them. Most kinds of plants, like most types of organisms generally, are tropical.

These losses are not trivial ones from any point of view. There are many uses for plants other than food: for example, oral contraceptives for many years were produced chiefly from Mexican yams; the muscle relaxants used in surgery come from an Amazonian vine, traditionally used in poison darts for hunting (curare); the cure for Hodgkin's disease comes from the rosy periwinkle, native to the Indian Ocean island of Madagascar; and the gene pool of corn recently was enriched by the discovery of a wild relative in the mountains near Guadalajara, Mexico. Among the undiscovered or poorly known plants are many possible sources of additional medicines, oils, waxes, fibers, and other commodities that we would value if we knew of their existence. However, we are losing them faster than we are finding them.

How fast is extinction proceeding? Nearly half of the world's species of plants, animals, and microorganisms occur in areas in which the vegetation will be destroyed quite thoroughly during the next 25–30 years. If half of these are at immediate risk, we might stand to lose a quarter of all species—some 60,000 plants, for example—during the lifetimes of most people who are alive today. Anyone who attempts to counter the sheer horror of such a projection by saying, for example, that extinction is normal simply fails to realize the dimensions of the problem we are facing. Considering the ultimate sources of our livelihood, the loss we are facing literally is incalculable.

Unfortunately, the percentage of people in the U.S., or elsewhere in the world, who are even remotely aware of these realities is disturbingly small, and the possibilities for effective action correspondingly limited. One of the key steps in any rational approach to world problems is to promote internationalism—a common understanding that all human problems are interconnected. From the vantage point of the U.S., attaining this objective is more difficult than it sounds; like most people everywhere, we tend to operate as if we were alone.

Nonetheless, it is very much in the medium- and long-term interests of countries like the U.S. to cooperate with developing nations and encourage the growing cooperation that exists between them. Our record in this area is not strong, however. When the U.S. deals with its neighbor, Mexico, for example, the primary issues discussed tend to be confrontational ones, emphasizing drug trafficking, illegal immigration, debt repayment, protective trade practices, and respective national policies toward the Central American conflict. Why could we not begin to move the agenda toward cooperative initiatives in science, technology, and the humanities; sustainable development and conservation; and mutual cultural understanding? Wouldn't a deep and mutually considerate discussion of subjects of this sort help to prepare us better for the increasingly intense interaction that will characterize our relationships in the next century?

As the richest country on Earth, we have the most to gain from global stability, yet we do little to promote it. On a per capita basis, our development assistance is the lowest of any industrial nation. In a trillion-dollar budget, we argue about a few billion dollars for this purpose as if allocating it would permanently destroy all other possibilities for our country, even though the opposite is closer to the truth. How will we find stable trading partners, reap the benefits of biological productivity, achieve political stability, avoid the recurrent necessity for military intervention, and solve the immigration problem unless we realize that we share a common destiny with other nations, and act on that exceedingly important fact? We need to use our institutions, such as universities, to help improve conditions in the Third World, remembering that only six percent of the world's scientists and technicians work in countries with three-quarters of the world's population—another mark of global inequality. At the same time, subsidizing our own crops by about $25,000,000,000 to achieve a like amount in farm exports, while not helping to build the stability of the countries that accept the exports, simply will not accomplish our aims in the long run.

The search for biological diversity, and for ways to save it for our own benefits, should become a consuming international effort. Parks and other protected areas can survive only in an economic atmosphere that can afford them, a relationship that the U.S. has been testing. For our common good, however, such areas must be made a part of every development scheme. Plants and other organisms must be catalogued rapidly through the world and saved by any means possible. A small investment in this process now will yield incalculable benefits for the future; once they are gone, we never can get them back.

In the tropics, the way we meet the needs of the poorest of the poor today profoundly will affect the contours of the world we leave to our children. The single most important step that could be taken to preserve the productivity of the remaining forests would be to use lands that already are deforested to produce timber, pulp, beef, firewood, and other products, thus alleviating the pressure on the remaining forests. The role of biotechnology in providing cheap, efficient ways to improve Third World crops should be exploited fully; improved crops that might enhance greatly the prospects for peasant agriculture could be made available at an accelerated rate in this way.

We cannot avoid profoundly modifying the Earth that supports us all, and, in fact, already have done so. Nevertheless, we should not allow ourselves to respond only when the crises we are causing are so extensive that they threaten our lives. To do so is to be thoroughly immoral, in the fullest sense of the term.

*Do We Need a Massive Program to Improve the Environment?*

## NICOLAS S. MARTIN

### Environmental Myths and Hoaxes:
### The Evidence of Guilt Is Insufficient

Most of you are probably too young to remember the first Earth Day. Quite an occasion it was, if for no other reason than it substituted for the normal classroom stupor. Instead of conjugating verbs and dissecting triangles we took a look into an apocalypse. Man—many of us learned for the first time—was maliciously intent on destroying his habitat, and those of his fellow planet dwellers in the animal and plant kingdoms.

On top of Vietnam War protests, rioting in the ghettos, and the recent assassinations of Martin Luther King and Robert Kennedy, this was pretty heady stuff. What we were told in the Earth Day handbooks, news reports, and speeches was essentially that man was a plague on the face of the planet. He was an infestation of the universe.

*Now* it all sounds pretty ordinary, not very different from what we hear nightly on the news. But in 1970 it sounded like a ghastly science fiction novel.

Today I am here to tell you that that perception was half right. It was indeed fiction, but it had little to do with science.

In the intervening two decades we have been pounded relentlessly with stories of man's environmental depravity. Before images of spewing waste, oil-drenched birds, deformed infants, and poisoned fields normal people are rendered mute and helpless (though the cacophony of activists is never stilled). None but the most callous soul could fail to be humbled and moved by the trail of environmental sin.

Well, it's atonement time, and either I have grown a very hard callous on my soul, or the evidence of guilt is insufficient, because I'm no longer touched by the pleadings of the environmental evangelists, among whose numbers I was once included. When the ecological prophet of doom says that without your tax-deductible contribution the earth will perish, I am reminded of the evangelist up in that tower—where he could talk to God better—notifying the faithful that only their *donations* could prevent his tragic demise. Or the famous *National Lampoon* cover which said: "Buy this magazine or we'll shoot this dog."

As Earth Day II rolls around, the evangelist is still alive, the dog is probably no longer with us, through no fault of poor readership, and the planet earth is a more congenial place for humanity than ever in history. Almost without exception, the doomsayers have been wrong, their prophecies flawed, and all of us the better for it.

Allow me to offer some specifics.

First: The asbestos scare.

Sadly, before we knew of the connection between certain types of asbestos and lung cancer, many shipyard workers and those applying insulation, were exposed to large concentrations of the mineral. About thirty years after exposure, somewhere between 3,300 and 12,000 people are dying from the asbestos-induced cancer mesothelioma each year in the U.S. There has been a great deal of totally justified concern over this natural environmental tragedy. Unfortunately, it has also led to one of the most ridiculous and expensive public health hysterias in history.

Initially, it must be noted that a very high percentage of mesothelioma-afflicted people were also heavy cigarette smokers, which increases the asbestos cancer risk by more than 50 times. Smoking is such a critical co-factor that last year the *New England Journal of Medicine* reported that "it remains uncertain whether *any* type of asbestos acting alone can cause lung cancer in nonsmokers."

Due to the worker's plight, though, concern was raised about the effects of asbestos exposure on the rest of us, especially those who work in buildings insulated with asbestos. Ralph Nader, the Sierra Club, and the Audubon society, among others, convinced Congress and President Reagan to require an asbestos inspection of all school buildings in the United States. Many cities and states followed up with their own *even more* stringent requirements for asbestos inspection and removal. The reality is that America was driven berserk by asbestos, largely due to the perpetual wailing of environmentalists, and in direct contradiction of the facts.

In one single San Francisco school $18 million (the annual cost of about 300 teacher salaries) was spent on asbestos removal and repairs, an event duplicated first at school after school, and then at offices and malls. The same governments which legally required the use of asbestos as a public health measure were now demanding its removal.

This play will run for many years. The cost of asbestos abatement at New York's World Trade Center and LaGuardia Airport will run to $1 billion. The total cost for removal in California's schools will probably exceed $1 billion. The cost of removing asbestos from the country's offices is estimated to run to $200 billion.

So what are we getting for our money? The answer is virtually nothing.

Besides generally being smokers, the workers who contracted cancer were regularly exposed to concentrations of the mineral *100,000 to 1 million times higher* than the amount normally present in a building insulated with asbestos. The risk of fatality to people who work in buildings insulated with asbestos has been estimated by a commission of the Canadian government in the following way. "Even a building whose air has a fiber level up to 10 times greater than that found in typical outdoor air would create a risk of fatality that was less than one-fiftieth the risk of having a fatal accident while driving to and from the building." The authors went on to state, "We deem the risk which asbestos poses to building occupants to be insignificant and therefore find that asbestos in building air will almost never pose a health hazard to occupants."

The New Jersey Asbestos Policy Committee reported to the governor in the midst of all this fiasco, "There are no documented cases of lung cancer associated with low-level asbestos exposure over a lifetime." Definitively, the World Health Organization, after exhaustive analysis concluded: "In the general population, the risks of mesothelioma and lung cancer attributable to asbestos cannot be quantified reliably and are probably undetectably low." The great asbestos scare is a hoax, and a big one, but only one of many.

In 1984, Americans were frightened out of their wits to learn that traces of the pesticide ethylene dibromide (EDB) were found in food products. The accusation was all too familiar. It causes cancer, the activists said—in rats.

EDB was used as a fumigant for protecting grains against contamination by molds and fungi and infestation by worms and insects. The only substitutes available were either known to be more toxic or had never been tested for carcinogenicity.

The amount of EDB found in foods was 10 to 100 times less carcinogenic than the dose of the natural chemical safrole present in a typical daily amount of black pepper. The amount of EDB being ingested by the average consumer was less than one-quarter millionth as much on a body-weight basis as was fed to the rats.

Nevertheless, Americans were bamboozled by what I call the Jim Bob Effect. My friend Jim Bob is an ardent environmentalist who thinks we are doing ourselves in with all of our chemicals and technology. He wants to turn back the clock.

Recently, Jim Bob bought a loaf of bread which, soon enough, was crawling with worms. Enraged, he wrote a letter to the manufacturer demanding to know why they would foist an infested loaf off on him. "I don't like my bread with worms," he barked. The Jim Bob Effect is when someone is so far removed, so ignorant, of food production, that he can on the one hand demand chemical-free food, and on the other hand become addled at the sight of a worm in his "preservative-free" bread.

I've seen the Jim Bob Effect many times in health food stores. These purveyors of chemical-free goods have turned back the clock and are constantly caught in the throes of a war against predators. I have seen a store so infested with maggots hatching from the food that it looked like a possum two days after being squashed on the roadway. I've seen the look on a chemical-free purist's face when the granola she just popped inside began to wiggle. Let me tell you, if she wasn't a victim of the Jim Bob Effect she would have begged for the fumigants and chemicals which would have prevented her distasteful experience.

But most people think we can just do without EDB and the other chemicals. They don't understand that they would have to eat 400 tons per day of EDB-laced foods to equal the amount fed the rats, and that chemicals like EDB are all that stand between us and a mouthful of maggots. So EDB was banned and the activists went on to the next chemical scare.

And by now the scares are abundant. In 1959, the government informed Americans that cranberries were contaminated by a cancer-causing weed killer. They neglected to mention that this chemical replaced paint thinner as the previous weed killer of choice in cranberry bogs at far lower cost and toxicity and dose. And they downplayed the real victim of the killer chemical, another poor little rat fed a dose that would choke a horse. The cranberry industry lost, in 1959 dollars, $30 million.

Deja vu 1989. The eminent scientist Meryl Streep, TV's "60 Minutes," and the National Resources Defense Council let fly with a report claiming that the chemical Alar, used to keep apples from maturing before reaching the stores, and to prevent internal decay, caused cancer—in mice.

Never mind that Alar helped keep a nutritious food within the price range of the economically less advantaged. Never mind that it kept apples from rotting before getting to the stores. When fed in gargantuan doses to mice it causes cancer.

There was resistance to the anti-Alar onslaught. The farmers bought TV time to plead their case. The Environmental Protection Agency determined that the amount of Alar eaten during a 70 year lifetime increased the risk of cancer by 5 in 1,000,000, an estimate many scientists consider high. They consider the risk to be zero. Forget all that. Dr. Streep wanted Alar banned and banned it was. After things quieted down, an influential biochemist estimated that the risk in a glass of apple juice from apples treated with Alar was 18 times less than the cancer risk in a peanut butter sandwich; 50 times less than the hazard of one edible mushroom; 1000 times less than the risk of one beer. But by that time nobody cared.

Something very interesting was happening in the science labs while the activists were standing in front of the cameras proclaiming the virtues of nature and the vices of man. Scientists at top universities were discovering that nature herself is teeming with toxins. Every single bite of food we take is laced with pesticides brewed not in the laboratory of Monsanto, but in the laboratory of nature.

Little by little they found things like nitrate in celery, tannin in tea, and arsenic in potato. Gradually the research accumulated until they identified tens of thousands of the natural pesticides plants generate to protect against predators. Plants most definitely are not subject to the Jim Bob Effect.

By 1984 a prominent scientist who was a favorite of the environmentalists proclaimed that Americans eat 10,000 times as much of natural toxins as we do synthetic. Or to put it another way, more than 99.99 percent of all toxic chemicals ingested are natural. One of nature's carcinogens, allyl isothiocynate, is present in cabbage at a level tens of thousands of times higher than the amount necessary to damage chromosomes, mutate cells, and produce tumors.

So, while the activists continued their love-fest with nature and their hate-fest with man, their entire paradigm was being rendered obsolete by the development of scientific research placing the real threat squarely at nature's door. In comparison, the hazard of man-made chemicals like EDB and Alar is utterly trivial.

What has the reaction of the activists been? They've done two things: They've simply ignored the facts, and they defamed the character of some of the finest scientists in the world.

The discovery of nature's toxins dovetails nicely with another environmental disaster hoax: The Great Dioxin Scare.

Dioxin is a group of the most enervating chemicals known to environmentalists. They have delighted in discovering it lurking in waste dumps, rice fields, drinking water, and, most especially in the forests of Vietnam, in the form of the defoliant Agent Orange. The discovery of small amounts of dioxin led to the depopulation of entire neighborhoods, not due to a genuine threat, but due to fear induced by earth activists.

Despite the fact that over $1 billion has been spent researching its effects, not a single case of chronic illness or death has even been attributed to dioxin in the U.S. Despite an unparalleled media outcry over dioxin concentrations in New York's Love Canal, and Times Beach, Missouri, including the government purchase of abandoned homes, no evidence was offered linking dioxin to unusual rates of sickness, birth defects, or death. On the sidelines, *Science* magazine reported: When administered orally dioxin is highly toxic, "but when bound to soil it does not pose much of a hazard." Love Canal was another environmental hoax. This was emphasized in 1987 when researchers discovered that nature's darling broccoli contained a chemical which precisely mimics the toxic effects of dioxin on human cells. The twist in the tale is that the amount of this natural chemical present makes it 20 million times as toxic as the dioxin level declared safe by the EPA. Not one activist has spoken out in favor of banning broccoli.

Let me offer just a few more examples of environmentalist myths and hoaxes.

As recently as December, NBC News science correspondent Robert Bazell wrote in the *New Republic* that Americans should be concerned because certain cancer rates were going up rapidly. He didn't offer a source for his opinion, but he listed a lot of cancer statistics which turned out to be utterly wrong.

Bazell says that bladder cancer is up 15 percent. But the authoritative statistics show it down 15 percent for men and 42 percent for women in the past 30 years. The same for liver cancer. Bazell has it up 16.2 percent, but the American Cancer Society says that liver cancer deaths are down 21 percent for men and 54 percent for women. If there was an epidemic of cancers caused by synthetic chemicals in food, the liver is the first place it would show up. In fact, the opposite has occurred.

The numbers go on like this. Bazell is using his fictitious proof to scare Americans into thinking that there is a man-made chemical epidemic. In fact several important cancers have declined, and the cancers which have risen precipitously are almost exclusively related to cigarette smoking, which accounts for one-third of all cancer deaths. Deaths from heart disease, incidentally, have declined by 30 percent since 1970.

Bazell's myth-making is common practice in the media. In 1975, Dan Rather led off a documentary with this statement: "The news tonight is that the United States is number one in cancer. The National Cancer Institute estimates that if you're living in America your chances of getting cancer are higher than anywhere else in the world." That was sheer fantasy, with the truth being that the U.S. was about 15th among industrialized countries, and would have been considerably lower if smoking-related cancers were subtracted.

Take the case of nuclear power. Much ado has been made about the risks of the atomic radiation hazard. Rarely is it mentioned that scientists estimate that as many people die every year due to the burning of fossil fuel as would die in a worst-case nuclear accident. In the worst accident we have ever had in this country, Three Mile Island, not a single person was killed. The same environmentalists who proclaim the dangers of nuclear power are the ones—like Ralph Nader—who claimed that home smoke detectors were a radiation hazard, despite the fact that they contain roughly the same total radiation as the dirt in a potted plant. They are people like writer Paul Brodeur, whose 1977 book *The Zapping of America* tried preposterously to convince Americans that their microwave ovens would wreak havoc on their nervous sytems. The truth is that both smoke detectors and microwave ovens have saved many lives by reducing the hazard of fires in the home. Thank goodness for radiation.

Another kind of radiation, food irradiation, would save many more lives by exterminating hazards like trichinosis and by keeping food fresh and nutritious longer, but predictably the environmentalists object.

They objected to the use of DDT, which in the single example of Ceylon—now Sri Lanka—reduced the number of people killed by malaria by 2 million per year. The environmentalists didn't lose any sleep about these real people dying. They were more concerned with the miniscule hypothetical risks of DDT which never materialized, and by claims of bird-shell thinning which were later proven to be false.

Overpopulation is said to be at the root of many environmental problems. The more people, it is said, the more suffering.

I think most of us have the image of mainland China as the epicenter of overpopulation misery. This image has been fostered by years of Zero Population Growth propaganda.

But before you accept this image, consider that mainland China has a population density only half as great as another starvation-brutalized state, where people await only death's beck and call. I refer, of course, to the famine-infested state of Maryland.

Overpopulation is supposedly the key to the poverty of the mainland Chinese, who have an annual per capita income of just $300. Why, then, do their Chinese kin across the river in Hong Kong—with 30 times as many people per square mile—have a per capita income of $8,260?

Why do the Chinese of Taiwan—with 3 times the population density—have 9 times the income of the mainland Chinese?

These few numbers are sufficient to disprove the activist claim that high population density produces poverty.

Let me finish with the most glamorous environmental hoax of our time. I refer to none other than the Greenhouse Effect.

The alleged destruction of the ozone layer and the accompanying heating of the earth is used by environmentalists as the quintessential example of man's technological folly. It proves once and for all that we have produced a system whose ultimate byproduct is suicide. The goods we buy to protect, feed, and transport ourselves, are, the environmentalists say, killing us. The chickens are coming home to roost. Doom is at hand, and hopefully the contribution is in the mail. And the media all agree. This is the big one. The earth's revenge.

But some strange things have happened in the scientific community in recent months. Atmospheric scientists who have been studying the greenhouse effect are rapidly deserting the computer models which predicted great climatic changes. They are repudiating the rash statements made earlier by some scientists and almost all environmentalists.

For instance, a top climate modeler from the University of Illinois recently reported to a conference that, "Confidence among climatologists in detection of the Greenhouse Effect is now down near zero." Dr. Reid Bryson, founder of the Institute for Environmental Studies at the University of Wisconsin, states, "The very clear statements that have been made that the greenhouse warming is here, and that the globe will be 4 degrees warmer in 50 years cannot be accepted."

Scientists at the National Oceanographic and Atmospheric Administration reviewed the best climate statistics available for the U.S. and concluded, "There is no statistically significant evidence of an overall increase in annual temperature or change in annual precipitation for the contiguous U.S. 1895–1987." Said one, "If there is a greenhouse warming effect you can't find it in the U.S. records." Says an MIT meteorologist, "The absence of any trend in the record of the contiguous U.S. leads to the suspicion that all the trends in the global record may be spurious." By trends, he is referring to those manufactured by the environmentalists.

The Greenhouse Effect is the latest but not the last environmental hoax. They will go on as long as we are willing to allow ourselves to be scared by activists parading as scientific experts. The risks of listening to political nonsense are great. The food supply is threatened, we are goaded into disposing of technologies which save lives, such as certain drugs, pesticides, and nuclear power. And worst of all, we are deceived into accepting changes in our political institutions which reduce our liberty. As famous environmentalist Paul Ehrlich puts it in calling for mandatory sterilization: "Coercion, perhaps. But coercion in a good cause." There is no good cause for coercion of a free people.

The Tiananmen Square massacre brought to mind the long-buried comment of the anti-industrial guru, Ralph Nader, offering his prescription for a healthy society about a decade ago.

He said: "One of the best solutions is to get people at the top of institutions to go through what their victims go through. The coal magnate should work a couple of weeks in the coal mine each year. That was the main thrust of the

Cultural Revolution. Mao said that they were becoming like the Russians—a bureaucracy, remote, elite. He really broke it. It hadn't been done before in history. He was seventy years old when he decided that. *He had fantastic sensitivity.*" It reveals the entire nature of Mr. Nader's vision for society that he refers to the architect of the most brutal and murderous government in history as *sensitive.* He made this comment after 50 to 100 million Chinese lost their lives so that the communists could realize their vision. Fifty million deaths are nothing to the man who lays awake at night worrying about the risk of lawn darts.

## Questions for Discussion

1. How will population increases affect the environment?
2. Why do scientists disagree about global warming?
3. What are the economic consequences of the solutions posed by environmentalists?
4. What criteria should be used in evaluating the seriousness of an environmental problem?
5. What should a prudent policy maker do in evaluating the threat of global warming?

## Suggested Readings

Bookchin, Murray. "Death of a Small Planet: It's Growth That's Killing Us." *Progressive,* 53, no. 8 (August 1989), 19–23.
Commoner, Barry. *Making Peace with the Planet.* New York: Pantheon, 1990.
Easterbrook, Gregg. "Everything You Know about the Environment Is Wrong." *New Republic,* 202, no. 18 (April 30, 1990), 14, 16–27.
Eisenberg, Evan. "The Call of the Wild." *New Republic,* 202, no. 18 (April 30, 1990), 30–38.
Fessler, Pamela. "A Quarter-Century of Activism Erected a Bulwark of Laws." *Congressional Quarterly Weekly Report,* 48, no. 3 (January 20, 1990), 153–156.
Heppenheimer, T. A. "Keeping Your Cool." *Reason,* 21, no. 8 (January 1990), 22–27.
McKibbin, Bill. *The End of Nature.* New York: Random House, 1989.
Postrel, Virginia I. "The Green Road to Serfdom." *Reason,* 21, no. 11 (April 1990), 22–28.
Russell, Cristine. "Escape from the Doomsday Predictions?" *Washington Post,* April 17, 1990, Health Sec., pp. 8–10.
Safire, William. "Earth Day's 'Planetism.'" *New York Times,* April 16, 1990, p. A19.

U.S. Cong., Senate. *The Global Environmental Protection Act of 1988.* Joint Hearings before the Subcommittee on Hazardous Wastes and Toxic Substances and the Subcommittee on Environmental Protection of the Committee on Environment and Public Works, 100th Cong, 2nd Sess., 1988.

Wald, Matthew L. "Guarding [the] Environment: A World of Challenges." *New York Times*, April 22, 1990, pp. 1, 24, 25.

# Chapter 20

*Should Puerto Rico Be Granted Statehood?*

The United States began with thirteen states along the eastern seaboard. Through war and purchase, the nation enlarged its territory, and new states came into the Union. In 1959 Alaska and Hawaii became the country's forty-ninth and fiftieth states. The quest for statehood did not end in 1959, however. Today a statehood movement exists in the District of Columbia and in Puerto Rico.

The Constitution grants Congress exclusive control of the District. Congress was, in effect, the city council for the District until 1974, when a system of governance was established which provided for a mayor and city council. Congress, however, retained the right to rescind Council actions. The adoption of the 23rd Amendment to the Constitution in 1961 enabled residents of the District to vote in presidential elections, and the District now has three electoral votes. A law enacted in 1970 allows District residents to also elect a nonvoting delegate to the House of Representatives.

Many Washingtonians have felt they have been disenfranchised by being denied the representation that the federal government allows states. So far, at least, the quest for statehood for the District has been unsuccessful, but that could change in coming years.

The status of Puerto Rico is entirely different from that of the District. Puerto Rico, an island in the Caribbean Sea with a population in 1991 of about 3.6 million people, was acquired by the United States in the Spanish-American War.

Puerto Rico has a Commonwealth status, which is a legal relationship to the United States. This status gives its citizens advantages and disadvantages. Puerto Rican citizens are U.S. citizens, but they are unable to vote in presidential contests. They can visit and live anywhere in the United States that they choose. If they live in Puerto Rico, they pay no federal income taxes. Many U.S. corporations have branches in Puerto Rico because they do not have to pay federal taxes on their profits. The economy of Puerto Rico has done well. Its living standard is above that of any Caribbean or Latin American nation.

In 1989 and 1990 Congress considered permitting a plebiscite in Puerto Rico to determine whether the Commonwealth should retain its present status, try for independence, or seek statehood.

The debate below considers the statehood issue. Carlos Romero Barcelo, a former governor of Puerto Rico, makes the case for statehood. He contends:

1. Puerto Rico seeks the same rights as citizens of the fifty U.S. states, including the right to participate in federal lawmaking and the right to vote in presidential elections.
2. Puerto Ricans have earned statehood because of their contributions in fighting wars in which the United States was engaged.
3. Statehood will strengthen U.S. national security and improve relations with Latin America.
4. The future of the United States will be greater, freer, and even more prosperous if Puerto Rico becomes the fifty-first state, just as the nation improved as it expanded from thirteen states to fifty.
5. The arguments against statehood cannot be substantiated.

Jaime Benítez, a former resident commissioner of Puerto Rico, opposes statehood. He contends:

1. Puerto Rico is part of a different cultural tradition from the United States, with a different language and different ways of going about its business.
2. The present status of Puerto Rico allows for democratic values to grow.
3. Commonwealth status has shown that the intelligent cooperation of a great power and a small nation can work without degredation or submission but with respect, encouragement, and mutually advantageous development.

 ☑ *Y E S*

## Should Puerto Rico Be Granted Statehood?

### CARLOS ROMERO BARCELO
#### *The Case for Statehood*

I want to devote my first comments to the legislation pending before this Committee. Having the Congress invite the people of Puerto Rico to express their will on their preferred status is a significant gesture. More than that, it is a governmental exercise of surpassing importance.

Congress' initiative to enact this legislation enjoys the New Progressive Party's full endorsement. We believe the people of Puerto Rico will exercise this franchise to select statehood. Whatever the result, the time has come to gauge the will of the U.S. citizens in Puerto Rico.

Mr. Chairman, you will hear from three very dedicated political leaders in these hearings.

We differ strongly on matters of policy.

But each of us loves the island of Puerto Rico and its people. Each of us wishes to promote the economic development of Puerto Rico. Each of us wishes to preserve and enhance the free institutions and traditions that have made our island a beacon of liberty in the Caribbean.

Our differences have to do with how best to promote these ends. One of us believes the way is through independence. Another, that it lies in a mixed relationship with the United States known as "Commonwealth." I believe the best way is the same as that chosen by our fellow citizens of the United States— through statehood.

If Congress passes plebiscite legislation, we will campaign hard for our positions. Just as in campaigns in the states, there will be some hard punches thrown and received. But the purpose of that hard campaigning will not be for personal gain or political aggrandizement. It will be to enhance the well-being of our fellow Puerto Ricans by the best means we know.

It is important to keep this in focus. The debate over statehood versus the other two options is absorbing and, because the definitions of each status have been incorporated in the legislation, is an indispensable element. But let us not lose sight of the overall objective: that Congress enact this legislation inviting the plebiscite. Whatever the merits of our differences, this result is a common goal.

Having said that, everyone knows I represent an ever-growing number of Puerto Ricans who believe statehood is the only viable status. Faithful to my beliefs and my constituency, I advocate that cause.

These hearings are being televised in Puerto Rico, where they will be watched with intense interest. However, it will come as a surprise to many Americans that there is much debate about Puerto Rico's political future. After all, for the near-century since the Spanish-American War, the United States and Puerto Rico have shared a common bond, a common heritage, and an uncommon interweaving of our societies.

In every war since World War I, Puerto Ricans have fought under the American flag.

Nearly 200,000 Puerto Rican citizens have served the United States faithfully in this century's major wars. Many paid the ultimate price for the Cause of Democracy. In the Korean War, for example, Puerto Rico was second among all states in the number of wounded and third in the number of battle deaths.

The American naval base at Roosevelt Roads is the largest in the world outside the mainland U.S. and it is vital to our hemispheric and international security.

More than two million Puerto Ricans live, work, and vote as full-fledged citizens all across the United States, in addition to the 3.3 million Puerto Ricans who live on our island.

Our cultures exchange the best of both worlds with musicians like Pablo Casals, opera singers like Justino Diaz, actors like José Ferrer and Raul Julia, and athletes like Roberto Clemente, Chi Chi Rodriguez, and Angel Cordero, achieving fame not only in America, but around the world.

Our economies have virtually become one. More than 75 percent of our consumer goods are produced in the 50 states. More than 90 percent of our industry derives from mainland U.S. businesses.

Since 1917, Puerto Ricans have been citizens of the United States. We have 3.3 million American citizens living in Puerto Rico: more than live in 27 states now represented in Congress.

With such a close bond, with so much progress, some people ask why Puerto Rico would ever want to change the current status and become the 51st State.

The answer is simple—because we do not have equal rights.

Puerto Ricans are a talented people, a hard-working people, a proud people.

We are U.S. citizens who have given their lives for our country and have worked hard to enrich our nation.

But we are U.S. citizens with a difference—we are second-class citizens who have no voice in our Nation's future, who have no vote in Washington.

For more than two hundred years, the United States has been the world's shining example of democracy. And today the torch of the Statue of Liberty is burning brightly in Beijing.

So it should surprise no one that American democracy burns brightest in Puerto Rico.

We already are U.S. citizens. What we seek is to become full-fledged citizens, with the same rights and responsibilities as Americans in New Orleans or Boise or any American city or state.

I believe the case is compelling for Puerto Rico to become the 51st State.

President Bush agrees. George Bush is a strong supporter of statehood for Puerto Rico. Many Democratic and Republican members of Congress also believe that the State of Puerto Rico will strengthen this country just as Alaska and Hawaii did, and just like the other 35 states who joined the Union after the Revolution.

Let me briefly spell out the reasons why Puerto Rico should become the 51st State. And let me also discuss some of the misconceptions about what this would mean.

There are four compelling reasons why Puerto Rico should become the 51st star on the American flag.

The first reason goes back to the first thirteen stars on that American flag. The American Revolution was fought to give people the right to decide their own destiny. Puerto Ricans seek no less.

We are subject to the laws of Congress. But three million Puerto Ricans, three million U.S. citizens, have no vote here in Congress. That is not right. It was not right in the thirteen colonies in 1775, and it is not right in Puerto Rico in 1989.

Puerto Rico is subject to a patchwork of Federal laws, some of which are the same as they are here on the mainland, some of which are specifically written for our island. But all these laws governing Puerto Rico share a common feature—not one Puerto Rican had a vote to determine what those laws were going to be.

If Puerto Rico becomes the 51st State, the motto which adorns the Supreme Court, "Equal Justice under Law," will finally have real meaning on our island.

The second reason why Puerto Rico should be the 51st State is because we have earned the right to become full-fledged American citizens—and many Puerto Ricans earned it the hard way, with their lives. I mentioned earlier the numbers of Puerto Ricans who have served and died fighting under the American flag.

But behind those numbers are heroes, Puerto Rican heroes, American heroes. When American planes sought to avenge the bloody terrorism of Muhammar Quadafi's Libya, a Puerto Rican Air Force Commander was in the eye of the raid. And Major Ribas-Dominicci gave his life for his country.

His mother did not vote for the President who gave the order to take action against Libya. She has no *right* to vote—she lives in Utuado, Puerto Rico.

The United States, in its long march to overturn inequality, has historically reversed past patterns of discrimination. Other men and women have fought in the Nation's wars when they too were disenfranchised. In World Wars I and II and Korea, men and women served and died at a time when neither they nor their parents could vote. They came from Alaska and Hawaii, they came from southern states; they were below the age of 21. They could fight, but not until the 1960s and early 1970s were they granted full voting rights.

The nature of the "Commonwealth" or territorial status is undemocratic in itself. It seems preposterous to suggest that the Congress of the Nation which is the example of democracy throughout the world can sponsor, encourage or support a relationship between the fifty states and a territory of 3.3 million U.S. citizens based on permanent disenfranchisement.

The third reason for Puerto Rican statehood is international relations and national security. Just as Puerto Rico needs the United States, the United States needs Puerto Rico. Earlier I mentioned the critical role played by Roosevelt Roads Naval Base.

Puerto Rico is at the crossroads of the Caribbean and North, South, and Central America. If the security of twentieth century America focused on Europe and Asia, then it is clear that the security of twenty-first century America could well center on this hemisphere. We need look no further than Cuba, Panama, Nicaragua, and the drug lords in South America to realize the foreign policy challenges we face.

Admission of Puerto Rico as a state will demonstrate to Central America and South America, in an irrefutable way, that the United States is genuinely hospitable to Hispanic language and culture. The present territorial relationship— using the Supreme Court's word in 1980—is one in which decisions are made for the territorials in the national capital, without their participation. That sends one signal to Latin America. Statehood, in which Puerto Ricans take part in choosing the American President, and elect actual voting members to the Senate and the House, sends quite another kind of signal. I do not know how many billions in foreign aid and debt forgiveness such a signal is worth, but surely it has great value for America's standing in the eyes of Latin Americans.

It will place a part of the American Union in an area of great strategic interest to the United States, the Caribbean. Granting statehood to Hawaii achieved the same result in the Pacific. A territorial outpost is one thing. Even an enormous military facility such as Roosevelt Roads cannot transform it into something organically linked to the mainland. By its very nature, statehood does that.

It will, for all practical purposes, end the debate that has sometimes erupted in the United Nations over the alleged "colonial" status of Puerto Rico.

And the fourth reason why Puerto Rico should become a state can be summed up in two words—the future. The first thirteen of these United States made a great, free and prosperous Nation. And that Nation became greater, freer, and even more prosperous with each new state that was added. When the Louisiana Purchase was made, many Americans scratched their heads and asked what would they ever do with all that worthless land. When William Seward committed his "folly" of buying Alaska, people thought he was crazy.

But today you cannot imagine what America would be like without the states of the Louisiana Purchase, without the State of Alaska. I am confident that, in a few decades time, the citizens of the United States will look back and not be able to imagine a time when Puerto Rico was not the 51st State of our union.

The genius of the American experiment in democracy is that the United States has never stopped growing, not just in size and population, but in the diversity, strength, and freedom of its people.

Senators serve on this panel from the great states of Oklahoma and New Mexico. How many American citizens know that those states were admitted as late as 1907 and 1912, and that one of the obstacles they had to overcome was the objection that they were bilingual? How many American citizens know that Alaska, whose Senator also sits on this panel, had to fight for admission for over 40 years and overcome the serious objection that Alaska might never be able to pay its way? For that matter, how many members know that the enabling legislation to admit Colorado to the Union was vetoed over that same issue? How many know that the State of Ohio was the first state admitted to the Union with a special grant from the federal government to ensure that the citizens of Ohio would be able to live according to the same standards enjoyed by the other states who already were members of the Union?

Puerto Rico has been a member of the Union, although on a hybrid basis, since 1898. The Puerto Rican people have been United States citizens since 1917. They have bled for their country and they have earned the opportunity that the pending bills would bestow: the chance to express their preference regarding the type of relationship they should have with the mainland with an advance knowledge that Congress has blessed their endeavor.

Equal Justice, Patriotic Service, International Relations, National Security, and the Future. All good reasons why Puerto Rico will be a great State in a great Nation.

Let me address some of the arguments some people make against Puerto Rican statehood. Just as I believe there are compelling reasons for statehood, others find arguments to oppose it.

The first argument they cite is why upset the status quo, why not just remain a territory tied to the United States, getting a free ride.

Puerto Rico has made progress as a territory. But no matter how much economic progress we make as a territory—no matter if we call it Commonwealth—we can never solve the fundamental problems of that status—we will never be equal, we will always be second-class citizens without participation in the decisions that affect our Nation's future. We will never know when Congress will withdraw what it has given.

Independence would give us total control of our own destiny, but the overwhelming majority of Puerto Ricans believe our destiny, our families, and our future, are inextricably bound with that of the United States. Only a relative handful of Puerto Ricans favor independence.

Only one option will endow Puerto Ricans with the full rights of American citizens. That option is statehood.

The status issue is a voting rights issue. It is also a civil rights issue. The present territorial relationship violates a basic principle of democracy; that is, the principle of government by consent of the governed.

Governor [Rafael] Hernandez-Colon stated correctly on February 26, 1989: "Due to our unique relationship with the United States, Puerto Rico has no participation in making laws that apply to us. A lack of democratic legitimacy in the application of those laws is a basic problem in the political structure of the Commonwealth we have been aware of since 1952."

Statehood is the challenge. It is the inevitable choice of those who place a high value on representative government, and who believe that Puerto Rico's real economic development will occur not as a territory, under the plenary power of Congress to grant or withdraw various benefits, but as a state inextricably bound to the union of other states.

From the Congress' point of view, statehood is the only option of the three under which Puerto Rico will contribute to the Federal Treasury, and not simply make claims upon it. The difference is dramatic. Under the present "Commonwealth" status—to say nothing of the proposed "enhancement" of that status—the net deficit to the Treasury that is attributable to Puerto Rico will be at least $160 billion over the next 25 years. The net deficit under our statehood proposal will be about $17 billion over the same 25-year period—and in the latter years, under statehood, there should not be a deficit at all, but a surplus beginning in the eighteenth year. So fiscal prudence is one reason why Congress should wish to make statehood possible for Puerto Rico.

The second argument against statehood is economic. Opponents of statehood claim Puerto Rico would suffer serious economic side effects from the imposition of federal income taxes and the loss of Section 936 tax incentives.

The facts are exactly the opposite. It is under territorial status that Puerto Rico's economic development is uncertain. Commonwealth status is the most serious threat to Section 936. Congress may eliminate the Section, and would be under pressure to do so, in consideration of every future tax bill.

We are not proposing to end Section 936 precipitously. We are proposing instead that it be guaranteed for a period of time after the beginning of statehood and then be phased out gradually at a rate and in an environment that will continue to attract business and jobs to Puerto Rico.

Whatever accommodation may be agreed upon would be protected more fully within a statehood enabling act than Section 936 is now. Statehood would provide certainty not possible under the territorial status.

For the long term, the best way to assure continued economic growth in Puerto Rico is statehood. Businesses grow and create jobs where there is long-term stability. And nothing would do more to build business confidence in Puerto Rico than the ultimate stability of statehood.

The argument of economic chaos and additional tax burdens of statehood are repetitious of the arguments raised against statehood in the case of Tennessee, Indiana, Illinois, Michigan, Florida, Iowa, Wisconsin, Oregon, Nevada, California, Nebraska, Colorado, South Dakota, North Dakota, Montana, Washington, Idaho, New Mexico, Arizona, Alaska, and Hawaii. Particularly in Alaska and Hawaii, the last two to be admitted, the economic arguments were very similar to those used against Puerto Rico becoming a state. In Alaska they argued at a local level that statehood would be too costly and that increased taxes would destroy the economy. In Hawaii the opponents of statehood at a local level argued that increased taxes would bring economic collapse.

At page 967 of *Breakthrough from Colonialism,* the principal argument in opposition to Hawaii statehood is summarized as follows: "Statehood would bring rising expenditures and increased taxes which in turn would make it difficult to attract new industries and would also drive away from the Islands many established firms. In short, statehood would bring about the economic collapse of Hawaii."

Another argument which appears in the same book on page 969 was summarized as follows: "Independence or Commonwealth status was preferable to statehood especially since the latter offered certain tax advantages which no state could enjoy."

And what happened when Hawaii became a state? Did Hawaii suffer an economic collapse as predicted?

No. On the contrary. In 1970, the First Hawaiian Bank published a report called "Hawaii in 1969: After a Decade of Statehood." The growth rates of Hawaii under statehood shown in that publication are incredible.

- The per capita personal income jumped from $1,987 in 1959 to $3,513 in 1969.
- Bank Private Demand Deposits rose from $220.3 million in 1959 to $524.2 million in 1969.
- Total Personal Income rose from $1,178 million in 1959 to $2,705 million in 1967.
- Civilian employment rose from 204,450 in 1959 to 294,850 in 1969.

The growth of tourism was remarkable.

- In 1959 visitors to Hawaii numbered 243,000. In 1969, Hawaii had 1.4 million visitors, an increase of 476 percent in ten years.
- In 1959 Hawaii had 6,802 rooms for visitors. In 1969 Hawaii had 25,822 rooms.
- Hotel employment in 1959 was 3,700 persons. In 1969 hotel employment was 13,150.

This kind of economic expansion is precisely what can be and should be expected in Puerto Rico as soon as we become a state.

The third argument against statehood is language. Some people argue that our Spanish heritage and language are a barrier to statehood. I could not disagree more. Puerto Rico is a bilingual society, proud of both our Hispanic and American cultures.

By accepting Puerto Rico as a state and guaranteeing that we shall maintain English and Spanish as official languages and that we preserve our right to enrich and strengthen our cultural heritage, the Congress and the Nation will be sending a strong message of friendship and brotherhood to all of Latin America.

The two principal languages in America are Spanish and English. It is in our national interest to improve our relations, politically, economically, and otherwise with Latin America. Accepting a Hispanic community as an equal partner in the Nation, with two Senators, seven Congressmen, and at the same time respecting our language and cultural heritage, will go a long way in helping to crumble down the walls of misunderstanding, walls of misunderstanding that have been nourished through the years by a feeling in Latin America that North Americans look down upon them.

The fourth argument against statehood is simple—that a majority of the Puerto Rican people do not support it. Well, that is what plebiscites are all about. It has been 22 years since the last plebiscite and an entire new generation of Puerto Ricans have come on the scene. They deserve the chance to choose, for once and for all, where Puerto Rico's future lies.

In the 1967 plebiscite, 39 percent supported statehood. Since that time our numbers have grown significantly. If I were not convinced that a new plebiscite will result in statehood, then I would not be here with you today.

Members of the Committee, complete the task you have initiated. Let the people of Puerto Rico speak. Puerto Ricans will speak loud and clear for equal justice, for patriotic service, for international relations, for national security, and for the future.

Puerto Rico will speak for statehood.

I think it is about time we added a new star on the American flag.

## Should Puerto Rico Be Granted Statehood?

### JAIME BENÍTEZ
### A Permanent Autonomous Relationship

I have come to testify as a concerned citizen on behalf of Puerto Rico's quest for self-affirmation, autonomy and democracy. We are seeking to stabilize a relationship within the culture of freedom in accordance with our own political experience. I believe these goals are best served by an enhanced form of Commonwealth. The present political arrangements are as yet in a historical sense recent and fluid.

Ours has been a historical odyssey, a century-old struggle to establish ourselves as a distinct political community, entitled to exercise autonomous self-government and to establish lasting and mutually acceptable interrelations, in the nature of a compact, with the metropolitan authority, be it Spain in the 19th century or the United States in the 20th.

Since early in the 19th century, the ideological alternatives for Puerto Rico have been, at least in theory, the same three:

1. Incorporation as an equal province or state.
2. Separation as an independent republic.
3. Recognition as a self-governing unit, linked to its former metropolis, in common citizenship, common defense, common currency, common trade, and, may I add, common sense.

There are no utopias. Thomas More's dream was creative and legitimate shortly after Columbus discovered America; by the end of the 20th century it is no longer tenable as a political objective.

For the first time this year, official representatives of these three alternatives have joined hands with representatives from the United States in proposing adjudication of the issue of political status, to be made by the Puerto Rican electorate itself. Such an approach has received full support in Puerto Rico. We trust it will also be approved by Congress and by the President of the United States.


## AUTONOMY

I now turn briefly to four crucial moments when choices were made for or by Puerto Rico: 1897, 1952, 1967 and 1991, when—I hope—a decision will be made for Enhanced Autonomy.

Puerto Rico's search for autonomy was organized while still a Spanish possession, on March 6, 1887, when political, intellectual and social leaders met in Ponce and created Puerto Rico's Autonomous Party. It became the majority party.

Following a ten-year campaign, and after a compact was reached between Puerto Rico's Autonomous Party and the Liberal Party of Spain, the Charter of Autonomy was granted on November 25, 1897, by Queen María Cristina. It was a broad grant, for Puerto Rico retained at the same time ample representation in the Spanish Parliament. The Preamble to the Charter of Autonomy states: "For when it is proposed to intrust the direction of their affairs to peoples that have attained their majority, either autonomy should not be offered to them at all, or it should be given to them complete, in the conviction that they are thus put on the path to prosperity, unhampered by restrictions or impediments springing from mistrust or suspicion."[1]

Pursuant to the Charter of Autonomy, Puerto Rico's Legislature was elected in March, 1898. It chose Luis Muñoz Rivera, Puerto Rico's great leader, as Prime Minister.

## HISTORY TURNS AROUND

Then came the War of 1898. "The Splendid Little War," as Secretary of State John Hay said, went much beyond the Congressional declaration of war of March 25, 1898. After Admiral Cervera's fleet was destroyed in Santiago and Queen María Cristina and Prime Minister Sagasta requested peace on July 23rd, offering to grant the independence of Cuba, President McKinley rejected the Armistice Proposal. The invasion of Puerto Rico initiated, on the 25th of July, was continued until the 12th of August, when Queen María Cristina and Prime Minister Sagasta finally agreed to grant Puerto Rico to the United States and to study conditions for the possible cession of the Philippines. Both were included in the Treaty of Paris of December 10, 1898.

This time, Puerto Rico did not participate at any stage in the transaction. The recommendation made to President McKinley by Puerto Rico's outstanding educator and writer, Eugenio María de Hostos, that a plebiscite be held in Puerto Rico offering annexation or independence, was ignored by the White House.

In Puerto Rico, political leaders assumed that the long-established Northwest Ordinance of 1787, concerning territories, would be applied to Puerto Rico as it had been to Louisiana, Florida, and Texas. From 1889 to 1896 seven territories had been admitted into the Union. They were North Dakota, South Dakota, Montana, Washington, Idaho, Wyoming and Utah. Those familiar with American expansion anticipated that Puerto Rico, too, would be incorporated as a territory, its inhabitants would be accorded citizenship and self-government, and shortly thereafter Puerto Rico would become the 46th state of the Union.

All these expectations were shattered with the approval, in 1900, by Congress and the President, of the first Organic Act of Puerto Rico, known as the Foraker Act, which was in force from May 1, 1900, to March 2, 1917. American citizenship was included in the original draft but was eliminated in the final bill. Instead Puerto Ricans were to be "citizens of Puerto Rico and as such entitled to the protection of the United States." The President, with the advice and consent of the Senate, appointed the Governor, his six cabinet members plus five citizens of Puerto Rico to serve as his Executive Council, all to serve four-year terms. The President, with the advice of the Senate, would also appoint the Supreme Court of Puerto Rico and a Federal District Court for Puerto Rico. The Governor, with the advice of the Executive Council, would make all other appointments.

Every two years, the qualified voters of Puerto Rico would elect a House of Delegates of 35 members. The Executive Council would also serve as a Senate, and with the House of Delegates would constitute the Legislative Assembly of Puerto Rico. Every two years, Puerto Rico would elect "a resident commissioner to the United States entitled to official recognition as such by all departments." It took our first resident commissioner four years to be admitted to the House of Representatives as an additional non-voting member. Puerto Rico's status was obviously colonial then, one which our Independentista and Statehood friends claim prevails to this day. This we fully deny.

From an economic standpoint the Foraker Act was most fair and even puritanical. The principle that taxation without representation is tyranny was explicitly incorporated. No federal taxes have ever been imposed on Puerto Rico. Free trade has been the rule ever since 1901. However, the Foraker Act provided that, effective for one year, 15 percent of the Dingley tariff would apply to articles from Puerto Rico entering the United States and vice versa, with such returns going to Puerto Rico's treasury in order to fill the empty coffers resulting from the War of 1898. That provision led to a number of law suits questioning its constitutionality, what are known as the Insular Cases. In *Downes* v. *Bidwell* 182 U.S. 244 (1901) in a 5 to 4 opinion the Supreme Court validated the extension of the tariff to Puerto Rico since "The island of Puerto Rico is not a part of the United States" within that provision of the Constitution which declares that "all duties, imposts and excises shall be uniform throughout the United States" (Art. I, Sec. 8).

Justice Brown went on to explain that "Puerto Rico belongs to but is not part of the United States." That imperial expression offended all of us deeply. It required and has received ample rectification. Seventy years later it was my opportunity as Resident Commissioner for Puerto Rico to persuade Congressman Wilbur Mills to take advantage of the fact that Puerto Rico is not part of the United States to establish what came to be Section 936 of the Revenue Tax Code of the United States.

The rectifications have been more de facto than de jure.

I should indicate at this point that one of the main sources of misunderstandings between the Anglo and Latin cultures relates to the fact that our legal systems have followed completely different patterns of development through their histories. The Anglo American system comes from the case method. In it, decisions are reached in an inductive manner in accordance with each particular situation. The Latin system centers upon the codification of general and universal declarations, applied later to cases by deduction. Under the Latin system we normally start with general principles and definitions.

To avoid possible confusions resulting from using both approaches at the same time, I will recommend later that in the revision of the enhanced Commonwealth proposal the general definition be broad, such that the twelve specific requests which the Governor has presented can be encompassed in the general presentation.

The shock of the setback of the Foraker Act and the Insular Cases was offset in part by many improvements in day-to-day life. Outstanding among these new benefits were the Bill of Rights, the separation of Church and State, the emphasis on Public Schools, the establishment of the University of Puerto Rico in 1903, and the overwhelming assistance provided by the Red Cross and the Navy when the greatest hurricane of the 19th century, San Ciriaco, devastated Puerto Rico.

I quote from *The Great Book of Worldwide Disasters: From Ancient Times to the Present, Darkest Hours,* by Jay Robert Nash:

> The greatest hurricane of the nineteenth century (or any other, for that matter) was the storm that moved directly over the entire length of Puerto Rico on August 8, 1899. Known as the "San Ciriaco," the storm first struck Arroyo at about 8:00 a.m. The port of Humacao was inundated by tidal waves, and Aguadilla, a town of considerable size, was all but wiped out by winds gusting to 125 m.p.h. Only San Juan escaped the more brutal punishment of the storm. By the time the hurricane reached this city, its winds had slackened to 90 m.p.h.
>
> One account reported that "there was no escape. The winds would rise to a hundred miles an hour, and you could not stand up before them. You couldn't see either. The roofs would come off tile by tile and plank by plank and go whizzing through the air. Plates and metal strips soared through the streets like giant razor blades, cutting and slicing, decapitating, amputating, maiming, killing."
>
> More than 3,000 persons were slain by this monster, which also destroyed $20 million in property.

San Ciriaco destroyed the principal coffee plantations, at the time the main source of wealth and of employment in Puerto Rico. Since it takes five years for new coffee trees to produce again, the hurricane disaster threw the coffee industry out from its position of prominence. It facilitated the intensification of the sugar cane plantations and factories. The five-hundred-acre limitation on corporate ownership established by Congress in 1900 was honored in the breach only until 1940. By that time four absentee sugar corporations monopolized the industry and the trade.

The Republican Party of Puerto Rico, founded on the 4th of July, 1899, by our leading statehood advocate Dr. José Celso Barbosa, is our oldest party and lives to this day under the name New Progressive Party. It has never, in its long history, attained on its own as much as 50 percent of the electorate, although through coalitions and the presence of more than two electoral contenders it has achieved legislative and executive control on several occasions.

By 1904 the social and political irritation caused by the American governors' exercise of political control and the intense policy of Americanization led to the creation of the Unionist Party under the leadership of Luis Muñoz Rivera, Rosendo Matienzo Cintrón and José de Diego. It called for unity against colonialism and demanded that the Federal Government grant autonomy, statehood or independence, the very same three alternatives involved in this proposed Plebiscite, 87 years later. The Unionist Party won all the elections from its founding in 1904 to its demise in 1930. The Unionist Party sent Muñoz Rivera to Washington as Resident Commissioner in 1910, where he worked until his death to replace the Foraker Act with a new organic charter—the Jones Act—which became effective on March, 1917, six months after his death. Twenty of its provisions are effective to this day under the name of the Puerto Rico Federal Relations Act.

The Jones Act of 1917 did extend American citizenship to Puerto Rico, and it eliminated the Executive Council, provided for an elected Senate, and allowed the Governor to appoint 4 of the 7 members of his Cabinet with the advice and consent of the Puerto Rican Senate. The President retained the power to appoint the Commissioner of Education, the Attorney General and the Comptroller until 1948 when the Elective Governor Amendment went into effect.

Second to the extension of American Citizenship, the most important modification was the creation of the Senate with confirmation power over the governor's appointments. Under well-disposed governors—there were not many—it permitted the development of a semi-parliamentary system under which the President of the Senate became a working partner with the American Governor.

Under this system, life in Puerto Rico underwent significant ups and downs. On the positive side, health, education, religious freedoms, labor unions, citizen rights were improved. On the negative side, the goal of Americanization was over-emphasized; the teaching in English in public schools from the first grade up became an all but unacceptable imposition and one which served to provoke an understandable reaction against "Americanization."

While the economic situation had improved and sugar had become the main insular agricultural and industrial activity, the basic feudal situation continued to prevail until the forties.

You can appreciate the massive social and economic changes affecting Puerto Rico if you think of these general figures. In 1899, out of a total population of 953,243, 85 percent was classified as rural and only 15 percent as urban. It was within the urban population where the social ruling class resided. By 1940, the population had almost doubled to 1,869,255 while its distribution changed to 70 percent rural and 30 percent urban. Compare the present population, which stands at 3,350,000, and the geographic distribution, which is estimated to be 80 percent urban and 20 percent rural. Our population density now stands at 960 per square mile, the highest anywhere in America and among the highest worldwide.

After the Jones Act of March 2, 1917, came the United States' declaration of war on Germany on April 6, 1917. Puerto Ricans joyously supported the Congressional action and our young men entered the Army with enthusiasm and pride. Unfortunately the North American class segregation prevailing then was extended to our men and for the first and last time in our common history such an obscenity was implemented in our midst. The end of the war was followed by a few years of what was called "Republican prosperity," inter-rupted in 1928 by another devastating hurricane—San Felipe—followed by a much greater crisis, the depression of 1929, followed in Puerto Rico by another hurricane—San Ciprián—in 1932.

I provide you with this catalog of particulars so that you can best perceive the background from whence we had to face and deal with a completely new reality.

## THE SECOND WORLD WAR

Toward the end of the dreadful decade of the 30s, the greatest holocaust in history—the Second World War—was to begin. Germany invaded Poland on September 1, 1939. England and France declared War on Germany two days later. Germany proceeded to invade Denmark, Norway and Belgium. After December 7, 1941, our own young men were engaged within the American Army in that life and death struggle to preserve the possibilities of democracy.

At the same time, we in Puerto Rico were involved in a decisive quest for internal decolonization at home. Under the exceptional leadership of Luis Muñoz Marín, flying the banner of *Pan, Tierra y Libertad* (Bread, Land and Freedom) and depending exclusively upon the electoral strength of the ill-housed, ill-clothed and ill-fed, the Popular Democratic Party gave birth to what came to be known as Puerto Rico's "peaceful revolution." The electoral man-date, which was reaffirmed with even greater strength every four years from November 1940 to November 1964, transformed what President Hoover had described as "the poor-house of the Caribbean" into what President Truman called "the show-place of democracy."

During the decisive first five years of social and political reorganization, the new program was aided significantly by our last and best American Governor, the outstanding economist and leader of the New Deal approach, Rexford Guy Tugwell.

As the defeat of the Axis was sealed with the suicide of Hitler, the hanging of Mussolini in the public square of Milan, and the atomic bombs in Hiroshima and in Nagasaki, it became our responsibility in Puerto Rico to come to grips once more, and now in a new world, with the issue of our own political status. It had been held in abeyance for two elections. In 1948 it could no longer be.

We had witnessed how after the Second World War European colonial power came to an end in Africa and in Asia, as well as in the British Caribbean colonies. The process of establishing independent states began within the framework of traditional Western political thought. Simultaneously, in Europe, Russia claimed and won the power to incorporate small countries within its political structure. Such incorporation included national groups with centuries behind them of independent or autonomous political identities.

Japan was occupied by American troops. China went its way into the Communist world. Germany was divided within its boundaries. The United States emerged as one of the two superpowers, together with Russia.

Nuclear energy was unleashed and for the first time the achievement of man brought tragically into question the biblical words "Nothing is new under the sun."

In the words of the American writer John Steinbeck—who won the Nobel Prize in Literature in 1962—"Fearful and unprepared man has assumed lordship over the life and death of the whole world of all living things."

It was a very difficult and anguishing period of research and soul-searching, exploring old and new alternatives with one primary consideration in mind: In this world of flux, with old certainties melting away before one's eyes, what would be best for Puerto Rico? Finally, by June of 1946, we knew which goals we could not pursue. Independence was out for three basic reasons:

1. The large majority in Puerto Rico do not want it. It cannot be imposed.
2. We cannot afford it. Common trade with the United States is indispensable for Puerto Rico.
3. The times are out of joint and they do not call for additional separations. They call at best for interdependence with the United States.

Why not statehood? Because we would have to stop being ourselves. We—Puerto Ricans and mainlanders—are too different, to be in a position to carry out without excessive losses a merger into statehood in Puerto Rico.

I believe Commonwealth works out best not only for Puerto Rico but also for the United States.

## THE PERTINENCE OF COMMONWEALTH TODAY

In the 19th century, as a new and growing nation, the United States was frankly committed to expansion across the continent. In the dawn of the 21st century as a mature nation, the expansions ahead are more a matter of ideas than of geography. Manifest Destiny, the concept under which the United States pressed west to the Pacific and south to its present border with Mexico, has come to an end.

The United States long ago reached what could be thought of as its natural geographical limits, and it began to experiment with non-contiguous as well as overseas lands. Alaska and Hawaii figure prominently here.

Puerto Rico is also an overseas territory, and its people are citizens of the United States, but Puerto Rico is different from the two non-contiguous states in crucial ways. It is also essentially different from the United States, and as a result bears—and I think must necessarily bear—a different relation to the nation than do the two overseas states.

Puerto Rico is part of a different cultural tradition with a different language and different ways of going about its business. Unlike Hawaii, it has a clear and historically unbroken relation to a particular cultural, legal and language tradition. Though quite uniform in its population, its cultural stock and language are, unlike Alaska, Hispanic rather than Anglo-Saxon. The presence of the United States for 91 years has not broken this tradition. It has, rather, accentuated the differences, while at the same time new political values have been added, and new cultural approaches have evolved.

Unlike the other non-contiguous areas, Puerto Rico has a kind of unity of its own, a style of working and living, and a deep historical continuity to which American traditions have been added without replacing the valuable ones already here. This has led Puerto Ricans to embrace American democratic values wholeheartedly and at the same time to keep a sharp eye out to preserve the cultural traditions in which they are rooted. I am thinking here, particularly, of the Spanish language, one of the great languages of the world, into which we have been born, and of institutions such as the family, which has proven our mainstay in the difficult adjustments of modern, urban life, in which we now take full part.

It is sometimes difficult for a mainlander who has not lived among us to understand in what ways we are different from him and in what ways we are also like him. What I have to say here will, I hope, be useful in helping to understand the value of the present form of Puerto Rico's political life, which is neither statehood nor independence, but commonwealth, an enduring relation between two peoples who share certain common political principles.

Democratic men and women throughout America need and hope that a democratic style of life be finally extended throughout the hemisphere. But we know that that achievement cannot take place by force, economic imposition, or incorporation. It must take place internally in keeping with national and local interests, concerns and developments.

From the mainlander's point of view, the United States has achieved so much and its citizenship confers such great advantages that it has come to seem only natural and rational that other peoples would, if given a chance, choose to be a part of the United States. For Americans, this idea is constantly reinforced by the influx of both legal and illegal migrants, people who have chosen to make drastic changes in their lives and sacrifice some of their traditional ways in order to benefit from life in the United States. For the mainlander it is difficult to imagine that any reasonable person would choose not to become an integral part of his great society.

It is a mistake, however, to think that what people do individually they would, or should, choose to do as a whole people. When an individual uproots and resettles elsewhere, it is a choice for himself. When a whole people chooses to establish a permanent link with another, locations, distances, historical backgrounds, variations are significant considerations to be explored and taken into account. It is a choice that affects one's children and one's children's children, and the whole of a way of life. The two are not the same. Think of the thousands of Irish immigrants that came to the States in the 19th century. They are millions now of loyal American citizens and think of the Irish Free State as a distinct affectionate reality.

National expansion by acquisition of territory gave way to a general program of fostering democratic values. The need for geographical contiguity and complete incorporation has become less and less important. There are not only limits to the amount and distribution of the land that one can acquire and control, but there are limits to the number and kinds of political entities that can reasonably be incorporated without affecting the functioning or the character of the nation.

First of all—and this will perhaps seem a very obvious thing to say—it is simply not possible or even desirable for all the world to be incorporated into the United States, nor for all who share America's vision of human possibility to come to live in the United States. Second, if not all the world can or should become part of the United States, a question arises: How can what is liberating and hopeful in America's distinctive vision be spread to other traditions?

The proof, if you will, of that vision is how it works in the larger world, among other peoples and traditions. It is in this that Puerto Rico, in its present status, is very significant, not only to itself and to the United States, but to the larger progress of democracy in the world. In its present form, it constitutes a proof that America's vision is applicable to and can enrich, without rooting out or substituting, what other peoples value in their own traditions.

The present status of Puerto Rico can be said to have provided a new dimension to this matter, for it is a place where democratic values of the kind the United States espouses have taken root, have grown and have prospered. We are in the presence, here, of a noble, and I believe singular reality in the spreading of democratic values in the world at large. This is not a frozen format but a basic approach, flexible, adjustable to changing realities within mutually acceptable modifications for the common good.

In the long view, it is these historical facts that will count, rather than the difficulties that have arisen here and there in this vital process of two nations finding a way to live together in a world that simply must be just and harmonious. The alternatives—strife, misunderstanding and conflict—are deeply repugnant and dangerous to us all, and are clearly visible in many parts of the world today.

The experimentation with democratic forms which has arisen in this process has been a rather pragmatic matter. It has not been focussed on abstract systems so much as on the betterment and well-being of the peoples concerned.

In modern times, it has been incumbent on virtually all nations to find new forms to meet their changed circumstances. At this time, the European nations are reexamining the very idea of what it is to be a nation, and by 1992 will have fused into one confederated body. It is of essential interest to us here that this confederation will safeguard for the foreseeable future the distinctness of its constituent peoples, their cultures, languages and traditions. In this, and in our common concern to find peaceful, mutually beneficial and democratic solutions to human problems, the present relationship of the United States and Puerto Rico is similar.

The scale, of course, is very different, for Puerto Rico is tiny beside its partner. Its progress has been achieved by the United States and Puerto Rico working together, and this, in itself, is enormously hopeful, for it signifies, for any who want to see the fact, that dissimilarity of scale and power need not lead to the crushing or subjugation of the smaller partner. It signifies that one can make strengths of presumed weaknesses and that real human needs can be met through imaginative, innovative political thought, and that all of this can be done without depriving the members of either society of their most fundamental freedoms or rights.

I would argue, in this way, that the present status of Puerto Rico has, for the United States, a significance far beyond the partnership itself. It represents a way to prove the pertinence and applicability of our shared, democratic way of life to other places and peoples. The message is clear for the many peoples of the world who would embrace democratic practice, if they could be sure that to do so would not mean merely copying the lifestyle of Americans or the end of traditions they depend on and revere.

It seems to me that commonwealth's opponents fall into a common error of human thought: when they say that Puerto Rico must be one thing or another, a republic or a state, either this or that, they let some set of opposing ideas— abstractions of some kind, tricks of the mind—get in the way of looking at the facts, so that they do not see the human and historical problems to which the political organization of societies is supposed to attend.

In the case of Puerto Rico, there is every reason to cultivate the deep Hispanic tradition of which it is a respected part. If we do not, we risk depriving generations of their heritage. There is every reason, too, to protect and cultivate the democratic tradition of which Puerto Rico is also a respected and thriving part.

What the political thinkers of any society must do, perhaps the essential thing, is to look long and hard at the real, not the imagined needs of the people who live, and will in the future live, in the framework it provides. It must discover political forms that meet these needs in a real world, which we now know to be necessarily and intricately interdependent.

For Puerto Rico, and for its great partner, the United States, there are abundant reasons to preserve the experiment and achievements of the Commonwealth, a form which speaks to the needs and to the condition not only of these two different peoples who share democratic values, but to the hopes of other nations and individuals straining toward their own forms of democratic organization.

What matters here, I believe, is the principle of mutual respect of each for each, a respect in which difference is not taken for hostility, and the choice to continue to be different in some ways is not taken as rejection of the principles that unite us.

So, I urge mainland Americans to give their understanding, appreciation and support to this unique and fruitful formula, which unites us and speaks to the whole world of respectful collaboration. I urge them to recognize the immediate and future value of Commonwealth, as a living political institution and as a symbol of hope for the world.

And I urge my fellow Puerto Ricans, Americans too, to support and give their best for this imaginative experiment, which preserves our own best traditions and makes us not a mere part but a partner in the democratic enterprise. This is, in fact, where the action is. We are living the experiment, and what we do will signify beyond any of our lifetimes.

## CONCLUSION

Let me sum up my argument now. We are a small nation; yet from 1887 to 1952—in 65 years—we have achieved an important degree of autonomy not once but twice, first with Spain and then with the United States. We have successfully merged two different legal systems and political traditions. Today ours is a modern, working democracy of the kind that Americans everywhere can recognize as concordant with their own.

The autonomy to which I have referred repeatedly is in keeping with democratic values, and it is certainly not hostile to the United States. It is, instead, a kind of proof of the applicability of democratic principles to a much larger and more varied world than the mainland itself or for that matter to Puerto Rico.

In this turbulent post-war period, a period of world-wide experimentation in political forms, Puerto Rico has been on the cutting edge. The principle of interdependence is present today [1989] in Europe, in Central America, in the Asiatic World, in varying forms but nonetheless as an expression of unity within pluralism. Commonwealth has shown that the intelligent cooperation of a great power and a small nation can work without degradation or submission, but with respect, encouragement and mutually advantageous development.

This interdependent relationship—which has in fact worked exceedingly well in guaranteeing liberty and in vastly improving conditions of life in Puerto Rico—is always susceptible to criticism. But there are quite different modalities in critical assessments and we must be clear about them. There are, on one side, the ideological opponents and there are, on the other, the members of the same basic group who nonetheless differ among themselves concerning one or several points of variance.

The ideological argument comes from two sources: There are those who believe that independent nationhood is indispensable, uniform and universally desirable. This, I hold, distances theory from reality, formulae from fact. Then there are those who favor assimilation, at the risk of diluting our culture in the vastly different culture of the mainland. The other arguments, if you examine them closely, are of the same kind that have arisen in modern democracies everywhere. As such they should not be used as condemnation of this particular working form. Nor should we confuse the basic Commonwealth's continued development with the merits or demerits of specific instances of development which may or may not be advisable. Let us not forget that even at the Constitutional Convention there were significant variations among the fathers of the Constitution.

The fact that there is criticism from the other parties, which enjoy the benefits of Commonwealth, should not confuse us as we try to shape Puerto Rico's future. That there is open criticism is proof that Puerto Rico has, with its experience under Commonwealth, become strong, confident, and committed to the responsibilities as well as the rights of a democratic political life.

The essential argument is the success story itself. I hope that the Congress and the people of Puerto Rico will not be distracted by the frustrations of modernity but will grant Commonwealth its due for the fundamental successes which it has afforded our people and for what it promises for the future.

---

NOTE

1. Marcos Ramírez Lavandero (ed.), *Documents on the Constitutional Relationship of Puerto Rico and the United States*, 3rd ed., Washington, D. C.: Puerto Rico Federal Affairs Administration, 1988, p. 15.

## *Questions for Discussion*

1. Which status should a Puerto Rican favor for the island? Defend your answer.
2. Is statehood for Puerto Rico beneficial to the United States? Why or why not?
3. What should the U.S. Congress do if Puerto Rico votes for statehood?
4. How is a difference in culture relevant to the issue of statehood?
5. What arguments over statehood for Puerto Rico are relevant to the issue of statehood for the District of Columbia?

## Suggested Readings

Carr, Raymond I. *Puerto Rico: A Colonial Experiment.* New York: New York Univ. Press, 1984.

Falk, Pamela, ed. *The Political Status of Puerto Rico.* Lexington, Mass.: Lexington Books, 1986.

Kane, Brian A., and Ruel Bernard. "Puerto Rico: Nation or State?" *Progressive,* 53, no. 9 (September 1989), 32–35.

Meléndez, Edgardo. *Puerto Rico's Statehood Movement.* New York: Greenwood Press, 1988.

Passell, Peter. "Debate on Puerto Rico's Future Has a Bottom Line." *New York Times,* May 15, 1990, p. A18.

Perusse, Roland I. *United States and Puerto Rico: The Struggle for Equality.* Malabar, Fla.: R. E. Krieger, 1990.

Stevens-Aroyo, Antonio M. "Prisoners of Many Myths." *Nation,* 250, no. 3 (January 22, 1990), 86–90.

U.S. Cong., Senate. *Political Status of Puerto Rico.* Hearings before the Committee on Energy and Natural Resources, 101st Cong., 1st Sess., 1989.

Weisman, Jack. "An Island in Limbo." *New York Times Magazine,* February 18, 1990, pp. 29–32, 34, 36–37, 40.

# Chapter 21

## *Does U.S. National Interest in the Post–Cold War Era Require a Policy of Globalism?*

When the United States achieved its independence in the late eighteenth century, it was a small country, with thirteen states along the eastern seaboard. In protecting itself from hostile countries, it benefited from the Atlantic Ocean, which made sustained military operations difficult. At the time, Europe was the most likely candidate to generate serious security threats to North America.

And so U.S. foreign policy was based on isolationism, or noninterference in the kinds of foreign policy concerns that mattered most to European nations. George Washington stated the position squarely in his Farewell Address to the nation as he concluded his second term of office: "It is our true policy to steer clear of permanent alliance with any portion of the foreign world."[1] Until the twentieth century, the United States concerned itself more with its own internal economic and political development than it did with foreign policy. Not only did distance protect the United States, but so, too, did the global political situation and lack of military technology.

The strongest military powers in the world were in Europe, but Europe was not united. Instead it was marked by rivalries and alliances that pitted European nations against each other. The fact that European nations were more concerned with each other than with the United States made it easier for the United States to continue its policy of isolationism.

Lack of military technology, too, served to protect the United States. Air power did not have military application until the twentieth century. For a country to marshal its forces and conquer the United States, moreover, would require much time.

But the twentieth century saw great changes. When World War I broke out in 1914, the United States remained aloof and sought to continue its traditional policy of isolationism. But when German power became too strong, the United States intervened on the side of Great Britain, France, and their allies and helped to bring victory to the Allied Powers.

The United States tried to return to its policy of isolationism. When World War II started in Europe in 1939, the United States again tried to remain aloof. It was not until 1941, when Japan, a new military power in the world, attacked Pearl Harbor, that the United States became directly involved in that war. The United States faced two major enemies—Japan and Germany.

By 1945, Americans accepted the fact that their country could no longer maintain its isolationist position. New technology—air power and atomic bombs—had shown that distance no longer served to protect the nation as it had for more than a century. So now the United States was prepared to play a permanent role as a global power.

Soon after World War II came to an end in 1945, the cold war began. The term, "cold war," describes the conflict between the United States and its allies against the Soviet Union and its allies in which the two blocs regarded each other as mortal foes but sought to achieve advantages for the most part through political, economic, and propaganda means rather than through direct military confrontation. Both sides, moreover, created huge military establishments with nuclear weapons and sought to build global alliances.

World War II had so devastated Europe that the United States and the Soviet Union became the strongest military powers in the world. They were superpowers, and their foreign policies were preoccupied with each other.

The United States built a vast alliance system, with the cornerstone being the North Atlantic Treaty Organization (NATO). That alliance reversed George Washington's view and established a permanent relationship between the United States and other Western nations. As the leader of the Western alliance, the United States sought to protect countries facing domination by the Soviet Union and other communist countries.

A consensus developed in the United States that globalism—a belief that the United States should be involved in countries everywhere—was the correct policy. Although Americans divided on specific foreign policy issues, such as the Korean War and the Vietnam War, for the most part there was an American consensus that the United States could not withdraw from the world.

But starting for the most part in 1989, the Soviet system began to crumble. The Soviet economy was in a shambles. Soviet domestic politics was in disarray as most of the Soviet republics sought independence or greater autonomy. Soviet influence over Eastern Europe diminished, and communist regimes toppled within a year, to be replaced in many cases by democratic governments.

Although differences exist between the United States and the Soviet Union, it was clear by late 1990 that the cold war was over. Now the United States would have to devise a foreign policy geared to the new global political order.

But what should that foreign policy be? Americans grappled with an answer. The selections below capture the flavor of the debate. Carl Gershman, president of the National Endowment for Democracy, contends that the United States must follow its traditional foreign policy goal of supporting freedom everywhere. The endowment is a private, grant-making government-financed organization committed to promoting democracy around the world. He argues:

1. There is a worldwide movement recognizing that democracy is the best form of government.
2. The United States should not impose democracy on the world but should encourage it.
3. The United States should promote democracy because it strengthens political stability, peace, and friendly relations with other governments—all goals of U.S. foreign policy.

Syndicated columnist Patrick J. Buchanan argues that the interests of the United States require it to concern itself with the nation's own security and not the security or political system of other nations. He contends:

1. Once the cold war has definitely ended, the United States should disengage from Europe and Asia.
2. The United States should strengthen its own military forces, including strategic defense.
3. It should maintain dominance over the Western hemisphere.
4. The United States will lead the world by avoiding global intervention.
5. The United States should not seek to promote democracy everywhere in the world.
6. Americans need to support a new American nationalism.

---

NOTE

1. George Washington, "Farewell Address to the People of the United States," first published in *Daily American Advertiser* (Philadelphia), September 19, 1796, reprinted as U.S. Cong., House Document 504, 89th Cong., 2nd Sess., 1966, p. 24.

✓ *YES*

---

*Does U.S. National Interest in the Post–Cold War Era Require a Policy of Globalism?*

---

### CARL GERSHMAN

#### *Freedom Remains the Touchstone*

With the stunning collapse of communism in Central Europe, it is appropriate to reconsider the goals of American foreign policy in a post–Cold War world. It is true, of course, that the communist regime in the Soviet Union remains in place, that in military terms Moscow is still a superpower, and that it continues to give military assistance to Afghanistan, Cuba, Angola, and other Third World client states. Nonetheless, the Soviet Union is exhausted economically and ideologically, and is in the throes of a profound systemic crisis. The challenge ahead is not to defend against its expansion but to manage its decline.

In this altered world, the policy of containment is clearly outdated. It does not respond to the immediate challenge of consolidating democratic systems in the liberated countries of Central Europe and facilitating their eventual integration into an expanded European Community. It is rapidly becoming obsolete in the Third World as well.

That said, however, it does not follow that the United States must define a new "central purpose" for its foreign policy. Containment itself was not the central purpose of U.S. policy but rather a response to a specific geopolitical situation in which the United States found itself challenged by a formidable military and ideological rival. The central purpose, as stated in the Truman Doctrine, was to "support free peoples" in defense of a "way of life" based upon "the will of the majority" and "distinguished by free institutions, representative government, free elections, guarantees of individual liberty, freedom of speech and religion, and freedom from political oppression." Support for this way of life against its totalitarian alternative was the purpose for which containment was designed. The attenuation of the totalitarian challenge does not invalidate this purpose, which was enunciated before the Cold War by Woodrow Wilson and Franklin Roosevelt. It only raises the question of whether a policy of support for free institutions and for adherence to democratic political norms around the world can and should be sustained in the absence of a grave threat that necessitates U.S. action.

In answering that question, it may be helpful to recall that the consensus supporting the containment policy broke down as a result of the debate over U.S. involvement in Vietnam and was not reestablished during the following two decades. At issue was the policy of the United States toward non-communist authoritarian governments threatened by communist attack or subversion. In effect, one side in this debate favored withdrawing the containment shield from such governments if they did not take meaningful steps to improve their human rights performance. The other side favored retaining the shield not only to resist communist expansion but also in the belief that authoritarian systems were less repressive and more open to democratic reform than the totalitarian alternative.

The debate sharpened in the 1970s when it appeared that the United States faced the bleak prospect of having to choose between these two options only. It came to a head in 1979 over the Nicaraguan revolution, but the bitter lesson that each side came away with from that experience—that authoritarianism is not a bulwark against communism, and that the overthrow of authoritarianism is not a guarantee of democracy—actually laid the foundation for a new policy fostering peaceful transitions to democracy. As the democratic wave of the 1980s in Latin America and elsewhere in the Third World gained momentum, and despite the bitter dispute over funding the armed resistance to the Sandinista government in Nicaragua, a new bipartisan consensus began to form around this pro-democracy policy. In March 1986, following the peaceful revolution in the Philippines, President Reagan enunciated the new consensus by committing the United States to the "democratic revolution" taking place in the world. The core of his message to Congress was that "The American people believe in human rights and oppose tyranny in whatever form, whether of the Left or the Right."

The collapse of communism has given this policy renewed support as Republicans and Democrats outdo each other in calls for assistance to the democratic revolution in Central Europe, and as the fear of another Vietnam—still a cautionary factor in any policy expressing global support for democracy—recedes. Nonetheless, strong reservations persist about the merits of such a policy. They are associated with no single political camp, but can be found among both conservatives and liberals, as well as among foreign policy "realists" who have always been skeptical of American universalism.

The reservations may be summarized as follows: Democratic globalism, or Wilsonian internationalism if you will, betrays an ethnocentric point of view that mistakenly assumes democracy is an appropriate system for everybody. It is not, and the desire to implant it where it does not exist reflects cultural arrogance, missionary zeal, and a dangerous tendency to impose abstract principles on political reality. Moreover, a policy of globalism implies unlimited commitments along the lines of President Kennedy's pledge to "pay any price" to support freedom. If commitments exceed power and resources, policy will become insolvent, as Walter Lippmann once wrote. On top of this, there is no compelling, tangible national interest that is served by such a policy. The United States should not go abroad, in the famous words of John Quincy Adams, "in search of monsters to destroy," but only in pursuit of clearly defined interests to protect.

The response to this line of argument begins with the democratic revolution which demonstrates that successful democratic systems, as well as the aspiration for democracy, now extend far beyond the industrial democracies of the West. The last months of 1989 alone saw not only communist dictatorships overthrown in Central Europe but the holding of transitional elections in Chile, Namibia, and Taiwan; the peaceful transfer of power following sharply contested elections in the two largest Third World democracies, India and Brazil; and the installation of a democratically-elected government in Panama (by U.S. troops, to be sure, but with the overwhelming approval of the Panamanian people). These dramatic events were the culmination of a period of unprecedented democratic gains that began in the 1970s with the democratic transitions in Greece, Spain, and Portugal, then spread across most of Central and South America and to a large part of Asia before it reached Central Europe. While the democratic movement in China was brutally suppressed, it probably did more than any single event to signal to the world that the democratic idea is truly universal and that there are young people continents and cultures away from the historic centers of democratic life who are prepared to lay down their lives for freedom. The democratic movement in Burma (which was suppressed) demonstrated the same point.

No single factor accounts for this worldwide phenomenon. The technological and communications revolutions have made the attributes of modern democratic society accessible and discernible throughout the world, thereby introducing into non-Western societies expectations and aspirations for democracy not present before. Moreover, the decline of traditional forms of authority in modernizing societies, combined with the more recent collapse of Marxism, has left democratic consent as the only means of conferring legitimacy on governments. Developing countries are also discovering that democracy, while by no means a panacea, offers a way to limit and decentralize state power, to expose corruption, to reduce the potential for civil violence by integrating different economic and ethnic groups into the system, and to achieve economic growth. As the alternative to tyrannical force in the management of increasingly complex societies, democracy would have to be invented, as Peter Berger has written, if it did not already exist.

If democracy is developing indigenously within countries because it offers the best way to manage the affairs of society and to achieve national objectives, the issue for us to decide is whether we should assist and encourage this process, not whether we should seek to impose our system on others. We cannot force others to do what they are not prepared or willing to do for themselves; the American people would not support this approach in any event. But we can insist upon adherence to political norms and provide support and encouragement to those seeking to establish democratic systems. Such a policy is consistent with American values—pluralism as well as democracy—and it does not risk insolvency because it can be pursued with relatively limited resources.

In fact, the basic elements of such a policy are already in place, having been assembled in the course of more than a decade of attempts to find common ground between liberals and conservatives, and between the executive branch and Congress, on these questions. They include the integration of human rights issues into the fabric of U.S. policy through such mechanisms as the establishment of a Human Rights Bureau at the State Department; the annual preparation of "country reports" on human rights; the conditioning of economic and security assistance, trade benefits, and votes in international lending agencies on human rights performance; and the provision of funds under the Foreign Assistance Act for programs that encourage respect for human rights. They also include instructions to U.S. ambassadors to carry out this policy by maintaining close contacts with democratic groups and by encouraging wherever possible steps toward stable democratic transitions. (The results of this activist approach have already been evident in such countries as the Philippines, Chile, Paraguay, Poland, and Hungary.)

An additional element in this policy has been the establishment of the National Endowment for Democracy which enlists the involvement of private U.S. organizations—principally institutes associated with our two political parties, the AFL-CIO [American Federation of Labor–Congress of Industrial Organizations], and the Chamber of Commerce—in assisting the development of democratic political and social institutions abroad. Military force is also an element in the policy, though its use is circumscribed by criteria, set forth by Defense Secretary [Caspar] Weinberger in 1984 and now widely endorsed, that favor the commitment of U.S. forces only as a last resort and only with broad bipartisan backing. Significantly, the recent commitment of U.S. forces in Panama and the show of force in the Philippines during the coup attempt against the [Corazon] Aquino government were justified in terms of supporting democracy.

But does this policy serve a compelling, tangible national interest? Or is it, to borrow the phrase of one commentator, "a special kind of international social work"? The events of the last months offer the most eloquent answer to this question, for it was the democratic revolution in Central Europe, more than any military or diplomatic factors, that brought the postwar era to a close and redrew the political map of the world. Despite all the attention devoted to disarmament over the last decades by governments and demonstrators alike, it was the success of the democratic struggles in the communist world that made meaningful disarmament a real possibility.

Beyond these immediate issues, the United States has a clear interest in the establishment of democratic governments abroad. Such governments are more likely than dictatorships to enjoy political stability and to establish peaceful relations with their neighbors. In addition, while governments that share our values may not agree with us on every issue, they are likely to be our friends and to desire a close mutual relationship. Just as important, we would be able to sustain such a close and collaborative relationship with *them*, something we have difficulty doing (given the nature of our polity and the importance we attach to democratic values) with countries that are not democratic. Moreover, given our position as the world's first and leading democracy, we have a unique opportunity to exercise leadership in supporting the progress of democracy, arguably the foremost political issue of our time. Our prestige and morale would inevitably suffer if we were to relinquish this responsibility.

Is the objective of supporting democracy sufficient to serve as a "central purpose" for the United States in its relations with the world? The question should answer itself, for this already *is* our central purpose and has been since our nation was founded on the basis of universal democratic principles. The moments when we strayed from these principles—during the Vietnam malaise, for example, when many Americans ceased to believe in our national purpose—have not been happy times for America. More recently, our national self-confidence and sense of purpose have been restored. The fact that this restoration coincided with the world democratic revolution may have been purely coincidental. More likely, however, these developments were mutually reinforcing; the former giving renewed impetus to the idea of freedom in the world, and the latter reminding us that our heritage does, indeed, have a universal meaning. That is a useful thing to recall as we set our course at the beginning of a new era.

*Does U.S. National Interest in the Post–Cold War Era Require a
Policy of Globalism?*

## PATRICK J. BUCHANAN

## *America First—and Second, and Third*

On the birthday of Thomas Jefferson, dead half a decade, the President of the
United States [Andrew Jackson] raised his glass, and gave us, in a six-word
toast, our national purpose: "The Union," Old Hickory said, "it must be
preserved."

It was to "create a more perfect Union" that the great men came to Philadelphia; it was to permit the Republic to grow to its natural size that James K. Polk
seized Texas and California; it was to preserve the Union—not end slavery—
that Lincoln invaded and subjugated the Confederate states.

"A republic if you can keep it," Franklin told the lady in Philadelphia. Surely,
preservation of the Republic, defense of its Constitution, living up to its
ideals—that is our national purpose. "America does not go abroad in search of
monsters to destroy," John Quincy Adams said. "She is the well-wisher of the
freedom and independence of all. She is the champion and vindicator only of
her own."

Yet, when the question is posed, "What is America's national purpose?",
answers vary as widely as those who take it. To Randall Robinson of
TransAfrica, it is the overthrow of South Africa; to Jesse Jackson, it is to advance
"justice" by restoring the wealth the white race has robbed from the colored
peoples of the earth; to AIPAC [American Israel Public Affairs Committee], it is
to keep Israel secure and inviolate; to Ben Wattenberg, America's "mission" is
a crusade to "wage democracy" around the world. Each substitutes an extra-
national ideal for the national interest; each sees our national purpose in another continent or country; each treats our Republic as a means to some larger
end. "National purpose" has become a vessel, emptied of original content, into
which ideologues of all shades and hues are invited to pour their own causes,
their own visions.

In Charles Krauthammer's "vision" (in the Winter [1989/1990] issue of *The
National Interest*), the "wish and work" of our nation should be to "integrate"
with Europe and Japan inside a "super-sovereign" entity that is "economically,
culturally, and politically hegemonic in the world." This "new universalism,"
he writes, "would require the conscious depreciation not only of American
sovereignty but of the notion of sovereignty in general. This is not as outrageous
as it sounds."

While Krauthammer's super-state may set off onanistic rejoicing inside the
Trilateral Commission, it should set off alarm bells in more precincts than

Belmont, Massachusetts. As national purpose, or national interest, like all of the above, it fails the fundamental test: Americans will not fight for it.

Long ago, Lord Macaulay asked:

> And how can man die better
> Than facing fearful odds
> For the ashes of his fathers,
> And the temples of his gods?

A nation's purpose is discovered not by consulting ideologies, but by reviewing its history, by searching the hearts of its people. What is it for which Americans have always been willing to fight?

Let us go back to a time when the establishment wanted war, but the American people did not want to fight.

In the fall of 1941, Europe from the Pyrenees to Moscow, from the Arctic to North Africa, was ruled by Hitler's Third Reich. East of Moscow, Stalin's gulag extended across Asia to Manchuria, where it met the belligerent Empire of the Rising Sun whose domain ran to mid-Pacific. England was in her darkest hour. Yet, still, America wanted to stay out; we saw, in the world's bloody conflict, no cause why our soldiers should be sent overseas to spill a single drop of American blood. Pearl Harbor, not FDR [Franklin D. Roosevelt], convinced America to go to war.

The isolationism of our fathers is today condemned, and FDR is adjudged a great visionary because he sought early involvement in Britain's war with Hitler. But even the interventionists' arguments were, and are, couched in terms of American national interest. Perhaps we did not see it, we are told, but our freedom, our security, our homes, our way of life, our Republic, were at risk. Thus do even the acolytes of interventionism pay tribute to the true national interests of the United States, which are not to be found in some hegemonic and utopian world order.

When Adams spoke, he was echoing Washington's Farewell Address that warned his fickle countrymen against

> inveterate antipathies against particular nations, and passionate attachments for others. . . . The Nation which indulges toward another an habitual hatred or an habitual fondness, is in some degree a slave. It is a slave to its animosity or to its affection, either of which is sufficient to lead it astray from its duty and its interest.

For a century after Washington's death, we resisted the siren's call of empire. Then, Kipling's call to "Take up the white man's burden" fell upon the receptive ears of Bill McKinley, who came down from a sleepless night of consulting the Almighty to tell the press that God had told him to take the Philippines. We were launched.

Two decades later, 100,000 Americans lay dead in France in a European war begun, as Bismarck predicted it would begin, "because of some damn fool thing in the Balkans."

"To make the world safe for democracy," we joined an alliance of empires—British, French, and Russian—that held most of mankind in colonial captivity. Washington's warning proved prophetic. Doughboys fell in places like the Argonne and Belleau Wood, in no small measure to vindicate the Germanophobia and Anglophilia of a regnant Yankee elite. When the great "war to end war" had fertilized the seed bed that produced Mussolini, Hitler, and Stalin, Americans by 1941 had concluded a blunder had been made in ignoring the wise counsel of their Founding Father.

After V-E Day and V-J Day, all America wanted to "bring the boys home," and we did. Then they were sent back, back to Europe, back to Asia, because Americans were persuaded—by Joseph Stalin—that the Cold War must be waged, because Lenin's party had made the United States the "main enemy" in its war against the West. As the old saw goes, you can refuse almost any invitation, but when a man wants to fight you have to oblige him.

If the Cold War is ending, what are the terms of honorable peace that will permit us to go home? Are they not: withdrawal of the Red Army back within its own frontiers; liberation of Central Europe and the Baltic republics; reunification of Germany; and de-Leninization of Moscow, i.e., overthrow of the imperialist party that has prosecuted the Seventy Years War against the West?

Once Russia is rescued from Leninism, its distant colonies, Cuba and Nicaragua, must eventually fall, just as the outposts of Japan's Empire, cut off from the home islands, fell like ripe apples into the lap of General MacArthur. Withdrawal of the Red Army from Europe would remove from the hand of Gorbachev's successor the military instrument of Marxist restoration.

The compensating concession we should offer: total withdrawal of U.S. troops from Europe. If Moscow will get out, we will get out. Once the Red Army goes home, the reason for keeping a U.S. army in Europe vanishes. Forty years after the Marshall Plan, it is time Europe conscripted the soldiers for its own defense.

As the Austrian peace treaty demonstrates, troop withdrawals are the most enduring and easily verifiable form of arms control. If we negotiate the 600,000 troops of the Red Army out of Central Europe, they cannot return, short of launching a new European war.

There is another argument for disengagement. When the cheering stops, there is going to be a calling to account for the crimes of Tehran, Yalta, and Potsdam, where the Great Men acceded to Stalin's demand that he be made cartographer of Europe. In the coming conflicts—over Poland's frontiers east and west, over Transylvania, Karelia, Moldavia, the breakup of Yugoslavia—our role is diplomatic and moral, not military.

In 1956, at the high water mark of American power, the U.S. stood aside as Soviet tanks crushed the Hungarian revolution. With that decision, Eisenhower and Dulles told the world that, while we support freedom in Central Europe, America will not go to war with Russia over it. The year of revolution, 1989, revealed the logical corollary: From Berlin to Bucharest to Beijing, as Lord Byron observed, "Who would be free, themselves must strike the first blow."

Would America be leaving our NATO [North Atlantic Treaty Organization] allies in the lurch? Hardly. NATO Europe contains fourteen states, which, together, are more populous and three times as wealthy as a Soviet Union deep in an economic, social, and political crisis. Moreover, NATO would have a new buffer zone of free, neutral, anticommunist nations between the Soviet and German frontiers. Our job will have been done.

To conquer Germany, the Red Army would have to cross a free Poland of 500 miles and 40 million people, before reaching the frontier of a united Reich of 80 million, whose tradition is not wholly pacifist. In the first hours of invasion, Moscow would see her economic ties to the West severed, and a global coalition forming up against her, including Germany, France, Britain, China, Japan, and the United States. As the Red Army advanced, it would risk atomic attack. To what end? So the Kremlin can recapture what the Kremlin is giving up as an unwanted and unmanageable empire?

The day of the realpoliticians, with their Metternichian "new architectures," and balance-of-power strategems, and hidden fear of a world where their op-ed articles and televised advice are about as relevant as white papers from Her Majesty's Colonial Office, is over.

Why seek a united Germany? Because it is consistent with our values, our promise to the German people, and our national interest. Moreover, the Germans desire it, and will attain it. "Conditions" set down by President Bush and Secretary Baker will prove as ineffectual as they are insulting. (If the Germans decide to unite, what, exactly, would we do to stop them: Occupy Munich until they yield to our demand that they stay in NATO?)

A free, united Germany in the heart of Europe, inoculated against Marxism by forty-five years of the disease, would be a triumph of American policy, a pillar of Western capitalism, and the first line of defense against a resurgent Russian imperialism. For the United States to permit itself to be used by London, Paris, and Moscow to impede reunification is to reenact, seventy years later, the folly of Versailles. Deny Germans the unity they rightly seek, and we shall awake one morning to find the Russians have granted it.

But, disengagement does not mean disarmament.

Still the greatest trading nation on earth, the U.S. depends for its prosperity on freedom of the seas. The strength of the U.S. navy should be non-negotiable; and, when the President is invited to enter naval arms control negotiations, the answer should be no, even if it means Moscow walks out.

With the acquisition of ballistic missiles by China, Iran, Iraq, Syria, and Libya, with atomic weapons work being done in half a dozen countries of the Third World, the United States needs—nay, requires—a crash research and development program for missile defense, to protect our homeland, our warships, our bases. No arms control agreement is worth trading away SDI [Strategic Defense Initiative, or "Star Wars"].

An island-continent, America should use her economic and technological superiority to keep herself permanent mistress of the seas, first in air power, first in space. Nor is the cost beyond our capacity. For, it is not warships and weapons that consume half our defense budget; it is manpower and benefits. When defense cuts are made, they should come in army bases no longer needed for homeland defense, and ground troops no longer needed on foreign soil.

As U.S. bases close down in Europe, we should inform Moscow we want all Soviet bases closed in the Caribbean and Central America, all Soviet troops out of the Western hemisphere. They have no business here. This is our hemisphere; and the Monroe Doctrine should be made again the cornerstone of U.S. foreign policy.

As the U.S. moves off the mainland of Europe, we should move our troops as well off the mainland of Asia. South Korea has twice the population and five times the economic might of North Korea. She can be sold the planes, guns, missiles, and ships to give her decisive superiority; then, U.S. troops should be taken out of the front line.

We are not going to fight another land war in Asia; no vital interest justifies it; our people will not permit it. Why, then, keep 30,000 ground troops on the DMZ [demilitarized zone, in Korea]? If Kim Il Sung attacks, why should Americans be first to die? If we must intervene, we can do so with air and sea power, without thousands of army and marine dead. It is time we began uprooting the global network of "trip wires" planted on foreign soil to ensnare the United States in the wars of other nations, to back commitments made and treaties signed before this generation of American soldiers was born.

The late Barbara Tuchman wrote of the Kaiser that he could not stand it if somewhere in the world a quarrel was going on and he was not a party to it. Blessed by Providence with pacific neighbors, north and south, and vast oceans, east and west, to protect us, why seek permanent entanglement in other people's quarrels?

The beginning of the end of the Cold War is surely time for that "agonizing reappraisal" of which Dulles only spoke. As Chesterton said, one ought not tear down a wall until you know why it was put up, but we must begin asking why some walls were built, and whether maintaining them any longer serves our interests.

As we ascend the staircase to the twenty-first century, America is uniquely situated to lead the world. Japan has a population older and not half so large as ours; her land and resources cannot match California's. Even united, the two Germanies have but a third of our population, a fifth of our GNP [gross national product], and a land area smaller than Oregon and Washington. Neither Japan nor Germany is a nuclear power; neither has a navy or air force to rival ours; even their combined GNP is dwarfed by ours. While the Soviet Union has the size, resources, and population to challenge us as a world power, she is a prison house of nations whose ethnic hatreds and unworkable system mean a decade of turmoil. Who is left? The corrupt, bankrupt China of Deng Xiaoping? It will not survive the decade. Nakasone was right: The twentieth century was the American century. The twenty-first century will also be the American century.

But America can only lead the world into the twenty-first century if she is not saddled down by all the baggage piled up in the twentieth.

For fifty years, the United States has been drained of wealth and power by wars, cold and hot. Much of that expenditure of blood and treasure was a necessary investment. Much was not.

We cannot forever defend wealthy nations that refuse to defend themselves; we cannot permit endless transfusions of the life blood of American capitalism into the mendicant countries and economic corpses of socialism, without bleeding to death. Foreign aid is an idea whose time has passed. The communist and socialist world now owe the West a thousand billion dollars and more, exclusive of hundreds of billions we simply gave away. Our going-away gift to the globalist ideologues should be to tell the Third World we are not sending the gunboats to collect our debts, but nor are we sending more money. The children are on their own.

Americans are the most generous people in history. But our altruism has been exploited by the guilt-and-pity crowd. At home, a monstrous welfare state of tens of thousands of drones and millions of dependents consumes huge slices of the national income. Abroad, regiments of global bureaucrats siphon off billions for themselves, their institutions, their client regimes.

With the Cold War ending, we should look, too, with a cold eye on the internationalist set, never at a loss for new ideas to divert U.S. wealth and power into crusades and causes having little or nothing to do with the true national interest of the United States.

High among these is the democratist temptation, the worship of democracy as a form of governance and the concomitant ambition to see all mankind embrace it, or explain why not. Like all idolatries, democratism substitutes a false god for the real, a love of process for a love of country.

When we call a country "democratic," we say nothing about whether its rulers are wise or good, or friendly or hostile; we only describe how they were chosen, a process that produced Olaf Palme, Lopez Portillo, Pierre Trudeau, Sam Nujoma, Kurt Waldheim, and the Papandreous, *père et fils,* as well as Ronald Reagan.

Raul Alfonsín, elected president, led Argentina to ruin; while General Pinochet, who seized power in a coup, rescued Chile from Castroism, and leaves her secure, prosperous, and on the road to freedom. Why, then, celebrate Alfonsín, and subvert Pinochet?

As cultural traditions leave many countries unsuited to U.S.-style democracy, any globalist crusade to bring its blessings to the natives everywhere must end in frustration; and will surely be marked by hypocrisy. While the National Endowment for Democracy meddles in the affairs of South Africa, the State Department props up General Mobutu. Where is the consistency?

Democracies, too, place their own selfish interests first. India, the world's largest, supported Moscow's genocidal war of annexation in Afghanistan, while General Zia, an autocrat, died aiding the resistance. Who was the true friend of liberty?

In 1936, Franco rescued Spain from a corrupt "democracy"; in 1937, Hitler received a "democratic" mandate from the German people; in 1941, Britain declared war on Finland, a democracy, at the behest of Stalin; in 1942, we deprived our own fighting men of needed weapons to send them to the USSR [Union of Soviet Socialist Republics], the most contemptuous enemy democracy has ever known.

How other people rule themselves is their own business. To call it a vital interest of the United States is to contradict history and common sense. And for the Republic to seek to dictate to 160 nations what kind of regime each should have is a formula for interminable meddling and endless conflict; it is a textbook example of that "messianic globaloney" against which Dean Acheson warned; it is, in scholar Clyde Wilson's phrase, a globalization of that degenerate form of Protestantism known as the Social Gospel.

"We must consider first and last," Walter Lippmann wrote in 1943, "the American national interest. If we do not, if we construct our foreign policy on some kind of abstract theory of rights and duties, we shall build castles in the air. We shall formulate policies which in fact the nation will not support with its blood, its sweat, and its tears." Exactly.

What do Tibetans, *mujabeddin*, UNITA [National Union for the Total Independence of Angola] rebels, and *contras* have in common? Not belief in a bicameral legislature, or in separation of church and state, but love of liberty and a hatred of communism. Is it not the spirit of patriotism that brought down the vassal regimes of Central Europe, that today threatens to tear apart the Soviet Empire?

"Enlightened nationalism" was Mr. Lippmann's idea of a foreign policy to protect America's true national interest. What we need is a new nationalism, a new patriotism, a new foreign policy that puts America first, and, not only first, but second and third as well.

## Questions for Discussion

1. How should the national interest of the United States be determined?
2. What is the relationship between democracy and the conduct of foreign policy?
3. What foreign policy interests does the United States have in the post–cold war era?
4. What would be the consequences to the United States if it pursued an isolationist foreign policy?
5. How would the Gershman view affect world politics?
6. How would the Buchanan view affect world politics?

# Suggested Readings

"Human Rights around the World." *Annals of the American Academy of Political and Social Science*, 506 (November 1989), entire issue.

Jervis, Robert, and Seweryn Bialer. *Soviet-American Relations after the Cold War.* Durham, N.C.: Duke Univ. Press, 1990.

Katz, Mark N. "The Decline of Soviet Power." *Survival* (London), 32, no. 1 (January–February 1990), 15–28.

Kegley, Charles W., Jr. "The Lost Legacy: Idealism in American Foreign Policy." *USA Today Magazine*, 117, no. 2526 (March 1989), 25–27.

Kelley, Donald R., and Hoyt Purvis, eds. *Old Myths and New Realities.* New York: Praeger, 1990.

Krauthammer, Charles. "Universal Dominion: Toward a Unipolar World." *National Interest*, no. 18 (Winter 1989–1990), 46–49.

Kristol, Irving. "In Search of Our National Interest." *Wall Street Journal*, June 7, 1990, p. A14.

Manes, Charles William. "America without the Cold War." *Foreign Policy*, no. 78 (Spring 1990), 3–25.

Markowitz, David M. "Strategic Weapons in the Third World." *Harvard International Review*, 12, no. 1 (February 1989), 56–59.

Roberts, Brad. "Human Rights and International Security." *Washington Quarterly*, 13, no. 2 (Spring 1990), 65–75.

U.S. Cong., House of Representatives. *U.S. Power in a Changing World: Proceedings of a Seminar Held by the Congressional Research Service, September 19–20, 1989.* Report prepared for the Subcommittee on International Economic Policy and Trade of the Committee on Foreign Affairs, 101st Cong., 2nd Sess., May 1990.

Vlahos, Michael. "Look Homeward." *National Interest*, no. 20 (Summer 1990), 49–53.

# Contributors

HERBERT M. LEVINE *taught political science at the University of Southwestern Louisiana for twenty years. He has written and edited several political science textbooks, including* What If the American Political System Were Different? *(1992),* World Politics Debated *(1992), and* Political Issues Debated *(1990). He is currently a writer who lives in Chevy Chase, Maryland.*

BRENT H. BAKER is executive director of the Media Research Center, Alexandria, Virginia. The Center publishes a newsletter which documents liberal media bias.

CARLOS ROMERO BARCELO is president of the New Progressive Party of Puerto Rico, the pro-statehood party. He served two terms as governor of Puerto Rico.

RYAN J. BARILLEAUX is an associate professor of political science at Miami University, Oxford, Ohio. He is the coauthor (with Barbara Kellerman) of *The President as World Leader* (1991), and author of *The Post-Modern Presidency* (1988) and *The President and Foreign Affairs* (1985).

JAIME BENÍTEZ is a former resident commissioner of Puerto Rico.

JUDITH BEST is Distinguished Teaching Professor at the State University of New York at Cortland. She is the author of *The Case against Direct Election of the President: A Defense of the Electoral College* (1975).

DAVID BOAZ is vice president for public policy affairs of the Cato Institute. He is the editor of *The Crisis in Drug Prohibition* (1990).

DAVID L. BOREN, a Democratic senator from Oklahoma, is chairman of the Senate Select Committee on Intelligence.

JAMES BRYCE (1838–1922) was a British historian, diplomat, and political leader.

PATRICK J. BUCHANAN, former presidential assistant to Richard Nixon and Ronald Reagan, is a syndicated columnist and a nightly commentator on CNN.

STUART M. BUTLER is director of Domestic Policy Studies at the Heritage Foundation. He is the author of *Privatizing Federal Spending: A Strategy to Eliminate the Deficit* (1985).

350

NOAM CHOMSKY teaches linguistics at the Massachusetts Institute of Technology. He is the author of *On Power and Ideology* (1987), *Towards a New Cold War* (1982), *American Power and the New Mandarins* (1969), and other works.

COMMITTEE ON THE CONSTITUTIONAL SYSTEM is a nonpartisan, nonprofit organization devoted to the study and analysis of the U.S. constitutional system.

JUDY CROCKETT is a legislative representative of the Washington office of the American Civil Liberties Union.

DAVID W. CROSLAND is co-chair of the American Bar Association's Representation of the Homeless Project.

ROBERT DEYLING is a Washington, D.C., attorney.

ROBERT C. ELLICKSON is Walter E. Meyer Professor of Property and Urban Law at Yale Law School.

JOSEPH J. FANELLI is president of Business-Industry Political Action Committee.

BRUCE FEIN is an attorney and partner in Blaustein & Fein. He writes frequently on legal issues.

DANIEL P. FRANKLIN is an assistant professor at Colgate University. He is the author of *Extraordinary Measures: The Exercise of Prerogative Powers in the United States* (1991).

CARL GERSHMAN is president of the National Endowment for Democracy, a private organization that seeks to promote worldwide development of democratic values.

MARK GREEN is consumer affairs commissioner of New York City. He was head of Congress Watch, a consumer lobby, in the 1970s and is coauthor of *Who Runs Congress?* (1984).

NAT HENTOFF is the author of *The First Freedom* (1980) and many other books. He writes regularly on civil liberties matters.

EDWARD S. HOCHMAN is a political consultant and a lawyer with the Law Offices of Edward S. Hochman in New York and Newark, New Jersey.

GORDON HUMPHREY served as a Republican senator from New Hampshire from 1979 to 1990.

ALBERT R. HUNT heads the *Wall Street Journal*'s Washington bureau.

JOHN E. JACOB is president and chief executive officer of the National Urban League.

GARRISON KEILLOR is a humorist and is the author of *We Are Still Married* (1989) and *Lake Wobegon Days* (1985).

MICHAEL KINSLEY writes a regular column for *New Republic*.

EDWARD I. KOCH served as mayor of New York City from 1978 to 1989. He was a member of the House of Representatives from 1969 to 1972.

ROBERT KUTTNER is economics editor of *New Republic*.

LAWRENCE LONGLEY is an associate professor of government at Lawrence University in Appleton, Wisconsin.

THURGOOD MARSHALL is an associate justice of the U.S. Supreme Court.

NICOLAS S. MARTIN is executive director of the Consumer Health Education Council.

ROGER MORRIS was a staff member of the National Security Council in the administrations of Lyndon Johnson and Richard Nixon.

KARY L. MOSS is a staff attorney of the Women's Rights Project of the American Civil Liberties Union.

LYNN M. PALTROW is a staff attorney of the Reproductive Freedom Project of the American Civil Liberties Union.

J. A. PARKER is editor of *Lincoln Review.*

PETER H. RAVEN, director of the Missouri Botanical Garden, St. Louis, is also home secretary of the National Academy of Sciences, a member of the Committee on Research and Exploration of the National Geographic Society, and a director of the World Wildlife Fund–U.S.

WILLIAM BRADFORD REYNOLDS is a partner in the District of Columbia office of Chicago's Ross & Hardies. He served as counselor to the attorney general and assistant attorney general in the Civil Rights Division of the Justice Department in the Reagan administration.

JEFFREY M. SHAMAN is director of the Center for Judicial Conduct Organizations of the American Judicature Society and a professor of law at De Paul University.

RICK SZYKOWNY is the associate editor of *The Humanist*. He has written extensively on political issues and popular culture.

JOHN UPDIKE is the author of numerous novels, including *Rabbit at Rest* (1990).

J. CLIFFORD WALLACE is a judge on the United States Court of Appeals for the Ninth Circuit.

JAMES Q. WILSON is Collins Professor of Management at the University of California at Los Angeles. He is the author of numerous books, including *Bureaucracy: What Government Agencies Do and Why They Do It* (1989).

**Acknowledgments** (continued from p. ii)

"Does the Separation of Powers Still Work?" by James Q. Wilson. *Public Interest*, no. 86 (Winter 1987), 36–52. Reprinted by permission of the copyright holder, James Q. Wilson.

"The Withering away of the States," (TRB) by Michael Kinsley. *The New Republic*, March 28, 1981. Reprinted by permission of *The New Republic*, © 1981, The New Republic, Inc.

"Knocking over Voter Barriers," by Robert P. Deyling. *Legal Times*, 12, no. 16 (September 18, 1989), 35–36. Reprinted by permission of the copyright holder, Robert P. Deyling.

"Tuned-out Voters Won't Turn out at the Polls," by Edward S. Hochman. *Legal Times*, 12, no. 23 (November 6, 1989), 25–26. Reprinted by permission of the copyright holder, Edward S. Hochman.

"The Case against Political Action Committees," by Mark Green. Prepared statement in U.S. Cong., Senate, *Proposed Amendments to the Federal Elections Campaign Act of 1971*, Hearings before the Committee on Rules and Administration, 99th Cong., 2nd Sess., 1986, pp. 190–193.

"The Case for Political Action Committees," by Joseph F. Fanelli. Prepared statement in U.S. Cong., Senate, *Proposed Amendments to the Federal Elections Campaign Act of 1971*, Hearings before the Committee on Rules and Administration, 99th Cong., 2nd Sess., 1986, pp. 304–308.

"The Case for the Electoral College," by Judith Best and "The Case against the Electoral College," by Lawrence Longley. In J. Jackson Barlow, Dennis J. Mahoney, and John G. West, Jr., eds., *The New Federalist Papers* (Lanham, Md.: University Press of America, 1988), 404–409. Copyright © 1988 by University Press of America.

"Media's Liberal Slant on the News," by Brent H. Baker. Reprinted from *USA Today Magazine*, 118, no. 2530 (July 1989), 64–66. Copyright © 1989 by Society for the Advancement of Education.

"Bewildering the Herd: An Interview," by Rick Szykowny. *The Humanist*, 50, no. 6 (November/December 1990), 8–17. Copyright © 1990 by The American Humanist Association.

"Addicts, Their Babies, and Their Liability," by Bruce Fein and William Bradford Reynolds. *Legal Times*, 12, no. 50 (May 12, 1990), 20, 22. Reprinted by permission of the copyright holders, Bruce Fein and William Bradford Reynolds.

"No Criminal Prosecution of Alcohol- or Drug-Dependent Women Who Choose to Continue Their Pregnancies," Testimony of Kary L. Moss, Lynn M. Paltrow, and Judy Crockett on behalf of The American Civil Liberties Union, before the Select Committee on Children, Youth and Families of the United States House of Representatives, May 17, 1990. Notes have been renumbered and note 25 has been omitted.

"Free Speech on the Campus," by Nat Hentoff. *Progressive*, 53, no. 5 (May 1989), 12–13. Reprinted by permission of the copyright holder, Nat Hentoff.

"Shunning Racial, Religious Bigotry," by Bruce Fein. *Washington Times*, May 1, 1990, p. F3. Reprinted by permission of the copyright holder, Bruce Fein.

"Major Issues Facing African-Americans," by John E. Jacob. *Vital Speeches of the Day*, 56, no. 1 (October 15, 1989), 7–12. Reprinted by permission of City News Publishing Co.

"The Growing Irrelevance of the Civil Rights Movement," by J. A. Parker. *Lincoln Review*, 9, no. 1 (Fall 1988), 1–9. Reprinted by permission of the copyright holder, J. A. Parker.

"The President Is Too Powerful in Foreign Affairs" by Daniel P. Franklin. Copyright © 1988 and 1990 by Daniel P. Franklin. Printed by permission of the author. This article, which was specially written for the third edition of *Point-Counterpoint*, has been revised and updated by the author.

"Seeing Presidential Power Clearly," by Ryan J. Barilleaux. Copyright © by Ryan J. Barilleaux. Printed by permission of the author. This article, which was specially written for the third edition of *Point-Counterpoint*, has been revised and updated by the author.

"Rejoinder," by Daniel P. Franklin. Copyright © 1988 by Daniel P. Franklin. Printed by permission of the author. This rejoinder, which was specially written for the third edition of *Point-Counterpoint*, has been revised and updated by the author.

"Rejoinder," by Ryan J. Barilleaux. Copyright © by Ryan J. Barilleaux. Printed by permission of the author. This rejoinder, which was specially written for the third edition of *Point-Counterpoint*, has been revised and updated by the author.

"Limit Congressional Terms," by Gordon Humphrey, *Congressional Record*, 136, no. 1 (January 23, 1990), S157–S158.
"Congress's Terms: Just Fine As They Are," by Albert R. Hunt. *Wall Street Journal*, April 24, 1990, p. 18, 54–59. Reprinted by permission of *Wall Street Journal*.
"Privatizing Federal Services: A Primer," by Stuart M. Butler. *Backgrounder*, no. 488 (February 20, 1986). Reprinted by permission of The Heritage Foundation, Washington, D.C.
"False Profit: The Perils of Privatization," by Robert Kuttner. *The New Republic*, 200, no. 6 (February 6, 1989), 21–23. Reprinted by permission of *The New Republic*, © 1989, The New Republic, Inc.
"CIA—Costly, Inept, Anachronistic," by Roger Morris. *The New York Times*, June 10, 1990, Sec. IV, p. 23. Copyright © 1990 by the New York Times Company. Reprinted by permission.
"New World, New CIA," by David L. Boren. *The New York Times*, June 17, 1990, p. 21. Copyright © 1990 by the New York Times Company. Reprinted by permission.
"The Case for Judicial Restraint," by J. Clifford Wallace. *Judicature*, 71, no. 2, (August/September 1987), 81–84. Copyright © 1987 by The American Judicature Society. Reprinted by permission of The American Judicature Society.
"The Supreme Court's Proper and Historic Function," by Jeffrey M. Shaman. *Judicature*, 71, no. 2, (August/September 1987), 80, 84–87, 122. Copyright © 1987 by The American Judicature Society. Reprinted by permission of The American Judicature Society.
"The Case for Legalizing Drugs," by David Boaz. Statement of David Boaz in U.S. Cong., House of Representatives, *Legalization of Illicit Drugs Part II*, Hearing before the Select Committee on Narcotics Abuse and Control, 100th Cong., 2nd Sess., 1988, pp. 144–153.
"The Case against Legalizing Drugs," by Edward I. Koch. Testimony of Edward I. Koch in U.S. Cong., House of Representatives, *Legalization of Illicit Drugs: Impact and Possibility, Part I*, Hearing before the Select Committee on Narcotics Abuse and Control, 100th Cong., 2nd Sess., 1988, pp.231–239.
"Housing and Homelessness," by David W. Crosland. Statement of David W. Crosland, U.S. Cong., House of Representatives, *Homelessness in America—The Need For Permanent Housing*, Hearings before the Subcommittee on Housing and Human Development of the Committee on Banking, Finance and Urban Affairs, 101st Cong., 1st Sess., 1989, pp. 785–793.
"The Homelessness Muddle," by Robert C. Ellickson. Reprinted with permission of the author from *The Public Interest*, no. 99 (Spring 1990), 45–60. © 1990 by National Affairs, Inc.
"The Case for Government Support," by Garrison Keillor. Remarks by Garrison Keillor in U.S. Cong. Senate, *Reauthorization of the National Foundation on the Arts and Humanities Act, National Endowment for the Arts*, Hearing before the Subcommittee on Education, Arts and Humanities of the Committee on Labor and Human Resources, 101st Cong., 2nd Sess., 1990.
"The Case against Government Support," by John Updike. Statement of John Updike, U.S. Cong., *White House Conference on the Humanities*, Joint Hearings before the Subcommittee on Select Education of the Committee on Education and Labor, House of Representatives; and the Subcommittee on Education, Arts and Humanities of the Committee on Human Resources, Senate, 95th Cong., 1st and 2nd Sess., 1977 and 1978, pp. 852–854.
"A World in Crisis," by Peter H. Raven. Reprinted from *USA Today Magazine*, 117, no. 2528 (May 1989), 48–50. Copyright © 1989 by permission of the Society for the Advancement of Education.
"Environmental Myths and Hoaxes: The Evidence of Guilt Is Insufficient," by Nicolas S. Martin. *Vital Speeches of the Day*, 56, no. 14 (May 1, 1990), 434–437. Reprinted by permission of the author, Nicolas S. Martin.
"The Case for Statehood," by Carlos Romero Barcelo. Statement by Carlos Romero Barcelo in U.S. Cong., Senate, *Political Status of Puerto Rico*, Hearings before the Committee on Energy and Natural Resources, 101st Cong., 1st Sess., 1989, Part 1, pp. 123–142.
"A Permanent Autonomous Relationship," by Jaime Benitez. Testimony by Jaime

Benitez in U.S. Cong., Senate, Hearings before the Committee on Energy and Natural Resources, 101st Cong., 1st Sess., 1989, Part 2, pp. 44–60.

"Freedom Remains the Touchstone," by Carl Gershman. © *The National Interest*, no. 19 (Spring 1990), Washington, D.C. Used with permission.

"America First—and Second, and Third," by Patrick J. Buchanan. © *The National Interest*, no. 19 (Spring 1990), Washington, D.C. Used with permission.